Research in Practice for Forensic Professionals

Edited by
Sheldon, Dr Jason Davies
Kevin Howells

Routledge
Taylor & Francis Group

LONDON AND NEW YORK

D1141557

First published 2011
by Routledge
2 Park Square, Milton Park, Abingdon, Oxon, OX14 4RN

Simultaneously published in the USA and Canada
by Routledge
711 Third Avenue, New York, NY 10017

*Routledge is an imprint of the Taylor & Francis Group, an informa
business*

British Library Cataloguing in Publication Data
A catalogue record for this book is available from the British Library

Library of Congress Cataloging in Publication Data

Research in practice for forensic professionals / edited by
Kerry Sheldon, Jason Davies and Kevin Howells.
    p. cm.
ISBN 978-0-415-67271-9 (hbk.) – ISBN 978-0-415-67272-6 (pbk.)
1. Criminal justice, Administration of–Research–Methodology.
I. Sheldon, Kerry. II. Davies, Jason. III. Howells, Kevin.
HV7419.5R47 2011
363.25072–dc22   2011008100

ISBN 13: 978-0-415-67271-9 (hbk)
ISBN 13: 978-0-415-67272-6 (pbk)
ISBN 13: 978-0-203-80532-9 (ebk)

Typeset in Times New Roman
by Cenveo Publisher Services.

KS: For Imogen
JD: For Susie, Bryn and Freya
KH: For Maya and Jay, natural investigators

Contents

Figures

Tables

Boxes

Editors

Dr Kerry Sheldon trained in Investigative Psychology at the University of Liverpool before obtaining her PhD in Psychology at Loughborough University. At the time of writing, Kerry worked as Research Fellow at Rampton High Secure Hospital. Since publication she has commenced her professional Doctorate in Clinical Psychology (DClinPsy) at the University of Nottingham. She has worked in the Probation Service in sex offender treatment and has worked as a Lecturer in Psychology and Criminology. She is a Fellow of the Higher Education Academy and has held a number of honorary academic and research appointments. Her areas of specialism are Internet sex offenders and service evaluation. In addition, her research interests include paedophilia, violent and sexual fantasies and self-harm. She has academic publications in the field of paedophilia including *Sex Offenders and the Internet* (Wiley and Sons, 2007) as well as a number of journal papers and book chapters covering a wide variety of Forensic Psychology topics.

Dr Jason Davies is a Consultant Forensic and Clinical Psychologist with ABM University Health Board. He has worked in the Personality Disorder Directorate at Rampton High Secure Hospital, in DSPD services and as Service Lead for Psychology and Psychological Therapies in a Medium Secure Hospital. Jason currently is Lead Psychologist in a Rehabilitation/Recovery and Low Secure Service in South Wales. He has worked as a part time lecturer (at the University of Sheffield) and currently holds a number of honorary academic and research appointments. His areas of specialism are working with complex needs including offending behaviour, dual diagnosis and personality disorder; service development; training and individual and service evaluation. He has an interest in engagement and motivation, clinical supervision, staff development and working with staff teams. His research interests include psychometric assessment, sadistic attitudes and behaviour and idiographic assessment. He has published qualitative and qualitative research on forensic and non-forensic topics and chapters on methods for evaluating individual change.

Professor Kevin Howells trained initially as a Clinical Psychologist before specialising in forensic work. His career has alternated between professional and academic roles. He has worked as a practitioner in a range of forensic mental health services in the United Kingdom and the United States, including high and medium security hospitals and recently in the service for personality disordered offenders at Rampton hospital (the Peaks Academic and Research Unit). He has worked extensively in prison and criminal justice settings, including for a ten year period in Australia. He has been a prolific researcher and publisher and has held a number of academic positions, including being Professor of Clinical Psychology (Birmingham University), Professor of Forensic Psychology (University of South Australia) and Professor of Forensic Clinical Psychology (Nottingham University and the Institute of Mental Health). His current interests include treatment readiness and engagement, therapeutic climate, anger problems and mindfulness.

Contributors

Professor Neil Brewer is Professor and Dean of the School of Psychology at Flinders University, Australia. His research is primarily located in the areas of eyewitness memory and identification. He is a member of the editorial boards of a number of the leading international journals that publish psychology-law research, including *Law and Human Behavior*; *Journal of Experimental Psychology: Applied*; *Psychology, Public Policy and Law*; *Legal and Criminological Psychology*; and *Applied Cognitive Psychology*. He is an Elected Fellow of the Academy of Social Sciences in Australia, and a regular invited presenter of professional development workshops on eyewitness memory and judgments of credibility for conferences of judges and magistrates throughout Australia.

Professor Jennifer Brown is a visiting professor at the London School of Economics where she is also the Deputy Director of the Mannheim Centre for Criminology. Her research interests lie in the area of psychological aspects of police investigation of serious crime such as rape and murder. Her interest in Facet Theory as a method was inspired by Louis Guttman who gave a workshop to PhD students at the University of Surrey in 1979.

Dr Michael Daffern is a clinical psychologist by training. He completed his training in clinical psychology at the University of Newcastle and was awarded his PhD from the University of South Australia in 2004. The focus of his PhD research was on the development of a functional analysis of psychiatric inpatient aggression. Michael has worked as a clinical and forensic psychologist within mainstream adult psychiatry, forensic mental health and in correctional settings. Presently, he is Senior Lecturer in Clinical Forensic Psychology in the School of Psychology, Psychiatry and Psychological Medicine and Principal Consultant Psychologist with the Victorian Institute of Forensic Mental Health (Forensicare), Australia. His research interests include violence, risk assessment and behavioural assessment methods. He has published widely in these areas. He recently co-edited *Offence Paralleling Behaviour: A Case Formulation Approach to Offender Assessment and Treatment*.

Professor Andrew Day is a Professor of Psychology at Deakin University in Victoria, Australia having previously worked as a psychologist for prison and mental health services in both Adelaide and the UK. His research interests centre around the development of effective rehabilitation programmes for offenders, with a particular focus on the treatment and management of violent offenders and the role that anger plays in serious violent offending. His most recent books include *Writing Court Reports* (2007, Australian Academic Press), *Anger and Indigenous Men* (2008, Federation Press), *Integrated Responses to Domestic Violence: Research and Practice Experiences in Working with Men* (2009, Annandale NSW: Federation Press) and *Transitions to Better Lives: Offender Readiness and Rehabilitation* (2010, Cullompton, UK: Willan Press). From 2004 until 2008, Professor Day was the leader of the Forensic Psychology Research Group at the University of South Australia before moving to Deakin University where he is the acting Director of the Deakin Forensic Psychology Centre. As a practising clinical and forensic psychologist he maintains a small private practice in Adelaide, working with both forensic and mental health referrals.

Dr Michael Doyle is currently in the post of Clinical Researcher and Programme Director for the recently developed MSc Forensic Mental Health at the University of Manchester. He is also Nurse Consultant for Clinical Risk at North West Adult Forensic Services at Greater Manchester West NHS Trust. He is the project manager for a national study funded by National Institute of Health Care Research evaluating post-discharge outcomes and he is Treasurer for the International Association of Forensic Mental Health. He has research experience in a range of areas and has published widely on psychosocial risk assessment, formulation, management and training. He also provides training, consultancy and advice to health and social care organisations and criminal justice agencies across the UK, Europe and beyond. Accredited as a behavioural and cognitive psychotherapist, he continues with clinical practice, supervision and mentorship.

Dr Michael Ferriter is joint Lead for Research in the Forensic Division of Nottinghamshire Healthcare NHS Trust, UK. For the past 15 years he has worked in research in forensic mental health. His research interests are case and disease registers, the physical health of people with mental health problems and systematic reviews. His most recent work has been a portfolio of Cochrane reviews on interventions for people with personality disorders, a review of the literature on forensic services in England and Wales and primary research on the impact of a total smoking ban in a high security hospital.

Dr Neil Gordon is a psychotherapist who works as a senior clinician and supervisor in a high secure forensic setting and is Head of Doctoral programmes at the Institute of Mental Health, Nottingham, where he is the Master's Programme Lead for the National Personality Disorder, Knowledge and

Understanding Framework (KUF) commissioned by the Department of Health and Ministry of Justice. He is a Fellow of the Higher Education Academy, an Honorary Teaching Fellow at Sheffield Hallam University, a member of the International Society of Schema Therapy and an accredited Schema therapist. Neil has published articles on a wide range of topics including personality disorder, organisational change, mental health education and qualitative research. He has recently co-edited a textbook, *Working Positively with Personality Disorder in Secure Settings*, published by Wiley in 2010.

Dr Sean Hammond is a Statutory Lecturer in the School of Applied Psychology, University College Cork, Ireland. Prior to that he was the Head of the Clinical Decision Support Unit of Broadmoor Hospital in the UK. His primary interests are in forensic assessment and he has particular expertise in psychometrics and multivariate statistics. He is involved in research into risk assessment and management and is a co-developer of the RAMAS approach to risk appraisal. He is also involved in research projects on sexual offending, in particular on offenders using internet and P2P technologies. His most recent research projects involve the use of implicit methods of assessment and the application and utility of idiographic techniques in clinical practice.

Professor Clive R. Hollin is Professor of Criminological Psychology at the University of Leicester, UK. He wrote the best-selling textbook *Psychology and Crime: An Introduction to Criminological Psychology* (1989, Routledge). His most recent book, edited with Graham Davies and Ray Bull, is *Forensic Psychology* (2008, John Wiley & Sons). In all, he has published 21 books alongside 300 other academic publications. He is also co-editor of the journal *Psychology, Crime & Law*. Alongside his various university appointments, he has worked as a psychologist in prisons, the Youth Treatment Service, special hospitals and regional secure units. In 1998 he received The Senior Award for Distinguished Contribution to the Field of Legal, Criminological and Forensic Psychology from The British Psychological Society.

Dr Ruth Horry is a postdoctoral research associate in the School of Psychology at Flinders University, Australia, where she is collaborating in several ongoing research projects on eyewitness identification. She previously held a post as a research associate at Royal Holloway, University of London, also in the area of eyewitness identification. She completed her PhD at the University of Sussex in 2009. Her thesis was on cross-cultural face recognition and meta-cognitive judgements. She has published several papers in leading international journals including *Memory and Cognition, Psychonomic Bulletin and Review* and *Behavior Research Methods*.

Dr Dennis Howitt is at Loughborough University in the Department of Social Sciences. He is a Fellow of the British Psychological Society and a chartered (forensic) psychologist. He was a graduate of Brunel University and the University of Sussex. His research career began with the study of mass communications but has developed into a broader interest in the application of psychology to social issues. His primary research areas are the effects of mass communications especially with reference to crime, violence and pornography; racism and the profession of psychology; paedophiles, sex offenders and child abuse; and forensic psychology. His books in the field of crime and sexual abuse include *Sex Offenders and the Internet* (co-authored with Kerry Sheldon; Wiley, 2007) and *Paedophiles and Sexual Offences against Children* (Wiley, 1995). He is the author of *Introduction to Forensic and Criminal Psychology* (Pearson Education) and has published widely in the field of race and racism, statistics, computing and research methods. His latest book is *Introduction to Qualitative Research in Psychology* (2010, Pearson Education).

Professor James McGuire is Professor of Forensic Clinical Psychology and Director of the Doctorate in Clinical Psychology at the University of Liverpool. He also holds an honorary consultant post at Mersey Care NHS Trust. He previously worked in a high security hospital and has carried out psycho-legal work involving assessment of individuals for criminal courts, for the Mental Health Review Tribunal, Parole Board and Criminal Cases Review Commission. He has conducted research in probation services, prisons and other settings on aspects of psychosocial rehabilitation with offenders, has published widely on this and related issues, and he has acted as a consultant to criminal justice agencies in a number of countries.

Dr Matthew A. Palmer is a postdoctoral research associate in the School of Psychology at Flinders University, Australia, where he received his PhD in 2009. His research is primarily in the psychology-law area, with a focus on eyewitness memory, and he has been published in several leading international journals including *Journal of Experimental Psychology: Applied, Legal & Criminological Psychology* and *Acta Psychologica*. He has several years of experience as a teaching assistant for undergraduate research methods classes.

Matt Tonkin is currently a PhD student at the University of Leicester. Previously he worked as a research assistant for the Peaks Academic Research Unit (PARU) at Rampton Hospital, where he contributed to research on self-harm, offence paralleling behaviour and social climate. His PhD research is focused on whether offender behaviour can be used to link crimes that have been committed by the same offender (comparative case analysis). Matt has published several papers in this area and has also published papers on geographical and offender profiling.

Professor Tony Ward is head of the School of Psychology and Professor of Clinical Psychology at Victoria University of Wellington, New Zealand. He is due to take up a research chair in Clinical Forensic Mental Health at Deakin University, Melbourne, in June 2011. Professor Ward has previously worked at the Universities of Canterbury and Melbourne and was director of Kia Marama, a specialist treatment centre for sex offenders in New Zealand. His research interests include reintegration and desistance processes in offenders, correctional rehabilitation models, ethical issues in forensic psychology, and cognition and emotion in offenders. He has published over 286 academic papers and books and his latest book (co-authored with Richard Laws) is *Desistance from Sex Offending: Alternatives to Throwing Away the Keys* (2011, Guilford Press).

Dr Gwenda Willis is a Post Doctoral Fellow in the School of Psychology, Victoria University of Wellington. In addition she is a clinical psychologist and has previously worked at Kia Marama, a prison-based treatment unit in New Zealand for men convicted of sexual offending against children. Her primary research interests revolve around sex offender rehabilitation and the promotion of desistance from sexual offending – including strengths-based approaches to rehabilitation, public attitudes towards sex offenders and policy responses to sexual offending.

Foreword

Finally, forensic researchers have a tool box with many useful tools and a user-friendly how-to manual in it. I am not talking about the metal contraption that the weekend handyperson, who happens to be a forensic researcher, carries around the house. I am referring to the present volume: *Research in Practice for Forensic Professionals.*

Research in forensic mental health and forensic social sciences has been expanding rapidly and is now much more multi-disciplinary. Many established academic disciplines now have a forensic hyphenated sub-discipline such as forensic–psychology, –psychiatry, –social work, –nursing and likely more to come. Researchers within these disciplines and, in particular, an increasing number of students, both undergraduates and postgraduates, are eager to undertake research projects and need methodological tools they can use and guidance on how to use them to answer research questions. As a discipline matures, more research questions will be put forth that require a wider range of sophisticated methodologies to investigate them. Most forensic reference books tend to focus on a discipline, such as forensic psychology; or a condition, such as antisocial personality disorder; or an intervention, such as a form of psychotherapy; or a theme, such as forensic mental health. The methodologies and techniques used as tools to investigate research questions within the discipline or the condition are scattered somewhere in the discourse and often are difficult to locate, particularly for students who are new to the area, or even for seasoned researchers who may not have ventured much beyond the tried and true. This book has brought together, under one cover, a wide array of forensic research methodologies and made them available at one's fingertips. Students, course instructors and researchers alike will welcome the arrival of this volume.

Just acquiring the tools of research is only the first step; selecting the right one and knowing how to use it properly is quite another. Many don't. As is often said, if you tried and tried and still couldn't make it work, read the manual. Tools are only useful if one knows what to use and how to use them effectively under real situations to solve real problems. The bumbling man standing ankle-deep in water with more gushing from the kitchen sink, looking at a non-descript tool in his hand with a bewildered look on his face, comes to mind; the instruction manual, of course, is floating unopened on the water behind him. This volume not only guides and informs the reader what tools are available to tackle different research questions but also how to use them intelligently and strategically under the very trying environments that most forensic researchers likely find themselves in. To do forensic research in applied settings researchers invariably have to navigate a bewildering maze of academic and bureaucratic hurdles before they can even sit in the same room with their research participants. And that is just the beginning.

I remember an occasion when I asked and then waited patiently to interview an offender inside a high security prison for a research project. Finally, I was taken to a room set aside for the interview. On entering the room, I found the offender waiting for me sitting literally inside a six-by-six-by-six cage made out of stainless steel bars! My heart sank as I knew that I needed to try to explain my research project, which was intended to be participatory and collaborative in nature, to a complete stranger and seek his written consent while he was staring at me from behind those inch-thick steel bars! Though many may not be as challenging as this example, most secure forensic settings are difficult environments in which to conduct research to say the least. This volume has done a splendid job in providing readers with guidance and information on conducting forensic research in real-life practical settings.

The editors – Kerry Sheldon, Jason Davies and Kevin Howells – and the contributors should be congratulated for undertaking this project to fill an important gap in forensic research methodology. They have carefully selected a range of established and useful methodological tools commonly used in forensic research and presented them to the readers in a clear and easy-to-understand way with the extensive use of case studies and examples, from ethical considerations to systematic review of the literature to quantitative and qualitative models to single case and large-scale evaluative research and more: what a treat! All of them written by recognised researchers with extensive hands-on experience. The next time someone asks me a methodological question I can't answer (and that is most of the time), I know where to look on my book shelf for an answer.

Some may say that methodologies are no more than mere implements to test and shape creative ideas; it is the ideas that rank supreme. But without the lowly hammer and chisel, we would not have the grand pyramids, would we? On occasions, after I read a useful and informative book, I say to myself, *Why didn't I think of this?* This volume is one of such.

Stephen C.P. Wong

Institute of Mental Health
University of Nottingham

Department of Psychology
University of Saskatchewan

Editors' preface

'Research is formalized curiosity. It is poking and prying with a purpose.'
– Zora Neale Hurston (American folklorist, anthropologist and author)

The intention in pulling this book together was to capture the 'poking and prying' in forensic settings; to produce a research textbook which contained practical assistance and guidance to the novice researcher who may have only limited or rudimentary social research experience. It was also intended to act as a reference resource for the forensic practitioner and as a useful source for those with more advanced research knowledge. However, this book is unique in that it provides a resource for the everyday forensic practitioner – rather than the academic researcher – providing a 'how-to' guide to using applied research methods in settings such as prison, probation, court and forensic mental health. The book is therefore intended, first and foremost, to be practical and useful; it should, if we've done our job correctly, speak to the methods that forensic researchers need to know about in detail. And while it is likely that aspiring researchers will gain the most from the book, many contributors have developed their points in a sophisticated way to also be of value to more seasoned researchers.

Our hope is to help readers develop or refine their knowledge and skills in the research process and, more importantly, to develop a critical and evaluative understanding of the problems, issues and ethics which can be specific to empirical research with forensic populations and in forensic settings. This is important as employers of forensic practitioners increasingly require that their staff should partake fully in research-led practice. As practitioners we do not just apply knowledge, we create it; although not always in systematic ways and often without wider dissemination. If practitioners understand research methods well then they are much more likely to be able to apply findings of other researchers into their therapy, assessment and when giving professional advice to clients, colleagues and other professionals.

In summary, this book is intended to provide social researchers with the tools and guidance necessary to undertake research within the challenging confines of forensic environments such as prisons and secure health facilities. What the books *does not* do, however, is provide guidance on the other strand of forensic practice represented most famously by the US crime drama *C.S.I.: Crime Scene Investigation*; this is a book aimed squarely at social scientists and psychiatric practitioners operating in a forensic setting, rather than forensic scientists undertaking work involving DNA profiling, ballistics, fingerprints or forensic pathology.

So how is the book structured? Well, we have attempted not to emphasise or recommend any one approach above another but rather each chapter attempts to provide a practical guide to the research approach or method it covers. The overall aim was to demythologise, systematise and summarise relevant information and advice which can be useful when the researcher comes to use a particular approach; to formalise the reader's curiosity, if you will. Readers are also encouraged to critically examine the methods proposed. While we have attempted to be as comprehensive and all-inclusive as possible, the simple breadth of research within forensic settings has meant that there are inevitably some approaches we have missed. For this we apologise and will attempt to put right in the next edition. Yet the following chapters include contributions from a wide variety of practitioners involved in social science research in forensic areas. Thus it reflects the multi-disciplinary nature of research utilised by them, whether they are nurses, psychologists, psychiatrists, probation staff or others. Our contributors have extensive experience of conducting applied research around the globe including in the United Kingdom, Ireland, America, Asia, Australia, New Zealand and Canada.

In Chapter 1 Jason Davies, Kerry Sheldon and Kevin Howells discuss some of the theoretical, philosophical and practical issues surrounding research in forensic settings. This includes the common steps taken from initial idea to dissemination of findings and consideration of the challenges that can be experienced. Continuing this theme in Chapter 2 Tony Ward and Gwenda Willis discuss some of the ethical issues surrounding how research should be conducted; how data in forensic and criminal justice services should be collected, analysed and reported; and how researchers should act towards participants in their research projects.

The next three chapters explore risk, investigative and criminal justice research. The task of assessing potential for serious harm and risk of future offending is intrinsically difficult and subject to error. Violence risk assessment and management are the principle justifications for the existence of specialised forensic services; therefore, it is imperative that the practice of risk assessment and management is supported by research evidence. In Chapter 3 Michael Doyle describes how risk assessment and prediction might be studied by the forensic practitioner. In Chapter 4 Jennifer Brown outlines an approach to research that can accommodate different research questions, varying types of data and alternative theoretical constructs. She describes Facet Meta Theory, its origins and developments and the use of its associated multi-dimensional scaling techniques, and works through design principles. Following this, in Chapter 5 Matt Palmer, Ruth Horry and Neil Brewer concentrate on research within court-based settings and discuss the methodologies used to conduct research in three prominent areas of relevance to the court: eyewitness identification tests, interviewing of witnesses and juror decision making.

Qualitative studies with forensic populations, particularly involving personality-disordered individuals and especially psychopaths, are limited since there was a view that such individuals have very little to say that will aid our understanding and theory development. In addition the use of qualitative research methods with offenders and forensic patients brings the challenge of how to present their perspectives. However, qualitative methods now represent an important suite of methods and approaches to aid the construction of knowledge and are becoming increasingly popular with practitioners and researchers. Neil Gordon in Chapter 6 and Dennis Howitt in Chapter 7 explore a sample of qualitative methods available to forensic practitioners and describe how they can be successfully applied, not simply as exploratory tools but in order to develop theory and practice. Neil Gordon describes a particular methodological approach – Grounded Theory. Dennis Howitt conducts a larger comparison of qualitative and quantitative methods. Consistent with some of the other authors in the present volume, both Howitt and Gordon stress the need for new research-ers to seek to develop an understanding between their epistemological position and their methodological choices.

Treatments should not be delivered if evaluation of their effectiveness is seen as hypothetical or only concerned with general effects or reported years after the intervention has been provided. However, establishing the 'value' of interven-tions and practice changes has traditionally been the preserve of group-based designs. In Chapter 8 Jason Davies and Kerry Sheldon discuss how single case experimental designs are ideal for answering research questions that aim to explore clinical treatment outcomes and discuss how single case methods have a range of applications which should be attractive to forensic practitioners. Continuing this individual change theme, in Chapter 9 Sean Hammond demon-strates how structured qualitative data can provide a good basis for actuarial assessment of change. In Chapter 10 Michael Daffern describes functional analytic methodology; an approach regularly used in forensic settings. Although there is very little published research using this assessment approach in this context, Michael introduces a novel application of it.

Chapters 11 to 15 explore research approaches at the group level and include a focus on treatment evaluation, regime evaluation and programme quality evaluation in forensic contexts. Randomised controlled trials (RCTs) are seen as the 'gold standard' when evaluating the efficacy of forensic programmes in the United Kingdom, but few have actually been conducted. RCTs also have a number of difficulties which are both conceptual as well as practical. In Chapter 11 Clive Hollin critiques some of the strengths and weaknesses of this approach. In particular the chapter focuses on the interplay between the different types of validity when research uses a randomised design. In Chapter 12 Matt Tonkin and Kevin Howells explore the types of method, design and analysis that might be used to evaluate forensic environments and regimes. This may be particularly important to consider as treatment programmes may operate in contexts (climates) which may be unhealthy, unsafe or unsupportive; factors which could negate benefits gained from treatment. In Chapter 13 Andrew Day outlines a relatively straightforward and efficient approach to quality assessment that allows both service providers and service managers to reflect on and review their current processes and services in terms of strengths and deficits. The final methods chapters discuss methods for aggregating data and drawing conclusions from findings reported by others. In this way they provide ways of reporting the cumulative knowledge and evidence base in a particular area. In Chapter 14 James McGuire outlines the kinds of methods employed in carrying out large-scale evaluation research, and describes how the findings of evaluation research can be combined and integrated. He focuses on meta-analysis, a procedure where data from several studies are statistically compared or combined. In Chapter 15 Michael Ferriter describes how systematic reviews are conducted and how they can be used to draw conclusions from a body of research evidence.

Ultimately, this book should provide you, as the reader, with the tools to conduct research within a forensic setting in an informed, conscientious and intelligent manner; it should allow you to formalise your curiosity, and ensure that your 'poking and prying' is done with purpose and success. And remember, as Einstein famously said, 'If we knew what it was we were doing, it would not be called research, would it?'

Kerry Sheldon
Jason Davies
Kevin Howells

Acknowledgements

We are grateful for the opportunity to prepare this book for Routledge and in particular thank Julia Willan and Kate Hill for their patience. We would also like to thank Lorraine Dubois for her assistance with proofreading. The editors would also like to thank the following for their help in reviewing the chapters and for their comments on earlier drafts of this textbook:

Miles Burger, Head of Research, APIL, Nottingham, UK
Jen Gallagher, University of Sheffield, Sheffield, UK
Tom Henwood, Abertawe Bro Morgannwg University Health Board, Swansea, UK
Mary Jinks, CLAHRC, Institute of Mental Health, University of Nottingham, Nottingham, UK
Hannah Jones, CLAHRC, Institute of Mental Health, University of Nottingham, Nottingham, UK
Rebecca Lovatt, Peaks Academic and Research Unit, Rampton Hospital, Retford, UK
Sara Morgan, Abertawe Bro Morgannwg University Health Board, Swansea, UK
Gita Patel, University of Nottingham, Nottingham, UK
Tamsin Short, Centre for Forensic Behavioural Science, Victorian Institute of Forensic Mental Health and Monash University, Melbourne, Australia
Amanda Tetley, University of Nottingham, Nottingham, UK.

Acknowledgements

Part I

Introduction to forensic research

1 Conducting research in forensic settings

Philosophical and practical issues

Jason Davies, Kerry Sheldon
and Kevin Howells

The purpose of this chapter is to give a context and sequence to the research process into which the methodological chapters in this book can be placed. Undertaking research in forensic settings requires the researcher to consider a wide range of issues from the point of the initial idea, through the planning and conducting phases to the final stages of dissemination. Whilst the process of research in forensic settings is the same as that found in any other area of social sciences research, the unique context places additional burdens, restraints and challenges upon the researcher. As we shall see, these include issues such as accessing participants, restrictions which impact on data collection and a wide range of ethical considerations (which are the specific focus of Chapter 2). This chapter will provide an overview of the research process; however, specific attention will be given to philosophical and theoretical issues, sampling and practical points.

Why do research in forensic settings?

This question is not intended to be flippant but rather to encourage the practitioner to carefully consider two interrelated issues – why is research needed in forensic practice and what might be the motivations and reasons for embarking upon research? Over the past 25 years a number of areas have become major topics of research activity within forensic practice, including research into specific personality factors such as psychopathy and anger; risk assessment and more recently management; violent and sexual offending; malingering; treatment outcome assessment; and the analysis of crime scene data. For the aspiring researcher, this range of topics is far from exhaustive and this means that there are a multitude of areas in which no or little research has been conducted – providing ample scope and opportunity to be the first to explore an idea or test a hypothesis through research. As with social sciences research in other areas much of the research conducted in forensic settings has one of two purposes: (a) *theory building* or inductive reasoning in which the researcher seeks to use observations and other data to generate explanations about the relationships or causal processes present; and (b) *theory testing* or deductive reasoning in which the researcher seeks to gather specific evidence which might disprove a particular theory (Breakwell, 1995). As you will see in the examples contained within the methodology chapters of this book, researchers start with some notion, curiosity or questions to which they seek an answer or a more robust understanding. Importantly, the relationship between theory building and testing is generally reciprocal with these two research goals feeding back and forth. However, as we shall see, when we look at research philosophy, theory may range from understanding the individual through to understanding some generalisable construct or idea.

Research has the potential to cause splits or rifts between researchers and practitioners unless the purposes and processes are carefully managed. In treatment settings this may be achieved in many ways including research being commissioned and/or conducted by practitioners in the settings in which they work, and by researchers being sensitive to the potential implications of their findings. Unfortunately, within many forensic disciplines practitioners and researchers have often been divided; practitioners applying knowledge and academics undertaking research. Despite these tensions and splits, the reality is that the relationship between practice and research is increasingly important. Furthermore, practice is enhanced through practitioners who have a good grasp of research methods (and are confident to undertake research) and research is improved when researchers understand the practice, issue and/or setting they seek to investigate. Because of this, the growing number of practitioner-researchers is to be welcomed, enabling the wisdom gained from research and practice to be integrated and to foster an interplay which enhances our understanding of forensic problems and questions.

Research philosophies and paradigms

The philosophical position of the social scientist (i.e. their beliefs about the nature of research, evidence, knowledge and science) will influence the way in which their research is defined and conducted. Although many forensic workers may be both researchers and practitioners and subscribe to the broad notion of being a scientist-practitioner this provides just a starting point to report one's philosophy of knowledge, understanding and research. The term *scientist practitioner* has a long and varied history; however, the ethos of this is the integration of scientific understanding and evidence into applied settings (Shapiro, 2002). In assessment and intervention settings this may be in the form of evidence-based practice (using research to guide practice) and practice-based evidence (gathering evidence alongside practice).

There are a multitude of terms used to describe the wide variety of philosophical research positions which is beyond the scope of this chapter. However, a basic discussion of the commonly used phrases and ideas which underpin research and the researcher is necessary. It is worth noting that research methods themselves may be embedded in a philosophical position and so a researcher moving from one method to another may need to adjust their stance to reflect this. However, it is important to accept that whilst the paradigms have been described below as discrete entities, there is an increasing blurring of research/inquiry methodology and genres (Guba and Lincoln, 2005). Anyone exploring the philosophical ideas outlined here will begin to appreciate the complex web of information available and the challenge of succinctly and clearly articulating research philosophy. This is probably one reason why many researchers avoid the question: 'What philosophies underpin your general approach to research?' It must be stated that whilst research methods may have a good fit with one philosophy or another, philosophies and paradigms themselves do not dictate methodology. Thus it is possible for qualitative and/or quantitative methods to be used for data collection and analysis across paradigms. Further quantitative methods may be underutilised by researchers within some paradigms (Guba and Lincoln, 2005).

A common starting point for describing philosophy is the positivist research position. *Positivism* describes the pursuit of 'models or laws of behaviour' which researchers working from this stance believe can be derived from observation or measurement of the social world. Thus knowledge in this paradigm is based upon empiricism ('direct evidence') and the theories developed typically focus upon understanding causation, which the positivist would seek to generalise from a sample to a population. The method has close links to those adopted in the physical sciences and much quantitative and experimental social sciences research takes a largely positivist approach. Critics of this approach argue that in pursuing objectivity, the subjective dimension of social research is overlooked. Core to this position are concerns with the reliability and validity of data and the generalisability of findings from samples to a wider population.

In contrast to the objectivity aspired to within the positivist tradition, anti-positivism locates itself firmly within the subjective nature of human experience (Dash, 2005). The anti-positivist position emphasises the ways in which individuals interpret the world and thus focuses upon the interaction between the individual and the world (or specific situations or experiences). The importance of the individual viewpoint and the ways in which these are influenced and shaped by individual experience inform many of the qualitative approaches widely used in social research, whether or not they subscribe to an anti-positivist stance.

The anti-positivist philosophy hides a more complex and subtle range of alternatives that have emerged in response to the positivist position. For the purposes of this chapter, the four positions described by Guba and Lincoln (2005) of post-positivism, critical theory, constructivism and participatory/action will be outlined.

Post-positivism can be viewed as a modification of the positivist stance in that rather than theories and models being viewed as absolutes they are accepted as approximations. However, the goal of 'describing reality' remains. Post-positivism acknowledges the subjectivity of the researcher, the influence of context and the limitations of measurement and data. The post-positivist stance supports the use of triangulation (i.e. testing the overlap between data of different types, of different kinds or from different sources) in order to develop and test theory. Although the post-positivist approach remains largely quantitative (concern with numerical information), qualitative (concern with subjective information) methods are sometimes used.

Critical theory encompasses a broad range of theoretical positions. Guba and Lincoln (2005) argue that all maintain a historical realist perspective i.e. that there is a reality 'out there' which is shaped by factors such as social and political values. The approach to uncovering knowledge is through subjective means. Critical theory is particularly concerned with issues of power and justice as they are enacted and create influence in people's lives. The efforts to critique the present (and how it came to be) and to engage in transformation (and the concern with 'what could be') underpin this paradigm (Kincheloe and McLaren, 2005). Thus, research within this philosophy seeks to promote social change and overcome social injustice.

Constructivism is concerned with the creation of models though the interaction between the researcher and the researched. This philosophical position takes a relativist stance (i.e. there are multiple realities 'constructed' by different people). Guba and Lincoln (1994) suggest that: 'The final aim [of constructivism] is to distill a consensus construction that is more informed and sophisticated than any of the predecessor constructions ...' (p. 111). In common with other 'new paradigms', the concept of validity concerns the rigor of the interpretation and whether the findings can be trusted.

Participatory / action research is a cyclical process of research where the findings of research are used to make direct changes even whilst the research is being conducted. It has been suggested that this paradigm arose from 'widespread non-utilization of evaluation findings ... [and from] a political and ethical commitment' to research leading to change (Guba and Lincoln, 2005; p. 201). Action research is a form of 'democratic enquiry in which professional researchers collaborate with local stakeholders to seek and enact solutions to problems of major importance to the stakeholders' (Greenwood and Levin, 2005; p. 54); thus neither the researcher nor stakeholder knowledge or power prevails over the other. Validity and credibility are measured by the willingness of the stakeholders to act on the findings (Greenwood and Levin, 2005).

Many researchers, especially those using qualitative methods, will seek to further define their research position. For example, a constructionist might subscribe to a phenomenolgical approach in which the study of experience is used in order to discover knowledge through unbiased description. For those wishing to explore the philosophy of research further, a number of articulate summaries exist; however, a comprehensive introduction is the edited text by Denzin and Lincoln (2005).

The research process in seven steps

1. Identifying a research topic/question

The first step in undertaking research is to define the research topic and subsequent questions which will be addressed (see Barrett, 1995). This will usually be based upon the researcher's curiosity, theory or previous research. For those new to research, the prospect can be both exciting and daunting. A novice researcher may follow their own interests; however, it is increasingly the case that junior researchers will develop a research idea based on a line of enquiry being pursued by a supervisor or senior colleague. This can be a good starting point, as it might assist with containing the size and scope of the project, enable the researcher to contribute to a larger 'scheme of work' and maximize the likelihood that the supervisors and collaborators will commit the necessary time and other resources to the project. Whatever the origins of the research, for those new to research (and for those with lots of experience!), having a good learning experience during the research process is at least as important as the exact nature of, and approach to, the research conducted.

Careful attention should be paid to developing the research question. Typically, this will include reviewing the literature to a) check that the research idea has not already been addressed in the way planned (or if it has, how the proposed research would fit) and b) help define the research. The extent to which the literature is used to define the research will vary according to the approach adopted. This is because some methods advocate using the data to lead analysis and interpretation stating that this is best achieved by minimising preconceptions or expectations generated from elsewhere such as past research and literature. Nevertheless, some review of the literature is necessary to test out the appropriateness, viability and possible utility of the research.

In this first phase, it is important to define the research purpose and question(s) as specifically as possible. Researchers should consider how the phrasing of the question might influence how it is addressed and ensure that the question(s) being asked can be operationalised (i.e. described in unambiguous detail) and that the assumptions made can be minimised. Sometimes, however, the research purpose and question will evolve during the course of the research activity based on the findings of the research along the way. This is particularly the case in research based on a participatory/action approach.

Time dedicated to defining the research purpose and questions is very well spent, potentially saving time, resources, effort and sanity later in the process. Underdeveloped research ideas (and questions) can result in research which is of poor quality or that fails to live up to the researcher's hopes and expectations. The importance of the research question being clearly specified can be illustrated through the following example. A review of the literature might lead a researcher to pose the question 'Do poor social skills increase the likelihood of sexual offending in men?' based on the argument that those who commit sexual offences lack social skills and thus fail to form appropriate and satisfying adult relationships. The researcher might be tempted to undertake a study in which sexual offenders are studied and data collected on their social skill (perhaps using questionnaire and observer report data) and number and nature of offences (based on conviction and self-report data). The findings may be that, in the sample of sexual offenders studied, they do indeed have poor social skills and that further analysis shows that those with the poorest social skills have the largest number of offences. Findings such as these might tempt the researcher to conclude that social skills are poor in sexual offenders and that these deficits increase the likelihood of sexual offending.

However, there are a number of very important limitations in this study which mean that the conclusions the researcher believed they could draw cannot be made with confidence. First, without a non-offending group, it is not possible to determine the number of people with poor social skills who do not offend. This is important to consider because if many people with poor social skills do not offend the proposition upon which the research question rests is challenged. Second, without controlling for age, the relationship between more offences and poorer social skills may simply reflect a difference in age between research participants. Older participants may have spent more time withdrawn from others (further impeding their social skills) and the increased number of convictions may simply reflect more lifetime opportunity to offend. Third, the self-report elements of the research might affect the reliability or validity of the data collected. For example individuals might be affected by reporting bias and so might provide answers which they believe the researcher wants or that puts them in a particular light. Fourth, people with poor social skills might be more likely to be caught for sexual offences committed rather than being any more likely to commit the offence in the first place. Thus the influence of gathering conviction data rather than data concerning whether or not an act has taken place significantly affects the conclusions that can be drawn. Other limitations are more theoretical in nature. Fifth, social skills may be relevant for some sexual offenders but not all. Thus a typography of individuals might be lost if the global (and simple) question of the relationship between social skills and offence conviction is investigated. Sixth, models typically include a multitude of factors which may have relevance. Investigating one without consideration of the others may mean that important relationships are missed or that one factor becomes seen as more or less important than it really is.

As can be seen from this simple exploration, developing and specifying the research question is an important first step, as is anticipating problems of inference and interpretation that may arise when data have been collected. Once the question is in place decisions can be made about the method.

2. Identifying the approach: analysis, sample and method

In order to address the question(s) the researcher has asked, an appropriate approach to data collection and analysis needs to be selected. It is essential that this phase comes *after* the research question has been developed, although in the authors' experience it is not uncommon for a novice researcher to ask for a research topic and question that they can apply a particular methodology to. Starting with the research question should, at least in theory, mean that the researcher needs to be versed in a range of methods so that they can pick the method to suit the question/research purpose. Often, however, the philosophical stance of the researcher will influence the types of question they ask or may lead them to discard questions which might require the use of an unfamiliar methodology or change in research approach. The subsequent methodology chapters in this book will assist the researcher to consider many of the possible approaches to research, enabling them to choose a method which might best suit the question they have posed.

Once the research method has been selected, other aspects of the research design need to be considered. The source(s) of the data and the criteria that will be used to guide the selection of data sources require attention. Certain parameters may be dictated by the question being asked. For example a *longitudinal* design, where data is collected from the same participants over time, allows individual development or change over time to be investigated or the influence that factor (A) measured at time one has on another factor (B) at a later time to be determined. Research on the 'course of committing crime and natural desistence' has often made use of such an approach (e.g. Simmons Longitudinal Study – see www.simmons.edu/ssw/sls (accessed 30/1/11); The Cambridge Study – see www.crim.cam.ac.uk/people/dpfl/csdd185.pdf (accessed 30/1/11)). Alternatively, if the researcher is interested in how a phenomenon might present itself or the relationship between specific factors, one or more cohorts of individuals may be studied at a single point in time. Such an approach is referred to as a *cross-sectional* study and is widely used in forensic research. One example is that of a study designed to measure the prevalence of domestic violence in a general practice setting (Richardson *et al.*, 2002). When researchers are interested in the difference between two groups they need to consider how far they wish to use *matched* (i.e. similar on key characteristics such as age, gender mix, educational attainment, ethnicity and income) or *unmatched* samples. Where samples are closely matched and only those who meet rigorous predetermined criteria are used, the sample may be said to be *controlled*. Useful discussion of the issues associated with this approach in forensic settings can be found in Hollin (Chapter 11) and Farrington and Jolliffe (2002).

Once the method has been selected (or narrowed down to a small number) other considerations such as the source of data and the approach to data collection should be introduced. Undertaking any research will require the identification, gathering or compiling of appropriate data. Typically, the question being posed will dictate the nature of the sample and the method being followed is likely to shape the sample size needed. For example if the researcher were to address the question 'How do prison officers come to terms with responding to a suicide in custody?' using an Interpretative Phenomenological Approach (Smith *et al.*, 2009) then the sample would need to be prison officers who have had this experience. Further, the researcher may be interested in a particular time frame following such an experience or the cumulative effect of three or more such experiences. These factors would further shape the sample and the approach would guide the size of the sample. Samples based on specific factors dictated by the researcher are described as *purposeful* samples.

In some circumstances the researcher may shape their question and determine their approach based on the information they have about the availability and access to a sample; however, the sample available should not be the starting point for research. For example, the researcher interested in the impact of alcohol on impulsivity, based on a theory that alcohol increases impulsivity which in turn increases the likelihood of violent or sexual offending, may need to develop their question so that they can use a general population sample rather than an incarcerated sample due to restrictions on alcohol consumption in the latter. Such *analogue* samples can be very useful for testing general ideas or in order to provide 'proof of a principle' which might then help demonstrate the case for investigating particular phenomena at a later time within other (e.g. convicted prisoner) population(s).

There are probably as many possible sources of data as there are research questions to be asked. However, data sources can be clustered into categories for consideration. First, data may be gathered from existing sources either where data have been collected for another purpose or, as in the case of meta analyses, where they are derived from the results of other (typically published) studies. These are generally referred to as secondary data. Whilst secondary data are suited to some research questions there are important potential limitations, not least that the data have been designed and collected by others for different purposes which may compromise how the data can be used.

Second, existing materials or information may be converted into data by the researcher, for example using existing text (e.g. news print), video or physical data such as crime scene information. In such circumstances the researcher needs to specify the inclusion criteria for the sources and then provide a detailed method for codifying the material (e.g. features present or absent).

Third, data may be collected directly from a chosen sample of individuals using a scheme designed specifically for the study. This is often the main data source used by forensic researchers. These data can take many forms such as interview transcripts, physiological measurements, observation or self-report psychometric information. In forensic practice, samples can come from a multitude of sources which frequently include convicted or remand prisoners, individuals in forensic mental health settings, criminal justice workers, witnesses or victims of crime. However, increasingly the use of internet mediated research (e.g. Davies *et al.*, 2007) enables researchers to access relevant participants in large numbers. Such an approach can be particularly helpful when the researcher is trying to move beyond conviction as a defining characteristic or when groups that can be difficult to access in other ways are required. Just like other methods there are limitations with this approach, such as self-selection and computer access (see Davies *et al.*, 2007).

Finally, non-forensic samples may be appropriate for some research questions. Whilst these are often drawn from student groups because of the ease of access to such populations, techniques such as snowballing (where individuals who complete the research are asked to encourage others to participate) can be useful. However, such convenience samples, which are based on those individuals available to the researcher, might also lead to the exclusion of particular groups. Convenience sampling can be method of choice where the question under study is a general one. Often researchers using this approach hope to gather a large volume of data which they can later organise into subgroups based on specific demographic information. However, limitations of this approach include possible systematic biases in respondents (e.g. all are students; over-representation of females) or that meaningful groups cannot be formed from the gathered data due to large variability in respondent characteristics. Careful consideration to the way(s) in which the sample will be accessed and any additional or specific issues which may be pertinent should be given at this stage (e.g. ability of minors to provide consent to participate in research; permissions to access individuals detained in particular establishments; logistics of collecting samples across a wide geographical area; likely drop out or refusal rate).

As researchers we need to be aware of the range of difficulties that can be faced in accessing participants and data, with no approach being immune from potential problems. Common issues include small numbers of potential participants eligible for inclusion; problems with access due to security conditions; willingness of participants to engage with research; and motivation for responses given by participants. Researchers need to invest time and effort into identifying potential difficulties, understanding the possible impact on the research to be conducted and considering what can be done to address these. A further complication can be the political influences that may be present in forensic settings. This can be at the meta level (i.e. research that is sensitive may require extensive review and authorisation at a high level) or the local level (e.g. findings may challenge service delivery). As with other issues such as those relating to samples and ethics, the researcher should explore these (e.g. to allow extra time for obtaining approval) before developing the research further.

3. Writing a research proposal

Once the researcher has considered existing research and literature, developed the research question and considered the approach and sample they will use to answer it, a protocol or proposal can be written which provides detail of the research to be undertaken. The proposal should provide an outline of the research context along with the purpose of the research (the research question and, where appropriate, hypotheses). Following this introduction, information about the method, including the research approach to be used, the approach to data collection, an outline of the desired sample source and size (including any inclusion and exclusion criteria), details of the materials (e.g. interview schedule; psychometric measures (including their appropriateness)) to be used to gather data and the ways in which the data will be analysed, should be described. The proposal should specify the resources needed for the study (e.g. cost of materials, amount of researcher time), any collaborators and supervisors, funding needed (or available), ethical issues and a timescale. Researchers should also consider the way(s) in which the research findings and implications will be reported and disseminated. Although the protocol might be a relatively brief document, it will help the researcher and others determine the feasibility, strengths and limitations of the study. Various outlines for writing a research protocol or proposal exist such as those at www.des.emory.edu/mfp/proposal. html (accessed 30/1/11) and www.education.monash.edu.au/students/current/ study-resources/proposalwriting.html (accessed 30/1/11).

4. Scientific and ethical review

Once the protocol is written, the study can be reviewed by others to consider its scientific and ethical merits. Scientific review may be through a formal process (e.g. a university or government committee or board) or an informal process where the researcher seeks views and feedback from senior colleagues about the proposed study. The purpose of such review is to ensure that limitations and weaknesses in the study can be considered and where possible addressed before any research is conducted. Ethical review generally follows scientific review (or may be part of the same process) and is generally formalised (e.g. health service or criminal justice research ethics processes; university research ethics committees). Further issues relating to research ethics can be found in Chapter 2.

Finally, before data collection starts, research governance, registration, sponsorship and necessary funding may need to be in place. Funding can have an important influence over research, especially as funding bodies may support one type of question or area of study over another or give preference to those with established research careers. Local funding or special grants from funding bodies (e.g. to undertake a PhD) can be useful sources for less experienced researchers to consider. The agency overseeing the research (e.g. university, health service, prison, employer) can provide advice on these aspects.

5. Undertaking data collection

Once the research has a favourable ethical opinion, formal requirements are in place (e.g. research governance procedures or research sponsorship), necessary funding is obtained and access to participants has been secured, data collection can begin. Data collection will be guided by the procedure specified in the protocol which will in turn be informed by the approach to research being taken. This part of the process is often anxiety provoking and time consuming, and monitoring and review should be used to ensure that the research remains on schedule. Often researchers who are gathering data directly from participants will specify in the protocol other (additional) possible sources of participants and/or data as backup in case recruitment problems arise.

6. Analysing data

Data analysis will be guided by the approach to research that has been selected. The methodology chapters in this book provide descriptions of a wide range of methods for analysing data of different kinds and from different sources.

7. Writing up and dissemination

Writing up and disseminating research findings is a very important stage. Where the research has been commissioned, funded or is part of an academic process the way in which the research should be reported may be specified. This may include providing progress reports during the research study as well as a report at the end. Researchers should also consider the range of other ways in which the research may be presented to others such as through service documents, training, in a newsletter, a poster or presentation at a meeting or conference, as a book chapter or as a journal article. Each of these will require the research to be presented in a particular way; however, the widely used structure of introduction, research purpose/questions, method, results, discussion and conclusions will be relevant for the majority of these.

For those who have not written up research in the format required obtaining examples is a good starting point. In addition resources such as 'Communication in Psychology' (Chapter 14; Shaughnessy *et al.*, 2009) and 'Publishing Your Psychology Research: A Guide to Writing for Journals in Psychology and Related Fields' (McInerny, 2001) may be helpful.

However, we are aware that contemplating and writing a submission for a journal can be daunting and so offer some pointers here. The starting point is to choose possible journals to submit to. This can be informed by asking experienced researchers for suggestions of journals that might be appropriate; reviewing your reference list to identify any journals which have published similar research and looking at the aims and scope of journals to identify whether your work might fit with their stated purpose. Typically, researchers will select a number of journals which might accept the paper and then put them in a 'submission sequence', i.e. which journal will be submitted to first and then where the work might be submitted next if not accepted (and so on). This order may be informed by the likely time a journal will take to make a decision; the reported 'impact factor' of the journal (the measure of the average number of citations per article; c.f. *H-index* which is the impact of a researcher); or the individual wishes of the researchers. It is very common for the research not to be accepted by the first (or even second or third) journals – however, the feedback received may be very helpful to modify the manuscript before it is submitted elsewhere. Acceptance rates for journals vary widely, influenced by factors such as the submission rates and the standing of the journal (and thus the standard of research required for publication).

Once the journal has been selected, the researcher should read the author guidelines which each journal will provide. These can be commonly found on their website. The website will also describe the type of research or content which is welcomed by the journal as well as their circulation (e.g. worldwide or UK). Author guidelines will also outline the maximum length of a paper and how manuscripts should be formatted and submitted. Increasingly this is via an online submission process. You should carefully consider who will be named as authors on the paper and any acknowledgements you wish to make. Again guidance can be found online.

The processes of peer review and production are often described on the journal's website too, but typically papers submitted to a journal are peer reviewed. Some are rejected without going through a peer review if the journal editor decides that they are unsuitable for the journal. If your paper is sent for peer review it will be sent to two or three reviewers (experts in the field of research or the methodology) to comment on the article and make a recommendation about its suitability for publication. This part of the process will commonly take three months if not longer. Consequently, a decision is made based on these comments and recommendations; there are several possible outcomes: *reject* (not suitable for publication – may be due to 'fit' with the journal or serious flaws in the research or write up); *reject and resubmit with substantial changes* (may be suitable if significant changes are made – this will often include reanalysis or further analysis of the data – the paper will then be reviewed again usually by at least one of the original reviewers); *accept with minor changes* (requirement to make changes to the way information is presented or changing / modifying text); and *accept in current form* (no changes necessary). A paper may go through several revisions before acceptance. Journals may have an appeal system if you feel your manuscript has been unfairly treated, misunderstood or important points overlooked. The editor may then decide to reconsider the decision.

Once your paper has been accepted you cannot introduce substantial new information or make substantive changes. The paper will then be sent to the publishers of the journal for copy-editing and layout and you will be sent a copy of these proofs for checking and approval. This part of the process may take several months depending on the number of papers the journal has waiting for publication. Journals are increasingly publishing papers online first in order to make the work formally available before it is available in printed journal form.

Conclusions

This chapter has attempted to set the scene of research by providing a focus on research philosophies and the general research process. It is hoped that this guide and structure will provide a useful support to the following chapters and provide those undertaking research in forensic settings with a helpful overview to which they can return as necessary.

Some useful resources

In addition to the web links contained within the chapter the following provide general information on social research:

http://changingminds.org/explanations/research/research.htm
www.socialresearchmethods.net/kb/index.php
www.celt.mmu.ac.uk/researchmethods/index.htm

References

Barrett, M. (1995). Practical and ethical issues in planning research. In Glynis M. Breakwell, Sean Hammond and Chris Fife-Schaw (Eds). *Research methods in psychology*. London: Sage.

Breakwell, G. M. (1995). Introducing research methods in psychology. In Glynis M. Breakwell, Sean Hammond and Chris Fife-Schaw (Eds). *Research methods in psychology*. London: Sage.

Dash, N. K. (2005). Selection of the research paradigm and methodology. Available from www.celt.mmu.ac.uk/researchmethods/Modules/Selection_of_methodology/index.php (accessed 30/1/11).

Davies, J., Oddie, S. and Powls, J. (2007). Using the internet to conduct research relevant to forensic practice. *The British Journal of Forensic Practice*, 9(4): 19–22.

Denzin, N. K. and Lincoln, Y. S. (Eds) (2005). *The handbook of qualitative research*. 3rd edn. California: Sage.

Farrington, D. P. and Jolliffe, D. (2002). A feasibility study into using a randomised controlled trial to evaluate treatment pilots at HMP Whitemoor. Home Office Online Report 14/02. Available from www.dspdprogramme.gov.uk/media/pdfs/Feasibility_HMP_Grendon.pdf (accessed 30/1/11).

Greenwood, D. J. and Levin, M. (2005). Reform of the social sciences, and of universities through action research. In Norman K. Denzin and Yvonna S. Lincoln (Eds). *The handbook of qualitative research*. 3rd edn. London: Sage.

Guba, E. G. and Lincoln, Y. S. (1994). Competing paradigms in qualitative research. In Norman K. Denzin and Yvonna S. Lincoln (Eds). *The handbook of qualitative research*. 3rd edn. London: Sage.

—— (2005). Paradigmatic controversies, contraditctions, and emerging confluences. In Norman K. Denzin and Yvonna S. Lincoln (Eds). *The handbook of qualitative research*. 3rd edn. London: Sage.

Kincheloe, J. L. and McLaren, P. (2005). Rethinking Critical Theory and qualitative research. In Norman K. Denzin and Yvonna S. Lincoln (Eds). *The handbook of qualitative research*. 3rd edn. London: Sage.

McInerny, D. M. (2001). *Publishing your psychology research: a guide to writing for journals in psychology and related fields*. London: Sage.

Richardson, J., Coid, J., Petruckevitch, A., Chung, W. S., Moorey, S. and Feder, G. (2002). Identifying domestic violence: cross sectional study in primary care. *British Medical Journal*, 324: 1–6.

Shapiro, D. (2002). Renewing the scientist practitioner model. *The Psychologist*, 15(5): 232–4.

Shaughnessy, J. J., Zechmeister, E. B. and Zechmeister, J. S. (2009). *Research methods in psychology*. 8th edn. New York: McGraw-Hill.

Smith, J. A., Flowers, P. and Larkin, M. (2009). *Interpretative phenomenological analysis: theory, method and research*. London: Sage.

2 Ethical problems arising in forensic and correctional research

Tony Ward and Gwenda Willis

Introduction

While the literature on ethical issues associated with social science research is rapidly growing and becoming increasingly sophisticated, few papers have been published on the ethics of forensic or correctional research (but see Adshead and Brown, 2003; Overholser, 1987). The literature that does exist is arguably narrow and superficial, and is overly reliant on professional ethical codes (Lavin, 2003; O'Donohue and Ferguson, 2003; Ward and Syversen, 2009). Articles that focus directly on forensic and correctional ethical concerns emphasise procedural matters and are preoccupied with practice related issues such as who is the client, safety, dual relationships, how to deal with duty to warn situations and so on (Bush *et al.*, 2006; Haag, 2006). More research oriented work tends to concentrate on matters of recruitment and barriers to research rather than systemically addressing the ethical questions confronting all social science researchers (Appelbaum, 2008).

Ethical norms for research are intended to ensure that the practice of social science is undertaken in ways that benefit rather than harm research participants, researchers and the rest of the community. These aims are well summarised by Symonette (2009):

> Social research ethics speaks to the morally responsible ways in which we should conduct ourselves as we design and engage in systematic inquiry, analysis, interpretation, and dissemination processes via-a-vis individuals, groups, organisations, communities, and so on. Ethical practice is reflected in the extent to which researchers conduct themselves and their research in ways that are respectful, are fairly representative (accurate and just) and ideally leave persons better off – or at least minimally, 'does no harm.'
> (p. 280–1)

The above quote directly raises an important ethical issue concerning the ethical competences that can be reasonably expected of a researcher and the degree to which norms ought be be rationally justified rather than arbitrarily asserted (Driver, 2006; Kitchener, 2000). This general issue can be usefully unpacked in the form of two fundamental ethical questions that social science researchers need to answer (Kitchener and Kitchener, 2009; Ginsberg and Mertens, 2009). First, how *should* research data be collected, analysed and reported? Second, how *should* researchers act towards participants in their research projects?

In this chapter we discuss some of the specific ethical challenges for researchers working in forensic and correctional domains, using the two questions outlined above as a guide. We consider how best to deal with ethical problems that arise in forensic and correctional contexts. In the final section, some attention will be given to how to address some of these concerns. Our aim will be to provide researchers with some *general ideas* of how to proceed in certain situations rather than come up with a final set of answers to every conceivable problem. The ethical problems and our responses emerging from the two questions overlap to some degree, as you would expect when dealing with practices (i.e. patterns of actions revolving around primary goals) and moral agents (Driver, 2006). The material covered in this chapter is intended to apply to forensic and correctional settings but it should be noted that there are unique challenges in the former. For one thing, the presence of severe mental illness creates an additional set of ethical pressures that relate to individuals' status as patients as well as offenders, for example elevated concerns about competency and vulnerability.

Ethical issues in forensic and correctional contexts

Human dignity

In a recent paper, Ward and Syversen (2009) developed an integrated ethical framework that covered the different levels of ethical tasks inherent in forensic and correctional work. The key argument of the Ward and Syversen paper is that researchers and practitioners ought to justify their ethical decisions in a stepwise process, typically first relying on their commonsense everyday reasoning and then in successive steps appealing to the standards of ethical codes, principles underling ethical codes (e.g. beneficence, autonomy, justice and integrity), ethical concepts and theory and ultimately the concept of human dignity. In essence, the concept of dignity designates the moral *worth* or value of all human beings (Sulmasy, 2007). Because of their inherent dignity (i.e. intrinsic worth) human beings are assumed to possess equal moral status and therefore are expected to receive equal consideration in matters that directly affect their core interests. According to the analysis by Beyleveld and Brownsword (2001), the dignity of human beings is located in their capacity to formulate and pursue their interests in the world (empowerment) without unjustified interference by other people. In order to actively pursue their core interests and goals individuals require a certain level of well-being and access to social, psychological and material resources, otherwise it would be impossible for them to function as autonomous individuals (i.e. dependence on resources and opportunities are constraints, their absence undermines a person's agency efforts). We will draw on the concept of dignity when discussing the various ethical dilemmas confronting researchers.

The design, collection, analysis and reporting of research data

The ethical problems in this section all revolve around the design of studies and the ways in which data are collected, analysed and presented in journals or reports. The various issues cluster into the following themes: (a) making theoretical assumptions explicit, (b) aims of research, (c) selection of research designs, (d) data presentation, (e) negative results, (f) analysis decisions and resource wastage, (g) self as an instrument and finally (h) participants and data.

Making theoretical assumptions explicit

A first problem involves the importance of ensuring that a researcher's theoretical assumptions are made explicit rather than remaining implicit (Brown and Hedges, 2009). The articulation of a research problem often will involve clarifying the nature of a phenomenon such as deviant sexual arousal in sex offenders or speculating about the causal mechanisms that generate a phenomenon, for example deviant sexual preferences (Ward et al., 2006). A more forensic mental health oriented example is describing the relationship between psychotic symptoms and aggression (Bartol and Bartol, 2008). Once researchers are clear about their assumptions it is then a question of ascertaining what kind of design will provide the data necessary to clarify or address the problem at issue. The danger is that failure to clearly specify the postulated relevant mechanisms may result in poorly directed investigation or else premature acceptance of current ideas and practice. An example of the latter is the past mistaken assumption that sex offenders only follow one offence and/or relapse process whereas empirical evidence revealed that there are in fact a number of distinct offence trajectories (Hudson et al., 1999; Ward et al., 2006; Yates and Kingston, 2006).

Research aims

A second point concerns the broader social aims of research in ethical and forensic contexts irrespective of whether its focus is on etiological or assessment and programme related matters. The design of a study and methods of data collection depend on the reasons for undertaking it and also arguably who is likely to benefit from the findings. For example if members of the public have a strong interest in ensuring that violence towards women and children is reduced then research priorities in the area of aggression are likely to reflect this concern. A difficulty may be that research into other, equally important, correctional and forensic issues is neglected or that there is pressure to develop programmes without the basic science being in place. Thus, in order to acquire funding researchers may prematurely accept clinically derived theory and treatment programmes based on this theory as warranted knowledge and proceed to design programme evaluation studies. An example of this is arguably the premature acceptance of suggestions that there is a causal relationship between sexual offending and negative affect whereas the actual research evidence for this relationship is comparatively weak (McCoy and Fremouw, 2010). Alternatively, the assumption that offender rehabilitation initiatives ought to focus predominately on risk reduction has resulted in a failure to consider the role of protective factors or well-being considerations in the reintegration process (Ward and Maruna, 2007).

Selection of research designs

A third ethical problem relates to decisions concerning the kind of research designs and analytical methods employed in a project. The choice between the use of ethnographic, interview based or experimental research designs is a crucial one and has ethical dimensions alongside epistemic considerations such as the degree to which causal inferences are facilitated or natural social processes respected. An example of how disagreement over design issues can be associated with ethical debate is the recent interchange between Marshall and Marshall (2007; 2008) and Seto *et al.* (2007) over whether or not the randomised controlled trial (RCT) is the gold standard for research into the effectiveness of sexual offending treatment. Marshall and Marshall argued that RCT designs lack ecological validity and also raised serious ethical concerns about allocating offenders to non-treatment conditions, thereby possibly placing future members of the community at risk from untreated men. Seto *et al.* took issue with Marshall and Marshall's conclusions and argued strongly for the value of RCT designs (suitably implemented) in providing robust evidence for treatment effectiveness. Seto *et al.*'s de facto assumption appears to be that the strongest possible design should always be implemented in treatment research whereas Marshall and Marshall state that ethical concerns may override scientific aims in some circumstances. Consistent with Marshall and Marshall's position, Mark and Gamble (2009) assert that despite constituting an extremely powerful research design sometimes RCT designs may not be desirable if reasonable evidence *already exists* that certain treatment approaches are likely to be useful. They conclude that for an RCT design to be implemented 'there needs to be real uncertainty about the best course of action, that is, about which alternative is preferable' (p. 204). There is certainly a question mark over whether this degree of uncertainty exists when it comes to the treatment of sex offenders with cognitive behavioural techniques. In fact, research indicates that offender programmes that target criminogenic needs (dynamic risk factors) and follow the principles of risk and responsivity are likely to reduce reoffending rates (Andrews and Bonta, 2003; Hanson *et al.*, 2009). If a treatment programme for sex offenders follows the principles of risk, need and responsivity it is possible that a quasi-experimental design of some kind is scientifically acceptable, and ethically supported.

Taking into account the current state of knowledge in the sexual offending field it is at least possible to use this argument to refute claims that RCTs represent the only ethically acceptable, and scientifically supported, research design for treatment outcome evaluations.

A problem that is especially relevant for researchers using interview based methods and qualitative designs is the danger of creating inappropriately intense and close relationships with participants which ultimately may prove harmful to the offender and also compromise the integrity of the research itself. Interview based approaches frequently require researchers to establish strong rapport with offenders and there is a danger in prison environments characterised by mistrust, loneliness and fear that such a relationship could cross the boundaries into a therapeutic one. A potential consequence of this boundary violation is that the interactions will lead to inevitable disappointment and possibly a sense of betrayal in the offenders concerned. Acknowledging the inherent value of offenders means taking their interests into account when undertaking research activities and appreciating the possible effects of some methods on the subsequent well-being and autonomy of offenders. We suggest that failure to consider the impact of data collection methods on what constitutes suitable boundaries between researchers and offenders indicates a lack of integrity on behalf of the former.

Data presentation

A fourth ethical issue related to design, data collection and analysis concerns the way data are presented. Researchers should be careful to take into account accepted findings that are relevant for their research questions and ensure that the data are analysed in ways that reflect these distinctions, and presented accordingly. For example research on sex offenders that fails to distinguish between risk levels and variables that are known to affect outcomes such as age, sexual deviancy, emotional regulation and so on is misleading and ethically unacceptable (Craig *et al.*, 2009). It may culminate in clinical and research decisions that unfairly disadvantage offenders such as unnecessarily long or overly intrusive parole conditions. This problem is particularly pertinent to research on risk assessment. An associated issue is the need to examine research results closely and never to rely on simple group effects when publishing or presenting the results (Bersoff *et al.*, 2003; Douglas and Skeem, 2005; Vess, 2008). A similar concern relates to risk assessment more generally with violent offenders and forensic mental health patients (Bartol and Bartol, 2008). In light of the above debate it is prudent for researchers when using risk bands for research purposes or conducting research on risk to take great care to communicate the extent and limitations of their findings. Offenders are already stigmatised and any research outputs that entrench public mistrust and negative stereotypes of this group without strong justification violate both scientific and ethical norms (Laws and Ward, 2011; Ward and Maruna, 2007). It goes without saying that the presentation of data that do not accurately depict the heterogeneity of offenders, and thus causes public outrage, is an affront to their moral equality and dignity.

It may culminate in the perception of offenders as less worthy, and of less intrinsic value than other members of the community.

Negative results

A fifth, associated issue concerns the failure to publish negative study findings whether they arise from assessment, etiological or programme evaluation research projects. This matter is as much the responsibility of journal editors and reviewers as individual researchers. For example it is a well-established recommendation that real efforts should be made to include both published and unpublished studies in meta-analysis in order to avoid the *file drawer* problem, where studies with negative effects are not published (Crombie and Davis, 2009). A difficulty in neglecting to make negative findings public is that erroneous conclusions about a measure or intervention programme's effectiveness may unduly influence subsequent funding decisions and possibly disadvantage offenders and community members. Such a situation could result in withdrawal of good programmes or the continuation of weak ones, a potential disaster from both policy and practice viewpoints. Publishing or making negative results readily available acknowledges the right of the public and offenders to have accurate information when making decisions about the value of research initiatives and any measures or treatment programmes that are linked with them.

Analysis decisions and resource wastage

A sixth problem emerging from data analysis and study design matters occurs when researchers embark on a large study without undergoing power analyses (estimating the number of participants needed to allow for the possibility of reliable, statistically significant effects – Bausell and Li, 2006) or fail to have explicit rules about what to do if an intervention is clearly effective or ineffective (Mark and Gamble, 2009). In some types of programme evaluation research it may be evident early on that a treatment is working and likely to help offenders enhance their quality of life and also reduce risk to the community. It could be argued that in these situations it is ethically and scientifically advantageous to terminate the study prematurely and introduce the programme more generally (Morris, 2007). The ethical benefits of terminating research in these circumstances are that (a) an effective intervention is implemented to reduce risk to the community and to enhance the lives of offenders, (b) valuable resources can be redirected to other worthwhile projects and (c) decisions about what to do given the promising results are placed in the hands of stakeholders (e.g. funding bodies, policy makers etc.) other than researchers. As an aside, issues relating to statistical power are unlikely to be relevant for single case and qualitative research designs. However, associated research concerns such as ensuring that sufficient numbers are recruited to enable saturation (i.e. when qualitatively derived categories are sufficient to account for the data) or ensuring that sufficient data points are included in a single case study ought to be kept in mind when using these types of research designs (Denzin and Lincoln, 2005).

Self as instrument

A seventh ethical issue arises from ethnographic and qualitative research traditions where the researcher's self is viewed as an instrument and therefore subject to concerns about reliability, sensitivity and validity (Symonette, 2009). Problems of bias, lack of reliability and validity arise when researchers' perceptions of participants play an important role in data gathering and interpretation. The source of bias and subsequent contamination of data analysis is most likely to originate in the theoretical allegiances and methodological commitments of researchers, and ultimately, their core values (Day and Ward, 2010). Values reflect fundamental commitments concerning what is worthwhile and best in life and as such underlie choices about how to behave. In this way, it is suggested that values are evident in the broad life goals individuals set for themselves and others and in the way in which these goals are pursued. The danger is that lack of critical scrutiny of theoretical and value assumptions may undermine the integrity of inquiry and result in data and subsequent publications that more reflect aspects of researchers' personal worlds and communities rather than accurately describe the phenomena in question.

Participants and data

A final ethical concern associated with research design, data collection and presentation revolves around the role of participants in gathering the data and to what degree they should be regarded as co-owners of the information and, potentially, co-authors of subsequent research publications. For both ethical and methodological reasons it could be argued that because research participants consent to become involved in a project they have a claim on the data yielded and therefore some entitlement to co-ownership (Ntseane, 2009). And if the data are seen as partly owned by the participants it follows that the publication of the results ought to appear in forms that they are likely to read and understand, and not simply appear in specialised academic journals. Indigenous offenders may have a particularly strong claim for co-ownership and control, especially when the research touches upon their cultural beliefs and practices (LaFrance and Bull, 2009). In forensic and correctional contexts this ethical concern is pressing because of the power imbalances that exist and reluctance to consider offenders as moral equals and potential research partners (Ward and Salmon, 2009). From a dignity perspective, it is easier to appreciate the force of participant claims to data ownership and to negotiate the tricky issues more adroitly.

Researchers and offenders: issues and problems

The ethical problems in this section spring directly from the face-to-face nature of researcher–participant relationships and essentially revolve around the themes of (a) ethical blindness, (b) offenders' moral status, (c) offenders' vulnerability,

(d) cultural/social differences, (e) researcher vices and virtues, and (f) assumptions about disorders and offender treatability (Howells and Day, 2007).

Ethical blindness

A first ethical concern evident in research and practice domains is that of *ethical blindness* (Ward and Syversen, 2009). What we mean by this term is that important ethical matters can remain undetected, in part due to the conceptual constraints imposed by the ethical resources relied on by researchers such as professional ethical codes. In other words, individuals' theoretical commitments influence their ethical judgements, and in part determine what counts as an ethical problem. In our experience, a problem with ethical codes is that because of their derivation from routine research and clinical experience they often do not have anything meaningful to say about some matters that can be legitimately viewed as ethical ones. That is, codes may ignore concerns that are outside the normal moral experience of practitioners and researchers. In our view, ethical codes are *backward* rather than *forward looking* and do not contain the theoretical resources to orientate clinicians to detect ethical flashpoints that have not yet been flagged in such encounters (Cooper, 2004; Ward and Syversen, 2009). A good example of this myopia is research that presupposes the acceptability of allocating offenders into treatment bands according to their assessed level of risk, often defended by reference to the Risk-Need-Responsivity model of offender rehabilitation (RNR; Andrews and Bonta, 2003). The problem with restricting research and treatment in these ways is that offenders can be denied legitimate access to treatment, access that they are ethically entitled to receive according to human rights declarations, and, more fundamentally, their moral equality (Ward and Birgden, 2007). Research projects that presuppose such a division arguably violate their norms and therefore are morally unacceptable.

The moral status of offenders

The above issue of moral blindness places the question of offenders' moral status directly in the foreground: do offenders possess the inherent dignity and hence value of the other members of the community? If so, does the fact they have received punishment erode their moral status (see Ward and Salmon, 2009)? We propose that offenders possess the inherent dignity of all members of the community because they are fellow human beings. This dignity is acknowledged and protected by human rights treaties and protocols and applies to offenders and non-offenders alike (Lippke, 2002; Ward and Birgden, 2007). In effect, this means that research with offenders should proceed in accordance with their equal moral status and only (a) be undertaken under conditions that meet the standards of acceptable punishment and confinement, and (b) be conducted in ways that demonstrate recognition for offenders' intrinsic value (e.g. full disclosure of the aims and consequences of research, do not involve implicit or explicit coercion and so on). Unfortunately, the harsh conditions of imprisonment and neglect of offenders' welfare apparent in many correctional jurisdictions throughout the western world implies a lack of acknowledgement of this inherent dignity (Lazarus, 2004; Travis, 2005). A lack of dignity recognition creates problems for researchers as such conditions render subsequent research with vulnerable individuals problematic (see page 25). Research with offenders incarcerated in prisons that impose unacceptably harsh conditions is thereby rendered unethical and ought to be avoided.

The matter of informed consent (i.e. ensuring that individuals are presented with enough information about a study so they can make reasonable decisions about whether to participate or not) with prisoners does raise the question as to whether it is ever appropriate to use prisoners as research participants. Perez and Treadwell (2009) address ethical issues inherent in using prisoners in biomedical research as participants in clinical trials. The authors highlight the vulnerable status of prisoners and the overrepresentation of physical and mental health problems in prison populations, and argue that 'until the question of adequate health care for prisoners is resolved, human experimentation should not be allowed' (p. 201). They go on to assert that 'for research in prisons to be ethical, it must be interested in upholding prisoners' constitutional right to appropriate quality care while in prison and ensure a stronger and more effective safety net for them when they return home' (p. 201). The authors therefore advocate for research with prisoners, but only when its focus is on the advancement of prisoners' welfare. It is possible, however, that sometimes the pendulum may swing too far in the other direction and correctional officials could be overly paternalistic and deny offenders the opportunity to decide for themselves whether or not to take part in research projects (Overholser, 1987). Issues related to informed consent and competency are to the forefront when prisoners are involved in research projects. There is a heavy burden of proof on researchers in forensic and correctional settings to establish that offenders were under no pressure to consent, and were indeed psychologically competent to do so.

A neglected ethical issue that emerges from a discussion of offenders' moral status and informed consent is how much information should a researcher impart to potential participants? Should all the aims of the research and their potential applications be raised with an offender, or is it sufficient to simply describe the major goals and not engage in such speculation (Chwang, 2010)? This conundrum is nicely illustrated in risk assessment research and the use of such research to inform policy in the management of sex and violent offenders (Vess, 2008). In many western jurisdictions sex offenders are assessed prior to release from prison and if deemed to be of high risk may have strict parole conditions imposed on them or even be committed to special treatment institutions until such time as their risk is significantly reduced. For some offenders, this incarceration could amount to a life sentence (Vess, 2008). In view of the possibility of risk assessment instruments being used in ways that could have adverse effects for (harm) offenders in the future we argue that it is obligatory for researchers to make this possibility explicit to potential study recruits. That is, researchers should state when describing a risk assessment study that one of the consequences of the refinement of the measure concerned is that it might be used in the evaluation and possible confinement (or imposition of strict parole conditions etc.) of offenders in the future. Failure do so would arguably constitute a breach of informed consent norms and a violation of an offender's inherent dignity and status as a moral agent.

The vulnerability of offenders

Offenders are a vulnerable population because of the fact that their core well-being and freedom interests are often neglected or put at risk when living within correctional and forensic institutions (Overholser, 1987; Regehr *et al.*, 2000). The Institute of Medicine (2006) report highlights the degree to which prisoners are a vulnerable population and outlines specific ethical considerations that are required for research involving prisoners as participants. For example potentially inadequate physical and mental healthcare in prisons presents a barrier to ethical research, as research participation might reflect a desperate attempt on the part of prisoners to obtain treatment. The vulnerability of prisoners and offenders more generally needs to be taken into account when it comes to research into mandated treatment programmes for offenders as well as ones where there is evidence of more subtle types of coercion (for a good recent review of issues related to coercion see Day *et al.*, 2004). The fact that offenders who are coerced into treatment may demonstrate favourable outcomes does not necessarily support such interventions because of the violation of offenders' autonomy and ultimately dignity as a human being (also Bonnie, 2006; Marlowe, 2006; McSweeney *et al.*, 2007; Miller, 1998).

A related ethical problem may occur in forensic and correctional settings where researchers may also function as practitioners and hence have dual roles (Munthe *et al.*, 2010). The difficulty in these types of situations is that allegiances formed in therapeutic relationships may exert subtle pressures on offenders to agree to participate in research projects without appropriate consultation and reflection. The fact that offenders have found therapy valuable, and taking into account the bond formed with the clinician-researcher, could combine to persuade him or her that involvement in research is a good option. The worry is that it is arguably never possible when dual relationships exist for offenders to be able to carefully consider the pros and cons of any research involvement. A related ethical problem is that of inducements for agreeing to take part in research projects in settings where 'good' behaviour may be viewed as contributing to early release or favourable treatment by correctional officials (Overholser, 1987). While we appreciate the point being made here, in our view it can be ethical to include offenders in research as long as care is taken to factor in issues of vulnerability and competency. To categorically deny them such opportunities could be regarded as unjustified paternalism and a violation of offenders' autonomy and a denigration of their dignity.

Cultural differences

Modern societies are frequently composed of ethnically diverse groups and this fact is reflected in the ethic mix of prison populations (Parekh, 2006). A glance at the proportion of indigenous prisoners around the world indicates that they are overrepresented in prison populations. To illustrate, as at 21 March 2010, Maori offenders comprised 50.68 per cent of the New Zealand prison population (Department of Corrections, personal communication, 24 March 2010) compared to 14.6 per cent of the general population (Statistics New Zealand, 2006). The key point is that such offenders are currently incarcerated or placed on community orders and that there are cultural differences between such offenders and those belonging to the majority ethnic group. These differences include issues such as informed consent or confidentiality that researchers need to be aware of. For example in some cultures the right to make decisions extends to family and even group members and therefore an offender is unlikely to want to make a decision about research participation unless he or she can consult with family and cultural representatives (Ntseane, 2009). In many prison environments this is likely to prove problematic and there is a danger that offenders' wishes may get ignored and they may consent to research because they feel pressured or undermined. It is typically the cultural challenges within a given society that are likely to prove most taxing for researchers and practitioners in the course of their day-to-day duties (Li, 2006; Ntseane, 2009; Parekh, 2006). It is also imperative that researchers establish that participants from minority cultures possess the necessary knowledge and mainstream cultural competency to fully appreciate the research aims and methods and therefore can make an informed decision about whether or not to take part in the project.

An ethical issue emerging from the social and cultural underpinnings of forensic and correctional research concerns what constitutes warranted knowledge, that is knowledge claims that meet what are considered to be acceptable standards (Denzin and Lincoln, 2005; Mertens and Ginsberg, 2009). Claims to knowledge from other cultures that may have merit could be too easily dismissed because they do not conform in terms of procedures or substance to received standards. Furthermore, research participants may feel that their world views and cognitive strategies are unfairly neglected or even ridiculed.

Virtues and vices

The question of what character traits are desired (virtues) or not desired (vices) in researchers is partly a question of the kinds of skill needed to engage effectively in research tasks, and the broader social aims underpinning forensic and correctional research more generally. In research contexts there are knowledge related virtues such as accuracy, carefulness or flexibility as well as ethical virtues like consideration, sensitivity and empathy. The type of qualities required depends on the specific investigatory tasks and these in turn reflect the research and broader community's core values and research priorities. In a society dominated by a conservative social justice agenda there may be little if any stress placed on offender well-being and therefore the virtues required to conduct research projects constrained by these assumptions will be different from those necessary in a culture dominated by broader humanistic commitments. The ethical problem is that the training researchers receive in formal academic settings and from more informal methods of knowledge transmission in conferences and workshops is likely to heavily influence their skill set and the kinds of research activities they are competent to engage in. For example researchers who are trained under the auspices of risk management assessment and intervention approaches may lack the orientating values and actions necessary to view and relate to offenders as fellow human beings (Denny, 2005; McNeill, 2004). This lack of knowledge could culminate in difficulty in (a) making justifiable ethical decisions and (b) implementing effectively some types of research methods (e.g. ethnographic research). Ideally, the choice of research methods should logically follow from the formulation of the research question rather than stem from the actual skill set possessed by a researcher. A further complication is that researchers' theoretical and methodological commitments could bias the way they formulate problems in the first place and distort any subsequent plan of inquiry.

Assumptions about disorders

A final ethical difficulty evident concerns the assumptions made about disorders and offender treatability (Howells and Day, 2007). Every research project is necessarily underpinned by core assumptions about the nature of the problems and participants being investigated. In the forensic and correctional arena there is the added complication of a strong ethical overlay, that is offenders have frequently inflicted serious harm on members of the community and are being punished as well as researched or treated (Duff, 2001). In light of what is at stake for both offenders and the wider community, it is incumbent on researchers and practitioners to examine their ethical and epistemic assumptions about offenders and their problems carefully (Ward and Maruna, 2007). For example psychopathy has been long regarded by researchers to be virtually untreatable, and as a consequence of this viewpoint there has been little sustained research into the development and evaluation of suitable programmes for individuals diagnosed as psychopathic (Howells and Day, 2007). The worry is that these assumptions may be incorrect or premature, and may instead simply express moral condemnation towards habitually violent and callous individuals masquerading as informed scientific opinion.

Addressing ethical conflicts

A difficult question concerns exactly how researchers should reason about the range of ethical dilemmas that confront them in correctional and forensic research. The nature of such conflicts and their complexity means that more often than not it is a question of engaging in an ethical balancing process. If so, exactly how should the process of ethical reasoning unfold in research contexts? It is clearly not possible to resolve this issue in a chapter intended to provide an overview of both underappreciated and noted ethical concerns in research, but there are some important conceptual constraints that ought to regulate any such attempts. According to Becker (1986) all moral practice is underpinned by two core justificatory assumptions, those of *generalisability* and *equality*. Thus when faced with the inevitable dilemmas generated by research any solutions should (a) generalise to other persons in similar situations and (b) treat every person involved as someone of equal moral status (i.e. as possessing inherent dignity). The later constraint means that unless there are good reasons it is presumed that the interests of all individuals will be equally considered and any decision should result in outcomes that are judged as fair. The two constraints of generalisability and equality will rule out some strategies for addressing research ethical problems. For example, mandated treatment (and associated research projects) would be ruled out for psychologically competent offenders because it overrides the equality assumption without adequate justification. Furthermore, it arguably also violates the assumption of generalisability as it is unlikely researchers would permit themselves or non-offenders to be forcibly treated. Similarly, the biased presentation of data would be ruled out because it could result in wasted research resources, which denies the opportunity for policy makers and the community to make balanced decisions about the allocation of funds. This failure ignores the equality of individuals as co-decision makers and, if universalised, could undermine research completely. Finally, when recruiting participants for a project neglecting relevant individual differences such as ethnicity, or overlooking the vulnerability of offenders to implicit or explicit coercion, does not succeed in meeting the requirements of both tests. It fails the generalisability assumption because most individuals would reject a general rule that allowed researchers to exploit vulnerable individuals for research purposes. Furthermore, the fact that the participants were (a) not provided with relevant information or (b) pressured to consent would also fail to meet the equality assumption.

From an institutional viewpoint, ethics review committees provide valuable feedback for researchers but they really only address a limited range of ethical concerns. In order to deepen ethical perception and improve decision making the following suggestions could be helpful. First, set up informal research groups to discuss projects from an ethical perspective alongside strictly scientific (methodological) matters. A related strategy is to give proposals to someone whose ethical competence researchers respect and ask for critique and feedback. Second, engage in a process of ethical education through study groups and personal reading. There are a number of recent introductory books on ethical thinking that cover both theoretical and practical issues and that should provide researchers with a deeper understanding of what ethics is about and how it can impact on the process of inquiry (e.g. Cooper, 2004; Driver, 2006; Kitchener,

2000; Mertens and Ginsberg, 2009; Nussbaum, 2006; O'Donohue and Ferguson, 2003; Orend, 2002; Ward and Syversen, 2009). Third, draw up a checklist of local (e.g. research governance procedures, institutional requirements), national (e.g. professional ethical codes) and international (e.g. human rights declarations) requirements and make sure that a project complies with them. Fourth, try to cultivate the ethical virtues outlined above by consistently thinking through the implications of a research project. Virtues are ingrained ways of thinking, feeling and acting that reliably result in ethically acceptable outcomes (Driver, 2006).

As we stated earlier, it is not practical or ethical (!) to attempt to approach ethical issues in forensic and correctional work settings by way of a cookbook or algorithmic approach. Because of the complexity and influence of context on ethical decision making, personal judgement is always required and should not be avoided. However, becoming familiar with ethical theories and concepts such as those of human rights, dignity and care should assist in orienting individuals to problems and point to ways of resolving them that are justifiable.

Conclusions

Ethical thinking in forensic and correctional research contexts is complex and demanding. The reason for this complexity and level of difficulty resides in the dual nature of forensic and correctional research and practice; it is both normative and descriptive. A culture's deep assumptions about moral accountability, punishment, the nature of moral agency, social justice and so on will inevitably colour the way researchers approach their investigatory tasks. As researchers we have an obligation to keep in mind our responsibilities to all those affected by crime and never forget that the fruits of such work can have lasting and potentially devastating consequences for all. In our view, ethical forensic and correctional research is more likely to emerge out of the virtues of compassion and an appreciation of the value of all human beings.

Further resources

There are a number of books on professional ethics and ethical theory available for practitioners but very little written on correctional or forensic research ethics. We suggest that the following papers and books in particular will prove helpful in providing researchers with an understanding of ethical concepts and their implications.

Bush, S. S., Connell, M. A. and Denny, R. L. (2006). *Ethical practice in forensic psychology: a systematic model for decision making.* Washington, DC: American Psychological Association. This is one of the few books on forensic ethics generally and its ideas can be generalised to the forensic and correctional domain.

Cooper, D. E. (2004). *Ethics for professionals in a multicultural world.* Upper Saddle River, NJ: Pearson Prentice Hall. This is an excellent book that works with levels of ethical theory approach.

Driver, J. (2006). *Ethics: the fundamentals.* Oxford, UK: Blackwell Publishing. A comprehensive overview of ethical theories and concepts.

Institute of Medicine (2006). *Ethical considerations for research involving prisoners.* Washington, DC: National Academies Press. A nice discussion of research issues associated with the use of prisoners.

Lavin, M. (2003). Ethical issues in forensic psychology. In W. T. O'Donohue and E. Levensky (Eds). *Handbook of forensic psychology: resources for mental health and legal professionals.* New York, NY: Elsevier Science. An accessible, sensible discussion of ethical ideas and their relevance for mental health professionals.

Mertens, D. M. and Ginsberg, P. E. (2009) (Eds). *The handbook of social research ethics.* Thousand Oaks, CA: Sage Publications. This is a useful collection of articles on ethical issues in social science research and is clearly applicable for those researching offenders.

References

Adshead, G. and Brown, C. (2003) (Eds). *Ethical issues in forensic mental health research.* London, UK: Jessica Kingsley.

Andrews, D. A. and Bonta, J. (2003). *The psychology of criminal conduct.* 3rd edn. Cincinnati, OH: Anderson.

Appelbaum, K. L. (2008). Correctional mental health research: opportunities and barriers. *Journal of Correctional Health Care,* 14: 269–77.

Bartol, C. R. and Bartol, A. M. (2008). *Introduction to forensic psychology: research and applications.* 3rd edn. Thousand Oaks, CA: Sage Publications.

Bausell, B. and Li, Y. (2006). *Power analysis for experimental research: a practical guide for the biological, medical and social sciences.* New York, NY: Cambridge University Press.

Becker, L. C. (1986). *Reciprocity.* Chicago, IL: University of Chicago Press.

Bersoff, D. N., Faust, D., Sales, B. D., Shuman, D. W., Heilbrun, K., Haas, L. J., *et al.* (2003). Forensic settings. In D. N. Bersoff (Ed.) *Ethical conflicts in psychology.* Washington DC: American Psychological Association.

Beyleveld, D., and Brownsword, R. (2001). *Human dignity in bioethics and law.* New York, NY: Oxford University Press.

Bonnie, R. J. (2006). Judicially mandated naltrexone use by criminal offenders: a legal analysis. *Journal of Substance Abuse Treatment,* 31: 121–7.

Brown, B. L. and Hedges, D. (2009). Use and misuse of quantitative methods. In D. M. Mertens and P. E. Ginsberg (Eds). *The handbook of social research ethics* (pp. 373–85). Thousand Oaks, CA: Sage Publications.

Bush, S. S., Connell, M. A. and Denny, R. L. (2006). *Ethical practice in forensic psychology: a systematic model for decision making.* Washington, DC: American Psychological Association.

Chwang, E. (2010). Against risk-benefit review of prisoner research. *Bioethics,* 24: 14–22.

Cooper, D. E. (2004). *Ethics for professionals in a multicultural world.* Upper Saddle River, NJ: Pearson Prentice Hall.

Craig, L. A., Beech, A. R. and Harkins, L. (2009). The predictive accuracy of risk factors and frameworks. In A. R. Beech, L. A. Craig and K. D. Browne (Eds). *Assessment and treatment of sex offenders* (pp. 53–74). Oxford, UK: Wiley-Blackwell.

Crombie, I. K. and Davis, H. T. (2009). *What is Meta-analysis? Evidence-based medicine*, 2nd edn. Available from www.whatisseries.co.uk/whatis (accessed 21/4/11).

Day, A. and Ward, T. (2010). Offender rehabilitation as a value-laden process. *International Journal of Offender Therapy and Comparative Criminology*, 54: 289–306.

Day, A., Tucker, K. and Howells, K. (2004). Coerced offender rehabilitation – a defensible practice? *Psychology, Crime & Law*, 10: 259–69.

Denny, D. (2005). *Risk and society*. London, UK: Sage.

Denzin, N. K. and Lincoln, Y. S. (2005). *The Sage handbook of qualitative research*. 3rd edn. Thousand Oaks, CA: Sage Publications

Douglas, K. S. and Skeem, J. L. (2005). Violence risk assessment: getting specific about being dynamic. *Psychology, Public Policy, and Law*, 11: 347–83.

Driver, J. (2006). *Ethics: the fundamentals*. Oxford, UK: Blackwell Publishing.

Duff, R. A. (2001). *Punishment, communication, and community*. New York, NY: Oxford University Press.

Ginsberg, P. E. and Mertens, D. M. (2009). Frontiers in social research ethics: fertile ground for evolution. In D. M. Mertens and P. E. Ginsberg (Eds). *The handbook of social research ethics* (pp. 580–613). Thousand Oaks, CA: Sage Publications.

Haag, A. M. (2006). Ethical dilemmas faced by correctional psychologists in canada. *Criminal Justice and Behavior*, 33: 93–109.

Hanson, R. K., Bourgon, G., Helmus, L. and Hodgson, S. (2009). The principles of effective correctional treatment also apply to sexual offenders: a meta-analysis. *Criminal Justice and Behavior*, 36: 865–91.

Howells, K. and Day, A. (2007). Readiness for treatment in high risk offenders with personality disorders. *Psychology, Crime & Law. Special Issue: Personality Disorder and Offending*, 13: 47–56.

Hudson, S. M., Ward, T. and McCormack, J. (1999). Offence pathways in sexual offenders. *Journal of Interpersonal Violence*, 14: 779–98.

Institute of Medicine (2006). *Ethical considerations for research involving prisoners*. Washington, DC: National Academies Press.

Kitchener, K. S. (2000). *Foundations of clinical practice, research, and teaching in psychology*. Mahwah, NJ: Lawrence Erlbaum.

Kitchener, K. S. and Kitchener, R. F. (2009). Social science research ethics: historical and philosophical issues. In D. M. Mertens and P. E. Ginsberg (Eds). *The handbook of social research ethics* (pp. 5–22). Thousand Oaks, CA: Sage Publications.

LaFrance, J. and Bull, C. C. (2009). Researching ourselves back to life: taking control of the research agenda in indian country. In D. M. Mertens and P. E. Ginsberg (Eds). *The handbook of social research ethics* (pp. 135–49). Thousand Oaks, CA: Sage Publications.

Lavin, M. (2003). Ethical issues in forensic psychology. In W. T. O'Donohue and E. Levensky (Eds). *Handbook of forensic psychology: resources for mental health and legal professionals*. New York, NY: Elsevier Science.

Laws, D. R. and Ward, T. (2011). *Desistance from sexual offending: alternatives to throwing away the key*. New York, NY: Guilford Press.

Lazarus, L. (2004). *Contrasting prisoners' rights: a comparative examination of England and Germany*. New York, NY: Oxford University Press.

Li, A. (2006). *Ethics, human rights, and culture*. Basingstoke, UK: Palgrave MacMillian.

Lippke, R. L. (2002). Toward a Theory of Prisoners' Rights. *Ratio Juris*, 15: 122–45.

McCoy, K. and Fremouw, W. (2010). The relationship between negative affect and sexual offending: a critical review. *Clinical Psychology Review*, 30: 317–25.

McNeill, F. (2004). Desistance, rehabilitation and correctionalism:developments and prospects in Scotland. *The Howard Journal*, 43: 420–36.

—— (2006). A desistance paradigm for offender management. *Criminology & Criminal Justice*, 6: 39–62.

McSweeney, T., Stevens, A., Hunt, N. and Turnbull, P. J. (2007). Twisting arms or a helping hand? Assessing the impact of 'coerced' and comparable 'voluntary' drug treatment options. *British Journal of Criminology*, 47: 470–90.

Mark, M. M. and Gamble, C. (2009). Experiments, quasi-experiments, and ethics. In D. M. Mertens and P. E. Ginsberg (Eds). *The handbook of social research ethics* (pp. 198–213). Thousand Oaks, CA: Sage Publications.

Marlowe, D. B. (2006). Depot naltrexone in lieu of incarceration: A behavioral analysis of coerced treatment for addicted offenders. *Journal of Substance Abuse Treatment*, 31: 131–39.

Marshall, W. L. and Marshall, L. E. (2007). The utility of the random controlled trial for evaluating sexual offender treatment: the gold standard or an inappropriate strategy? *Sexual Abuse: A Journal of Research and Treatment*, 19: 175–260.

—— (2008). Good clinical practice and the evaluation of treatment: a reply to Seto *et al. Sexual Abuse: A Journal of Research and Treatment*, 20: 256–60.

Mertens, D. M. and Ginsberg, P. E. (Eds). (2009) *The handbook of social research ethics.* Thousand Oaks, CA: Sage Publications.

Miller, R. D. (1998). Forced administration of sex-drive reducing medications to sex offenders: treatment or punishment. *Psychology, Public Policy, and Law. Special Issue: Sex Offenders: Scientific, Legal, and Policy Perspectives*, 4: 175–99.

Morris, M. (2007). *Evaluation ethics for best practice.* New York, NY: Guilford Press.

Munthe, C., Radovic, S. and Anckarsater, H. (2010). Ethical issues in forensic psychiatric research on mentally disordered offenders. *Bioethics*, 24: 35–44.

Ntseane, P. G. (2009). The ethics of the researcher-subject relationship. In D. M. Mertens and P. E. Ginsberg (Eds). *The handbook of social research ethics* (pp. 295–307). Thousand Oaks, CA: Sage Publications.

Nussbaum, M. C. (2006). *Frontiers of justice: disability, nationality, and species membership.* Cambridge, MA: The Belknap Press.

O'Donohue, W. T. and Ferguson, K. (Eds) (2003). *Handbook of professional ethics for psychologists: issues, questions, and controversies.* Thousand Oaks, CA: Sage Publications.

Orend, B. (2002). *Human rights: concept and context.* Ontario, Canada: Broadview Press.

Overholser, J. (1987). Ethical issues in prison research: a risk/benefit analysis. *Behavioral Sciences & the Law*, 5: 187–202.

Parekh, B. (2006). *Rethinking multiculturalism: cultural diversity and political theory.* 2nd edn. Basingstoke: Palgrave MacMillan.

Perez, L. M. and Treadwell, H. M. (2009). Determining what we stand for will guide what we do: community priorities, ethical research paradigms, and research with vulnerable populations. *American Journal of Public Health*, 99: 201–4.

Regehr, C., Edwardh, M. and Bradford, J. (2000). Research ethics and forensic patients. *The Canadian Journal of Psychiatry / La Revue Canadienne de Psychiatrie*, 45: 892–8.

Seto, M., Marques, J. K., Harris, G. T., Chaffin, M., Lalumière, M. L., Miner, M. H., Berliner, L., Rice, M. E., Lieb, R. and Quinsey, V. L. (2007). Good science and progress in sex offender treatment are intertwined: a response to Marshall and Marshall. *Sexual Abuse: A Journal of Research and Treatment*, 19: 175–260.

Statistics New Zealand (2006). 2006 census data. Available from www.stats.govt. nz/Census/2006CensusHomePage/QuickStats/quickstats-about-a-subject/maori/ maori-ethnic-population-te-momo-iwi-maori.aspx (accessed 24/3/10).

Sulmasy, D. P. (2007). Human dignity and human worth. In J. Malpas and N. Lickiss (Eds). *Perspectives on human dignity: a conversation* (pp. 9–18). Dordrecht, The Netherlands: Springer.

Symonette, H. (2009). Cultivating self as responsive instrument: working the boundaries and borderlands for ethical border crossings. In D. M. Mertens and P. E. Ginsberg (Eds). *The handbook of social research ethics* (pp. 279–94). Thousand Oaks, CA: Sage Publications.

Travis, J. (2005). *But they all come back: Facing the challenges of prisoner Reentry*. Washington, DC: The Urban Institute Press.

Vess, J. (2008). Sex offender risk assessment: consideration of human rights in community protection legislation. *Legal and Criminological Psychology*, 13: 245–56.

Ward, T. and Birgden, A. (2007). Human rights and correctional clinical practice. *Aggression and Violent Behavior*, 12: 628–43.

Ward, T. and Maruna, S. (2007). *Rehabilitation: beyond the risk paradigm*. London: Routledge.

Ward, T. and Salmon, K. (2009). The ethics of punishment: correctional practice implications. *Aggression and Violent Behavior*, 14: 239–47.

Ward, T. and Syversen, K. (2009). Vulnerable agency and human dignity: an ethical framework for forensic practice. *Aggression and Violent Behavior*, 14: 94–105.

Ward, T., Polaschek, D. L. L. and Beech, A. R. (2006). *Theories of sexual offending*. Chichester, UK: Wiley.

Ward, T., Yates, P. and Long, C. (2006). *The self-regulation model of the offense and relapse process: Volume 2: Treatment*. Victoria, BC: Pacific Psychological Assessment Corporation.

Yates, P. M. and Kingston, D. A. (2006). Pathways to sexual offending: relationship to static and dynamic risk among treated sexual offenders. *Sexual Abuse: A Journal of Research and Treatment*, 18: 259–70.

Part II

Risk, investigative and criminal justice research

3 Risk research

Michael Doyle

Researching risk in forensic settings

Assessing and managing risk to others is fundamental to the practice of mental health professionals in forensic services. The need for clear structured approaches to risk assessment that are based on research evidence has become more prominent in recent years (Royal College of Psychiatrists, 2008; Department of Health, 2007). In mental health services, there has been increasing concern in relation to violent behaviour. A relatively small, yet significant number of incidents involving people with mental illness have received considerable media attention (e.g. Ritchie *et al.*, 1994; NHS London, 2006). This has left a strong impression of the potential dangerousness to the public from individuals with various forms of mental disorder. This is fuelled by findings that patients recently in contact with mental health services commit around 9 per cent of all homicides in England and Wales. These figures translate to 52 homicides per year, of which 30 are committed by people diagnosed with schizophrenia (National Confidential Inquiry, 2006). Perceived failures support the widely-held perception of inadequate service provision and the growing concern that the public are not adequately protected from dangerous individuals by current legislation and practice.

Risk assessment and management are crucial in clinical and legal decision making in such areas as admission and discharge to hospital, commitment to prison and release, institutional and community management, child protection, probation orders, antisocial behaviour orders, multi-agency public protection panels, charges and bail conditions and notification and registration for lifers and sex offenders. The impact of risk assessments are profound, as individuals could be discharged or released prematurely to commit further offences or, conversely, they could be subject to unnecessary restrictions being placed on their freedom. Yet despite the widespread necessity of risk assessment it remains an inexact science. Ultimately, clinical decisions on the level of risk are based on clinical judgement although the debate continues as to the relative merits of clinical and actuarial approaches (see Hart *et al.*, 2007; Doyle and Dolan, 2007). The need for comprehensive and good quality research in this area is crucial given the ever-increasing need for evidence-based approaches for risk assessment and management (Buchanan, 2008; Taylor *et al.*, 2009).

Violence risk assessment and management are the principle justifications for the existence of specialised forensic services. It is imperative therefore that the practice of risk assessment and management is supported by research evidence to ensure assessments are conducted proficiently and documented accurately to reflect a high standard of clinical practice (Doyle and Dolan, 2008). This chapter will provide some background to violence risk assessment research, introduce research design principles and consider the different types of methodology and analyses. The strengths and limitations of different approaches will be reviewed and an example of risk research will be provided. The chapter will conclude with a consideration of future directions in risk research.

The nature of risk assessment in forensic services

In the past there has been substantial debate and controversy about the ability of mental health professionals to predict violence. Early research in this area concluded that mental health professionals' predictions of dangerous behaviour were 'wrong about 95 per cent of the time' (Ennis and Emery, 1978) and Faust and Ziskin (1988) argued that the accuracy of the judgements of psychologists and psychiatrists did not necessarily surpass that of laypersons.

Historically, the most common approach used for risk assessment is unstructured clinical or professional judgement. This approach involves professional 'opinion' or judgements where there is complete discretion over which information should be considered and there are no constraints on the information the assessor can use to reach a decision. This has the advantage of being flexible, allowing a focus on case-specific influences and violence prevention (Hart, 1998). Nonetheless, the clinical approach has been criticised for being unstructured, informal, subjective and impressionistic and is plagued by various sources of bias and error as information is highly dependent upon interviewing, observation and self-report.

Actuarial judgements are based on specific assessment data selected because they have been demonstrated empirically to be associated with violence and coded in a predetermined manner. However, there are limitations to the approach as actuarial approaches tend to focus the assessment on a limited number of factors thus ignoring potentially crucial case-specific, idiosyncratic factors (e.g. Violence Risk Appraisal Guide (VRAG), Webster *et al.*, 1994). There is a tendency to focus on relatively static factors, which are immutable, therefore leading to passive predictions. They also tend to be optimised to predict a specific outcome, over a specific time period in a specific population, leading to non-optimal, even bizarre, decisions when applied in different settings (Hart, 1998). For example, the VRAG item seriousness of index offence weights the more serious offence as protective so somebody committing murder would be seen as less of a risk than somebody committing a minor index offence.

Both clinical and actuarial approaches have definite advantages and disadvantages. The debate as to which approach is most relevant to clinical practice is complex. However, it would appear that a combination of the clinical and actuarial approach is warranted. Such an alternative, referred to as empirically validated, structured decision making (Douglas *et al.*, 1999) or structured clinical/professional judgement (Douglas et al., 2003; Department of Health, 2007) attempts to bridge the gap between the scientific (actuarial) approach and the clinical practice of risk assessment. With structured professional judgment, the emphasis is on developing evidence based guidelines or frameworks, which promote systemisation and consistency, yet are flexible enough to account for case-specific influences and the contexts in which assessments are conducted (e.g. Historical, Clinical and Risk Management – 20 items (HCR-20), Webster *et al.*, 1997). Such guidelines are based on sound scientific knowledge and can promote transparency and accountability, yet encourage the use of professional discretion and remain practically relevant (Hart, 1998; Douglas *et al.*, 1999). This approach also recognises the reality that the process of clinical risk assessment is a dynamic and continuous process, which is mediated by changing conditions (see Doyle, 2000, p. 144).

In summary, structured professional judgement involves a broad assessment approach, which is rooted in evidence that for the most part has been validated by research (Douglas *et al.*, 1999). To facilitate this approach, research-based instruments need to be developed that are grounded in well-substantiated research that may improve the clinical practice of risk assessment (Borum, 1996).

Approaches to investigating risk in forensic services

There are a number of approaches to investigating risk. Monahan and Steadman (1994, p. 3) identified three approaches to risk research that have been used in an attempt to improve the practice of violence risk assessment. As Figure 3.1 highlights, studies may address three distinct aspects of risk assessment: (a) the relationship between cues or risk factors and judgement or clinical prediction;

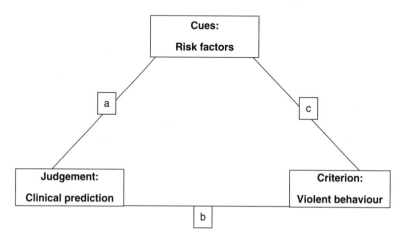

Figure 3.1 Approaches to risk research (Monahan and Steadman, 1994).

(b) the relationship between judgement or clinical prediction and the criterion (outcome) of violent behaviour; and (c) the relationship between cues or risk factors and the criterion of violent behaviour. These aspects of risk research can be reframed into research questions: (1) what factors influence decisions about future risk for violence? (2) how accurate are clinicians' predictions of future violent behaviour? and (3) what factors predict future violent behaviour?

There have been a number of studies which have considered the relationship between cues or risk factors and judgement or clinical prediction by reviewing how clinicians go about assessing the risk of violence and considering what factors and methods they utilise. Qualitative approaches to exploring clinical practice may be more appropriate to answer this research question (Doyle, 1996). The findings of these studies suggest that clinicians consider a multitude of factors with no consensus and little consistency across studies. Common factors include past history of violence, current hostility and impulsivity, and the presence of a serious mental or personality disorder as important risk factors for future violence (see Mulvey and Lidz, 1984, 1985; Doyle, 1996).

Extensive literature exists on the relationship between judgement or clinical prediction and violent behaviour, where the accuracy of clinical predictions of violent behaviour have been examined (See Monahan, 1981; Lidz *et al.*, 1993). Perhaps the most influential study of this type followed the *Baxtrom v Herold* case (1966), where a decision of the USA Supreme Court led to the release or reduction in security of over 900 patients adjudged to be criminally insane and dangerous. Steadman and Cocozza (1974) followed up these patients and found that only one out of three were actually violent and only seven out of 98 patients released to the community were violent in a two-year follow-up period. More recently, Mossman (1994) extracted 58 data sets from 44 published studies dating from 1972 to 1993 on violence risk prediction, and examined prediction accuracy using Receiver Operating Characteristics (ROCs). Mossman concluded that clinicians were able to distinguish violent from non-violent patients with a modest, better than chance level of accuracy.

Research on how clinicians assess risk and how accurate they are in predicting violent behaviour is certainly valuable, yet unless research can independently verify the predictive value of risk factors, their actual, as opposed to perceived, usefulness in violence risk assessment will remain unknown. Until clinicians are better informed of the factors that are actuarially associated with violent behaviour there is little chance of improving the accuracy of risk assessments (Monahan and Steadman, 1994, p. 7). Such research should lead to the development of instruments aimed at guiding clinical practice and further research. Before considering the content and format of any form of violence risk assessment instrument that will be of practical use in clinical practice, it is necessary to (1) identify the risk factors found to be the most predictive of violence and (2) review the reliability and validity of existing instruments and frameworks in predicting violent behaviour. This following section reviews some of the methodological issues involved in risk assessment 'experimental prediction studies' (Otto, 1992).

Methodological issues in risk research

Prospective versus retrospective design

By their very nature, risk assessment studies are generally prediction-outcome follow-up studies that attempt to evaluate predictive validity of risk factors and/ or measures of risk. The research paradigm focuses on the comparison between baseline measures and follow-up periods at subsequent time points. A first issue to address is therefore prospective versus retrospective design.

Retrospective studies generally rely on information that was not originally collected and recorded for research purposes. Retrospective studies can compare baseline measures with previous behaviour or preferably attempt to simulate a prospective design by comparing baseline measures at a certain time point (e.g. admission, pre-discharge) with future violent or other behaviour over a stipulated time period. This type of retrospective methodology is acceptable in preliminary studies in this area as it is well suited to time-limited studies and may be useful when controlling for interviewer bias and performance management (prevalent in forensic populations) and results can be generated cost-effectively (Doyle *et al.*, 2002). If there is adequate collateral information in case records then it is possible to complete risk measures such as the Psychopathy Checklist: Screening Version (PCL:SV; Hart *et al.*, 1995), the Violence Risk Appraisal Guide (VRAG; Webster *et al.*, 1994) and the Historical Clinical and Risk Management – 20 items (HCR-20: Webster *et al.*, 1997) without interview (Doyle *et al.*, 2002), as long as the limitations of such a method are noted in the research report (see Hart *et al.*, 1995).

Large sample epidemiological retrospective studies that are based on longitudinal data stored in large databases may offer more credible findings to influence policy, practice and future research. Examples of such studies investigating risk include the National Confidential Inquiry into Homicides and Suicides (National Confidential Inquiry, 2006), studies on the link between violence risk and substance use (Elbogen and Johnson, 2009; Fasel *et al.*, 2009) and birth cohort studies investigating links between schizophrenia, substance use and violence (Arseneault *et al.*, 2000). Access to such databases may be restricted and these studies are still subject to the limitations that apply to retrospective design generally which will now be considered.

As retrospective studies are concerned with events that have already happened, it is not possible for the researcher to control or manipulate the experimental variable and therefore retrospective studies provide less convincing evidence of causal relationships (Robson, 1995). Retrospective studies rely on comprehensive reviews of records, and the risk for bias is obvious; especially if measures are not taken to keep the person(s) collecting the data entirely blind to the subjects' follow-up status. It should be noted that ratings from case notes involve reliance on others' judgements that may be subjective and may lose some of their meaning in translation so researchers need to evaluate the adequacy and accuracy of the information used. There is no guarantee that all the notes/information will be available and the quality of reporting cannot be guaranteed. Also, reliance on records inevitably means that some information is difficult to obtain (e.g. current clinical and/or dynamic items). Retrospective studies are therefore best suited to preliminary studies to examine possible significant relationships in preparation for more robust prospective studies.

Prospective research design is generally considered the most desirable (Fowkes and Fulton, 1991; Monahan *et al.*, 2001). In prospective studies, baseline data collection may be conducted in a systematised specific-to-purpose fashion and the design is to some extent inherently safeguarded against errors of bias as baseline assessment is truly blind to subsequent follow-up status. Prospective studies tend to be epidemiological in nature where cohorts of patients, prisoners or other groups are followed up over one or more time points either in institutions, in the community, or both. An example of a rigorous research study design is provided in Box 3.1. Prospective studies tend to be more time consuming and more expensive than retrospective studies. They are also subject to selection bias as usually they will be dependent on the proportion of research participants providing consent. There is also the problem of the

---

Box 3.1 **Example of rigorous design for prospective study of community violence**

MacArthur Violence Risk Assessment Study (Monahan et al., 2001)

Background

Almost all existing studies of violence risk assessment suffer from one or more methodological problems: they considered a constricted range of risk factors, often a few demographic variables or scores on a psychological test; they employed weak criterion measures of violence, usually relying solely on arrest; they studied a narrow segment of the patient population, typically males with a history of prior violence; and/or they were conducted at a single site. Based upon this critical examination of existing work, the research was designed, to the greatest extent possible, to overcome the methodological obstacles identified.

Aims

The study was designed with three purposes in mind: (1) to improve the validity of clinical risk assessment, (2) to enhance the effectiveness of risk management and (3) to provide information on mental disorder and violence useful in reforming mental health law and policy.

Method

(I) Prospective cohort follow-up design. Admissions (*n* = 1,136) both male and female were sampled from acute civil inpatient facilities in the USA: Pittsburgh, Kansas City and Worcester.

Inclusion criteria: English-speaking patients between the ages of 18 and 40 were selected, who were of White, African American or Hispanic ethnicity, and who had a chart diagnosis of thought or affective disorder, substance abuse or personality disorder. The median length of stay was nine days. After giving informed consent to participate in the research, the patient was interviewed in the hospital by both a research interviewer and a research clinician in order to assess him or her on each of the risk factors. Baseline assessments of risk factors were then compared with violent outcome up to 20 weeks post-discharge.

(II) Comparison group of 519 people living in the same neighbourhood in which the patient sample resided after discharge. They were interviewed about their violent behaviour in the past ten weeks. Findings were then compared with the patient sample to see if the rate of violence varied between samples.

Predictor variables (risk factors)

A comprehensive range of 134 risk factors were assessed and considered under four domains:

1 Dispositional factors: demographic, personality and cognitive
2 Historical factors: social history, mental hospitalisation history, history of crime and violence
3 Contextual factors: perceived stress, social support, means for violence
4 Clinical factors: Axis I diagnosis, symptoms, Axis II diagnosis, functioning, substance abuse

The best of the existing measures of these variables were used and where no instrument to adequately measure a variable was available, the development of the necessary measure was commissioned.

Criterion variable (violent outcome)

Violence to others was defined to include acts of battery that resulted in physical injury; sexual assaults; assaultive acts that involved the use of a weapon; or threats made with a weapon in hand. Three sources of information were used to ascertain the occurrence and details of a violent incident in the community. Interviews with patients (by researchers blind to baseline assessment), interviews with collateral individuals (i.e. a person named by the patient as someone who would know what was going on in his or her life) and official sources of information (arrest and hospital records) were all coded and compared. Participants and collaterals were interviewed twice (every ten weeks) over the first twenty weeks – approximately four to five months – from the date of hospital discharge.

risk paradox as researchers will be duty bound to report imminent risks to the appropriate clinicians or authorities. This would result in a 'false positive' outcome if the behaviour is subsequently managed and the participant is effectively prevented from becoming violent. This can be controlled for in certain jurisdictions where researchers can apply for a Certificate of Confidentiality, although ethical and legal dilemmas will still remain (Monahan *et al.*, 2001). Despite the limitations of the prospective design, this remains the most rigorous approach. Methodological issues related to prospective research design will now be considered.

Selecting and categorising risk factors

The cause of violent behaviour is complex and as such there are many reasons why a person may become violent. The heterogeneous nature of violent behaviour means that risk research needs to investigate predictive risk factors from multiple domains. The most comprehensive prospective community violence study of its type, the MacArthur Violence Risk Assessment Study (MacVRAS: Monahan *et al.*, 2001) investigated the predictive validity of 134 risk factors that were hypothesised as predicting future violent behaviour. The risk factors were categorised as *Dispositional* (e.g. impulsiveness, anger), *Historical* (e.g. history of violence), *Contextual* (e.g. family or social support) or *Clinical* (e.g. mental illness, substance use). More recently, Monahan (2006) provided an alternative system to categorise these risk factors, related to (1) individual risk factors; what the person *is*; (2) clinical risk factors; what the person *has*; (3) historical risk factors; what the person *has done*; and (4) experiential risk factors; what *has been done* to the person. These factors are illustrated in Table 3.1. The challenge for researchers is how to reliably measure the risk factors under investigation, and valid and reliable measures are essential. Researchers need to evaluate existing established measures of a particular variable hypothesised to be linked to increased risk of future violent behaviour (e.g. anger, impulsiveness, psychopathy). Measures of risk that have previously been validated by research could also be used. These could be specific risk assessment instruments such as the VRAG, HCR-20 or the Violence Risk Scale (Wong and Gordon, 2003).

Table 3.1 Risk factors for violence

Category of risk factor	Risk factor
Individual: what the person *is*	• Age • Gender • Ethnicity • Anger • Impulsiveness • Personality
Clinical: what the person *has*	• Mental illness • Persecutory delusions • Misidentification delusions • Threat/control-override symptoms • Command hallucination • Personality disorder • Psychopathy • Substance abuse
Historical: what the person *has done*	• Prior crime and violent behaviour • Recency • Frequency • Severity • Pattern
Experiential: what *has been done* to the person	• Pathological family environment • Victim of childhood abuse • Childhood victimiser/delinquent

Violent outcome

The criterion variable is the outcome in terms of violent recidivism. The definition and classification of violence has been problematic in past research (Monahan, 1981; 2005; Volavka, 1995) and has been used interchangeably with the definition of 'aggression'. There are many definitions of violence in the literature, and an exhaustive review is beyond the scope of this chapter. The definition in the HCR-20 manual-version 2 (Webster *et al.*, 1997, p. 24) has been applied in numerous previous studies:

> Actual, threatened or attempted physical harm to others, which is deliberate and non-consensual. Threats of harm must be clear and unambiguous, rather than vague statements of hostility or verbal abuse, and this definition includes behaviour that is fear-inducing (e.g. stalking).

This definition would include all sexual assaults, kidnapping and arson as violent acts. Violence against animals or in self-defence would not be considered as violent behaviour, unless meeting the criteria identified in the definition given above. In the MacVRAS (Monahan *et al.*, 2001), the definition of violence was 'any acts that include battery that resulted in physical injury; sexual assaults; assaultative acts that involved the use of a weapon; or threats made with a weapon in hand'. This definition would appear more rigid, although it is worth noting that the authors of the MacVRAS modified their definition of violence in subsequent studies to include violent acts where physical injury could not be corroborated (Monahan *et al.*, 2005). The important principle is that a clear operational definition of violent behaviour that can be accurately measured is used as the criterion outcome measure in research.

Perhaps one of the most urgent methodological considerations in terms of measuring violence is what criminologists call the 'dark figure of crime' (Persson, 1980). The 'dark figure' is the discrepancy between crime rates based on convictions or other official records and actual crime rates. Several steps in the legal system act as filters on the way to a court conviction. Crimes may go undiscovered or unreported, and far from all police inquiries lead successfully to an arrest. Also, in the end the court may fail to convict due to insufficient evidence. Similarly, in mental health services reliance on reconvictions for the outcome measure will probably lead to an under-estimate of the true rate of violence. Research on violence among the mentally disordered has therefore begun to use and combine other data sources for the outcome measure other than official records to include self-report of the participant and reports from a collateral informant who knows the person well (Monahan *et al.*, 2001; Doyle and Dolan, 2006a).

In institutional settings most previous researchers have made the distinction between physical violence and verbal threats of violence, verbal attacks and violence to objects (for example, Doyle and Dolan, 2006b, McNiel and Binder, 1989) in order to capture violent incidents that may not have resulted in harm and/or physical assault on another. However, previous studies are inconsistent when defining, categorising and identifying incidents of violence and this can reduce the generalisability of findings across studies.

An outcome measure that is valid and reliable is desirable. Ideally, one would want the type of audit conductible only in a closed institution, where the behaviour of the subject(s) may be constantly monitored. For these reasons the rate of institutional violence should be more reliable than non-institutional violence. On the other hand, if the purpose is to learn about risk in the community, then data derived from an institution may be of limited value. The researcher will need to consider the aims of the study before selecting an appropriate outcome measure. Ongoing monitoring of violent behaviour can be implemented by using a monitoring instrument such as the Overt Aggression Scale (OAS) (Yudofsky *et al.*, 1986) or the Modified Overt Aggression Scale (MOAS). The MOAS was designed to be rated retrospectively once per week to reduce the burden on staff expected to complete measures (Sorgi *et al.*, 1991). The evidence suggests that when the method of data collection is adapted to the ward environment and staff demands are considered, the OAS and MOAS are useful measures of aggression (Doyle and Dolan, 2006b).

In community settings reliance on official records for information has plagued attempts to predict such violent behaviour. Failure to detect significant amounts of violence by using inappropriate measures can lead to the wrong conclusion about where to focus efforts to control violence by patients (Mulvey *et al.*, 1994; Doyle and Dolan, 2006a). Researchers have relied on a variety of instruments to measure violence, from self-report questionnaires to checklists based on observed aggression. This renders comparison between studies a difficult task. However, the MacVRAS developed a state-of-the-art instrument to improve the reliability of measuring violence. The MacArthur Community Violence Instrument (Monahan *et al.*, 2001) can be used with participant and collateral and reliability can be enhanced by electronic clinical information and paper records as necessary. Steadman *et al.* (1998) reported that using this method the prevalence of violence reported was six times higher, using the three independent information sources, self-report, records and collateral, rather than using agency records alone. However, if using this method one needs to ensure that independent sources are themselves valid and reliable records so that accurate data can be collected.

Sampling issues

The sample chosen for the research will depend upon the aims and hypotheses of the study and will need to reflect the characteristics of the population under investigation. Consideration will include whether it is inpatient or community violence that is under investigation and researchers will need to sample accordingly. In either situation it is important that the sample is truly representative of the general population of interest. This can be ascertained by comparing the research sample with the general population using key indices such as gender, age, ethnicity and diagnosis (see Doyle and Dolan, 2006a). At the outset of a study, inclusion and exclusion criteria are required to increase the representativeness of the sample and reduce risk of confounders such as age, disability and language difficulties (see Box 3.1). Failure to reflect the ethnic diversity within a population in a research sample will reduce the validity and generalisability of findings.

In some studies there may be a specific group or groups under investigation. For example, specific diagnostic groups such as people with personality disorder, ethnic groups (e.g. Caucasian versus Latino) or different genders. The sample could also include a control group to test whether there is an ecological effect where impact of interventions and management would decrease violence. In some situations, identifying a high-risk group of participants who have a previous and/or recent history of violence may be advantageous to ensure a high base rate of subsequent violence. However, this will preclude those who have never been violent and therefore the findings cannot be generalised to the population as a whole (Steadman *et al.*, 1998) and the research question will be focused on what predicts violence *recurring* rather than *occurring*.

The size of the sample is important and should be large enough to reliably answer the research questions or hypotheses. Reference to previous similar research is useful in determining the size of the sample and in some cases it may be possible to conduct a formal power analysis that will provide a probability (usually 80 per cent) of a similar change or difference in terms of violence between groups based on results from previous studies (see Bland, 2000).

Likely base rate of violence is also important as this can influence the findings. The likely percentage of those invited to take part who actually consent and possible attrition need to be taken into account when calculating sample size as these can be a threat to overall validity of the findings.

In general, a large sample is preferable in terms of representativeness, prevalence of the outcome of concern (e.g. violence), statistical power and generalisability (Monahan and Steadman, 1994). However, sample size alone is no guarantee of robust findings. In some cases, a smaller more rigorous design (e.g. Gray *et al.*, 2003: sample n = 34) could be more convincing than a large scale epidemiological study that only relies on official records and therefore fails to adequately detect the true rate of violence. Also, in qualitative exploratory research, the focus is often on the quality of responses from a small number of participants so that themes can be identified and theory generated and hypothesised. Qualitative approaches are of equal importance especially when investigating areas where there is little or no established theory (Doyle, 1996).

Reliability issues

Inter-rater reliability is perhaps the most important type of reliability that needs to be addressed in risk research. This is important to control for rater bias where researchers are expected to provide a judgement or clinical rating about a risk factor or outcome variable. The level of agreement between raters needs to be evaluated and this is usually achieved by getting different raters to code the same participants. Formal training and supervised practice in the measures need to be provided to raters before the study begins. Dual rating of items should be encouraged where any doubt exists, and consensus ratings with supervisor and colleagues can be used to maintain satisfactory agreement between raters. It may not be possible or desirable to include every study participant in reliability testing, although a sufficient number (20–30) or proportion (>20 per cent) would be required and all test cases should be selected at random.

Agreement between different raters needs to be evaluated throughout the study period so that both early and later ratings are considered to control for experience of the respective raters and possible drift. In some situations it may be necessary to evaluate inter-rater reliability with raters external to the study to ensure impartiality. Where this is deemed appropriate detailed information and taped interviews could be provided.

Other reliability issues relate to test-retest reliability and internal consistency. Test-retest reliability is important where participants are asked to rate items that are static or historical factors (e.g. past abuse, previous offending) and not expected to change. The participant would be expected to provide similar ratings on scores over two or more time points. With internal consistency the aim is to ensure that items on measures of an underlying construct (e.g. anger, psychopathy) are in fact homogeneous and reliable in rating the construct.

This only applies to instruments intended to measure an underlying construct and would not apply to risk measures such as the VRAG or HCR-20.

Validity issues

Evaluating the predictive validity of risk factors or risk instruments is a prerequisite of the evidence-base for inclusion of risk factors or measures in clinical practice. The question that needs to be answered is whether the risk factor or risk instrument will predict future violent behaviour and this is usually conducted by comparing violent and non-violent groups during follow-ups over one or more specific time periods.

Violent outcome can be measured as either dichotomous (yes/no violent) or continuous variables (frequency of violence), depending upon the research question and outcome measures selected. As a dichotomous variable (violent or not violent) the hypotheses tested would be that the violent group will score higher on the risk measures than the non-violent group. Statistical analyses may include receiver operating characteristics, chi square analysis, comparison of means, logistic regression and correlational procedures (see 'Data analyses', below). An alternative would be to use a continuous measure of violence, such as the frequency of violent incidents or the rate of violence between different risk categories (low, moderate, high). Here, multiple regression, bivariate correlations and analysis of variance procedures would be indicated.

Convergent and concurrent validity of risk factors and risk instruments have been considered in past research. Convergent validity exists when measures of constructs that theoretically *should* be related to each other are, in fact, observed to be related to each other (e.g. anger with violence); that is you should be able to show a correspondence or *convergence* between similar constructs. Concurrent validity exists when measures of the same construct (e.g. violence risk) are observed to be strongly correlated. For example relatively new and emerging risk instruments such as the Classification of Violence Risk (Monahan *et al.*, 2005) could be validated against existing established scales such as the HCR-20 or VRAG to see if there is a close association using correlational and regression procedures.

Incremental validity refers to the extent to which one variable improves upon the predictive validity of another variable or group of variables. This is important in risk research to establish whether one or more variables add to predictive accuracy. For example it may be useful to know if alcohol use and homelessness add to the predictive accuracy of personality disorder in predicting future violence. This can be investigated using regression procedures.

Data analyses

When researching risk, data from various sources are gathered, reviewed and then analysed to form some sort of finding or conclusion. There are a variety of specific ways to analyse data (see Bland, 2000 for guidance on using the following approaches).

Sensitivity, specificity, positive and negative predictive value

In risk prediction research it is necessary to determine the accuracy of independent variables (e.g. anger) in predicting dependent variables (e.g. violence). Sensitivity, specificity, positive predictive value (PPV) and negative predictive value (NPV) have been used to measure predictive validity in past studies. Sensitivity corresponds to the probabilities that a violent recidivist will actually score positive on the examined predictor(s)/test. Specificity corresponds to the probability that a non-recidivist will yield a negative result (not be violent). Whereas sensitivity and specificity are important primarily to the researcher/test-developer, the positive and negative predictive values may appeal primarily to the clinician/user. The positive predictive value is the probability that a subject presenting with a positive test result is actually a recidivist, and the negative predictive value is the probability that a subject who scores negative on the test is actually a non-recidivist. The categorisation is typically derived from a continuous scale that has been divided into two by a predefined threshold value. For instance, subjects scoring in excess of 19 on the HCR-20 are predicted to recidivate, while those scoring 19 or lower are not; or psychopaths (PCL-R scores ≥30) are predicted to be at higher risk for recidivism than non-psychopaths (PCL-R scores < 30).

These measures of predictive validity are illustrated using the classical two-by-two table, Figure 3.2). The drawback with two-by-two table measures is that they estimate predictive validity only at one cut-off at a time, and these techniques do have limitations as they are influenced by the base rate of violence. If the cut-off is too low then more subjects will be wrongly identified as violent

		Outcome *Violence*: Yes	Outcome *Violence*: No
Prediction *Violence*	Yes	True positive	False positive
	No	False negative	True negative

Figure 3.2 Two-by-two contingency table.

(false positives); too high then the measure may fail to detect those who are actually violent (false negatives).

Correlation coefficients such as Pearson's *r* are reported in risk research of this type in order to compare findings from different studies. The independent samples *t* test can be used to compare the means of measures of independent variables in violent and non-violent groups as long as there is reasonable compliance with the criteria for using parametric tests; that is the samples are normally distributed, variances are similar and the samples comprise scores of at least interval measurement.

Multiple and logistic regression

Regression analysis is a statistical technique that attempts to predict the values of the dependent variable using the values of one or more independent variables. It is superior to correlation analysis as regression procedures provide data on the transformation in the dependent variable as a result of the independent variable/s, rather than just giving the association. Multiple linear regression allows the prediction of a continuous outcome measure (e.g. frequency of violence) based on one or more explanatory variables (e.g. past history, HCR-20 scores). Stepwise multiple regression omits variables that do not add to the overall predictive model and provides the best combination of independent variables for the optimal prediction model. However, this does not necessarily mean the omitted variables are not good predictors of outcome as they may be 'knocked out' because they are highly correlated with another variable with stronger predictive validity.

Logistic regression is useful when attempting to predict the presence or absence of a dichotomous outcome (e.g. violence, yes/no) based on values of a set of predictor variables. The explanatory, independent variables can be continuous, categorical or dichotomous and their relative contribution to predicting group membership (e.g. violent or non-violent) is calculated. Odds ratios (OR) are the main statistics of interest in prediction studies as they provide the ratio of the probability of an event occurring. For example Doyle and Dolan (2006a) found that psychopaths were over three times more likely to be violent than non-psychopaths up to 24 weeks post discharge where the odds ratio was found to be 3.24. In relation to the predictive validity of continuous measures, the OR gives the amount of change in the outcome measure (e.g. violence) expected for a one point change in scale scores. The OR given for dichotomous variables gives the odds of the outcome occurring if the dichotomous variable is present, yes or no. The output from the logistic regression model also provides the percentage of correctly classified predictions, and the chi-square statistic and significance of individual variables of the entire model. As with multiple linear regression, a stepwise procedure can be used with logistic regression to identify the best predictors from multiple significant predictor variables. Several recent violence risk assessment studies have used regression procedures to determine the significance of predictor variables for violence (for example Monahan *et al.*, 2000; Doyle and Dolan, 2006a).

Survival analyses can be used to evaluate the time it takes for a criterion-outcome variable, such as readmission or violence, to occur after a specific time point such as admission, discharge or release. The Kaplan-Meir Log rank statistic can be used to demonstrate whether survival or desistance from violence or avoiding readmission are different when two groups (high versus low scorers on a measure such as the HCR-20) are compared (see Dolan and Khawaja, 2004). Survival analysis can also be used in treatment studies and randomised controlled trials in order to estimate relative risk (or hazard ratio) between treatment and control groups; for example where the trial outcome measure is a distinct event such as violence, relapse or readmission over the course of the study period.

Receiver operating characteristics

The statistical tests referred to so far are dependent on the base rate of violence and methods are required to compensate for fluctuations in base rate. A method that seems to have gained a state-of-the-art status when it comes to the estimation of the predictive validity of a continuous risk measure (for instance, HCR-20 score) to a dichotomous outcome (i.e. violence, yes or no) is Receiver Operating Characteristic Analysis, or ROC-analysis (Mossman, 1994; Rice and Harris, 1995). They are recommended in this area because they are less dependent on the base rate of the criterion variable in the sample (in the present case, violence) than are traditional measures of predictive accuracy derived from two-by-two contingency tables (such as sensitivity and specificity). ROCs allow for the comparison of various thresholds on the predictor measures for offering predictions of violence, an overall index of accuracy which accounts for all possible thresholds, the simple identification of the optimal cut-off and the comparison of two or more predictors.

ROCs are meant to be applied to data that comprise continuous predictor variables (e.g. HCR-20 scores) and a dichotomous dependent measure (e.g. violence, yes or no). They take the form of a figure with the sensitivity ('Hit Rate') of the predictor plotted as a function of the False Alarm Rate (1-specificity) (see Figure 3.3). For any given level of specificity, the receiver knows the sensitivity. Each point on the curve (which corresponds to a cut-off on the predictor) represents a different trade-off between sensitivity and specificity.

The area under the curve (AUC) of the ROC graph (see Figure 3.3) can be taken as an index for interpreting the overall accuracy of the predictor. Areas can range from 0 (perfect negative prediction), to .50 (chance prediction), to 1.0 (perfect positive prediction). A given area represents the probability that a randomly chosen person who scores positive on the dependent measure (in this study, is actually violent) will fall above any given cut-off on the predictor measure, and that an actually non-violent person will score below the cut-off.

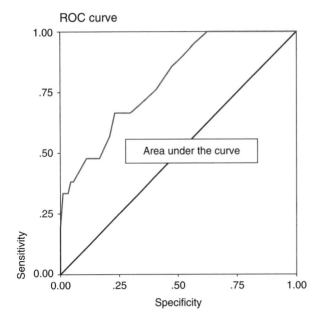

Figure 3.3 Receiver Operating Characteristics graph.

Thus, an area of .75 means that there is a 75 per cent chance that an actually violent person would score above the cut-off for violence on the predictor, and an actually non-violent person would score below the cut-off. AUC values of .70 may be considered moderate to large, and .75 and above may be considered large (Douglas *et al.*, 2001).

Predictive studies using group data are useful for identifying potential risk factors that may be tested and applied in future research and practice. However, these findings are limited when applied to individual cases in clinical practice as the findings will not tell us with any degree of certainty which individuals in the group are going to be violent. For example Doyle and Dolan (2006a) found that 38 per cent of psychopaths were violent compared to 16 per cent of non-psychopaths. This is a significant difference and psychopathy was found to be predictive. Nevertheless, when applied in clinical practice it would be impossible to know if an individual psychopath being assessed would be in the 38 per cent who will violent or the 62 per cent who are not.

Conclusion

Violence risk assessment is the *raison d'être* of forensic and related services. Debate regarding discretionary and actuarial approaches continues, although structured professional judgement has been proposed as a way of combining the strengths of both approaches. Research that is rigorous and of a high quality is required to provide the evidence-base for systematic approaches to risk assessment. Researchers need to consider a number of methodological issues and where possible should:

1 Clearly define research questions and hypotheses.
2 Use established, valid and reliable research instruments to assess a wide range of risk factors.
3 Aim to use a prospective design.
4 Control for threats to validity including attrition, selection and rater bias and level of professional and social support.
5 Identify existing databases (e.g. police national computer, Home Office database) that contain longitudinal data on large samples.
6 Clearly define violence in accordance with previous research (e.g. MacVRAS) and measure using multiple sources of information.
7 Provide clear rationale for sample inclusion and exclusion criteria and justify sample size.
8 Conduct inter-rater reliability analysis on measures of predictor and criterion variables before and during research study.
9 Consider predictive, concurrent and incremental validity of predictor variables.
10 Employ relevant procedures for statistical analyses.

Future directions for risk research

The field of forensic mental health is continuously evolving to meet the challenges of contemporary society and in response to innovative research and development. Much good quality and ground-breaking research has already been conducted in relation to violence risk assessment, although there are a number of areas that need to be considered for future research and development.

By reviewing change in clinical and risk management items it may be possible to assess the impact of current interventions and monitor progress while systematically tracking change in all key domains that have been identified as treatment targets. Characterising individual violence risk in the long-, medium- and short-term will enhance understanding of risk and help in the selection of future interventions.

The focus of most research to date in forensic services has been on risk factors that are linked to an increase in violence risk. There is a need to examine and refine our understanding of the factors that confer protection against risk of subsequent violent behaviour over and above pharmacological and specialist psychological treatments. In recent years some examples of good research in this area have emerged with samples of violent offenders (Haggard *et al.*, 2001), adult civil patients (Monahan *et al.*, 2001; Doyle and Doyle, 2008) and adolescents (Lodewijks *et al.*, 2009). De Vogel and colleagues have recently developed the *Structured Assessment of Protective Factors* (SAPROF; De Vogel *et al.*, 2009) which provides a measure of internal, motivational and external factors that are associated with a decrease in violence risk. More research needs to be done in this area to investigate and explore protective factors across different cultures, gender, crime types and mental/behavioural disorders. This should help to identify effective interventions for violence prevention that could be evaluated using randomised controlled trials (see Tarrier *et al.*, 2010).

In future research, consideration needs to be given to both the nomothetic studies of risk factors and the influence of idiosyncratic factors such as peer group, social factors and level of monitoring and supervision. In risk prediction the research question is aimed at determining the predictive accuracy of whether a person will be violent. However, in clinical practice there is a need to get an understanding of why the person might be a risk before prescribing treatment and management interventions to minimise the risk. Therefore future research in this area should aim to be theory based and where the theory is lacking this may need to be generated using more exploratory qualitative approaches. Evidence-based risk formulations should better explain reasons for risk, identify idiosyncratic 'causative' rather than risk factors, aid risk communication and result in formulation-based interventions (Doyle and Dolan 2006a). Research needs to consider how the evidence base may be developed to increase knowledge about risk formulation and its application in practice – which may include exploration of its utility, key features, process issues and what is helpful or unhelpful (Lewis and Doyle, 2009).

The generalisability of findings can be limited by the fact that in most prospective studies there are at least a significant minority of potential participants who refuse to participate (Monahan *et al.*, 2001; Doyle and Dolan, 2006a). It is also possible that those patients who do not consent are the group who are most likely to be non-compliant and antisocial and therefore more likely to be violent. This could seriously impact on the validity of any research and therefore the full benefits of the findings may be lost. Therefore, future studies may wish to consider using a confidential inquiry approach to overcome some of the methodological problems experienced in previous research while continuing to protect the legal rights and anonymity of the participants. This should maximise the validity and reliability of findings and subsequently lead to more effective approaches for the assessment and management of violence.

This chapter has focused on researching the assessment and management of violence risk, but many other risks confront forensic mental health services. The criterion variable in future research needs to be expanded to include risk of self-harm, suicide, sexual violence, absconding, fire-setting and exploitation. These areas warrant ongoing empirical investigation equivalent to research on violence risk.

Further resources

Martin Bland (2000). *An introduction to medical statistics.* 3rd edn. Oxford: Oxford University Press.

MacArthur Foundation (n.d.). MacArthur Foundation Violence Risk Assessment Study. Available at www.macarthur.virginia.edu/risk.html (accessed 21/4/11).
Tony Maden (2007). *Treating violence: a guide to risk management in mental health.* Oxford: Oxford University Press.
Randy K. Otto and Kevin S. Douglas (2009) (Eds). *Handbook of violence risk assessment.* NewYork: Routledge.
Keith Soothil, Paul Rogers and Mairead Dolan (2008) (Eds). *Handbook of forensic mental health.* Willan Publishing.
Christopher Webster (n.d.). Violence risk. Available at www.violence-risk.com (accessed 21/4/11).

References

Arseneault, L., Caspi, A., Moffitt,T. E., Taylor, P. J. and Silva, P. A. (2000). Mental disorders and violence in a total birth cohort: results from the Dunedin Study. *Archives of General Psychiatry*, 57: 979–86.
Baxstrom v. Herold, 383 U.S. 107 (1966).
Bland, M. (2000). *An introduction to medical statistics.* 3rd edn. Oxford: Oxford University Press.
Borum, R. (1996). Improving the clinical practice of violence risk assessment. *American Psychologist*, 51(9): 945–56.
Buchanan, A. (2008). Risk of violence by psychiatric patients: beyond the 'actuarial versus clinical' assessment debate. *Psychiatric Services*, 59(2): 184–90.
De Vogel, V., de Ruiter, C., Bouman, Y. and de Vries Robbe, M. (2009). *SAPROF: Structured Assessment of Protective Factors for Violence Risk.* Utrecht, NL: Forum Educatief.
Department of Health (2007). *Best practice in managing risk: principles and evidence for best practice in the assessment and management of risk to self and others in mental health services.* National Mental Health Risk Management Programme. June.
Dolan, M. and Khawaja, A. (2004). The HCR–20 and Post-discharge outcome in male patients discharged from medium security in the UK. *Aggressive Behavior*, 30: 469–83.
Douglas, K., Cox, D. and Webster, C. (1999). Violence risk assessment: science and practice. *Legal and Criminological Psychology*, 4: 149–84.
Douglas, K. S., Webster, C. D., Hart, S. D., Eaves, D. and Ogloff, J. R. P. (Eds) (2001). *HCR-20: violence risk management companion guide.* Burnaby, BC, Canada: Mental Health, Law, and Policy Institute, Simon Fraser University, and Department of Mental Health Law and Policy, University of South Florida.
Douglas, K. S., Ogloff, J. R. and Hart, S. D. (2003). Evaluation of a model of violence risk assessment among forensic psychiatric patients. *Psychiatric Services*, 54(10): 1,372–9.
Doyle, M. (2000). Risk assessment and management. In Chris Chaloner and Michael Coffey (Eds). *Forensic mental health nursing: current approaches* (pp. 140–70). London: Blackwell Science.
—— (1996). Assessing risk of violence from clients. *Mental Health Nursing*, 16(3): 20–3.
Doyle, M. and Dolan, M. (2006a). Predicting community violence from patients discharged from mental health services. *British Journal of Psychiatry*, 189: 520–6.

—— (2006b). Evaluating the validity of anger regulation problems, interpersonal style, and disturbed mental state for predicting inpatient violence. *Behavioral, Sciences and the Law*, 24(6): 783–98.

—— (2007). Standardized risk assessment. *Psychiatry*, 6(10): 409–14.

—— (2008). Understanding and managing risk. In K. Soothill, P. Rogers and M. Dolan (Eds) *Handbook of forensic mental health* (pp. 244–66). Willan Publishing.

Doyle, M., Dolan, M. C. and McGovern, J. (2002). The validity of North American risk assessment tools in predicting inpatient violent behaviour in England. *Legal and Criminological Psychology*, 7(2): 141–54.

Elbogen, E. and Johnson, S. (2009). The intricate link between violence and mental disorder. *Archives of General Psychiatry*, 66(2): 152–61.

Ennis, B. J. and Emery, R. D. (1978). *The rights of mental patients.* Rev. edn. New York, U.S.A.: Avon Books.

Fasel, S., Langstrom, N., Hjern, A., Grann, M. and Lichtenstein, P. (2009). Schizophrenia, substance abuse and violent crime. *Journal of the American Medical Association*, 301(19): 2,016–23.

Faust, D. and Ziskin, J. (1988). The expert witness in psychology and psychiatry. *Science*, 241: 31–5.

Fowkes, F. G. R. and Fulton, P. M. (1991). Critical appraisal of published research; introductory guidelines. *British Medical Journal*, 302: 1,136–40.

Gray, N., Hill, C., McGleish, A., Timmons, D., MacCulloch, M. and Snowden, R. (2003). Prediction of violence and self-harm in mentally disordered offenders: a prospective study of the efficacy of HCR-20, PCL–R, and psychiatric symptomatology. *Journal of Consulting and Clinical Psychology*, 71(3): 443–51.

Haggard, U., Gumpert, C. and Grann, M. (2001). Against all odds: a qualitative follow-up study of high-risk violent offenders who were not reconvicted. *Journal of Interpersonal Violence*, 16(10): 1,048–65.

Hart, S. D. (1998). The role of psychopathy in assessing risk for violence: conceptual and methodological issues. *Legal and Criminological Psychology*, 3: 121–37.

Hart, S., Cox, D. and Hare, R. (1995). *The Hare PCL: SV: psychopathy checklist: screening version.* New York: Multi-Health Systems Incorporated.

Hart, S., Michie, C. and Cooke, D. (2007). Precision of actuarial risk assessment instruments: evaluating the 'margins of error' of group v. individual predictions of violence. *British Journal of Psychiatry*, 190 (suppl. 49): 60–5.

Lewis, G. and Doyle, M. (2009). Risk formulation: what are we doing and why? *International Journal of Forensic Mental Health*, 8: 286–92.

Lidz, C., Mulvey, E. and Gardner, W. (1993). The accuracy of predictions of violence to others. *Journal of the American Medical Association*, 269: 1,007–11.

Lodewijks, H., de Ruiter, C. and Doreleijers, T. (2009). The impact of protective factors in desistance from violent reoffending: a study in three samples of adolescent offenders. *Journal of Interpersonal Violence*, 25(3): 568–87.

McNiel, D. E. and Binder, R.L. (1989). Relationship between preadmission threats and later violent behaviour by acute psychiatric inpatients. *Hospital & Community Psychiatry*, 40: 605–8.

Monahan, J. (1981). Predicting violent behaviour. *Sage Library of social research*, 114. California, Sage.

Monahan, J. (2006). A jurisprudence of risk assessment: forecasting harm among prisoners, predators and patients. *Virginia Law Review*, 92(3). May.

Monahan, J. and Steadman, H. (Eds) (1994). *Violence and mental disorder: developments in risk assessment.* Chicago: University of Chicago Press.

Monahan, J., Steadman, H., Silver, E., Appelbaum, P., Robbins, P., Mulvey, E., Roth, L., Grisso, T. and Banks, S. (2001). *Rethinking risk assessment: the MacArthur study of mental disorder and violence.* Oxford: Oxford University Press.

Monahan, J, Steadman, H., Robbins, P., Appelbaum, P., Banks, S., Grisso, T., Heilbrun, K., Mulvey, E., Roth, L. and Silver, E. (2005). An actuarial model of violence risk assessment for persons with mental disorders. *Psychiatric Services*, 56: 810–15.

Mossman, D. (1994). Assessing predictions of violence: being accurate about accuracy. *Journal of Consulting and Clinical Psychology*, 62: 783–92.

Mulvey, E. and Lidz, C. (1984). Clinical considerations in the prediction of dangerousness in mental patients. *Clinical Psychology Review*, 4: 379–401.

—— (1985). Back to basics: a critical analysis of dangerousness research in a new legal environment. *Law and Human Behavior*, 9: 209–18.

Mulvey, E. P., Shaw, E. and Lidz, C. W. (1994). Why use multiple sources in research on patient violence in the community? *Criminal Behaviour and Mental Health*, 4: 253–8.

National Confidential Inquiry (2006). *Avoidable deaths: five year report of the National Confidential Inquiry into suicide and homicide by people with mental illness.* University of Manchester. December.

National Health Service (NHS) (2006). The independent inquiry into the care and treatment of John Barrett. October. London: South West London Strategic Health Authority.

Otto, R. K. (1992). Prediction of dangerous behavior: a review and analysis of 'second generation' research. *Forensic Reports*, 5: 103–33.

Persson, L. G. W. (1980). *Hidden criminality – theoretical and methodological problems, empirical results.* Sweden: Department of Sociology, University of Stockholm.

Rice, M. E. and Harris, G. T. (1995). Violent recidivism: Assessing predictive validity. *Journal of Consulting and Clinical Psychology*, 53: 737–48.

Ritchie, J. H., Dick, D. and Lingham, R. (1994). The report of the enquiry into the care and treatment of Christopher Clunis. London: HMSO.

Robson, C. (1995). *Real world research: a resource for social scientists and practitioner-researchers.* Oxford: Blackwell.

Royal College of Psychiatrists (2008). *Rethinking risk to others in mental health services. Final report of scoping group.* CR150. June. London: RCP.

Sorgi, P., Ratey, J., Knoedler, D. W., Markert, R. J. and Reichman, M. (1991). Rating aggression in the clinical setting: a retrospective adaptation of the Overt Aggression Scale: preliminary results. *Journal of Neuropsychiatry and Clinical Neuro-sciences*, 3(2): S52-6.

Steadman, H. J. and Cocozza, J. J. (1974). *Carers of the criminally insane: excessive social control of deviance.* Lexington, MA: Lexington Books.

Steadman, H. J., Mulvey, E., Monahan, J., Robbins, P., Appelbaum, P., Grisso, T., Roth, L. and Silver, E. (1998). Violence by people discharged from acute psychiatric inpatient facilities and by others in the same neighbourhoods. *Archives of General Psychiatry*, 55: 393–401.

Tarrier, N., Dolan, M., Doyle, M., Dunn, G., Shaw, J. and Blackburn, R. (2010). *Exploratory randomized control trial of schema modal therapy in the Personality Disorder Service at Ashworth Hospital.* Ministry of Justice Research Series 5/10. March.

Taylor, P., Chilvers, C, Doyle, M., Gumpert, C., Harney, K. and Nedopil, N. (2009). Meeting the challenge of research while treating mentally disordered offenders: the future of the clinical researcher. *International Journal of Forensic Mental Health*, 8(1): 2–8.

Volavka, J. (1995). Neurobiology of violence. Washington, DC: American Psychiatric Press, Inc.

Webster, C., Harris, G., Rice, M., Cormier, C. and Quinsey, V. (1994). *The violence prediction scheme: assessing dangerousness in high risk men.* Toronto: University of Toronto, Centre of Criminology.

Webster, C. D, Douglas, K., Eaves D. and Hart, S. (1997). *HCR-20: assessing risk for violence – version 2.* British Columbia, Canada: Simon Fraser University.

Wong, S. C. P. and Gordon, A. (2003). *Violence risk scale.* Available from the authors, Department of Psychology, University of Saskatchewan, Saskatoon, Saskatchewan, Canada S7N 5A5, or online at www.psynergy.ca (accessed 21/4/11).

Yudofsky, S., Silver, J., Jackson, W., Endicott, J. and Williams, D. (1986). The overt aggression scale for the objective rating of verbal and physical aggression. *American Journal of Psychiatry*, 143(1): 35–9.

4 Facet Theory and multi-dimensional scaling methods in forensic research

Jennifer Brown

Introduction

Forensic psychological research covers many topics. Brown and Campbell's (2010) recent handbook indicates areas of attention that include assessment, treatment, investigation and prosecution of offences and offenders, different crime types, criminal justice practitioners' attitudes or stress levels as well as cognitive, social and developmental processes. The handbook shows interest is wide ranging and includes creating motivational or behavioural typologies of offenders through to evaluating offender treatment programmes or conducting empirical studies into decision making within criminal justice practice. Methods used range from laboratory based experiments to experiential interviews. Theoretical formulations are drawn from social, cognitive and developmental theoretical positions. Research may be exploratory or hypothesis testing. Thus there is neither a unitary method nor preferred theoretical starting point for conducting a forensic psychological research study.

The research investigator may be focusing on differences between people, describing behaviours and working in different settings and is interested in relationships between any or all of these (Figure 4.1).

As an example, the investigator may be looking at stress in different professions (Bar-On *et al.*, 2000) or may wish to describe lay understandings of stress (Toch, 2002) or measure potential burnout of operational police officers (Euwema *et al.*, 2004). This might involve psychometric scales, qualitative interviews or analysis of sickness absence records. Each type of study could have a different theoretical formulation and certainly is likely to be asking different research questions and employing different methods.

What this chapter will outline is an approach to research that can accommodate all these variations, i.e. different research questions, varying types of data and alternative theoretical constructs. The approach is Facet Meta Theory. It is called a meta theory because it is a structural framework within which potentially any topic (or content) may be propounded. It has a procedure for designing studies and a set of analytic techniques to analyse data. Data may be in the form of questionnaire items, interview responses or secondary sources such as newspaper archives or police witness statements. The facet approach requires a shift in

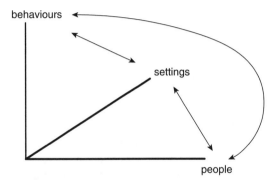

Figure 4.1 Foci of research investigations.

thinking as well as clarity of thought when utilising this as a means of conducting research. As a way to conduct research, Facet Meta Theory offers the novice researcher a set of tools that will help conceptualise the research problem, design measurement and offer a procedure for analysing and interpreting data. Not only does it force the researcher to define concepts when undertaking a study, but it presents data in the form of pictures or maps, often in three dimensions, and does not utilise tests of statistical significance as in chi-square or analysis of variance (ANOVA). The chapter will describe the origins and developments of Facet Meta Theory, the use of its associated multi-dimensional scaling techniques – most notably Smallest Space Analysis (SSA), Multi-dimensional Scalogram Analysis (MSA) and Partial Order Scalogram Analysis (POSA) – and take the reader through the design principles whereby questionnaires may be constructed or open-ended responses analysed. The chapter charts the pioneering research of David Canter and associates in the field of offender profiling. Thereafter the extension to wider arenas beyond sexual offending are described and developments in the theoretical understanding of offending within this approach are explained. Finally, there is a critique of the approach which draws attention to some of its strengths and weaknesses.

The Facet Theory approach

There are three aspects to this approach: theory, design and measurement. In essence the facet approach to research offers a set of methodological tools to facilitate theory construction (Guttman and Greenbaum, 1998). Donald (1995, p. 117) points out that Facet Theory places great emphasis 'on the definitions and hypotheses prior to data collection and analysis'. Any content theory can be developed through the scaffolding provided by the working method, in other words by focusing on the definitions of observations, then both explanations and predictions of the relationships between them can be undertaken. As Guttman and Greenbaum (1998) note in their review, Facet Theory has been applied to many areas of research including topics of interest to forensic psychology. Guttman's own definition of a theory is an 'hypothesis of correspondence between a definitional system for a universe of observations and an aspect of the empirical structure of those observations, together with a rationale for such an hypothesis' (Levy, 2005, p. 179). This means that there must be some reasoning or rationale, usually located in prior research findings, that identifies and defines the content of the phenomenon under study, and by means of facet design (to be explained later in the chapter) the relationships between aspects of the constituent parts are laid out and then, through the use of multi-dimensional scaling techniques, collected data are analysed to determine whether there is congruence between the conceptual and empirical domains. Guttman (1954) argues that where there is a clear specificity of key variables the specification (in the form of a mapping sentence) can be used to predict the statistical structure of empirical data. As a consequence Levy (2005, p. 179) observes that researchers thus have two things to worry about: the design of observations and the empirical structure of those observations. She notes 'the theoretical leap requires thinking about these two things in partnership'.

The versatility of the approach lies not only in its adaptability to any area of interest but also in its ability to handle both quantitative and qualitative data either collected from primary participants or derived through secondary sources such as law reports or police witness statements. It can be used both in top-down hypothesis testing or as bottom-up hypothesis generating. What this means simply is that a researcher may have a theoretical formulation such as the theory of planned behaviour (Ajzen, 1991) which is a model of attitudinal behaviour: i.e. evaluation of the behaviour; perception of social pressures to engage in the behaviour; and perception of controls thought to govern the behaviour. Norman, Bennett and Lewis (1998) used this framework to generate hypotheses about young people's binge drinking behaviours. Their findings supported the predictions arising from the theory with men more likely to be influenced by their own evaluation of drinking than by social pressures that do not endorse excessive drinking. Bottom-up approaches are where there is either no adequate theory or underdeveloped concepts from which to derive theoretical explanations. Frances Heidensohn used a Grounded Theoretical approach to analyse the experience of women police officers (Heidensohn, 1992). She conducted semi-structured interviews with policewomen and from this material constructed a number of explanatory concepts such as 'transformational scenes' which were devices used by women to engage in some heroic activity in order to gain acceptance from fellow police officers.

Methodological tools

The basic tools for designing a study using this approach are:

* identification of facets (or key variables) and their elements (exhaustive list of constituent aspects of the facet);

- construction of a mapping sentence (which lays out the facet structure by means of a notation system);
- specification of relationships between facets (which indicates the roles each facet plays with respect to each other, thereby constructing a geometric template);
- multivariate statistical analysis (that permits a reconstruction of the theoretical pattern by partitioning the distributed points, i.e. elements of the facets according to the template.

Facets are 'the conceptual categories that make up the universe of observations in an empirical investigation' (Brown, 2010b, p. 795). There are three types of facet: 1) background, which usually describes characteristics of the respondent such as gender or age or it could be their role such as police officer or civilian staff member; 2) domain, which specifies the content which could be motivation to commit a crime or different modus operandi; and 3) range, which indicates the common set of relevant response and could be a Likert type scale or simply presence or absence as a dichotomous response i.e. 1 or 0. The idea of a common range is that items should have some kind of order and there must be a uniform meaning to the order (Levy, 2005). Each facet has an exhaustive itemising of its constituent elements thus the facet sexual orientation contains the elements heterosexual, same sex and bi-sexual preferences.

A brief summary of the steps required to undertake a facet designed study are as follows:

1 Identify key papers/source literature in the area of research interest.
2 Identify theoretical concepts used to explain the phenomenon under scrutiny.
3 Construct a mapping sentence that converts the conceptualisations into facets with an exhaustive listing of all their component elements which have to be mutually exclusive and employing the facet notational system.
4 Hypothesise the roles that the respective facets play, e.g. a polar role in which facets have a qualitative relationship to each other and would therefore create a circular ordering in the multivariate analysis.
5 Using the mapping sentence, construct a questionnaire or coding dictionary in order to structure the collection of empirical data.
6 Having collected the data, create a data matrix for input into the appropriate multivariate statistical procedure.
7 Partition the multivariate space in line with the template set out in the mapping sentence.

So the starting point in a research investigation is to identify the broad area of interest, whether this be sexual offending, stress experienced by criminal justice practitioners or evaluating a programmed intervention. A search of the published literature will locate the theoretical ideas that have been used to try to explain the phenomenon under scrutiny. For example Salfati and Taylor (2006) examined the behaviours of sexual murders and rapists. They located a number of explanatory concepts used by previous researchers: interpersonal aggression, power and control, sexual fantasy. These then became the basic building blocks (facets) upon which they built their particular model of interpersonal interaction in violent sexual offending.

Next, the facets are laid out in the form of a mapping sentence which is a distinctive technique of facet design. Shye (1978, p. 413) defines a mapping sentence as 'a verbal statement of the domain and of the range of a mapping, including verbal connectives between facets as in ordinary language'. The mapping sentence should contain all three types of facet. Brown (2010b, p. 797) provides an example of a mapping sentence (see Figure 4.2).

In this example the population parameter specified is age (there could be others such as ethnicity, occupation etc.) Two domains or content facets, modus operandi and motivation, are identified and these are mapped into a dichotomous response of presence or absence. The convention for mapping sentences is to adopt a notation in which a capital letter denotes the facet and a lower case with subscript denotes the constituent elements.

From the mapping sentence, observations in the form of questionnaire items or content of qualitative interview material may be constructed. Table 4.1 illustrates how questionnaire items might be generated to undertake a study differentiating between the behaviours of adult and adolescent sex offenders. By drawing on the two content facets, modus operandi and motivation (2 x 3 = 6) combinations can be constructed, i.e. b_1c_1 to b_2c_3. These are known as structuples and are the profile of elements drawn from several facets. These form the template to design a questionnaire item (see Table 4.1). There would be a common opening section of the questionnaire in this case 'Does the offender engage in … ' followed by the verbal translation of the structuples. The answer would be yes (1) or no (0).

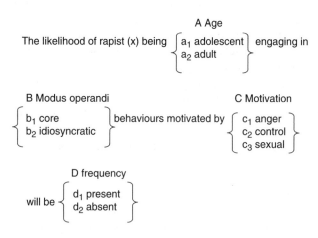

Figure 4.2 Illustrative mapping sentence.
　　　　　Source: adapted from Brown (2010b).

Table 4.1 Construction of questionnaire items from a mapping sentence

Verbal translation	Facet structuples
Core behaviours motivated by anger	b_1c_1
Core behaviours motivated by criminal intentions	b_1c_2
Core behaviours motivated by sexual intentions	b_1c_3
Idiosyncratic behaviours motivated by anger	b_2c_1
Idiosyncratic behaviours motivated by criminal intentions	b_2c_2
Idiosyncratic behaviours motivated by anger	b_2c_3

Table 4.2 Example of a data matrix in which scores are dichotomous (present or absent)

Respondent number	Adolescent = 1 Adult = 2	b_1c_1 question	b_1c_2 question	b_1c_3 etc.
1	1	1	1	0
2	1	0	1	1
3	1	1	0	0
4	2	1	1	1
5 etc.	2	1	1	0

In this way adolescent and adult offenders would amass a set of scores indicating presence or absence of the behaviours (see Table 4.2). Typically, a data matrix of behaviours as columns and rapists as rows would be constructed and submitted for analysis, and the modus operandi and motivation facets would be discernable as distinct regions in the multi-dimensional space if there was a correspondence between this way of conceptualising rape and actual rape behaviours.

Donald (2000) provides an accessible account of how questionnaire items are constructed by drawing a structuple profile. This enables the domain to be exhausted with all relevant questions being generated by means of the mapping sentence template.

Other times, data may be made up by questionnaire items in which the response is a Likert type scale, i.e. very satisfied (5); fairly satisfied (4); neither satisfied nor dissatisfied (3); fairly dissatisfied (2); and very dissatisfied (1). In this case the data matrix takes the form shown in Table 4.3.

Facets can also aid in the identification of themes underlying variables generated from secondary sources as in Canter and Heritage (1990). Here behaviours of rapists could be found that broadly were classified as criminal, sexual, impersonal, violent or intimate. They then set about describing the variables which could be classified under these broad themes (facets) to make a coding dictionary that enabled them to construct profiles for each rape described in a police witness statement.

Table 4.3 Example of a data matrix where scores are scale responses

Respondent no	Question 1	Question 2	Question 3	Question 4 etc.
1	3	4	5	2
2	5	3	4	4
3	2	5	5	5
4	3	2	2	3
5 etc.	1	3	1	2

Once questionnaire surveys have been completed, or qualitative material coded or data extracted from documentary sources, and the data entered into a matrix as described above, the matrix is submitted for analysis by one of three statistical procedures: Smallest Space Analysis (SSA), Multi-dimensional Scalogram Analysis (MSA) or Partial Order Scalogram Analysis (POSA). These produce outputs in the form of maps which then are partitioned to recover the facet structure. If this is successful then the correspondence is achieved between the conceptualisation as demonstrated in the mapping sentence and the structure of the data as revealed through the analysis.

Regional partitioning supports the general hypothesis of Facet Theory, i.e. the correspondence between the conceptual and empirical mapping. As Levy (2005, p. 182) explains: 'regional hypotheses relate to the roles that the content facets of the variables play in partitioning the SSA space. Three major roles emanate from consideration of order among elements in the facets: polar, modular and axial.' The polar role is described as being a facet whose elements are qualitatively related and would be expected to have a circular configuration emanating from a common point of origin. The modular role is partially ordered and would be expected to be represented as concentric rings from the centre of the configuration. An axial role is an ordered facet whereby the elements would be represented in some linear sequence across the plot. These roles may intersect and thereby create geometric structures; most typically the combination of a polar and modular facet constructs a radex. The addition of a facet playing an axial role creates a three-dimensional structure termed a cylindrex.

SSA, MSA and POSA are the suite of multi-dimensional scaling techniques derived by Louis Guttman and James Lingoes in the 1950s. Guttman's early research had led him to develop the Guttman Scale. This is a cumulative scale in which endorsement of later items is predicted by agreement with earlier statements, e.g. the social distance scale in which agreement that you would be happy for your son/daughter to marry someone from a different ethnicity would have predicted your agreement to items such as you would be happy to live next door to a black family, which itself predicts that you agree that you have friends or acquaintances of diverse ethnicity. Guttman was concerned with complexities of co-occurring relationships, and accordingly he set about developing a package of multi-variate statistics as the means to empirically verify sets of theoretically inspired relationships.

Smallest Space Analysis

SSA-I was the first of the Guttman-Lingoes series designed to analyse a symmetric data matrix. The data are often in the form of the sample data matrices given in Tables 4.2 and 4.3 above. The programme has a number of correlation co-efficient options depending on the type of data and thus generates a lower triangular correlation matrix. These are converted into linear distances such that the higher the correlation, the shorter the equivalent distance. The goodness of fit between the correlation coefficients and the relative distance is assessed by a measure called the coefficient of alienation (CoA) varying between 0 and 1 with the former designated a perfect fit. A rule of thumb suggest a coefficient of alienation of 0.15 is usually considered an acceptable fit, although interpretable SSA can be undertaken with CoA which are higher (Donald, 1995). The output of an SSA is in the form of a map with the variables projected as points in an n-dimensional space. Co-ordinates anchor the points in terms of the number of dimensions. Thus a two-dimensional solution may be anchored by co-ordinates that may be thought of as longitude and latitude or length and breadth. A third dimension such as time or depth could provide other co-ordinates thereby creating a three-dimensional space.

Perhaps an example might help. Imagine a bag of marbles of differing colours and sizes all connected with different lengths of elastic depending how similar the marbles are to each other. The marbles could be all slightly different hues of primary colours and described uniquely by their wavelength. They can also be classed as large or small. The first iteration of an SSA scatters the marbles and the slackness of the connecting elastic is the goodness of fit. The first iteration is not likely to be a good fit, so there are further scatterings until the connective elastic bands are as tight as possible. If the bands cannot be tightened within one dimension, the programme creates a second and third dimension into which to try to find the optimal fit. Once achieved, it should then be possible to draw partition lines in such a way as to differentiate the different coloured marbles conforming to a colour label and a further partition should allow a region of bigger and smaller marbles to be segregated. Colour might represent a qualitative facet, so having a circular ordering and size would represent a modulating ordering, thus the different colours, say blue, green and yellow, would be represented as slices of cake with the large marbles at the centre and the smaller ones pushed to the periphery. These together would make a radex as shown in Figure 4.3.

As this is an imaginary illustrative example, the partition lines are readily discernable and clear cut. Drawing partition lines is not unproblematic. As Guttman and Greenbaum (1998, p. 32) observe, 'where does one put the lines? Should they be smooth, curved, regular or irregular?' Without a prior facet design which hypothesises where the lines are drawn, researchers are often left to their own judgement. Moreover if the points at a and c are inspected they will be seen as suggesting greater similarity than between the marbles marked a and b. Thus a and c appear statistically more similar and are in different regions

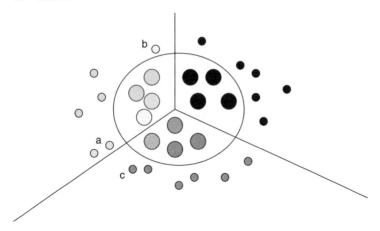

Figure 4.3 Hypothetical partitioning of an SSA.

than a and b which are in the same region. Partitions are based on substantive principles, e.g. the roles facets are hypothesised to play, and represent a departure from more traditional statistics because it is the regional hypothesis that is important.

Multi-dimensional Scalogram Analysis

MSA is described by Zvulun (1978) in which the input matrix is often in the form of participants making up the rows, and the columns are items that characterise them. Participants can be cities, as in a study by Bloombaum (1968) which sought to differentiate US cities involved in riots, or individuals, such as sex offender treatment managers in a study of stress by Brown and Blount (1999). MSA aims to create a geometric representation of a multivariate distribution, a scalogram, by taking into account the inter-relationships among all the items. In the Brown and Blount study, sex offender treatment managers were interviewed about the stressors they experienced. A total of 15 stressors were identified, e.g. seeing no change in a prisoner, prison governor's lack of understanding and becoming uncomfortable around children. Each manager was given a profile according to whether or not they had experienced this stressor. A matrix made up of the managers as rows against which was a series of ones and twos representing presence or absence of the columned stressor. MSA then compares all profiles and distributes the individuals as a function of how similar their profiles are. The first plot distributes individuals as points in the MSA overall mapping. Thereafter, the points representing the individual are anchored in subsequent plots of each variable, in this case the 15 stressors. Each stressor plot can then be inspected to see if there is a clear regional distribution of ones and twos, denoting presence or absence of that stressor for that individual.

Wilson (2000) has an accessible account of how this type of qualitative content analysis can be accomplished by means of an MSA. She explains how there is a literal reconstruction of a participant's profile in the MSA space and then how each plot representing the variable under consideration may be partitioned into identifiable regions. The analysis proceeds by providing some overview of the cumulative partitioning. If we use Wilson's approach to map the distinguishing characteristics of various professions, the progression from the mapping sentence, profiling of the occupation in question and analysis by means of an MSA can be shown. Recourse to the literature may reveal a number of ways occupations or professions may be distinguished. Having identified these, a mapping sentence such as that shown in Figure 4.4 might be constructed. If the researcher wished to profile a number of occupations, say police, social work, law, medicine, psychology or prison service, then various documents or other knowledge would enable profiles to be drawn and a data matrix constructed using the notation from the mapping sentence (see Table 4.4). The data matrix is then submitted to MSA with the resultant plots as illustrated in Figure 4.5.

From the overall plot we see that the prison officer and the police constable are quite close together, suggesting these to be similar occupations and rather different from the consultant. Each variable or facet plot shows the partition lines that represent the distribution of elements for that particular facet. This reveals the consultants and barristers as being highly paid whereas social workers and forensic psychologists are moderately paid and the police constable and the prison officer are the lowest paid. Consultants, social workers and forensic psychologists are not associated with any particular form of dress whereas barristers are garbed in gowns and wigs whilst police constables and

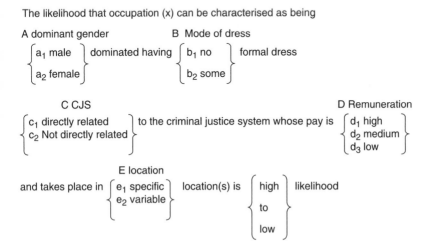

Figure 4.4 Mapping sentence for a classification of occupations.

Table 4.4 Specimen data matrix for an MSA

Occupation	Dominant gender	Mode of dress	CJS	Remuneration	Location
Police constable	1	1	1	3	2
Social worker	2	2	2	2	2
Barrister	1	1	1	1	1
Consultant	1	2	2	1	1
Forensic psychologist	2	2	1	2	2
Prison officer	1	1	1	3	1

Overall plot showing distribution of occupations

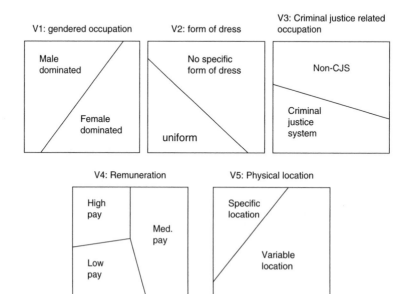

Figure 4.5 Partitioning of an MSA.

prison officers wear uniforms. Consultants, barristers and prison officers have specific locations, hospitals, courts and prison establishments within which they work and the other occupations undertake their work in variable locations. From this a multi-variate picture can be built up of how these occupations differ.

As with SSA, there is a goodness of fit measure for MSA. In this case congruence between the correlations and the linear distances is called the coefficient of contiguity and ranges between +1 and –1. Normally a measure of 0.9 is considered acceptable (Hammond and Brown, 2005).

Partial Order Scalogram Analysis

POSA is the extension of the original Guttman scale. A Guttman scale is often represented as follows:

11111
11112
11122
11222
12222
22222

This indicates some progressive and ordered endorsement of items. This is a perfect scale which rarely occurs in real data. POSA allows for other profiles to be represented. Supposing then a mapping sentence described the behaviour of a rapist as shown in Figure 4.6.

Then profiles can be constructed drawing on one element from each facet where $a_0b_0c_0$ denotes a rapist who engaged in none of these behaviours to $a_1b_1c_1$ where a rapist engages in all the behaviours. The mapping of these scales then conforms to a number of conventions; namely, that order relations are

The likelihood that rapist (x) engages in

A Theft
$\left\{ \begin{array}{l} a_1 \text{ stealing} \\ a_0 \text{ not stealing} \end{array} \right\}$

B Control
$\left\{ \begin{array}{l} b_1 \text{ controlling} \\ b_0 \text{ not controlling} \end{array} \right\}$

C Hostility
$\left\{ \begin{array}{l} c_1 \text{ displaying anger} \\ c_0 \text{ not displaying anger} \end{array} \right\}$

is $\left\{ \begin{array}{l} \text{high} \\ \text{to} \\ \text{low} \end{array} \right\}$ likelihood

Figure 4.6 Hypothetical mapping sentence of rapists' behaviour.

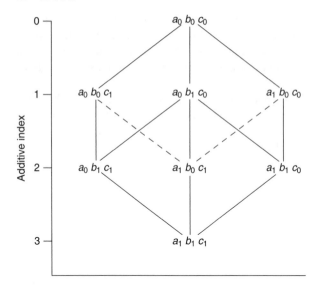

Figure 4.7 Hypothetical POSA of rapist behaviour.

represented by lines connecting profiles that logically increment in value. By summing the subscript value of a profile a joint or additive score can be computed. Profiles in the horizontal plane have similar additive scores but are qualitatively different. An example is shown in Figure 4.7.

Thus it is possible to type rapists by their behaviours such that either none, one, two or all three types of behaviour are displayed. Profiles to the left and right are progressive increments of additional and different types of behaviour being engaged in. Thus some rapists may only show one dominant facet of behaviour. An $a_0 b_1 c_0$ type rapist is controlling whereas an $a_1 b_0 c_0$ is motivated by criminality.

Beginnings

O'Neill and Hammond (2010) review the origins and application of multi-dimensional scaling techniques, noting in particular the work of Louis Guttmann and James Lingoes in producing a suite of procedures most commonly used within forensic psychology. Early US research making use of the then newly available multi-dimensional scaling techniques and applying them to forensic topics includes Bloombaum (1968) who reanalysed data in order to determine key demographic characteristics that predicted cities subjected to riots by using MSA. Cities in which riots had and had not occurred were considered and a matrix of demographic features constructed. Bloombaum's reasoning for using this technique was because it represented a generalisation of the unidimensional Guttman scale. In other words MSA enable multiple dimensions to adequately describe the conditions sufficient to discriminate cities in which riots occurred. Rafky (1975) used SSA to confirm Niederhoffer's police cynicism scale in which the SSA output confirmed the existence of two aspects of police cynicism, which was directed towards the public and that which occurred within and was aimed at the organisation itself. Such topics certainly fit under the rubric of forensic psychology interests, but perhaps the first application more readily recognised as such was David Canter's analysis of a series of rapes and three murders committed by John Duffy, the eponymous railway murderer (Canter 1988, 1989).

Canter was invited by Surrey police to assist in the investigation of the murder of Maartje Tamboezer at West Horsley in 1986. Canter approached this task from an application of an environmental psychological perspective, hypothesising that there would be discernable spatial patterns relative to where an offender lived in the commission of the crimes. The Tamboezer murder had been linked to two other killings and numerous rapes. Canter mapped the offences over time and showed a crescent shaped dispersion of rapes and the murders spreading out from a centre of gravity that indeed located Duffy's residence. Canter (1988, p. 14) concluded that this approach

> draws upon the development of statistical analysis procedures that can work with very crude, qualitative data, known in the trade as non-metric multi-dimensional scaling procedures. In a major investigation their great advantage is in summarising the large amounts of, often conflicting information. By reducing eyewitness statements to a matrix of categories, it is possible to use a form of statistical reduction that allows any pattern to become clearer.

Non-metric procedures are particularly helpful because they make no assumptions about the underlying structure of the data and can use a variety of input data, unlike the more restricted metric procedures (O'Neill and Hammond, 2010, p. 804).

The next development was an analysis of 66 rape offences by Canter and Heritage (1990). O'Neill and Hammond (2010) note that this analysis 'marked a shift within offender profiling away from an approach based on clinical judgement towards a more empirically established description of offender behaviour'. Canter and Heritage argued that if offender profiling, whereby psychologists were offering investigative advice in pursuit of an unknown offender, was to progress this should be undertaken systematically. Facet Theory offered a scientific method to undertake this task. According to Facet Theory design principles, Canter and Heritage provided a rationale by combing the existing research literature that suggested four facets had been found through various research studies to underpin sexual offence behaviours: sexuality; violence and aggression; impersonal sexual gratification; and interpersonal intimacy. They argued that if these theoretical constructs truly underpinned rape behaviours, then variables reflecting these aspects of behaviour should be found closer together and occupy distinct regions in a multi-dimensional space (i.e. SSA). Thus Canter and Heritage (1990, p. 190) hypothesed: 'An examination of the behaviours as they occur in actual sexual offences will reveal a structure that reflects the variety of modes of interpersonal interactions that underlie those offences.'

Thirty-three distinct behaviours were identified from the victim statements and police reports and the 66 offences were coded in terms of presence or absence of the itemised behaviour. The Jaccard co-efficient generated the correlations (used because this only accounts for agreement if behaviours co-occur rather than agreement if the behaviours are absent) and the resultant space was found to be partitionable into regions that corresponded with the rationale.

Canter and Heritage's (1990, p. 203) analysis presented a radex model of sexual offending (as discussed earlier in the marbles analogy). In other words, there was a set of core behaviours common to rapes and a further set of differentiating behaviours associated with particular types of rapist. This was at odds with previous typologies which had more discreet categories of rapist. O'Neill and Hammond (2010) suggest that Canter and Heritage's emphasis on the need to ground theories of criminal behaviour in quantifiable as well as verifiable ways continues to influence current thinking about general theories of criminal conduct. In the decade that followed Canter and associates applied these techniques to a variety of crime types such as arson (Canter and Fritzon, 1998) and paedophilia (Canter *et al.*, 1998). The radex structure reappeared in empirical analyses of these crime types. This led Canter (2000) to propose a hierarchy of criminal actions forming a radex structure. Thus at the centre are core aspects of criminality moving outwards to features that may be thought of as the modus operandi to more specific signature behaviours associated with particular individuals. Canter identifies a second aspect or facet called theme which distinguishes between different qualities of offences. He argues any class of crime can be described in terms of these core, modus operandi and signature behaviours. This structural model forms the basis of a theoretical positioning Canter calls offence differentiation.

In a further theoretical elaboration, Canter argues for the use of action systems developed by Shye (1985), an associate of Guttman. Canter (2010, p. 17) explains action systems as follows:

> The definition of an action system implies that any events in which it is engaged will have a source for its emergence and a location of the manifestation of that event. Furthermore the source may be within the system or external to it, as may be its manifestation. This gives rise to four possible forms of event: a) Those that emerge inside the system and are actualised outside – known as the *expressive mode*, which often reflect individualistic 'personality' aspects of the system, b) emerging outside and manifested outside – *adaptive mode*, which typically focus on shaping physical aspects of the environment, c) emerging within and actualised within the system – *integrative mode*, relating to intrapersonal processes, and d) emerging

outside and manifested inside the system – *conservative mode*, having cultural significance.

Canter and Fritzon (1998) demonstrated the uniting of the facet approach with the action system framework to differentiate arsonists. They proposed two facets supported by the rationale provide by the action system: sources of the motivation to set a fire, expressive and instrumental; and target, i.e. a person or an object. This gives rise to a combination of four types of arsonist: expressive person, expressive object, instrumental person and instrumental object. They were able to confirm this by their partitioning of an SSA of arson behaviours.

What Canter and Fritzon were then able to do was to argue that individuals who set fires according to this classification will share characteristics with those operating in the same mode and be distinctive from those operating in a different mode. They created scales according to the types demonstrated in the SSA and found distinctive patterns in terms of four aspects of arsonists: psychiatric history, being a young offender, having had a failed relationship and being a serial arsonist. Canter and Fritzon conclude that their findings had implications for the investigation of arson in that findings such as the object-oriented fire setter was more likely to be a repeat offender living close to the arson sites would suggest mounting surveillance in areas recently subjected to fire setting.

Further developments

In their review, O'Neill and Hammond (2010) demonstrate that the early use of MDS procedures *vis-à-vis* offender profiling later extended to other applications. These include:

- investigation of criminal networks (Porter and Alison, 2001);
- assessment and diagnostic measurement (Widiger *et al.*, 1987);
- examination of psychometric test structures (Bishopp and Hare, 2008).

Brown (2010b) notes further extensions of use, namely:

- intrafamilial homicides (Fritzon and Garbutt, 2001);
- conceptualisation of different types of sex offender (McGuickin and Brown 2001);
- identification of leadership styles amongst robbery gangs (Porter and Alison, 2006a);
- behavioural change in prisoners undergoing a therapeutic community intervention (Neville *et al.*, 2007).

Further applications of the approach were directed at exploring other topics of forensic psychological interest. Taylor (2002) utilised POSA to analyse the chronology of hostage negotiation from audio transcripts of real incidents. Salfati and Bateman (2005) examined behavioural consistency in homicide behaviours, adopting SSA as their main analytic tool to analyse data deriving from a US police database of murders. Porter and Warrender (2009) presented an MSA of data generated from archived court transcripts in order to empirically verify a facet model of police deviance. What is especially striking is the versatility of the procedures in dealing with a variety of research questions, areas of forensic interest and types of data. Thus Porter and Warrender (2009) pose their research aims as a series of exploratory questions in order to develop a multivariate model of police corruption. Salfati and Bateman (2005) asked the research question of whether serial homicide could be conceptualised in terms of expressive and instrumental aggression which in turn exhibits a degree of consistency within a series of offences. Taylor (2002) hypothesed that unsuccessful crisis negotiations will be characterised by an upward trend along a competitive scale and its converse that successful negotiations will be characterised by a downward trend of movement along a competitive scale.

Other examples include the work of Laurence Alison and Louise Porter (Porter and Alison, 2006b) looking at criminal leadership styles. They constructed a coding dictionary of variables drawn from law reports of commercial and personal robberies. Their mapping sentence contained content facets to reflect whether the gang member originated the idea for the robbery, selected the target, approached the victim, was involved in the criminal act itself and made critical decisions about the crime. They constructed a POSA to scale the presence of these features in determining the leadership attributes of individuals involved in robberies.

McGuickin and Brown (2001) undertook a card-sorting procedure to elicit categories that members of the public, police officers and journalists differentiated different types of sex offenders. Masochists, sodomites and sadists were viewed as engaging in seriously harmful activities, but which were not necessarily illegal and were often consensual. Fetishists, exhibitionists and voyeurs were thought to engage in less serious illegal activity whilst rapists, paedophiles and child molesters were viewed as carrying out serious criminal acts involving non-consenting victims. The focus of journalists' differentiations were offenders who were brought to attention by the media reporting in the public interest; the public differentiated offenders by risk to community safety; and police officers differentiated offenders in terms of interventions such as psychiatric treatment, community notification and long-term monitoring. The data in this study comprised a matrix of individuals' sorting criteria such that each respondent had a profile of how they distinguished the different types of sex offender. This was subjected to analysis by MSA. Once the individuals had been plotted in the MSA space, their role as journalist, police officer or member of the public was assigned. In other words the MSA distributed individuals in terms of how they sorted the cards representing the sex offenders and their role was an input variable but mapped on after the analysis was completed. That partitions were identified in which individuals belonging to the three groups were located in distinct regions of the MSA plot supported the hypothesis that role differentiated conceptualisation of sex offending.

The Neville, Miller and Fritzon (2007) research created behavioural categories from the reports on therapeutic community residents by therapy managers. These derived from the managers' observations of the residents on a daily basis. They invoked Shye's action system model, asking the following research questions:

(a) whether the four modes of action system functioning can be identified by analysing behaviours that occur in therapy sessions;
(b) whether an action system model of therapeutic behaviour is evident over the course of time;
(c) whether over the course of therapy there is a behavioural or modal shift (i.e. do residents either start to function in a different modality, or do they stay within one mode and begin to exhibit more positive examples of behaviour).

The analysis identified themes relating to the hypothesised action system structure within coded observed behaviours. Each participant was thus given a frequency score for each behaviour for the entirety of their time in therapy. These frequency scores were then inputted into a data matrix and subjected to Smallest Space Analysis (SSA). The authors reported that the analysis supported thematic groupings of behaviours that could be conceptually understood as representing the four modes of action systems functioning: expressive, conservative, integrative and adaptive. They suggested that expressive behaviours were communicative in nature, as well as somewhat attention seeking. Adaptive behaviours were aimed at removing perceived threats to the individual originating from the environment. The conservative mode contained behaviours redressing emotions triggered by external events. Finally, integrative behaviours tended to arise as a result of internal desires or conflicts, primarily associated with self-esteem. The study went on to look at behavioural change by classifying the individual's predominate mode of operating at six discrete points in time. The action systems model was found to hold, in that behaviours within each of the four modes co-occurred across time. Finally, t-tests were run on the behavioural frequency scores at time one and time six for the 30 participants who completed the full 18 months of therapy. They showed a shift from dysfunctional to functional behaviour within each mode, as was hypothesised.

Strengths

The facet approach is incredibly versatile. Guttman and Greenbaum (1998) enumerate a long list of applications including the criminal justice arena. This means there is now a corpus of research to draw upon to see how the method has been utilised, find examples of the different MDS procedures, build a growing body of theoretical formulations and substantiate research findings.

Facet design and the tenets of the approach 'force' researchers to engage in conceptual thinking and define their hypothetical constructs before collecting their data (Guttman and Greenbaum, 1998, p. 14). Much forensic research deals with complex issues, often 'messy' data. Some sources of data are held by criminal justice agencies and collection is time limited and may well only be possible under strictly controlled circumstances. Other data may deal with difficult and emotionally laden content. Engaging in detailed preparatory work that clarifies concepts before accessing primary or secondary sources is both ethically and methodologically sound practice. Horvath and Brown (2005) argued that drug-assisted rape was poorly defined and required both conceptual and definitional clarity. Given the trauma associated with this offence and difficulties in collecting data, it was important to be clear about the phenomena before either approaching victims or negotiating access to police sources.

The mapping sentence device is a disciplined and valuable way for clarifying the content of the research observations, and acts as a template for designing questionnaire items or creating a coding dictionary and also analysing the multivariate output. Hypotheses are stated in the mapping sentence and then may be employed to partition the empirical space to see if the facets correspond to regional partitions. Levy (2005, p. 180) argues that the definitional framework provided by the mapping sentence 'ensures clarity and reliability [and] continuities in research'. The specification of facets in mapping sentences allows researchers to learn what facets are common, and how to refine content and build support for a facet through confirmatory replication. This aids the cumulative project of research activity. Santilla and colleagues (Santilla *et al.*, 2003) were able to replicate the findings of Canter and Fritzon (1998) to confirm the action systems model of fire setting. Interestingly, Sturidsson *et al.* (2006) failed to replicate the original model. Thus both success and failure add to our store of knowledge and permit systematic inquiry.

O'Neill and Hammond (2010) suggest that the multi-dimensional scaling techniques of the facet approach have enabled offender profiling to move beyond clinical theorising to clarify understanding and offer the radex model of a diverse range of criminal behaviours. Indeed, Canter invites tests of his proposed model (Canter, 2000).

The Facet Theory approach is flexible. It has tackled a diverse range of content (see reviews by Brown, 2010b, and O'Neill and Hammond, 2010). Moreover it offers means to manage a wide variety of primary and secondary data sources, e.g.:

- conceptual data generated by means of a multiple card-sorting procedure (McGuickin and Brown, 2001);
- police witness statements (Parker and Brown, 2000);
- legal reports (Porter and Alison, 2005);
- newspaper archives (Wilson, 2010);
- semi-structured interviews (Brown and Blount, 1999);
- observations (Neville, Miller and Fritzon, 2007);
- psychometric scores (Brown and Andersen, 2000);
- audio tapes (Taylor, 2002).

Brown and Barnett (2000) argue that, whilst ideally the facet approach should incorporate design, theory and MDS analysis, particular tools may be used without reference to the total package. An analogy would be the use of the repertory grid method without reference to Kelly's personal construct theory. So Brown and Barnett (2000, p. 118) suggest 'no doubt purists would be bothered by the à la carte advice offered here in the uses and application of facet theory, but we suggest that various aspects of the approach can be profitably employed in a flexible manner'.

The mapping sentence may be used to aid conventional statistical analyses as in Murphy and Brown (2000). They were examining gender role identity, gender value orientation and biological gender in terms of attitudes towards male and female offenders. This rather convoluted set of potential influencing factors on attitudes towards offending was clarified by its specification in a mapping sentence. This then aided statistical analysis by means of Analysis of Variance to determine the significance of gender variations of attitudes.

Use of the MDS techniques can be extremely helpful in exploratory research prior to a specification formally in a mapping sentence. Smallest Space Analysis in particular has been used heuristically to derive broad themes of co-occurring behaviours. For example Horvath and Brown (2007) presented an exploratory SSA to reveal differences between rape victims who had voluntarily become intoxicated and those who were the subject of induced intoxication.

Disadvantages

Borg and Lingoes (1987) state there is no simple answer to how good or bad a representation is, it rather depends upon a complex combination of the number of variables and the amount of error in the data and the logical strength of the interpretation framework. Whilst there are goodness of fit measures (e.g. coefficient of alienation, coefficient of contiguity) there are different opinions as to what constitutes a good fit. Guttman (1954) recommends a coefficient of alienation of 0.15; Donald (1995) suggests 0.2.

There are problems associated with lines of partition demarcating regions in the multi-dimensional space. Should the lines be straight, and if not straight how 'wiggly' can or should they be? Hammond and Brown (2005) discuss the criticism that partitioning can be somewhat subjective. First, they suggest where possible straight lines should be drawn to capture items which are meaningfully related, whether this is a heuristic partitioning or one accomplished by means of a facet design. Shalit (1977) devised sensitivity and selectivity indices to measure the efficiency of the zoning in an MSA space. Selectivity is the exclusivity of the target items appearing in a partitioned zone as a function of all the items appearing in that zone. Sensitivity is the efficiency of the partitioning in enclosing the members of the target variable within a zone as a function of the total number of the target variable. In Hammond and Brown's (2005) analysis of a burglary series, they were able to calculate percentage hits for selectivity and sensitivity of partition for a series of variables describing burglaries. Thus the MSA partitioning was most effective in identifying a region in which ground entry was effected and least effective in partitioning burglaries committed during daylight or where jewellery was stolen. These measure are very infrequently used in the reported literature.

There clearly are general issues, not specific to facet designs, about using secondary sources which are not necessarily collected with academic rigor. Thus Farrington and Lambert (1997) discuss problems associated with use of police witness statements. They point out that data are often missing or incomplete or inaccurate. Lovett and Horvath (2009) draw attention to another problem; namely, that using police data for analysis of crime either only captures suspects and not unknown offenders or deals only with reported crime so there remains the unknowable aspects of unreported crime.

One of the assumptions underlying much of the mapping of offence behaviours is the homology principle (Mokros and Alison, 2002). This assumption suggests that the degree of similarity in offence behaviour of a given crime will match degree of similarity in offender characteristics. In other words, there is a correspondence between offence and offender such that the more similar offenders are the greater the resemblance of their crimes. Mokros and Alison tested the homology assumption with respect to rapists, i.e. rapists displaying similar styles of offending are also more similar in their background characteristics. They generated a coding dictionary of 28 dichotomous variables from 139 victim statements and extracted demographic offender details from police files including prior offence histories. Their subsequent SSA was unable to demonstrate any consistent links between age, socio-demographic or offence history variables with offence behaviours. They conclude that pragmatic or heuristic approaches to interpreting SSAs are likely to fail and that interpretative work should be associated with theoretical formulations (such as a facet design).

A further threat to the radex theorising by Canter has been the made by Taylor *et al.* (2011). They argue that the modular facet postulated by Canter to be a feature of criminal behaviour is in fact an artefact of the Jaccard co-efficient. This is calculated as a function of co-occurrence of behaviours and ignores matches based on co-occurring absence of behaviours. Canter's thesis is that common or core behaviours appear at the centre of an SSA and increasingly differentiating less frequent behaviour radiates out to the periphery. Taylor and colleagues suggest that the Jaccard co-efficient is inflated by the frequency of occurrence of a variable and will artefactually correlate more highly with other behaviours, resulting in the tendency to fall at the centre of the plot. Thus rather than being of theoretical significance, the core behaviours are a confound of their greater likelihood of correlating with all other variables. Again if SSAs are interpreted heuristically, i.e. without the benefit of a conceptual mapping, this artefactual hypothesis potentially confounds the demonstration of the radex model. This discussion is ongoing and is demonstrative of the productive debate called for by Canter (2000) in developing robust evidence, but as yet has not been resolved.

The statistical programmes are not universally available and not easily usable for the novice. O'Neill and Hammond (2010) suggest that limitations of in-house software hinder the propagation of use of the Guttman-Lingoes programmes. Donald (1995) suggests constructing a mapping sentence is a considerable challenge and difficult to do for the untutored. Often the packages do not have good mapping graphics and additional graphics software is required to present the results of analyses.

Conclusion

Accessible overviews of Facet Theory, design principles and MDS packages are available in Brown (1985, 2010a) and Brown and Barnett (2000). A more technical account is to be found in Levy (2005) and Guttman and Greenbaum (1998). Donald (1995) gives a helpful explanation of constructing questionnaire items from a mapping sentence, whilst Brown and Sime (1982) and Wilson (2000) show how qualitative data may be analysed by means of an MSA.

The following papers use particular MDS analyses associated with the facet approach:

- SSA: Fritzon (2001) on motivation and distances travelled in fire setting; Canter, Bennell, Allison and Reddy (2003) on classifying stranger rape behaviours; Salfati and Bateman (2005) on behavioural consistency in serial murder; Canter and Wentink (2004) on types of murder; and Brown, Hamilton and O'Neill (2007) on attrition in rape cases.
- MSA: Parker and Brown (2000) on detecting deception in rape statements; Wilson (2000) on terrorist hostage taking; Porter and Alison (2006b) on leadership roles in criminal groups; Porter and Warrender (2009) on police misconduct and deviance; and Wilson, Scholes and Brocklehurst (2010) on assassinations and bombings.
- POSA: Levy (1998) on typology of drug users; Porter and Alison (2001) on gang rape behaviour; Canter (2004) on criminal networks; Last and Fritzon (2005) on differentiating stranger, acquaintance and interfamilial murder; Porter and Alison (2006) on decision making by violent gang leaders; and Dancer (1990) on suicide behaviours.

Further resources

David Canter and Donna Youngs (Canter and Youngs, 2009) have recently published *Investigative psychology; offender profiling and the analysis of criminal action* published by John Wiley & Sons. This provides a detailed account of the application of Facet Theory to the empirical investigation of crime and gives many examples of multivariate analyses using SSA, MSA and POSA. The chapters by Ian Donald and by Margaret Wilson and Sean Hammond in the Breakwell, Hammond and Fife-Schaw (2000) *Research methods in psychology* book are accessible accounts of constructing mapping sentences, questionnaires and interpreting multi-dimensional space. Brown and Campbell's (2010) *Cambridge handbook of forensic psychology* has short informative essays covering Facet Theory and facet design, investigative psychology and the use of multivariate statistics arising from facet analysis.

Free downloads of the software are also available (at time of writing) at www. pbarrett.net/cfa-facet.htm.

References

Ajzen, I. (1991). Theory of planned behaviour. *Organisational Behaviour and Human Decision Making Processes*, 50: 179–211.

Bar-On, R., Brown, J. M., Kirkcaldy, B. D., and Thome, E. P. (2000) Emotional expressiveness and adaptation to occupational culture. *Personality and Individual Differences*, 28: 1107–18.

Bishopp, D. and Hare, R. D. (2008). A multidensional scaling analysis of the Hare PCL-R; unfolding the structure of psychopathy. *Psychology Crime and Law*, 14: 117–32.

Bloombaum, M. (1968). The conditions underlying race riots as portrayed by MSA; a re-analysis of Lieberson and Silverman's data. *American Sociological Review*, 33: 77–91.

Borg, I. and Lingoes, J. (1987). *Multidimensional similarity structure analysis*. New York: Springer.

Breakwell, G. Hammond, S. and Fife-Schaw, C. (Eds) (2000). *Research methods in psychology*. 2nd edn. London: Sage.

Brown, J. M. (1985). An introduction to the uses of Facet Theory. In D. V. Canter (Ed). *Facet Theory; approaches to research*. New York: Springer-Verlag, pp. 17–57.

—— (2010a). Facet Meta Theory. In J. M. Brown and E. A. Campbell (Eds). *Cambridge handbook of forensic psychology* (pp. 58–64). Cambridge: Cambridge University Press.

—— (2010b). Designing research using Facet Theory. In J. M. Brown and E. A. Campbell (Eds). *Cambridge handbook of forensic psychology* (pp. 794–802). Cambridge: Cambridge University Press.

Brown, J. M. and Andersen, K. (2000). Police experience of vicarious stress. *Forensic Update*, 6: 6–11.

Brown, J. M. and Barnett, J. (2000). Facet Theory; an approach to research. In G. Breakwell, S. Hammond and C. Fife-Schaw (Eds). *Research methods in psychology* (pp. 105–18). 2nd edn. London: Sage.

Brown, J. M. and Blount, C. (1999). Occupational stress in sex offender treatment managers. *Journal of Managerial Psychology*, 14: 108–20.

Brown, J. M. and Campbell, E. A. (Eds). (2010) *Cambridge handbook of forensic psychology*. Cambridge: Cambridge University Press

Brown, J. M., and Sime, J. (1982). Multidimensional scaling of qualitative data. In E. Shephard and J. P. Watson (Eds). *Personal meanings* (pp. 71–90). New York: Wiley.

Brown, J. M., Hamilton, C. and O'Neill, D. (2007). Characteristics associated with rape attrition and the role played by skepticism or legal rationality by investigators and prosecutors. *Psychology, Crime and Law*, 13(4): 355–70.

Canter, D. V. (1988). To catch a rapist. *New Society*, 4 March: 14–15.

—— (1989). Offender profiles *The Psychologist*, January: 12–16.

—— (2000). Offender profiling and criminal differentiation. *Legal and Criminological Psychology*, 5: 23–46.

———. (2004). A partial order scalogram anlaysis of criminal network structures. *Behaviormetrika*, 31: 131–52.

——— (2010). Action system applied to forensic topics. In J. M. Brown and E. A. Campbell (Eds). *Cambridge handbook of forensic psychology* (pp. 17–22). Cambridge: Cambridge University Press.

Canter, D. and Fritzon, K. (1998). Differentiating arsonists; a model of firesetting actions and characteristics. *Journal of Legal and Criminological Psychology*, 3: 185–212.

Canter, D. and Heritage, R. (1990). A multivariate model of sexual offence behaviour: developments in 'offender profiling'. *Journal of Forensic Psychiatry*, 1: 185–212.

Canter, D. and Wentink, N. (2004). An empirical test of Holmes and Holmes' serial murder typology. *Criminal Justice and Behaviour*, 20, 1–26.

Canter, D. and Youngs, D. (2009). *Investigative psychology; offender profiling and the analysis of criminal action*. Chichester: Wiley.

Canter, D., Bennell, C., Alison, L. J. and Reddy, S. (2003). Differentiating sex offences: a behaviorally based thematic classification of stranger rapes. *Behavioral Sciences and The Law*, 21: 157–74.

Canter, D., Hughes, D. and Kirby, S. (1998). Paedophilia; pathology, criminality or both? The development of a multivariate model of offence behaviour in child sexual abuse. *The Journal of Forensic Psychiatry*, 9: 532–55.

Dancer, L. S. (1990). Suicide prediction and partial order scalogram analysis of psychological adjustment. *Applied Psychology* 39, 479–97.

Donald, I. (1995). *Facet theory; defining research domains*. In Breakwell, G., Hammond, S. and Fife-Schaw, C. (Eds). *Research methods in psychology*. London: Sage.

Donald, I. (2000). *Facet Theory; defining research domains*. In G. Breakwell, S. Hammond and C. Fife-Schaw (Eds). *Research methods in psychology*. 2nd edn. London: Sage.

Euwema, M. C., Kop, N. and Bakker, A. B. (2004). The behaviour of police officers in conflict situations: how burnout and reduced dominance contributes to better outcome. *Work and Stress*, 18: 23–38.

Farrington, D. and Lambert, S (1997). Predicting offender profiles from victim and witness description. In J. Jackson and D. Bekerian (Eds). *Offender profiling; theory, research and practice*. Chichester: Wiley.

Fritzon, K. (2001). An examination of the relationship between distance travelled and motivational aspects of firesetting behaviour. *Journal of Environmental Psychology*, 21: 45–60.

Fritzon, K. and Garbutt, R. (2001). A fatal interaction: The role of the victim and function of aggression in intrafamilial homicide. *Psychology, Crime and Law*, 7, 309–331.

Guttman, L. (1954). An outline of some new methodology for social science. *Public Opinion Quarterly*, 18: 394–404.

Guttman, R. and Greenbaum, C. (1998). Facet Theory; its development and current status. *European Psychologist*, 3: 13–36.

Hammond, S. and Brown, J. M. (2005). Comparing three multivariate statistical procedures when profiling prolific residential burglaries. *Forensic Update*, 80: 9–16.

Heidensohn, F. (1992). *Women in control*. Oxford: Clarendon.

Horvath, M. A. H. and Brown, J. (2005). Drug-assisted rape and sexual assault; definitional, conceptual and methodological developments. *Journal of Offender Profiling*, 2: 203–10.

—— (2007). Alcohol as drug of choice; is drug assisted rape a misnomer? *Psychology Crime & Law*, 13: 417–29.

Last, S. K. and Fritzon, K. (2005). Investigating the nature of expressiveness in stranger, acquaintance and intrafamilial homicides. *Journal of Investigative Psychology and Offender Profiling*, 2(3): 179–93.

Levy, S. (1998). *Encyclopedia of social measurement*, Vol. 2, 175–88.

Levy, S. (2005). Guttman, Louis. *Encyclopedia of social measurement*, Vol. 2, 175–88.

Lovett, J. and Horvath, M. A. H. (2009). Alcohol and drugs in rape and sexual assault. In M. A. H. Horvath and J. M. Brown (Eds). *Rape; challenging contemporary thinking* (pp. 125–60). Cullompton: Willan.

McGuickin, G. and Brown, J. (2001). Managing risk from sex offenders living in communities; comparing police, press and public perception. *Risk Management: An International Journal*, 3: 47–60.

Mokros, A. and Alison, L. J. (2002). Is offender profiling possible? Testing the predicted homology of crime scene actions and background characteristics in a sample of rapist. *Legal and Criminological Psychology*, 7: 25–43.

Murphy, E., and Brown, J. (2000). Exploring gender role identity, value orientation of occupation and sex of respondent in influencing attitudes towards male and female offenders. *Legal and Criminological Psychology*, 5: 285–90.

Neville, L., Miller, S. and Fritzon, K. (2007). Understanding change in a therapeutic community: an action systems approach. *The Journal of Forensic Psychiatry & Psychology*, 18: 181–203.

Norman, P., Bennett, P. and Lewis, H. (1998). Understanding binge drinking from adolescent people; an application of the theory of planned behaviour. *Health Education Research*, 13: 163–9.

O'Neill, D. and Hammond, S. (2010). Drawing out the meaning in data; mulitidimensional scaling within forensic psychology research. In J. M. Brown and E. A. Campbell (Eds). *Cambridge handbook of forensic psychology* (pp. 803–12). Cambridge: Cambridge University Press.

Parker, A. and Brown, J. M. (2000). Detecting deception; statement validity analysis as a means of determining truthfulness or falsity of rape allegations. *Legal and Criminological Psychology*, 5: 237–59.

Porter, L. and Alison, L. (2001). A partially ordered scale of influence in violent group behaviour; an example from gang rape. *Small Group Research*, 32: 475–97.

Porter, L. and Alison, L. (2005). The primacy of decision-action as an influence strategy of violent gang leaders. *Small Group Research*, 36: 188–207.

—— (2006a). Behavioural coherence in group robbery; a circumplex model of offender and victim interactions. *Aggressive Behaviour*, 32: 330–2.

—— (2006b). Leadership and hierarchies in criminal groups; scaling degrees of leader behaviour in group robbery. *Legal and Criminological Psychology*, 11: 245–65.

Porter, L. and Warrender, C. (2009). A multivariate model of police deviance: examining the nature of corruption, crime and misconduct. *Policing and Society: An International Journal of Research and Policy*, 19: 79–99.

Rafky, D. (1975). Police cynicism reconsidered; an application of SSA. *Criminology*, 13: 168–92.

Salfati, C. G. and Taylor, P. (2006). Differentiating sexual violence; a comparison of sexual homicide and rape. *Psychology, Crime and Law*, 12: 107–25.

Salfati, C. G. and Bateman, A. L. (2005). Serial homicide; an investigation of behavioral consistency. *Journal of Investigative Psychology and Offender Profiling*, 2: 245–65.

Santilla, P., Häkkänen, H., Alison, L. and Whyte, C. (2003). Juvenile fire setters; crime scene actions and offender characteristics. *Legal and Criminological Psychology*, 8: 1–20.

Shalit, B. (1977). Structural ambiguity and limits to coping. *Journal of Human Stress*, 3: 32–45.

Shye, S. (1978) (Ed). *Theory construction and data analysis in behavioural research.* Thousand Oaks, CA: Sage.

——— (1985). Nonmetric multivariate models for behavioral action systems. In Facet Theory Approaches to Social Research. New York: Springer Verlag, 97–148.

Sturidsson, K., Langström, N., Grann, M., Sjöstedt, G., Asgård, U. and Aghede, E. (2006). Using multidimensional scaling for analysis of sexual offence behaviour; a replication and some cautionary notes. *Psychology, Crime and Law*, 12: 221–30.

Taylor, P. (2002). A Partial Order Scalogram Analysis of communication behaviour in crisis negotiation with the prediction of outcome. *The International Journal of Conflict Management*, 13: 4–37.

Taylor, P. J., Donald, I. J., Jacques, K. and Conchie, S. M. (2011). Jaccard's heel; radex models of criminal behaviour are rarely falsifiable when derived using Jaccard coefficient. *Legal and Criminological Psychology*. doi: 10.1348/135532510X518371.

Toch, H. (2002). *Stress in policing.* Washington: American Psychological Association.

Widiger, T. A., Trull, T. J., Hurt, S. W., Clarkin, J. and Frances, A. (1987). A multidimensional scaling of the DSM-III personality disorders. *Archives of General Psychiatry*, 44: 557–63.

Wilson, M. (2010). Terrorism research; current issues and debates. In Brown, J. M. and Campbell, E. A. *Cambridge handbook of forensic psychology.* Cambridge: CUP, pp. 571–78.

Wilson, M. A. (2000). Towards a model of terrorist behaviour in hostage taking situations. *Journal of Conflict Resolution*, 44: 403–24.

Wilson, M., Scholes, A. and Brocklehurst, A. (2010). A behavioural analysis of terrorist action;the assassination and bombing campaigns of eta between 1980 and 2007. *The British Journal of Criminology*, 50: 690–707.

Zvulun, E. (1978). Multidimensional Scalogram Analysis; the method and its application. In S. Shye (Ed). *Theory construction and data analysis in behavioural research* (pp. 237–64). Thousand Oaks, CA: Sage.

5 Court-relevant research methods

Matthew A. Palmer, Ruth Horry
and Neil Brewer

Background

Consider some of the key events that typically occur during a criminal court case. The jury will hear evidence relating to the events surrounding the crime in question. This evidence will usually be based, at least in part, on the recollections of one or more witnesses interviewed by police during their investigations. In many cases, the jury will also be presented with the results of eyewitness identification tests conducted by police. When considering evidence, jurors must evaluate the evidence – and the reliability of those presenting it – and come to a conclusion about the likely guilt of the defendant.

Given the important role that the courtroom plays in our legal system, it is not surprising that the various elements of court cases have prompted a considerable amount of psychological research. Court-relevant research first came to prominence with the publication of Münsterberg's *On the witness stand* (1908). Some important research was conducted over the following half century, before the work of Strodtbeck and colleagues (e.g. Strodtbeck *et al.*, 1957) precipitated a surge in research on juror decisions. Loftus' (e.g. Loftus, 1979) work on eyewitness memory represented another landmark in court-relevant research, and attention to eyewitness research within the legal system was increased further in the 1990s, when advances in DNA testing procedures – resulting in the exonerations of numerous innocent suspects – highlighted mistaken eyewitness identification as by far the leading cause of wrongful convictions (Innocence Project, 2010). At present, one of the most important challenges for researchers conducting court-relevant work is to improve communication with legal professionals so that research findings can translate to appropriate policies (Wells, 2005; Wells *et al.*, 2000).

In this chapter, we discuss the methodologies used to conduct research in three prominent areas of relevance to the court: eyewitness identification tests, interviewing of witnesses and juror decision making. It is worth noting from the outset that some aspects of research design are the same across the areas. For example experimental designs are the norm in each. Other aspects differ between areas. For example the type of stimuli typically used in eyewitness identification studies differs from that used in juror studies. Such similarities and differences will be highlighted throughout the chapter.

Eyewitness identification

Research aims

Mistaken eyewitness identification is the leading contributor to wrongful convictions (Scheck *et al.*, 2003). To date (16th August 2010), 258 falsely imprisoned men in the USA have been exonerated through DNA testing by the Innocence Project (www.innocenceproject.org). Mistaken eyewitness identification played a central role in 75 per cent of the first 239 cases. These eyewitnesses were not deliberately attempting to subvert the course of justice. They were using their memories of the culprit's face and appearance to make the best identification decision that they could. And while in many cases eyewitnesses *are* able to correctly identify the culprit, there is clearly a large margin for error.

Psychologists' aims in this area have been two-fold: protecting innocent suspects from mistaken identification, and increasing the chances that guilty suspects will be identified. The first aim has received the most attention, due to the dire consequences of mistaken identification. However, psychologists must ensure that any recommendations that they make to policy makers will not increase the likelihood of guilty suspects going free.

Before beginning an identification experiment, the researcher must have a clear research question in mind. For example does the presence of a weapon during a crime affect witnesses' abilities to accurately identify the perpetrator? Most identification experiments follow the same basic procedure. First, the participants are shown a staged crime, which could be live or videotaped. Some period of delay passes, after which the participants are given an identification test. The researcher must choose an appropriate population to sample (young adults, children, older adults, people with learning disabilities), and must develop appropriate stimulus materials. For example two similar videotaped crimes might be produced – one featuring a gun, and another with no visible weapon. The following section summarises some of the main methodological choices that must be made by any researcher who wishes to run an eyewitness identification experiment. This is followed by a brief discussion of the strengths and limitations of this kind of research, and a consideration of future directions in the field.

Methodology

The mock crime. Most eyewitness identification studies begin with a mock crime. This could be a live event (Valentine *et al.*, 2007) or a videotaped event (Semmler *et al.*, 2004). Videotaped events allow greater experimental control, while sacrificing some external validity. Mock crimes may not always be practical: field studies may use mundane encounters between the participants and a confederate (Carlucci *et al.*, in press; Wright *et al.*, 2001). The content of the mock crime or encounter will be guided by the research questions, constraints on resources and ethical considerations. For example showing a violent mock crime to a sample of children would be inappropriate.

Participants are shown this mock crime. They may view the crime individually on videotape. Alternatively, researchers interested in social influences on memory may show participants the crime in pairs or small groups. Some studies have even involved live events occurring in lecture theatres to groups of several hundred participants (e.g. Malpass and Devine, 1981a). Participants are generally not told that they will need to identify the perpetrator/confederate later. Rather, the mock crime is usually presented under some other guise (e.g. a study on memory for events).

Retention interval. Next follows some period of delay, which can range from minutes (Palmer *et al.*, 2010) to days (Lefebvre *et al.*, 2007), to weeks or even months (Malpass and Devine, 1981a). The delay period will largely be guided by practical considerations, and may require adjustment if the task is too difficult or too easy for the participants.

Selecting foils and measuring line-up fairness. To create a line-up, the researcher must select some appropriate distractor faces, or 'foils'. In a fair line-up, the foils should resemble the suspect. Foils can be selected in two ways: based on the physical resemblance to the culprit, or based on a witness's description of the culprit. Luus and Wells (1991) argued that investigators should match-to-description rather than matching-to-appearance. However, this is usually impractical for a researcher, as a new line-up would be required for each participant witness who potentially could provide a different description. With large sample sizes required in eyewitness identification studies (see for example Palmer *et al.*, 2010), this would be very costly and time-consuming. Most researchers, therefore, select foils to match the culprit's appearance. Others opt for a middle-ground approach, selecting foils based on descriptions from one or more independent participants.

Line-up fairness is as important in the lab as in the justice system. In the real world, unfair line-ups can lead to wrongful convictions; in the laboratory, unfair line-ups can create spurious results. Line-up fairness is evaluated using the mock witness paradigm. 'Mock witnesses' read a brief description of the suspect, and are asked to select the suspect from the line-up. In a fair line-up, the choices should be evenly distributed across all of the line-up members. In a very unfair line-up (e.g. an African-American suspect with White foils), all of the mock witnesses would choose the suspect. There are several statistical techniques for estimating line-up fairness, which make different assumptions (see Brigham *et al.*, 1999, for a review). A simple measure is *functional size*, calculated by dividing the total number of mock witnesses by the number of mock witnesses who chose the suspect (Wells *et al.*, 1979). For example if there are 100 mock witnesses, and 50 choose the suspect, then the functional size of the line-up is 2 (100/50). This means that there is one plausible foil in addition to the suspect. If the functional size is close to the actual line-up size, then the line-up may be fair (though there are other statistical considerations to be made; see Tredoux, 1998, for a detailed review of measures of line-up fairness).

Line-up presentation. Line-up presentation can vary in modality – for example photographic (Gorenstein and Ellsworth, 1980), video (Valentine *et al.*, 2007) or live presentation (Malpass and Devine, 1981b). Photographic line-ups are easy to create, and are used by many police forces around the world. They are therefore favoured by researchers. However, a few police forces now use video line-ups as standard, and so some researchers have followed suit.

Researchers must decide whether to use a *simultaneous* or *sequential* line-up (Lindsay and Wells, 1985). In a simultaneous line-up, all of the images are seen together. In a sequential line-up, each image is seen individually and the participant makes a yes/no decision for each image. In some versions of the sequential line-up the line-up ends as soon as a positive identification is made. Sequential line-ups tend to produce higher accuracy than simultaneous line-ups. Sequential line-ups encourage absolute judgements ('Does this person match my memory of the culprit?') whereas simultaneous line-ups encourage relative judgements ('Which person is the best match to my memory of the culprit?'). Some studies use simultaneous line-ups (e.g. Valentine and Mesout, 2009) and others use sequential line-ups (e.g. Sauer *et al.*, 2008b). This choice will often be guided by the research questions and by practical constraints.

Target present and target absent line-ups. Crucially, eyewitness identification studies should include both target *present* (TP) and target *absent* (TA) line-ups. TP line-ups contain the actual culprit from the crime event, while TA line-ups do not. In TA line-ups, the culprit can be replaced with a designated innocent suspect, chosen for high similarity to the culprit (e.g. Carlson *et al.*, 2008). Alternatively, the culprit can be removed without replacement. TA line-ups act as a vital control, allowing researchers to examine the behaviour of witnesses when the suspect is not the culprit. This is essential for making recommendations to policy makers and for drawing conclusions about eyewitness misidentification in the real world.

Instructions to witnesses. The instructions given to participants can dramatically influence choosing behaviour. *Unbiased* instructions, which state that the culprit *may or may not* be present, reduce inaccurate identifications of innocent suspects and foils (Brewer and Wells, 2006; Malpass and Devine, 1981b). Many police forces are required to give unbiased instructions to witnesses, so researchers often use unbiased instructions in the lab. However, there are situations in which researchers will not use unbiased instructions, such as when the research question requires high choosing rates, and high error rates (e.g. Brewer *et al.*, 2008). Caution should then be exercised when applying the results to real-world eyewitness behaviour.

Analysis

Participants' responses can be divided into several categories, shown in Table 5.1. A participant can make one of three responses. They can identify the suspect, they can identify a foil or they can choose to reject the line-up by not making an identification. In both TP and TA line-ups, foil IDs will always be inaccurate. Note, however, that in TP line-ups, the correct response is to identify the suspect, but in the TA line-up, the correct response is to reject the line-up

Table 5.1 Response categories for target present and target absent line-ups

Target present line-up	*Correct suspect ID*	Foil ID	Line-up rejection
Target absent line-up	Incorrect suspect ID	Foil ID	*Line-up rejection*

Note: correct responses are shown in italics.

(correct responses shown in *italics*). Also note that incorrect suspect IDs can only be observed when an innocent suspect was designated. Without an innocent suspect, this data cell will be empty.

The frequencies of the participants' responses are recorded. As these data are categorical, they should be analysed with χ^2 tests or log linear analysis, depending on the research design and questions (see Field, 2009, for an excellent introductory book on statistics for psychology). The observed frequencies are compared against some expected frequencies – for example chance performance. The analyses will tell the researcher whether the observed results significantly differ from the expected results.

Worked example

The following example is taken from Malpass and Devine (1981b). Note that some methodological details have been omitted here for brevity; a comprehensive description can be found in the original article. Malpass and Devine were interested in whether the instructions given to eyewitnesses would influence the accuracy of identification decisions. Specifically, they asked whether the rate of false identifications from line-ups could be reduced simply by reminding witnesses that the person they were looking for might not be in the line-up. To address this question, they used a two (line-up instructions: biased or unbiased) by two (line-up type: target-present or target-absent) between-subjects experimental design. The four conditions are shown in Table 5.2.

Malpass and Devine (1981b) had 100 participants view a staged mock-crime. The crime took place in a classroom setting and involved a male culprit (actually a confederate of the experimenters) interrupting a class presentation, arguing with the presenter and pushing over some EEG equipment before fleeing the scene. The participants were then informed that the crime had been staged and, later, were asked to attempt to identify the culprit from a line-up.

Table 5.2 The four experimental conditions created by a two-by-two between-subjects design

Unbiased instructions	Unbiased instructions
Target-present	Target-absent
Biased instructions	Biased instructions
Target-present	Target-absent

Participants viewed either a target-present or target-absent line-up. For the target-present line-up, the culprit appeared alongside four other males of similar height, build, hair colour and style. For the target-absent line-up, the culprit was replaced by another appropriate foil. None of the line-up members wore clothing similar to that worn by the culprit during the staged crime. The position of line-up members was rotated so that each person appeared in each position equally often. Live presentation was used, with the line-up members located approximately 7 metres from witnesses, who viewed the line-up through a two-way mirror.

Participants were randomly allocated to receive either biased or unbiased line-up instructions. In both conditions, instructions were standardised by having the line-up administrator read them aloud and participants indicated their identification decision on a response sheet. The biased instructions read:

> We believe that the person who pushed over the electronics equipment during the EEG demonstration is present in the line-up. Look carefully at each of the five individuals in the line-up. Which of these is the person you saw push over the equipment? Circle the number of his position in the line-up below.
>
> (Malpass and Devine, 1981b, p. 484)

The unbiased instructions read:

> The person who pushed over the electronics equipment during the EEG demonstration may be one of the five individuals in the line-up. Look carefully at each of the five individuals in the line-up. If the person you saw push over the equipment is not in the line-up, circle 0. If the person is present in the line-up, circle the number of his position.
>
> (Malpass and Devine, 1981b, p. 484)

Analyses were performed using a variation on the chi-square test (see Langer and Abelson, 1972). The results indicated that line-up instructions had a substantial effect on identification accuracy. When the culprit was not in the line-up, participants made more foil identifications if they received biased versus unbiased instructions. Importantly, however, when the culprit was in the line-up, the rate of correct identifications was not lower for unbiased instructions (83 per cent) than biased instructions (75 per cent). We now know that the use of unbiased instructions can reduce the occurrence of false identifications without markedly reducing the rate of correct identifications, thus improving overall accuracy.

Strengths and limitations

Laboratory studies allow us to control factors that cannot be controlled in the real world. To understand the effects of delay on eyewitness identification, we can hold all other factors constant, randomly allocating participants to different delay conditions. Individual studies will always be limited in their conclusions. However, psychologists have now created a rich empirical literature which has provoked real change in police practice (see Wells *et al.*, 2000).

Of course, there are many ways in which experiments differ from crimes witnessed by real witnesses. These differences have prompted concerns about low 'external validity'. That is, the worry that findings from the lab will not extend to real-world behaviour. For example lab studies rely on videotaped mock crimes, or on fairly mundane live events, perhaps involving theft of equipment from the lab (Carlson *et al.*, 2008, Experiment 1). It would be unethical to show participants deeply distressing violent events, or to make them feel personally endangered. However, some creative researchers have taken advantage of naturally occurring high-stress situations to examine eyewitness memory. For example Morgan and colleagues (2004) tested participants' memories for an interrogator from a high-stress interview which had formed part of a military training programme. Valentine and Mesout (2009) asked participants to identify a confederate who had approached them while walking through a section of the London Dungeon which was created to elevate stress and fear responses. Such research bridges the gap between the experience of participants in the lab and witnesses in the real world.

A common problem in eyewitness identification research is statistical power (see Cohen, 1992, for a discussion of statistical power). Eyewitness experiments often involve designs which require each participant to be allocated to a different group. Usually, each participant will only make one identification decision from a single line-up. As a result of this, required sample sizes can reach several hundred (see Palmer *et al.*, 2010; Sauer *et al.*, 2008a), making research time consuming and costly. Where possible, researchers can design experiments so that each witness sees more than one line-up to increase statistical power.

A crucial concept within experimental science is 'generalisability'. Researchers do not want to limit their conclusions to the specific set of conditions within a given experiment. Rather, they wish to extend their results to a more general set of circumstances. In the eyewitness domain, the generalisability of a study's results can be influenced by many factors, including the distinctiveness of the target. If the culprit is especially distinctive, or not at all distinctive, the results may not be replicable in other situations (Wells and Windschitl, 1999). These concerns are compounded when the same small set of stimulus materials are shared among different researchers. One often used remedy is to use two or more culprits, counterbalanced between participants, thereby permitting an examination of whether findings are robust across a wide variety of stimulus materials and conditions.

Future directions

Our understanding of memory has changed dramatically over the last few decades. Long gone are the days in which we believed that the brain was a video camera, able to perfectly record visual input which was neatly filed away for later viewing. We now know that memory is malleable and fragile, and that people make mistakes even when viewing conditions are optimal. Through communicating these ideas to policy makers, eyewitness identification procedures have improved (see Wells *et al.*, 2000).

However, there are limits to how much the basic line-up procedure can be improved. The UK uses some of the most advanced identification procedures in the world (see Kemp *et al.*, 2001). Yet archival analyses of real line-up outcomes in the UK show that suspect identifications remain low (41 per cent – 44 per cent; Memon, Havard, Clifford *et al.*, in press). Perhaps it is time to rethink the line-up entirely, and to come up with radically different alternatives which are grounded in theory (Wells *et al.*, 2006). For example, Sauer *et al.* (2008a) tested a procedure where, rather than being asked to make an absolute decision about whether the culprit is in the line-up, the participants rated how confident they were that each line-up member was the culprit. These confidence ratings were better able to predict the identity of the culprit than were standard binary identification decisions. This programme of research, still in its early stages, offers a promising new avenue of investigation for researchers interested in eyewitness memory.

The traditional line-up pre-dates any real scientific understanding of human memory (Davies and Griffiths, 2008). Psychologists have focused on improving this procedure because of its wide usage. However, we have a vast body of knowledge on human perception and memory which we can use to develop a new paradigm for eyewitness identification. It is possible that any such advance would be likely resisted by the courts. However, if the science is conducted rigidly, and the weight of evidence suggests a dramatic improvement in eyewitness accuracy, then an overhaul of identification procedures may be possible (see, for example, Brewer and Weber, 2008; Brewer and Wells, 2011; Sauer *et al.*, 2008a).

Interviewing witnesses

Research aims

An eyewitness's memory of an event is often crucial for investigators. But memory is fragile and vulnerable, prone to distortion and deterioration. Early research exposed the fallibility of eyewitnesses and their susceptibility to misinformation (e.g. Loftus and Palmer, 1974). Researchers then began developing interview techniques to maximise the amount of accurate information gained from witnesses without increasing inaccurate information. The most successful technique was the cognitive interview (CI), an interviewing framework grounded in psychological theory on memory encoding, storage and retrieval (Geiselman *et al.*, 1984). The original CI had four components:

1   *Context reinstatement.* The witness thinks about the physical environment and the personal context (thoughts and feelings) of the event. For example

a witness to a car accident would imagine themselves at the scene of the accident. They would be asked to recall physical aspects of the scene (where they were located in relation to other parts of the environment, weather conditions, sounds that they heard etc.) as well as the thoughts and emotions that they had prior to and immediately after the accident.

2   *Report everything.* The witness reports everything that they can remember, without interruption. For example the witness would tell the interviewer about the accident, in as much detail as possible. It is very important that the interviewer allows the witness to use their own words, and that this free recall is not interrupted.

3   *Change temporal order.* The witness recalls events in a different chronological order, hopefully cueing additional details. For example the interviewer could ask the witness to begin by describing what happened after the accident, then work their way back from that point.

4   *Change perspectives.* The witness recalls the event from different perspectives, potentially providing new memory cues. For example the witness could imagine what the accident would have looked like from the opposite side of the street, or from above.

The CI has been modified many times, often by omitting the 'change perspectives' component, and adding in rapport building (e.g. Dando *et al.*, 2009). This is when the interviewer establishes a rapport with the witness, putting them at ease and explaining the interview procedure to them. The original CI and its modifications are described in detail elsewhere (see Memon, Meissner and Fraser, 2010). This section will outline the major methodological considerations for eyewitness interviewing research. Strengths and limitations will be discussed, and future directions will be considered.

Methodology

Interview type. Researchers usually use the CI, often modified from its original format. The enhanced CI, for example, includes elements such as rapport building and transfer of control to the witness, where the interviewer makes it clear to the witness that they are in control of the interview, and that they have the knowledge that the interviewer is hoping to access (Fisher and Geiselman, 1992). If working with special populations (e.g. children, older adults, cognitively impaired), researchers may omit some components of the CI, such as the change temporal order and change perspectives components, as these are more cognitively demanding than the context reinstatement and report everything components, and may be difficult for such populations to understand (e.g. Wright and Holliday, 2007). Furthermore, the context reinstatement and report everything components together have been found to be more effective than any of the other components, even when interviewing children as young as five years old (Milne and Bull, 2002).

Control groups. To draw conclusions about an interview technique, there must be a control group. Control groups are essential for any experimental study, as

Table 5.3 Interview components featured in structured interviews and cognitive interviews

Structured interview	Cognitive interview
Rapport building	Rapport building
Transfer of control to the witness	Transfer of control to the witness
—	Context reinstatement
Free recall instructions	Report everything
—	Change temporal order
—	Change perspectives
Specific, non-leading questions related to content of free recall	Specific, non-leading questions related to content of free recall

they allow the comparison of one group who received the experimental treatment (the CI) with another group who did not receive the experimental treatment. If all other variables are kept equal, and if the participants are randomly allocated to the groups, then the researcher can infer that any differences between the groups are due to the treatment (the CI). The control group usually receives a structured interview (SI), which shares some common features with the CI – rapport building, free recall, follow-up questions related to the content of the free recall. However, a SI excludes many features of the CI, including context reinstatement, 'report everything' instructions and 'change in temporal order'/'change perspectives' (e.g. Wright and Holliday, 2007). The components featured in SIs and CIs are compared in Table 5.3.

Coding and scoring. Before accuracy can be assessed, a comprehensive list of all of the details in the crime event must be made. This must be done carefully, and the responses of several researchers can be pooled together (see Davis *et al.*, 2005). This list then serves as a template against which the interviews can be scored.

Each detail mentioned within an interview is scored (with each unique detail scored only once). Commonly used scoring categories include correct details, errors (recalling a red hat instead of a green hat), confabulations (details which were not present) and intrusions (details which came from some other source, such as a leading question; see Memon *et al.*, 1996). Details may also be coded by content, such as person, action, and object details (e.g. Akehurst *et al.*, 2003). Two or more naïve coders should code the interviews separately. Inter-rater reliability is then checked using statistical indicators of agreement, such as Cohen's kappa (see Field, 2009). Any coding discrepancies are resolved, usually through discussion between the coders. If any disagreements remain, these can be resolved by an independent third party.

Analysis

For each witness, the number of details in each response category is summed. These scores can be compared using a range of statistical methods, including *t* tests, ANOVAs and regressions (Field, 2009). The statistics will depend upon the experimental design, the number of experimental groups and the hypotheses.

Worked example

The following example is taken from Larsson, Granhag, and Spjut (2003). Again, some of the methodological and analytical details have been omitted here for brevity. Larsson *et al.* tested children aged 10–11 years old either one week or six months following a videotaped event. The children were randomly allocated to receive a CI or a SI. The experiment therefore had a two-by-two between-subjects design. The four experimental conditions are summarised in Table 5.4.

Forty-nine participants took part, recruited from a local school. All of the children watched a videotaped event, in which a fakir performed several amazing feats, including playing with fire and laying on a bed of nails. The children were instructed to pay close attention to the video, but were not told that they would receive an interview on the contents of the video.

Following other researchers, the change temporal order and change perspectives components were excluded from the CI, to make it more suitable for use with children. The context reinstatement and report everything components were included, and these components were the key differences between the CI and the SI. After a delay of one week, one quarter of the original sample were given a CI and one quarter were given a SI. The remaining children were interviewed with either a CI or a SI after six months. The interviews were conducted by three interviewers, all of whom received training in the CI, and all of whom had previous experience in interviewing children.

A checklist of all of the information in the film was prepared. The checklist contained 224 distinct units of information. Two raters then coded the children's interviews, recording each unique detail mentioned. These details were then compared to the checklist to provide the following measures: correct information, incorrect information and confabulations (details which were not in the video). Percentage accuracy and completeness of the reports were then calculated for each participant. One rater coded all of the interviews, and a subset were randomly selected to be coded by a second rater. Inter-rater agreement was high (93 per cent), and any discrepancies were resolved by discussion.

Larsson *et al.* (2003) compared recall performance in the four conditions with a series of between subjects ANOVAs (one for each measure). They found that

Table 5.4 The four experimental conditions

One week delay	Six month delay
Cognitive interview (CI)	Cognitive interview (CI)
One week delay	Six month delay
Structured interview (SI)	Structured interview (SI)

Source: Larsson *et al.* (2003)

children who received the CI recalled more correct information and gave more complete and accurate accounts than children who received the SI. Children interviewed after six months recalled less correct information and reported fewer confabulations than children interviewed after one week. Longer delays led to lower overall accuracy and less complete accounts. Interview type and delay did not interact on any measure – that is, the effect of delay was not influenced by the effects of interview type. The authors concluded that the (modified) CI is a useful tool for interviewing children, even after long delay periods.

Strengths and limitations

Interviewing research shares many limitations with identification research. Reliance on videotaped mock crimes or low arousal staged events still raises concerns of low external validity. Specifics of the mock crime which is used could also create results which do not generalise to other stimulus materials. In addition, researchers must ensure that the standard of the interviews is high, and that the interview style is consistent if multiple interviewers are used. Interviewers should therefore be trained in the CI. This can create some practical difficulties: training can be expensive and time consuming to run, and the research team must gain access to appropriate training materials. However, despite these difficulties, proper training in CI techniques is essential for any group wishing to research eyewitness memory using the CI, to ensure that their procedures conform to the recognised standard. The exact interview procedure used should be reported explicitly when publishing, as there are so many modified versions of the CI in the literature. So, for example, details of any components which are included (e.g. context reinstatement, report everything), and details of any components which are excluded (e.g. change temporal order, change perspectives) must be presented in publications.

Memon *et al.* (2010) discuss some of the gaps in our current knowledge of interviewing, such as how real frontline investigators use the CI. Most studies use student or academic interviewers, with only a small minority recruiting trained law enforcement professionals as interviewers (see Geiselman *et al.*, 1985). There are practical reasons for this: law enforcement agencies can be difficult to recruit into research programmes due to high demands on their time and already over-stretched budgets. However, to convince policy makers, more researchers should recruit police interviewers in eyewitness research.

Future directions

A promising new line of research is the grain-size interview (Weber and Brewer, 2008), which builds on a theoretical framework of memory reporting. Goldsmith, Koriat and Weinberg-Eliezer (2002) noted that information varies in 'grain size', from coarse ('He was wearing a dark jacket') to fine grained ('He was wearing a navy blue jacket with a white logo on the right sleeve'). When reporting details, the individual controls the grain size of the information, aiming for an optimum balance between informativeness and accuracy. Weber and Brewer asked participants to provide both a fine grained response and a coarse response to a series of questions about a mock crime. The participants rated their confidence in each answer, and chose which they would like to volunteer as their preferred answer. Fine grained answers were chosen 35 per cent of the time, and were volunteered when the benefits of informativeness were likely to be large, and the costs to accuracy were likely to be small. While still in its infancy, grain size interviewing offers interesting possibilities for maximising information gain from witnesses. For example preliminary research suggests that the technique has the capacity to elicit a large amount of accurate coarse grained information that witnesses would not otherwise report (Brewer *et al.*, 2010; Hope *et al.*, 2010).

Juror decision making

Research aims

In this section, we concentrate mainly on decisions made by individual jurors (cf. collective verdicts arrived at by juries after deliberation), which have been the focus of the majority of research in this area. The study of juror decisions is concerned with several prominent questions, such as: What are the factors that influence jurors' decisions? How do jurors process information during a trial? How well do jurors comprehend judicial instructions about points of law? And, are jurors competent decision makers? Approaches for addressing such questions fall broadly into two categories: field studies and mock-juror experiments. In the next section, we discuss some key methodological aspects of each.

Methodology

Field studies. Field studies deal with data from actual trials and, hence, are excellent in terms of realism. However, field studies give researchers little or no experimental control over variables of interest. For example a researcher cannot, practically or ethically, arrange for a particular piece of evidence to be given to one randomly-selected half of a jury but not the other half. This problem limits the extent to which causal conclusions can be drawn from field studies.

In addition, because jurors are typically not allowed to discuss their opinions during an active case with anyone – including researchers – field studies often involve collecting data via post-trial interviews or surveys of jurors. One drawback of this approach is that it relies heavily on jurors' memories. To solve this problem, some studies (e.g. McCabe and Purves, 1974) have employed a *shadow jury* paradigm, whereby a second jury is selected by the researcher (ideally from the same pool that the actual jury was drawn from) to sit in the gallery of the court and listen to the case. The researcher is then able to obtain data from shadow jurors during the course of the trial.

Mock-juror experiments. Mock-juror experiments deal with decisions made by participants (typically jury-eligible individuals) who are presented with evidence and asked to behave as if they are jurors in a real case. The mock-juror paradigm allows researchers to experimentally manipulate a wide range of variables, some examples of which are discussed later.

Presentation mode. The degree of realism involved in mock-juror experiments varies widely, from having live actors present evidence in a real courtroom setting (e.g. Borgida *et al.*, 1990) to having student participants reading relatively brief portions of written transcript from a fictitious trial (for reviews, see Bornstein, 1999; Bray and Kerr, 1979). Constraints on time and financial resources usually dictate the choice of presentation mode.

Defendant characteristics. Juror decisions have been shown to be affected by certain characteristics of the defendant, such as attractiveness (e.g. Baumeister and Darley, 1982) and race (e.g. Johnson *et al.*, 1995). Apart from investigating the direct effects of defendant characteristics on juror decisions, researchers may wish to consider whether the effects of other variables are moderated by defendant characteristics.

Evidentiary variables. Researchers have innumerable options when it comes to manipulating aspects of the evidence presented to mock-jurors. A few examples of evidentiary factors include the complexity of evidence (e.g. Heuer and Penrod, 1994); the number of inconsistencies in a witness's testimony (e.g. Berman and Cutler, 1996); the presence of testimony from expert witnesses (e.g. McKimmie *et al.*, 2004); and the confidence with which witnesses deliver testimony (e.g. Brewer and Burke, 2002). Importantly, the choice of variables to be manipulated – and specific details of the manipulations – should be guided by the research questions being addressed.

Collective juror decisions. Although the majority of research has examined decisions made by individual jurors, collective jury decisions (i.e. verdict delivered after deliberation) have also been investigated. Studies of collective juror decisions have taken numerous approaches. For instance the consistency and competency of jury decisions has been examined by comparing the verdicts given by actual juries with those given by mock juries (McCabe and Purves, 1974) and presiding judges (Kalven and Zeisel, 1966). Other researchers have investigated the occurrence of social psychological phenomena in the context of jury decisions. For example several mock juror experiments (e.g. Bray and Noble, 1978; Hastie *et al.*, 1983) have found evidence of group polarisation, whereby the views held by jurors tend to become stronger and more extreme as the jury interacts. Although not widely used, one interesting option open to researchers in this area is to use confederates who pose as participants but have been asked to act in a certain pre-determined manner during jury deliberations (e.g. to steadfastly oppose the majority opinion). The use of confederates affords researchers experimental control over a wider range of variables that come into play during the deliberation stage of juror decisions.

Judicial instructions. One important area of research addresses the impact of judicial instructions (i.e. about relevant points of law) on juror decisions. Such research can be conducted via field studies or mock-juror experiments. Some issues examined include the extent to which jurors comprehend judicial instructions (Ogloff and Rose, 2005), and whether comprehension is affected by the timing (ForsterLee *et al.*, 1993) and mode of presentation of instructions (Brewer *et al.*, 2004).

Deception detection. Because witnesses are not always co-operative, jurors may sometimes attempt to make judgments about truthfulness based on verbal or non-verbal cues exhibited by a witness. Similarly, jurors in some countries may be presented with results from physiological lie-detection tests as evidence that bears on the truthfulness of a witness's account. Readers who are interested in conducting research in this area (e.g. examining the ability of jurors – or police investigators – to detect deception or interpret polygraph results) are encouraged to refer to Vrij (2008) for an excellent coverage of the extensive deception detection literature, which will guide the selection of research questions and variables to be manipulated.

Manipulation checks. In many mock-juror experiments, it is appropriate for researchers to include checks to test whether their experimental manipulations have been successful. Manipulation checks are often straightforward. For example a manipulation of testimonial consistency (high versus low) might be assessed by asking participants to recall the number of inconsistencies that occurred in the evidence they were presented with (as per Brewer and Burke, 2002). If the manipulation was successful, participants in the high consistency condition should, on average, recall fewer inconsistencies than those in the low consistency condition. To reduce the chances of participants becoming aware of the purpose of a study, researchers should have participants complete any manipulation checks after the more important measures have been obtained. For example mock-jurors might be asked to recall the number of inconsistencies in a witness's testimony (i.e. the manipulation check) after rating the credibility of the witness and giving a guilty/not guilty verdict (i.e. the measures of greatest interest to the researcher).

Analyses

For field studies and mock-juror experiments, the most common dependent measures are dichotomous verdicts (i.e. guilty or not guilty) and continuous ratings of probable guilt (e.g. from 0 per cent (*definitely not guilty*) to 100 per cent (*definitely guilty*)). Analyses of verdict data involve chi-square tests and hierarchical loglinear analysis, while analyses of probable guilt ratings involve *t*-tests and factorial ANOVA. One important point to note is that, in field studies, variables that are presumed to be causal must be measured rather than manipulated. For example Heuer and Penrod (1994) were interested in the effects of trial complexity on jury decisions in actual cases. The researchers obviously had no control over the complexity of actual cases and, therefore, had to measure complexity instead of manipulating it. They did this by asking the trial judge in each case to rate the complexity of that case – compared to an average case – in terms of a variety of aspects (e.g. the evidence presented, the relevant points of law and the arguments made by the prosecution and defence counsels).

Worked example

The following example is taken from Brewer and Burke (2002), who investigated the effects of testimonial inconsistency and eyewitness confidence on verdicts in a mock-juror experiment. (Again, some methodological details have been omitted here for brevity; a comprehensive description appears in the original article.) Their focus was on the interaction between the two independent variables. For example would the presence of inconsistencies affect juror judgements regardless of witness confidence, as suggested by surveys of police, lawyers and jury-eligible individuals, in which inconsistencies are rated as a strong indicator of inaccuracy (e.g. Brewer *et al.*, 1999)? Alternatively, would inconsistencies affect juror decisions only when witness confidence was low, as implied by the results of Lindsay, Wells and Rumpel (1981)? Or would confidence 'trump' inconsistency, as suggested by the results of Cutler, Penrod and Stuve (1988)?

The stimulus materials (based on materials developed by Berman and Cutler, 1996) comprised a 20-minute, audio-taped transcript of a prosecution witness being questioned by prosecution and defence attorneys during a bank robbery trial. Brewer and Burke (2002) developed four versions of the materials, one for each experimental condition in their two (testimonial consistency: consistent or inconsistent) by two (witness confidence: high or low) design. Each participant heard one version of the transcript: a high-confidence witness giving consistent testimony, a high-confidence witness giving inconsistent testimony, a low-confidence witness giving consistent testimony or a low-confidence witness giving inconsistent testimony.

For the consistency manipulation, the critical items were the witness's answers to four questions that were asked twice, first by the prosecution attorney and then by the defence attorney during cross-examination. In the consistent testimony condition, the witness's responses to these four questions did not differ between the first and second time they were asked. In contrast, in the inconsistent condition, the witness's responses under cross-examination clearly contradicted their earlier responses (e.g. the robber threw the money into a canvas bag versus the robber put the money in his pocket). These differences were highlighted by the defence attorney.

Confidence was also manipulated via the witness's responses to questions. In the high-confidence condition, the witness answered all questions without hesitation or qualification of her responses (e.g. 'Yes, exactly'; 'No'). In contrast, in the low-confidence condition, the witness did hesitate and qualify when answering some questions (e.g. 'Yes, I guess so'; 'Ummm ... I don't think so').

Brewer and Burke (2002) recruited 130 jury-eligible participants. Each participant was asked to imagine that they were a juror in an actual case, and was randomly assigned to hear one of the four versions of the transcript. Participants were then asked to indicate the probability that the defendant committed the crime (on a scale from 0 per cent (*I am not sure at all that the defendant committed the crime*) to 100 per cent (*I am 100 per cent sure that the defendant committed the crime*)), and to give a guilty/not guilty verdict. As manipulation checks, participants were then asked to rate the confidence with which the defendant delivered her testimony (on a scale from 1 (*not very confidently*) to 7 (*extremely confidently*)) and to recall how many, if any, contradictions occurred in the testimony. These items were embedded among several questions unrelated to the purpose of the experiment. The results of the manipulation checks suggested that the manipulations had the desired effects: on average, participants in the high confidence condition rated the witness as more confident than those in the low confidence condition ($M = 5.98$ vs. 3.02), and participants in the inconsistent condition recalled more contradictions than those in the consistent condition ($M = 3.31$ vs. 0.94).

The results for the central dependent measures suggested that, in line with the results of Cutler *et al.* (1988), participants' decisions were influenced primarily by witness confidence. A two (witness confidence) by two (testimonial consistency) loglinear analysis of verdicts indicated that participants gave more guilty verdicts when the prosecution witness was high in confidence (39.4 per cent guilty) versus low in confidence (9.4 per cent guilty), and this pattern held regardless of whether the testimony was consistent or inconsistent. Similarly, a two (witness confidence) by two (testimonial consistency) factorial ANOVA showed that participants gave higher probable guilt ratings when the witness was high (57.50 per cent) rather than low (32.50 per cent) in confidence, and this pattern occurred in both testimonial consistency conditions. (See Brewer and Burke, 2002, for a detailed interpretation of these results.)

Strengths and limitations

Compared to mock-juror experiments, field studies have a clear advantage in realism. For example the decisions made by jurors in actual cases carry real consequences, while those made by mock-jurors and shadow jurors do not. The lack of realism in many mock-juror experiments has given rise to a considerable amount of criticism (e.g. Weiten and Diamond, 1979). However, there is evidence suggesting that at least some of this criticism is not valid. For example some studies have found no meaningful difference in the verdicts given by jurors who anticipate that their decisions will carry real consequences for defendants, and jurors who do not (Kerr *et al.*, 1979). In addition, as outlined earlier, one very important disadvantage of field studies is that they do not afford researchers experimental control over variables, which limits the extent to which causal conclusions can be drawn. In contrast, well-conducted mock-juror experiments do enable researchers to draw causal conclusions.

Future directions

Given the methodological and practical advantages of mock-juror experiments, it is important for future research to further investigate the extent to which results found using such methods can be generalised to more realistic jury settings.

Some researchers (e.g. Kerr and Bray, 2005) have advocated a compromise, whereby psycho-legal research is conducted using a variety of field study and experimental methods. In this vein, researchers might begin by attempting to answer a question using relatively simple, well-controlled experiments before trying to replicate the results in increasingly more realistic scenarios. This approach might be particularly fruitful for areas of juror decision making research that have the potential to guide policy, such as the development of procedures that lead to better processing of evidence or comprehension of law by jurors (e.g. Brewer *et al.*, 2004).

Further reading

In this chapter, we have given an overview of the methodological questions that arise in three prominent areas of court-relevant research. However, these are not the only such areas. Productive research has been conducted on a wide range of topics that we have only considered briefly (e.g. deception detection; Vrij, 2008) or have not covered at all, such as the effects of pre-trial publicity on juror decisions (e.g. Studebaker *et al.*, 2000) and persuasive techniques used by attorneys during courtroom trials (e.g. Williams *et al.*, 1993). There are some excellent sources for readers who are interested in a broader and more detailed coverage of court-related research, including Brewer and Williams (2005), Hastie (1993), Hastie, Penrod, and Pennington (1983), Loftus (1979) and Vrij (2008). In addition, we highly recommend Pelham and Blanton (2007) as a useful starting point for any readers interested in learning more about the general principles of research methodology for psychology.

Author note

This research was supported by Australian Research Council Grant DP36065.

References

Akehurst, L., Milne, R. and Köhnken, G. (2003). The effects of children's age and delay on recall in a cognitive or structured interview. *Psychology, Crime, & Law*, 9: 97–107.
Baumeister, R. F. and Darley, J. M. (1982). Reducing the biasing effect of perpetrator attractiveness in jury simulation. *Personality and Social Psychology Bulletin*, 8: 286–92.
Berman, G. L. and Cutler, B. L. (1996). Effects of inconsistencies in eyewitness testimony on mock-juror decision making. *Journal of Applied Psychology*, 81: 170–77.
Borgida, E., DeBono, K.G. and Buckman, L.A. (1990). Cameras in the courtroom: the effects of media coverage on witness testimony and juror perceptions. *Law and Human Behavior*, 14: 489–509.
Bornstein, B. H. (1999). The ecological validity of jury simulations: Is the jury still out? *Law and Human Behavior*, 23: 75–91.
Bray, R. M. and Kerr, N. L. (1979). Use of simulation method in the study of jury behavior: Some methodological considerations. *Law & Human Behavior*, 3: 107–20.

Bray, R. M. and Noble, A. M. (1978). Authoritarianism and decisions of mock juries: Evidence of jury bias and group polarization. *Journal of Personality and Social Psychology*, 36: 1,424–30.

Brewer, N. and Burke, A. (2002). Effects of testimonial inconsistencies and eyewitness confidence on mock-juror judgments. *Law & Human Behavior*, 26: 353–64.

Brewer, N. and Weber, N. (2008). Eyewitness confidence and latency: Indices of memory processes not just markers of accuracy. *Applied Cognitive Psychology*, 22: 827–40.

Brewer, N. and Wells, G. L. (2011). Eyewitness identification. *Current Directions in Psychological Science*, 20: 24–7.

Brewer, N. and Wells, G. L. (2006). The confidence-accuracy relationship in eyewitness identification: effects of line-up instructions, foil similarity and target-absent base rates. *Journal of Experimental Psychology: Applied*, 12: 11–30.

Brewer, N. and Williams, K. D. (Eds) (2005). *Psychology and law: an empirical perspective*. New York: Guilford.

Brewer, N., Harvey, S. and Semmler, C. (2004). Improving comprehension of jury instructions with audio-visual presentation. *Applied Cognitive Psychology*, 18: 765–6.

Brewer, N., Potter, R., Fisher, R. P., Bond, N. W. and Luszcz, M. A. (1999). Beliefs and data on the relationship between consistency and accuracy of eyewitness testimony. *Applied Cognitive Psychology*, 13: 297–313.

Brewer, N., Muller, T., Nagesh, A., Hope, L. and Gabbert, F. (2010, March). Interviewing eyewitnesses: enhancing outputs by controlling the grain size of reports. American Psychology-Law Society Conference, Vancouver, Canada.

Brewer, N., Weber, N., Clark, A. and Wells, G. L. (2008). Distinguishing accurate from inaccurate eyewitnesses with an optional deadline procedure. *Psychology, Crime, & Law*, 14: 397–414.

Brigham, J. C., Meissner, C. A. and Wasserman, A. W. (1999). Applied issues in the construction and expert assessment of photo line-ups. *Applied Cognitive Psychology*, 13: S73–S92.

Carlson, C. A., Gronlund, S. D. and Clark, S. E. (2008). Line-up composition, suspect position, and the sequential line-up advantage. *Journal of Experimental Psychology: Applied*, 14: 118–28.

Carlucci, M. E., Kieckhaeffer, J. M., Schwartz, S. L., Villalba, D. K. and Wright, D. B. (in press). The South Beach study: bystanders' memories are more malleable. *Applied Cognitive Psychology*.

Cohen, J. A. (1992). Power primer. *Quantitative Methods in Psychology*, 112: 155–59.

Cutler, B. L., Penrod, S. D. and Stuve, T. E. (1988). Jury decision making in eyewitness identification cases. *Law & Human Behavior*, 12: 41–56.

Dando, C., Wilcock, R., Milne, R. and Henry, L. (2009). A modified cognitive interview procedure for frontline police investigators. *Applied Cognitive Psychology*, 23: 698–716.

Darling, S., Valentine, T. and Memon, A. (2008). Selection of line-up foils in operational contexts. *Applied Cognitive Psychology*, 22: 159–69.

Davies, G. and Griffiths, L. (2008). Eyewitness identification and the English courts: a century of trial and error. *Psychiatry, Psychology, & Law*, 15: 435–49.

Davis, M. R., McMahon, M. and Greenwood, K. M. (2005). The efficacy of mnemonic components of the cognitive interview: towards a shortened variant for time-critical investigations. *Applied Cognitive Psychology*, 19: 75–93.

Field, A. (2009). *Discovering statistics using SPSS*. 3rd edition. London, UK: Sage Publications.

Fisher, R. P. and Geiselman, R. E. (1992). *Memory enhancing techniques for investigative interviewing: the cognitive interview.* Springfield, IL: Charles C. Thomas.

ForsterLee, L., Horowitz, I. A. and Bourgeois, M. J. (1993). Juror competence in civil trials: effects of preinstruction and evidence technicality. *Journal of Applied Psychology*, 78: 14–21.

Geiselman, R. E., Fisher, R. P., Firstenberg, I., Hutton, L. A., Sullivan, S., Avetissian, I. and Prosk, A. (1984). Enhancement of eyewitness memory: an empirical evaluation of the cognitive interview. *Journal of Police Science & Administration*, 12: 74–80.

Geiselman, R. E., Fisher, R. P., MacKinnon, D. P. and Holland, H. L. (1985). Eyewitness memory enhancement in the police interview: cognitive retrieval mnemonics versus hypnosis. *Journal of Applied Psychology*, 70: 401–12.

Goldsmith, M., Koriat, A. and Weinberg-Eliezer, A. (2002). Strategic regulation of grain size in memory reporting over time. *Journal of Experimental Psychology: General*, 131: 73–95.

Gorenstein, G. W. and Ellsworth, P. C. (1980). Effect of choosing an incorrect photograph on a later identification by an eyewitness. *Journal of Applied Psychology*, 65: 616–22.

Hastie, R. (Ed) (1993). *Inside the juror: the psychology of juror decision making.* New York: Cambridge University Press.

Hastie, R., Penrod, S. D. and Pennington, N. (1983). *Inside the jury.* Cambridge, MA: Harvard University Press.

Heuer, L. and Penrod, S. (1994). Trial complexity: a field investigation of its meaning and its effect. *Law & Human Behavior*, 18: 29–52.

Hope, L., Gabbert, F., Brewer, N., Tull, M., and Nagesh, A. (2010, June). Interviewing eyewitnesses: enhancing output quality and diagnosing accuracy using the Grain Size technique. 20th Conference of the European Association of Psychology and Law. Gothenburg, Sweden.

Innocence Project (2010). *Eyewitness misidentification.* Available from www.innocence-project.org/understand/Eyewitness-Misidentification.php (accessed 19/7/10).

Johnson, J. D., Whitestone, E., Jackson, L. A. and Gatto, L. (1995). Justice is still not colorblind: differential racial effects of exposure to inadmissible evidence. *Personality and Social Psychology Bulletin*, 21: 893–8.

Kalven, H. J. and Zeisel, H. (1966). *The American jury.* Boston: Little, Brown.

Kemp, R. I., Pike, G. E. and Brace, N. A. (2001). Video-based identification procedures: Combining best practice and practical requirements when designing identification systems. *Psychology, Public Policy, & Law*, 7: 802–7.

Kerr, N. L. and Bray, R. M. (2005). Simulation, realism and the study of the jury. In N. Brewer and K. D. Williams (Eds). *Psychology and law: an empirical perspective* (pp. 322–64). New York: Guilford.

Kerr, N. L., Nerenz, D. and Herrick, D. (1979). Role playing and the study of jury behavior. *Sociological Methods and Research*, 7: 337–55.

Langer, E. J. and Abelson, R. P. (1972). The semantics of asking a favor: how to succeed in getting help without really dying. *Journal of Personality and Social Psychology*, 24: 26–32.

Larsson, A. S., Granhag, P. A. and Spjut, E. (2003). Children's recall and the cognitive interview: do the positive effects hold over time? *Applied Cognitive Psychology*, 17: 203–14.

Lefebvre, C. D., Marchand, Y., Smith, S. M. and Connolly, J. F. (2007). Determining eyewitness identification accuracy using event-related brain potentials (ERPs). *Psychophysiology*, 44: 894–904.

Lindsay, R. C. L. and Wells, G. L. (1985). Improving eyewitness identification from line-ups: Simultaneous versus sequential line-up presentations. *Journal of Applied Psychology*, 70: 556–64.

Lindsay, R. C. L., Wells, G. L. and Rumpel, C. M. (1981). Can people detect eyewitness-identification accuracy within and across situations? *Journal of Applied Psychology*, 66: 79–89.

Loftus, E. F. (1979). *Eyewitness testimony*. Cambridge, MA: Harvard University Press.

Loftus, E. F. and Palmer, J. C. (1974). Reconstruction of automobile destruction: an example of the interaction between language and memory. *Journal of Verbal Learning & Verbal Behavior*, 13: 585–89.

Luus, C. A. E., and Wells, G. L. (1991). Eyewitness identification and the selection of distracters for line-ups. *Law & Human Behavior*, 15: 43–57.

McCabe, S. and Purves, R. (1974). *The shadow jury at work*. Oxford: Blackwell.

McKimmie, B. M., Newton, C. J., Terry, D. J. and Schuller, R. A. (2004). Jurors' responses to expert witness testimony: the effects of gender stereotypes. *Group Processes and Intergroup Relations*, 7: 131–43.

Malpass, R. S. and Devine, P. G. (1981a). Guided memory in eyewitness identification. *Journal of Applied Psychology*, 66: 343–50.

—— (1981b). Eyewitness identification: Line-up instructions and the absence of the offender. *Journal of Applied Psychology*, 66: 482–89.

Memon, A., Havard, C., Clifford, B., Gabbert, F. and Watt, M. (in press). A field evalua-tion of the VIPER system: a new technique for eliciting eyewitness evidence. *Psychology, Crime, & Law*.

Memon, A., Holley, A., Wark, L., Bull, R. and Köhnken, G. (1996). Reducing sugges-tibility in child witness interviews. *Applied Cognitive Psychology*, 10: 503–18.

Memon, A., Meissner, C. A. and Fraser, J. (2010). The cognitive interview: a meta-analytic review and study space analysis of the past 25 years. *Psychology, Public Policy, & Law*, 16: 340–72.

Milne, R. and Bull, R. (2002). Back to basics: a componential analysis of the original cognitive interview mnemonics with three age groups. *Applied Cognitive Psychology*, 16: 743–53.

Morgan, C. A., Hazlett, G., Doran, A., Garrett, S., Hoyt, G., Thomas, P., Baranoski, M. and Southwick, S. M. (2004). Accuracy of eyewitness memory for persons encountered during exposure to highly intense stress. *International Journal of Law & Psychiatry*, 27: 265–79.

Münsterberg, H. (1908). *On the witness stand*. New York: Doubleday.

Ogloff, J. R. P. and Rose, V. G. (2005). The comprehension of judicial instructions. In N. Brewer and K. D. Williams (Eds). *Psychology and law: an empirical perspective* (pp. 407–44). New York: Guilford.

Palmer, M. A., Brewer, N., McKinnon, A. C. and Weber, N. (2010). Phenomenological reports diagnose accuracy of eyewitness identification decisions. *Acta Psychologica*, 133: 137–45.

Pelham, B. W. and Blanton, H. (2007). *Conducting research in psychology: measuring the weight of smoke*. 3rd edn. Belmont, CA: Thomson Wadsworth.

Sauer, J. D., Brewer, N. and Weber, N. (2008a). Multiple confidence estimates as indices of eyewitness memory. *Journal of Experimental Psychology: General*, 137: 528–47.

Sauer, J. D., Brewer, N. and Wells, G. L. (2008b). Is there a magical time boundary for diagnosing eyewitness identification accuracy in sequential line-ups? *Legal & Criminological Psychology*, 13: 123–35.

Scheck, B., Neufeld, P. and Dwyer, J. (2003). *Actual innocence: when justice goes wrong and how to put it right*. New York: New American Library.

Semmler, C., Brewer, N. and Wells, G. L. (2004). Effects of postidentification feedback on identification and nonidentification confidence. *Journal of Applied Psychology*, 89: 334–46.

Strodtbeck, F., James, R. and Hawkins, C. (1957). Social status in jury deliberations. *American Sociological Review*, 22: 713–19.

Studebaker, C. A., Robbennolt, J. K., Parthak-Sharma, M. K. and Penrod, S. D. (2000). Assessing pretrial publicity effects: Integrating content analytic results. *Law & Human Behavior*, 24: 317–36.

Tredoux, C. G. (1998). Statistical inference on measures of line-up fairness. *Law & Human Behavior*, 22: 217–37.

Valentine, T. and Mesout, J. (2009). Eyewitness identification under stress in the London Dungeon. *Applied Cognitive Psychology*, 23: 151–61.

Valentine, T., Darling, S. and Memon, A. (2007). Do strict rules and moving images increase the reliability of sequential identification procedures? *Applied Cognitive Psychology*, 21: 933–49.

Vrij, A. (2008). *Detecting lies and deceit: pitfalls and opportunities*. Chichester: John Wiley & Sons.

Weber, N., and Brewer, N. (2008). Eyewitness recall: regulation of grain size and the role of confidence. *Journal of Experimental Psychology: Applied*, 14: 50–60.

Weiten, W. and Diamond, S. S. (1979). A critical review of the jury simulation paradigm: the case of defendant characteristics. *Law and Human Behavior*, 3: 71–93.

Wells, G. L. (2005). Helping experimental psychology affect legal policy. In N. Brewer and K. D. Williams (Eds). *Psychology and law: an empirical perspective* (pp. 483–500). New York: Guilford.

Wells, G. L. and Windschitl, P. D. (1999). Stimulus sampling and social psychological experimentation. *Personality & Social Psychology Bulletin*, 25: 1,115–25.

Wells, G. L., Lieppe, M. R. and Ostrom, T. M. (1979). Guidelines for empirically assessing the fairness of a line-up. *Law & Human Behavior*, 3: 285–93.

Wells, G. L., Malpass, R. S., Lindsay, R. C. L., Fisher, R. P., Turtle, J. W. and Fulero, S. M. (2000). From the lab to the police station: a successful application of eyewitness reearch. *American Psychologist*, 55: 581–98.

Wells, G. L., Memon, A. and Penrod, S. D. (2006). Eyewitness evidence: improving its probative value. *Psychological Science in the Public Interest*, 7: 45–75.

Williams, K. D., Bourgeois, M. J. and Croyle, R. T. (1993). The effects of stealing thunder in criminal and civil trials. *Law & Human Behavior*, 17: 597–609.

Wright, A. M. and Holliday, R. E. (2007). Interviewing cognitively impaired older adults: How useful is a cognitive interview? *Memory*, 15: 17–33.

Wright, D. B., Boyd, C. E. and Tredoux, C. G. (2001). A field study of own-race bias in South Africa and England. *Psychology, Public Policy, & Law*, 7: 119–33.

Part III

Approaches at the qualitative level

6 Qualitative research with staff in forensic settings

A Grounded Theory example

Neil Gordon

Introduction

In this chapter I will reflect on a research study exploring staff experiences in a high security forensic setting, focusing on the use of Grounded Theory (GT) methodology, and including an exploration of how the epistemological debates in the GT literature informed the approach. The research explored the experiences of therapists working in high security environments, examining how these individuals adapted and managed their therapeutic style in response to the demands of clinical work. The aim of the study was to examine how the distinct boundaries and structures of the high security forensic setting influence and shape the nature of psychotherapeutic activity. This includes the complex difficulties experienced by the patient group and the uncertain and unpredictable nature of therapeutic work, leading to what Schön (1987) calls 'swamp like' practice conditions. Such conditions have to be managed and survived on a daily basis. I selected a GT approach to address this issue as I felt this was an under-researched phenomenon that would be usefully explored by an in-depth analysis of the experiences of the practitioners who inhabited these *swampy lands* (Schön, 1994).

The methodological approach taken was an *adapted* version of GT combined with an innovative interview approach based on the work of the educational researcher Irving Seidman (2006). I will set the scene by introducing qualitative approaches and their theoretical underpinnings before elaborating on the *nuts and bolts* of Grounded Theory, going on to discuss the uniqueness of forensic environments and indicating why qualitative research methods can be so helpful in increasing our understanding of what goes on within them. I will then critically review the origins and development of GT including a brief review of contemporary debates related to the differing epistemological and theoretical underpinnings of this approach advocated by different writers in the field (Charmaz, 2006; Willig, 2001; Strauss and Corbin, 1998). I will illustrate the data management and analysis strategies of GT with reference to the study outlined above. As the aim of this chapter is to encourage researchers to develop their skill repertoire I will also discuss how my *constructionist* approach to GT shaped my interaction with the data before exploring how you might judge the quality of this type of

qualitative research. Key reading and seminal texts will also be identified to h
readers extend their understanding of the GT approach.

The increasingly important contribution of qualitative approaches

Qualitative research approaches have only recently become a feature wit
forensic environments as recognition is growing of the important part they
play in exploring the complex interpersonal and organisational dynamics that
characteristic of these settings. In exploring, understanding and making sense
these dynamics the researcher needs to employ a range of methodologies with
capacity to focus on the phenomenology of personal experience while attend
to the social structures and behaviours of those who inhabit these social worl
The qualitative research tradition incorporates many epistemological standpoi
that tend to focus on developing our understanding of situated human experie
and have a particular interest in issues related to subjectivity, interpretation a
meaning making (Silverman, 2000).

For many years the research agendas within forensic settings were primar
informed by a positivist philosophical perspective resulting in the production
research reports dominated by statistics and measurement. While these stud
provided important data about patient experience they did little to illuminate
roles and meaning making of the staff who struggle to make sense of and mana
this often *hidden world* (Franciosi, 2001) of human experience. Those w
employ the active agent model (Blaikie, 1993) of human functioning tend
utilise its associated interpretivist and hermeneutic underpinnings in understa
ing the dynamics of organisational life. Acknowledging that the subjects of yc
research are actively constructing and making sense of the social world th
inhabit encourages forensic researchers to utilise methodologies that are design
to explore the meanings and interpretive frameworks that staff are utilising. T
focus on meaning making is particularly important as those working in
complex cultural milieu of the high security environment need to respond to
demands of an ever-changing interpersonal and organisational context. In und
standing and exploring these responses qualitative methodologies are particula
useful. Although this chapter focuses on GT methodology many of the points a
issues raised about analysis and the trustworthiness of the research report
relevant to other qualitative approaches where the interpretation of transcrib
data is the central concern. Where other approaches might use coding of tra
scripts and detailed field notes as part of the analytical process, GT methodolo
uses such approaches and other systematic and detailed analytical strategies
order to *generate theory*.

Key philosophical ideas that inform methodological debates

Before discussing the GT approach and how it has evolved, it is necessary
examine the relationship that exists between ontological perspectives and
guiding epistemologies that inform a researcher's methodological choic

Ontology can literally be defined as the *study of being* and in this context I will use the term (after Blaikie, 1993, p. 6) to mean the assumptions a particular approach to social inquiry makes about the nature of social reality. This includes beliefs about what exists in the world, what it looks like, what units make it up and how these interact with one another. The related concept of *epistemology* can be defined as 'a theory of knowledge' and is concerned with assumptions about how we acquire knowledge, about the social realities conceptualised in particular ontological perspectives, including what can be known, and how and what criteria we use to determine the status of such knowledge. *Realist epistemology* is a complex and diverse philosophical perspective that at some level postulates that social reality exists independently of perceiving subjects and that this reality is not only ordered, but also these uniformities can be observed, studied and explained. In contrast *constructionist epistemology* postulates that active human agents produce and reproduce social reality in a pre-interpreted inter-subjective world of shared meanings, cultural norms and social institutions (Gergen, 2001). Any researcher approaching this complex literature needs to be able to understand the relationship between epistemological and ontological roots of their chosen methodology (Crotty, 1998) and use this to inform their implementation of the selected method. These philosophical constructs have particular relevance to the novice GT researcher as the methodological debates that inform GT research practice are often represented in terms of tensions between realist or constructionist epistemologies (Charmaz, 2006; Bryant and Charmaz, 2007; Glaser, 2009).

Grounded Theory methodology – origins, evolution and debate

As Charmaz (2006, p. 2) observes, 'grounded theory methods consist of systematic, yet flexible guidelines for collecting and analysing qualitative data to construct theories grounded in the data themselves'. This approach was pioneered by the American sociologists Barney Glaser and Anslem Strauss and articulated in their seminal text: *The discovery of Grounded Theory* (1967). This publication was viewed as a counterbalance to what at that time was seen as the dominant quantitative and positivist perspectives shaping social science research. Increasingly this 'founding manifesto' (Charmaz, 2006, p. 49) has been exposed to a more sustained philosophical critique taking account of epistemological developments and debates in the sociology of science associated with constructionist accounts. Glaser (2009) himself has recently re-entered the debate (Strauss died in 1996) with a scathing attack on what he has called Bryant and Charmaz's (2007) 'jargonizing' text which he believes has confused the original GT method with more general qualitative data analysis (QDA). Bryant and Charmaz (2007) acknowledge that as the original GT work emerged in a particular social and disciplinary context, it encouraged the founders to articulate their approach as an alternative to the dominant hypothetico-deductive method. However, they conclude that the need to situate this alternative methodology within the discourse of the dominant paradigm discouraged a more radical review of positivist assumptions regarding the interpretive role of the researcher and the constructed nature of observational and interview data. This debate is at the heart of more recent attempts to address the accusations of naïve reductionism (Layder, 1993) aimed at the more positivist versions of GT, with Charmaz (2006) and others arguing for a more constructionist epistemology to inform qualitative research practice.

Those criticising the GT method have tended to focus on the philosophical limitations of the original text or the specific iterations produced by Strauss and Corbin (1994, 1998, and 2008) rather than engaging with the wider methodological literature. Other methodological critiques have centred on the acknowledged philosophical differences between Glaser and Strauss emanating from their own research trainings and affiliation with particular schools of thought (i.e. Glaser's quantitative positivist leanings as a survey researcher and Strauss's more symbolic interactionist perspective based on his affiliation with the Chicago School of Sociology). It is well documented that over the years Glaser and Strauss's thinking about GT diverged significantly based on their philosophical commitments and methodological concerns. For Charmaz (2006) part of this continuing tension was related to the fact that throughout the intervening period both men made only limited comments on these issues.

Getting to grips with epistemological and methodological debates, including how they have been shaped by historical developments, is an essential task for the novice researcher who has decided to use GT methodology. The following account is based primarily on the writing of Anslem Strauss and Juliet Corbin; however, it is also influenced by the more recent contributions of the constructionist grounded theorist Kathy Charmaz and the psychotherapy researcher David Rennie. It should be apparent with reference to the above debates that any attempt to outline the application of GT methodology is always in danger of oversimplifying methodological practices and the epistemological debates that have informed researcher choices.

The 'nuts and bolts' of Grounded Theory

The overall aim of a GT approach is to generate a substantive 'theory' about social phenomena that helps us to understand and make sense of what might be going on in a specific social context. The theory produced is described as *substantive* rather than *higher order* or *grand* theory (Gordon-Finlayson, 2010), in that it tends to provide a contextualised account of a particular set of social circumstances rather than some generalisable conceptual framework that can be applied universally. Hypothetico-deductive models of research design usually begin with a theory and then develop hypotheses to test this theory. In contrast, GT starts with detailed analysis of different cases and moves from this starting point to develop a theory that takes account of the variation within these cases and the relationships between them. Data can be obtained from different sources including interviews, documents and written texts, focus groups and field observations. The original 'raw data' or field notes are converted into transcribed text. It is when working with this textual data that the techniques of data interpretation and analytical strategies of GT are particularly useful.

In identifying what distinguishes the GT approach, Gordon-Finlayson (2010) suggests that there are three major traits that need to be evident in the researcher's approach to data; namely that this should be theoretical, analytical and cyclical. First, GT should be self evidently *theoretical* in that it culminates in the production of a theoretical account that attempts to communicate a new understanding of the phenomena under investigation. Achieving this outcome is dependent on the researcher's *theoretical* sensitivity to the area of study. This sensitivity is required to perceive 'subtle nuances and meanings in data and to recognise the connections between concepts' (Strauss and Corbin, 1998, p. 43). Strauss and Corbin (1998) consider that sensitivity means being able to see beneath the obvious to discover the new, recognising that insights and interpretations represent an interplay between the researcher and the data. This is informed in various ways including who the researcher is and his or her personal experience (Crotty, 1998), the professional experience and knowledge of the researcher and the use of literature from multiple sources. Another important concept is 'theoretical sampling' (Glaser and Strauss, 1967), i.e. using theoretical leads that emerge in the data (guided by the analyses already conducted) to inform further sampling and data collection. This collection has the specific purpose of 'sampling' for instances of the concepts in question. Some researchers have taken theoretical sampling to indicate testing out concepts from one interview to the next (for example Rennie, 1998), as well as the moving from site to site suggested by Glaser and Strauss, eventually leading to theoretical saturation, where new data confirms rather than extends the emerging categories.

Second, GT is *analytical* in that the theoretically sensitive researcher constantly interacts with the data, using a range of coding strategies to ask questions, reflect on content and produce theoretical and analytical memos about data themes and relationships. Over time, through the process of constant comparison, these memos become further developed by integrating relevant literature, thus creating the building blocks of the emerging theory.

Third, GT is *cyclical* in that as the researcher analyses the data through coding and memoing he/she is constantly reflecting on the relationship between what is being found and existing theoretical ideas. A further cyclical process involves the activity of theoretical sampling itself which may lead the researcher to new participants or encourage a reinterpretation of already analysed data through a newly created theoretical lens that has emerged from the constant comparative analysis. This cycling is also evident in the way GT researchers utilise literature; rather than conduct an exhaustive review at the outset of the study, which could impose an existing theoretical framework on the data, the researcher will return to the literature as the analysis proceeds as a way of developing the theory and connecting with existing perspectives. This does not mean the researcher enters the field as a blank slate with no sensitivity to the phenomena of interest. For example, in one study, I was entering the field as a psychotherapist who inhabited a similar therapeutic world to my interviewees and was therefore sensitised to key issues that might emerge. The important thing is that the researcher remains reflective and sensitive to this familiarity, attempting to manage it in ways that do not distort or lead to an imposition of the researcher's perspective on the data. The impact of researcher subjectivity on data generation and analysis represents an area of ongoing debate with the community of GT researchers who align with different philosophical and ontological perspectives. For those unfamiliar with this approach, describing the abstract analytical strategies does little to inform how one needs to proceed so it is worth illustrating them in more detail before discussing theoretical and philosophical debates about the GT method. Figure 6.1 offers an overview of the key tasks which are then illustrated further with reference to segments of data from my study of the high security therapists' experience.

The central principle of data management and analysis in GT research is the strategy of *constant comparison*. As incidents or issues of interest are noted in the data, they are compared against other examples for similarities and differences. Through the constant comparison process, emerging theoretical constructs are continually being defined and compared with fresh examples from ongoing data collection. This produces the richness that is typical of GT analysis. Initially, incidents or issues with similarities are grouped together into themes or categories, which are named according to meaning units in a process called open coding. This can be within segments of data, within entire transcripts and across different transcripts. For example in my study although the initial code of 'checking in' came from an early interview, as the theme was touched on in later interviews I 'cycled' back to the original transcripts where I found several references to this concept that I had missed. This is a common experience as the researcher's sensitivity to the data increases and encourages a comparison of new and old data.

Open coding involves reading the transcript line by line and constantly comparing and categorising segments of data by naming/labelling these in ways that both summarise and account for the data. 'Open coding' is taken to indicate that concepts suggested in the data are labelled according to the interpretation of the researcher. This is a process of conceptualising or abstracting incidents in the data by giving these incidents a label that represents them. In some cases the labels applied indicate 'in vivo codes' (Glaser and Strauss, 1967), utilising words used by the participants themselves, and in other cases the label or code came from the researcher's own interpretations of the data theme. Corbin and Strauss (2008) suggest this is an active process that involves various analytical strategies and a rigorous questioning of the raw data. At this stage it is essential that the researcher 'dwells with the data', that is, reads it over many times, thinks about it and interrogates it before beginning to impose an interpretive coding frame on the text. At this stage the researcher is examining the data line by line staying close to the text and asking questions about what the data might be saying. As illustrated below, further data excerpts from later interviews that can be

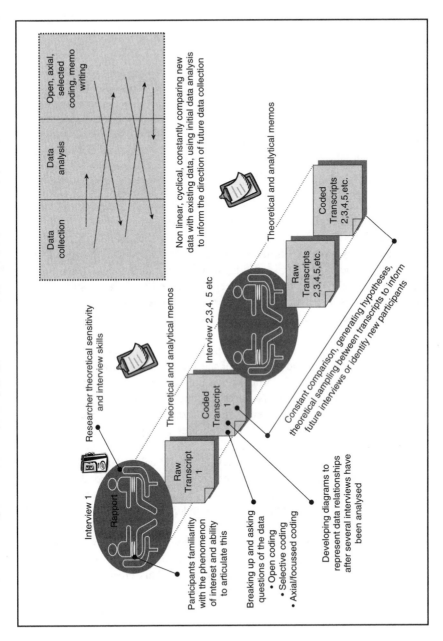

Figure 6.1 Nuts and bolts of Grounded Theory.

connected with this code are identified. It is important to highlight, as indicated in Figure 6.1, that in GT data analysis and collection are concurrent and initial coding is used to direct and inform future data collection. Each piece of data is constantly compared with all other pieces of data and over time segments of data may become connected through the interpretive frame of the researcher's analysis. This active engagement with the text is described by Rennie (2001) as reflecting a hermeneutic approach to analysis, as the researcher uses his/her analytical skills to interpret the key messages within the transcript/text.

Axial coding or focused coding involves working with the initial open codes by looking for related ideas and concepts across different transcripts or within a single transcript. The term *axial* relates to the idea of moving around an axis to develop and substantiate the code and its capacity to capture the meaning within the data. The initial code of 'checking in' is related to several key concerns for the therapist such as managing risk and assessing staff attitudes and relational dynamics. Strauss and Corbin (1998) refer to this process as axial or selective coding. However, Charmaz (1995, p. 40) elaborates the concept of 'focused' coding. This, she explains, indicates the next developmental step in theory building from open coding. Focused coding takes the analysis forward by considering the open codes for their theoretical promise and uses the open codes appearing to be the most promising in the data to drive further data generation, a form of 'theoretical notion chasing'; the researcher begins to ask questions in the interviews that 'test out hypotheses' to 'verify' the codes. Thus subsequent data collection becomes more focused, as does the subsequent analytical coding procedures.

Theoretical and analytical memos represent the researcher's attempts to articulate the dimensions and elements of the specific code by writing about its different features. Strauss and Corbin (1998) indicate that memos vary in length, content and degree of conceptualisation according to the phase of research. The purposes of memo writing are to raise the data to a level of conceptualisation, to develop the properties of each category, to present hypotheses about connections between categories, to integrate categories to generate theory and to locate emerging theory within other relevant theoretical perspectives (Rennie, 2001). Early memos may consist of the researcher's theoretical 'ponderings', the asking of questions, the surmising of meanings and formulation of hypotheses and notes to him- or herself that contain reminders of what he or she felt was happening in the data (Miles and Huberman, 1994). Charmaz (2006) suggests bringing raw data into memos to ground the abstract analysis fully, a technique adopted in the present study where I sorted data codings into groups through the 'cut and paste' facility of the word processor. This created files with all data segments coded under a particular label from each interview grouped together. This meets with advice to 'recontextualise' data by presenting data relating to a particular code or category all together so they are accessible for reading and exploring (Miles and Huberman, 1994; Coffey and Atkinson, 1996).

The analytical memo tends to be written based on a critical review of the way the code appears in the data and the different issues it refers to. Gradually, as analysis proceeds the memos become increasingly focused and begin to record the connections between concepts and to go beyond individual cases and to define patterns (Charmaz, 1995). The theoretical memo is made up of analytical reflections infused with relevant theory from the literature and memos, and the raw data they relate to, eventually becoming the writing up of the theory. So, for example, the idea of checking in or checking out might be connected with psychotherapist behaviours in different contexts, such as pre-therapy briefings with colleagues to prepare for a session. These memos are the building blocks of the emerging theory that help the researcher identify and articulate core categories in the data. Further discussion on identifying categories and themes can be found later in the chapter.

An extract from an analytical memo:

The code *checking in* relates to the way several respondents discussed the importance of talking with the ward staff before meeting with the patient. As therapists journey into the ward environment to see the patient, they commonly make time for talking to the staff on duty. This checking in process is partly related to security regulations where all visitors to the ward must let the staff know of their arrival. However, this encounter also provides an opportunity to explore what has been happening on the ward and how the patient they are going to see has been since the last encounter. Although entering the environment as a visitor, the therapists, like ethnographers, seek out the insider perspective and several talked about trying to get a 'feel' for what was going on in the ward and how the staff viewed the patient.

A further strategy I employed was the drawing of diagrams. The researcher uses *diagramming* to articulate and make visible different categories and the constant comparative method encourages connections between the different categories to examine and illustrate relationships between the different concepts and ideas. The purpose of diagrams is to provide a visual device to show the relationships between data themes. These relationships are represented in diagrammatic form as a useful way of holding different ideas up to scrutiny and showing the interrelatedness of data themes.

Grounded Theory diagrams are visual rather than written memos (Strauss and Corbin, 1998) and they provided me with a means of mapping out the issues that arose in early interviews. This facilitated a comparison of interview against interview. Later diagrams (each core theme had an associated diagram to show relationships between data themes) demonstrated an ordering and linkage of concepts, and a sorting of elements to form categories and to show linkages between them. To illustrate the usefulness of diagrams the final summary of the core categories and their related categories and sub categories is presented in Figure 6.2.

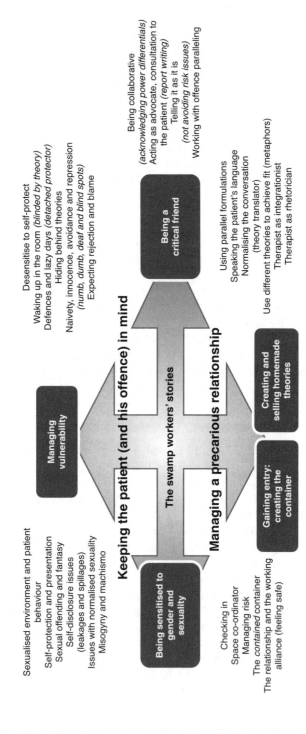

Figure 6.2 A diagram of the theoretical model and the core categories.

Identifying the categories

Focused coding guides the analysis towards increasing abstraction as codings are grouped together to become elements (or subcategories) of higher-level concepts that are termed categories. This indicates that the researcher is involved in a process of considering whether a higher-level concept (category) is suggested by the grouping of these codes, or which concepts in the data are best included in this category. The inclusion of the concepts representing sub-categories or elements of the more major category demonstrates the dimension of each category. It can be seen that the aim of these coding procedures is the development of categories, of demonstrating their dimensions through determining their elements and the identification of a core category. These operations are assisted through the writing of theoretical memos and the drawing of diagrams.

Figure 6.2 represents the GT emerging from my study including the core categories of 'Keeping the patient (and his offence) in mind' and 'Managing a precarious relationship'. Core categories represent the central abstraction that indicates the main theme of the study, consists of all the products of analysis and explains 'what this research is all about' (Strauss and Corbin, 1998, p.146). As discussed previously, in GT core and main categories emerge from the analysis and process of constant comparison, using the different coding strategies, writing analytical and theoretical memos and diagramming to show relationships between themes and concepts.

The first *core category* in my study was *keeping the patient and his offence in mind*. This related to the ways therapists in this setting found themselves constantly thinking about their patients (sometimes whether they wished to or not) and the negative and positive impacts this could have. Gabbard and Wilkinson (1994, p. 19), when discussing the challenges of working with personality disorder, list the potential impact on therapists in terms of powerful countertransference feelings which include 'guilt feelings, rescue fantasies, rage and hatred, worthlessness and helplessness, anxiety and even terror'. It was clear from the therapists' accounts that as a consequence of their work with patients they often found themselves carrying feelings, concerns and anxieties that were at times difficult to process and make sense of. This situation is compounded in the high security setting by the issue of risk associated with the patient's perceived dangerousness and potential for violence. Information about the individual's offence and potential for harming others are also continually held in the therapist's mind to help her/him manage the risk associated with working with this person. The data vividly illustrated how therapists in this setting had to keep in mind the potential dangers of working within this environment. It is not surprising that these thoughts are in conscious awareness as the individual the therapist is meeting is likely to have a history of violence towards others and this behaviour will probably be a central theme of the therapeutic conversation. Going into the therapy room is therefore potentially an anxiety provoking event that the therapist may come to perceive differently as the therapeutic relationship develops and she/he feels increasingly safe.

The second *core category* was related to *managing the precarious nature of this relationship*, which therapists highlighted as a characteristic feature of their work. This was a constant feature of the therapists' work as they became sensitised to and constantly vigilant to the patients' fluctuating levels of engagement and resistance to the therapeutic endeavour. This is particularly relevant as many of the workers acknowledged ambivalence (if not paranoid resistance in some cases) in relation to their involvement in therapeutic work. Additionally, because of their personality difficulties (and often abusive histories) the patients in this setting struggle with forming relationships and find the potential demands of the therapeutic encounter a frightening prospect. They also may not see the relevance of therapy for them but interpret this as a demand that the institution is making of them in order to achieve release to conditions of lesser security. This creates a potentially complex environment in which to develop a working alliance that gains the commitment of the patient and motivates him to carry on working on his problems.

Working with such patients (who are by definition often impulsive and easily emotionally dysregulated) can mean that when the therapist goes into a session he/she is never quite sure with what they will be presented. For example all of the therapists spoke of the fact that in this setting the patient's engagement with treatment and commitment constantly fluctuated. These fluctuations mean that people with histories of offending behaviour and personality difficulties often struggle to maintain their treatment motivation and commonly withdraw from, or reject, therapists with whom they are working (Jones, 2002). The reasons that patients in this setting withdraw from therapy are complicated and need to be understood with reference to engagement histories and behaviour in previous therapeutic contexts (Jones, 2002). It is perhaps useful to make the reader aware of some of the common issues that can lead to these ruptures. These can include a heightening of distress associated with offence disclosure (as part of an offence-focused treatment group); anger with the institution regarding regular infringements of privacy as part of risk management security checks (e.g. room searching); or setbacks associated with discharge or a request for an external visit refused and issues in relationships with peers (e.g. fights, sexual assault, bullying and intimidation) and ward-based staff (conflicts and disagreements about inappropriate behaviour and ward rules). At these points in the patient's life it is very difficult for him to separate the therapist from what he sees as the punitive organisation, resulting in the patient displacing his anger and frustration into the therapeutic encounter.

An example of how the findings are presented

When a specific category and its component parts are being presented in the research report, the researcher usually integrates direct quotes to show how the theme is grounded in the data. A short extract from the findings of the research report discussing the category of *managing vulnerability* and the theme of *desensitising to self-protect* are presented in Box 6.1 to illustrate this.

Box 6.1 **Managing vulnerability**

This category relates to protecting oneself from the inevitable corrosive effects of being exposed to the narratives of patients who have committed violent and sexual offences and have themselves experienced various levels of physical and sexual abuse. As Ryan and Lane (1997, p. 457) observe, 'professionals who interact with dysfunctional populations are at risk personally, socially and professionally'. These risks stem from the realities, the beliefs and attributions of each individual and how they meet the challenge of integrating these experiences into their personal worldview.

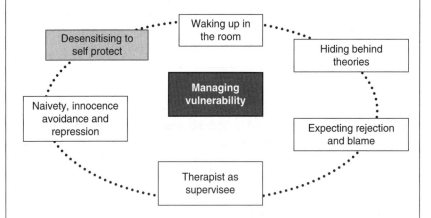

Part of the process of protecting oneself from and integrating these extremes of experience is to become desensitised to the horror of the story being told, as one of the therapists observed, much as a soldier in the front line becomes hardened to the idea of death and killing in order to survive the horrors of war.

> I think sometimes we become dehumanised and insensitive to the actual offences these guys have committed, [it's] easy to see the positive side of them, we are a bit like soldiers who have to deal with death, we deny the reality of what took place.

This individual then went on to explain that this was a necessary feature of working with these men as you need to have some capacity to protect yourself from the overwhelming horror associated with some of the offences they have committed. Other therapists spoke about their sense of at times finding themselves minimising and avoiding thinking about what the person had done as a way of maintaining capacity to work with the person.

Gillian Straker (1993) discusses the concept of 'vicarious traumatisation' of therapists associated with hearing accounts of abuse and violence in routine clinical work. This concept seemed to have some resonance with the participants' accounts where it was acknowledged how their experiences over time (and personal levels of energy) can impact on their capacity to hear (and listen to) offence narratives or the abuse that these men had experienced. Several people spoke of their own struggle to comprehend the accounts of the patients that seemed so alien to their own understandings of human behaviour and experience. As one therapist explained:

> A basic rule for me is that there is a huge amount of the picture that I can't hear, in the same way that I couldn't hear about abuse before [when first being exposed to narratives of abuse before it was realised how prevalent it was]. There is a lot of stuff I am not hearing now and I have got to try and keep open to these other possibilities.

You can see from the illustration in Box 6.1 how the raw data and the researcher's interpretations are integrated with the contemporary literature to create the narrative of the research report. The importance of including the direct quotes is that they demonstrate how the theoretical account has remained 'grounded' and has been developed directly from the data.

The status of interview data and the challenges of constructionist GT analysis

Referring back to the philosophical debates about GT methodology at the beginning of this chapter, I need to acknowledge that the approach I took in this study was situated in the constructionist paradigm. My access to narratives of practice involved the conducting of interviews with 12 selected expert practitioners from a range of forensic mental health disciplines. In the first phase of the project I used an innovative interview methodology to access these personal accounts of clinical experience (Chirban, 1996; McLeod, 2001). This activity was informed by a social constructionist approach to the development of knowledge, which maintains that the interview is an active interpersonal encounter where knowledge, rather than being discovered, is created (Kvale, 1996). In support of this claim Shotter (1994) suggests that a common feature of constructionist thought is the central assumption that, rather than study the inner psychic world of the phenomenologists or the external 'given' reality of the empiricists, we need to concentrate upon and explore the constant communicative activity that takes place *between* human beings. This is an important insight as it challenges the naïve notion that what we obtain in interviews is either some deep inner psychic truth or the objective truth about some observable reality (Miller and

Glasner, 1997). Alternatively, those adopting a constructionist perspective perceive the interview as a social conversation in which versions of 'reality or truth' are not so much accessed as actively constructed (Holstein and Gubrium, 1995, 1997).

A key issue in conducting the interviews was to ensure the participant's account was contextualised. To address this concern I met with all respondents prior to the interview to establish rapport and obtain key biographical data and information related to the individual's current role and clinical approach within the secure environment. The focus in these initial contacts was based on an exploration of the participants' professional and personal approach with particular reference to their therapeutic work. This autobiographical focus helped to situate the participants' accounts of the research phenomena in a social and cultural context, which reflected their personal and professional experience, and use of language. The second interview was tape-recorded and transcribed in full. In this encounter the participant was encouraged to articulate in detail his/her experience of the psychotherapeutic dimension of their client work. This interview was informed by the concept of experiential reflection and critical incident analysis commonly used in the interpersonal process recall methodology of psychotherapy researchers (Toukmanian and Rennie, 1992).

In this study the notions of narrative and participants' meanings were explicitly worked within the structure of the interview process (Seidman, 2006). For example at the biographical starting point I asked participants to adopt a narrative position that offered an account of why they were attracted to working in a secure environment. The second interview encouraged a narrative 'reconstruction' (Etherington, 2001, p. 120) of recent clinical experiences in as much detail as possible. Such an emphasis on narrative structuring was, in my view, particularly helpful as Polkinghorne (1988) suggests this is one of the most common ways humans represent their experience to themselves.

Judging the quality of qualitative research

Current attempts to establish acceptable criteria for judging qualitative research has led to a lively, and at times heated, philosophical discussion regarding how these may be different in emphasis from the more realist-positivist criteria used for quantitative research (see Lincoln and Guba, 1985; Seale, 1999; Hammersley, 2000). When conducting qualitative research, researchers often operate under alternate paradigms such as constructivism and interpretivism. Under the axioms or assumptions that inform these philosophical positions there are multiple realities or multiple truths based on our construction of that reality (Lincoln and Guba, 1985). Furthermore, because the constructivist and interpretivist paradigms dispute that access to reality can be independent from our perceptions of it, claims regarding the truthfulness of accounts become more complex and problematic.

It is important that the criteria that are developed by qualitative researchers acknowledge the methodological and philosophical differences between qualitative and quantitative approaches. For example some of the criteria currently utilised (e.g. member checking and triangulation) assume that different perspectives can be combined to verify 'the truth claim'; on the contrary, qualitative researchers who consider themselves constructivists or interpretivists would accept that because of the subjective positioning of researchers different investigators and participants may yield different versions of 'truth'. What is important is that critical appraisal criteria for assessing qualitative research not only address differences *between* qualitative traditions, but also the variants *within* each of those traditions (Hammersley, 2000). The criteria I used in this research were based on the seminal work of Lincoln and Guba (1985) but further informed by the constructionist critiques of GT (Charmaz, 2006).

Lincoln and Guba consider that terms such as objectivity, reliability and internal and external validity relate to criteria used for judging what they term the 'conventional' paradigm (Lincoln and Guba, 1985, p. 290). These criteria, they assert, are not appropriate for judging actions taken from a different perspective. They suggest that more appropriate criteria with which to judge the trustworthiness of qualitative work, of whether the findings of the study are worth paying attention to, are credibility, transferability, dependability and confirmability. Other writers have taken up these issues (for example Miles and Huberman, 1994; Seale, 1999; Hammersley, 2000) but here Lincoln and Guba's work (1985) will be used as a framework to discuss how issues of trustworthiness were attended to with respect to the present study.

Credibility, according to Lincoln and Guba, takes the place of internal validity of the conventional paradigm and refers to the 'truth value' of the findings. They suggest that activities which make it more likely that credible findings and interpretations are produced are prolonged engagement to learn the culture and gain the trust of the participants, persistent observation in order to identify those elements in the situation most relevant to the research interest and triangulation (using multiple methods and data sources). Lincoln and Guba discuss other issues relating to credibility. These include peer debriefing to provide an external check on the processes of inquiry and member checking to provide a direct test of findings and interpretations from the human sources from which they came, the participants.

When establishing the trustworthiness of qualitative data the researcher attempts to check out that his/her analysis is credible and remains grounded in the data. The use of *peer review* is advocated as one way of managing this process (Lincoln and Guba, 1985). My peer was an experienced qualitative researcher who taught and supervised qualitative research methods within master's and doctoral level programmes in a higher education setting. She reviewed my work in her capacity as a qualitative research expert who did not know the core issues or details of the clinical world I was researching. She provided feedback concerning how my analysis of the data remained grounded in the interview data and was conceptually coherent and understandable to someone who was unfamiliar with this context and the work that therapists were involved with. Willig (2001) argues that peer review is one dimension of ensuring the trustworthiness of one's work.

One of the main strategies I adopted was *member checking* (McLeod, 2001) where I took the analysis of the data back to the participants and asked them to comment on the categories that had emerged. In the first instance each participant was given a copy of their interview transcript before it had been analysed and they were then given a brief diagrammatic representation of the themes that emerged in their accounts. As the researcher, this enabled me to check out and clarify how consistent my interpretations remained with the participants' perspective. When the theory was more developed I invited all the participants to a focus group where we spent two hours discussing and reviewing the emergent theoretical account. These processes enabled me to check the credibility of the account with those who had contributed to the research and then use this feedback in finalising the theory. I also presented the theory at two professional conferences where the audiences responded with positive feedback about how the theory 'spoke to them' and seemed to accurately reflect some aspects of their own clinical experiences.

As a final critical reflection on this member checking process I am aware that the inputs from various sources (participants, peers, professional colleagues) were very confirming of the theory and I did not receive feedback that suggested it was way off the mark or missing things that needed to be said. It could be argued that this may be partly related to the narrative authority that a well-articulated story can acquire when it reveals or touches an individual's experience (McLeod, 2001). Alternatively, my personal and professional relationships with those involved may have inhibited more negative responses. In conclusion I recognise that this type of 'respondent validation' (Silverman, 2001, p. 235) where research participants agree with or confirm the theory may also be reliant on the researcher's analysis remaining compatible with the participants' self-image. I accept that the swamp workers' theory is based on a positive (and therefore flattering) account of the skills and knowledge these practitioners were using in their everyday work, and this may have influenced their willingness to be more critical.

The limitation of returning to the participants to validate the researcher's theory has been humorously addressed in the recent writing of Jennifer Mason (2002, p. 193). In her chapter on making convincing arguments to demonstrate the credibility of qualitative methods she addresses the idea of member checking in terms of people claiming 'epistemological privilege', that is having the right to decide on the truthfulness of a research account. She discusses the experience of the feminist researcher Beverly Skeggs who when returning with her theory to her participants was most commonly faced with the comment 'I can't understand a bloody word of it'. Mason concludes that you cannot assume that asking the participants in your research to check your interpretations provides a quick fix to the problem of interpretative validity! I am therefore comforted by the knowledge that my interpretations of the swamp workers' accounts seemed to have such strong resonance with their personal experiences and epistemological perspectives.

Transferability, in Lincoln and Guba's view, replaces the concept of external validity and so generalisability from the conventional paradigm refers to whether the findings arising from the context studied can be transferred to another. ˹ qualitative researcher makes no claims for his or her context-bound interpr˹ tions being generalisable across contexts, this not being an interest of qualita˹ designs. Rather, the aim is to provide sufficient descriptive data for the reade decide whether it is possible for the findings to be transferred to another con˹ with which the reader is familiar. For me the provision of segments of raw d within the findings while providing as rich a description as possible enables reader to make judgements regarding transferability.

Dependability is the qualitative researcher's equivalent of 'reliability'. Linc and Guba contend that there can be no dependability without credibility, nevertheless consider that a study's dependability should be established al˹ with its credibility. The dependability and the confirmability of a study may a be addressed by an audit trail, which Lincoln and Guba liken to fiscal au˹ undertaken by accountants. They suggest that qualitative researchers can, in or to establish dependability and confirmability and so provide for some open-en˹ judgement of the trustworthiness of the study, employ a research auditor review all documentation: tapes, transcripts, memos, diagrams, theoretical no˹ records of analytical theorising, in fact everything concerned with the study. determine an analytical trail and to attest that the researcher has remained true the data when writing up the findings. If researchers do not have the financial material resources to employ an external auditor, as suggested by Lincoln ˹ Guba (1985), the involvement of a colleague as a peer reviewer could prov˹ you with this.

Lincoln and Guba also suggest that it is necessary that the auditor be able judge the extent to which the researcher's biases may have influenced the fi˹ ings. The technique they suggest is the writing of a reflexive account. Through˹ the research process I remained sensitive to the need to engage reflexively w˹ the way my personal and professional biography informed and influenced ˹ methodological choices and interpretation of the data. I am acutely aware that ˹ personal and professional life course has raised my awareness of key philosop˹ cal and practical dilemmas in the field of psychotherapy practice and resear˹ In recognising this I acknowledged that the interview process and analysis w˹ shaped by my personal constructions and interpretations. It is my belief t˹ I used this theoretical sensitivity in a reflexive and open way, helping ˹ audience(s) to see my part in the construction of the theoretical narratives practice. As advised by Lincoln and Guba, I also provided a reflexive acco˹ showing how my situated understandings emerged from my personal valu˹ beliefs and professional biography.

Some writers (McLeod, 2001) suggest that the trustworthiness of qualitati data can be confirmed by using multiple methods or triangulation of differe methods (e.g. interviews plus participant observation or comparisons with ot˹ data sets). With respect to this study this type of credibility check was not und˹ taken, partly because of the nature of the project and partly because the m˹ constructionist influenced approach to grounded theorising I have adopt encourages scepticism about the notion of triangulation. This ambivalence associated with the implicit positivist assumption that reality is out there and will eventually reveal itself if the researcher employs a diversity of methods and looks hard enough! This is not to suggest that qualitative researchers would not see the usefulness of combining different methods, but rather, they agree with Hammersley and Atkinson (1983, p. 199) who state, 'assuming that aggregating different sources of data will eventually reveal an overall truth is naively optimistic'. As Willig (2001) argues, constructionist grounded theorists acknowledge that they are not so much categorising an existing reality but constructing a version of what is going on through the processes of their research activities.

Conclusion

This chapter has explored the usefulness of using qualitative methodologies in forensic contexts using the example of a GT study that explored the way therapists in high security environments adapt their therapeutic style to meet the challenges of clinical work. It has highlighted how important it is for novice researchers to develop their understanding of the relationship between epistemological positions and methodological choices, showing how different perspectives shape and guide research practice and their justification and defence within the wider academic community. I hope I have shown that whilst one can provide guidance on *how to* conduct GT research, it is essential that those intending to use these methods familiarise themselves with debates in this field and ensure they have the support of a well-informed research supervisor with direct experience of using the approach.

Further resources

Regarding *key resource material* that will help on this journey I feel the following would be particularly useful:

Bryant, A. and Charmaz, K. (Eds) (2007). *The Sage handbook of Grounded Theory*. London: Sage. (Chapter 1.)

Charmaz, K. (2006). *Constructing Grounded Theory: a practical guide through qualitative analysis*. London: Sage. (Chapter 6.)

Coffey, A. and Atkinson, P. (1996). *Making sense of qualitative data: complementary research strategies*. Thousand Oaks, CA: Sage.

Corbin, J. and Strauss, A. (2008). *Basics of qualitative research: techniques and procedures for developing Grounded Theory*. 3rd edn. Thousand Oaks, CA: Sage.

Crotty, M. (1998). *The foundations of social research: meaning and perspective in the research process*. London: Sage. (Chapters 3 and 4.)

Forrester, M. A. (Ed) (2010). *Doing qualitative research in psychology: a practical guide*. London: Sage. (Chapters 2 and 9.)

Glaser, B. G. (1992). *Basics of Grounded Theory analysis*. Mill Valley, CA: Sociology Press.

Glaser, B. G. and Strauss, A. L. (1967). *The discovery of Grounded Theory: strategies for qualitative research*. Chicago: Aldine.

Rennie, D. L. (2001). Grounded theory methodology as methodological hermeneutics: reconciling realism and relativism. *Theory and Psychology*, 10(4): 481–502.

Strauss, A. (1987). *Qualitative analysis for social scientists*. New York: Cambridge University Press.

Strauss, A. and Corbin, J. (1998). *Basics of qualitative research: techniques and procedures for developing Grounded Theory*. 2nd edn. Thousand Oaks, CA: Sage.

References

Blaikie, N. (1993). *Approaches to social enquiry*. Cambridge: Polity Press.

Bryant, A. and Charmaz, K. (Eds) (2007). *The Sage handbook of Grounded Theory*. London: Sage.

Charmaz, K. (1995). Grounded theory. In J. A. Smith, R. Harre and L. V. Langenhove (Eds). *Rethinking methods in psychology* (pp. 27–49). London: Sage.

——(2006). *Constructing Grounded Theory: a practical guide through qualitative analysis*. London: Sage.

Chirban, J. T. (1996). *Interviewing in depth: the interactive relational approach*. London: Sage.

Coffey, A. and Atkinson, P. (1996). *Making sense of qualitative data: complementary research strategies*. Thousand Oaks, CA: Sage.

Corbin, J. and Strauss, A. (2008). *Basics of qualitative research: techniques and procedures for developing Grounded Theory*. 3rd edn. Thousand Oaks, CA: Sage.

Crotty, M. (1998). *The foundations of social research: meaning and perspective in the research process*. London: Sage.

Etherington, K. (2001). Writing qualitative research – a gathering of selves. *Counselling and Psychotherapy Research*, 1(2): 119–26.

Franciosi, P. (2001). The struggle to work with locked up pain. In J. Williams Saunders (Ed). *Life within hidden worlds, psychotherapy in prisons*. London: Karnac Books.

Gabbard, G. O. and Wilkinson, S. M. (1994). *Management of countertransference with borderline patients*. New Jersey: Jason Aronson.

Gergen, K. J. (2001). *Social construction in context*. London: Sage.

Glaser, B. G. (1992*). Basics of Grounded Theory analysis*. Mill Valley, CA: Sociology Press.

—— (2009). *Jargonizing: using the Grounded Theory vocabulary*. Mill Valley, CA: Sociology Press.

Glaser, B. G. and Strauss, A. L. (1967). *The discovery of Grounded Theory: strategies for qualitative research*. Chicago: Aldine.

Gordon-Finlayson, A. (2010). Grounded theory. In M. A. Forrester (Ed) (2010). *Doing qualitative research in psychology: a practical guide*. London: Sage.

Hammersley, M. (2000). *Taking sides in social research: essays on partisanship and bias*. London: Routledge.

Hammersley, M. and Atkinson, P. (1983). *Ethnography: principles in practice*. London: Tavistock.

Holstein, J. A. and Gubrium, J. F. (1995). *The active interview*. Thousand Oaks, CA: Sage.

—— (1997). Active interviewing. In D. Silverman (Ed). *Qualitative research: theory, method and practice* (pp. 113–29). London: Sage.

Jones, L. F. (2002). An individual case formulation approach to the assessment of motivation. In M. McMurran (Ed). *Motivating offenders to change*. Chichester, UK: Wiley.

Kvale, S. (1996). *Interviews: an introduction to qualitative research interviewing.* London: Sage.

Layder, D. (1993). *New strategies in social research: an introduction and guide.* Cambridge: Polity Press.

Lincoln, Y. S. and Guba, E. G. (1985). *Naturalistic enquiry.* Beverly Hills, CA: Sage.

Mason, J. (2002). *Qualitative researching.* London, Sage.

McLeod, J. (2001). *Qualitative research in counselling and psychotherapy.* London: Sage.

—— (2002). *Qualitative researching.* London: Sage.

Miles, M. B. and Huberman, A. M. (1994). *Qualitative data analysis: an expanded sourcebook.* 2nd edn. Thousand Oaks, CA: Sage.

Miller, J. and Glasner, B. (1997). The inside and the outside: finding realities in interviews. In D. Silverman (Ed). *Qualitative research: theory, method and practice* (pp. 99–112). London: Sage.

Polkinghorne, D. E. (1988). *Narrative knowing in the human sciences.* New York: New York University Press.

Rennie, D. L. (1998). Qualitative research: a matter of hermeneutics and the sociology of knowledge. In M. Kopala and L. A. Suzuki (Eds). *Using qualitative methods in psychology* (pp. 3–14). Thousand Oaks, CA: Sage.

—— (2001). Grounded theory methodology as methodological hermeneutics: reconciling realism and relativism. *Theory and Psychology*, 10(4): 481–502.

—— (1994). *Educating the reflective practitioner.* San Francisco: Jossey Bass.

Ryan, G. and Lane, S. (1997). *Juvenile sex offending: causes, consequences and correction.* San Francisco, Jossey Bass.

Schön, D. A. (1987). *Educating the reflective practioner.* San Francisco, Jossey Bass.

Seale, C. (1999). *The quality of qualitative research.* London: Sage.

Seidman, I. E. (2006). *Interviewing as qualitative research: a guide for researchers in education and the social sciences.* 3rd edn. New York: Teachers College Press.

Shotter, J. (1994). Conversational Realities: constructing life through language. Sage: London.

Silverman, D. (2000). *Doing qualitative research: a practical handbook.* London: Sage.

—— (2001). *Interpreting qualitative data: methods for analysing talk text and interaction.* 2nd edn. London: Sage.

Straker, G. (1993). Exploring the effects of interacting with survivors of trauma. *Journal of Social Development in Africa* 8(2), 33–47.

Strauss, A. (1987). *Qualitative analysis for social scientists.* New York: Cambridge University Press.

Strauss, A. and Corbin, J. M. (1994). Grounded Theory methodology: an overview. In N. K. Denzin and Y. S. Lincoln *Handbook of qualitative research* (pp. 273–85). London: Sage.

—— (1998). *Basics of qualitative research: techniques and procedures for developing Grounded Theory.* 2nd edn. Thousand Oaks, CA: Sage.

Toukmanian, S. G. and Rennie, D. L. (1992). *Psychotherapy process research paradigmatic and narrative approaches.* London: Sage.

Willig, C. (2001). *Introducing qualitative research in psychology: adventures in theory and method.* Buckingham: Open University Press.

7 Using qualitative methods to research offenders and forensic patients

Dennis Howitt

The importance of qualitative methods

Throughout most of its history, psychology has been profoundly influenced by the quest for quantification which characterised physical sciences such as physics, chemistry and biology. In contrast, other social sciences disciplines were less influenced by the quantitative imperative. Consequently, disciplines such as sociology were more inclined towards qualitative perspectives. Qualitative research methods have increasingly been seen as an important, if small, part of the agenda for psychological research since the 1980s onwards. Studies indicate that it constitutes just a small percentage of psychological research output (Howitt, 2010). Nevertheless, qualitative methods now represent a clear alternative to the previous dominant forms of research in psychology and can be expected to expand in the future.

Forensic research on offenders and patients would gain from adopting qualitative perspectives. In particular, research benefits from the contextualization that qualitative research can bring. Forensic psychology may have a long past but the substantial part of its history is only three decades or so long (Howitt, 2009). There are topics which are ripe in terms of research potential about which remarkably little is known. A good example of this is theft, which constitutes just about the most frequent crime but is the focus of very little of the research output of psychologists. Qualitative research, with its emphasis on exploration and in-depth data, offers a fertile approach to enhancing our understanding of this everyday and commonplace crime as well as many other aspects of the criminal justice system.

The background of qualitative research in psychology

One fundamental misunderstanding of qualitative methods is that they consist of a number of techniques which can be employed to gather data. So discourse analysis, for example, is regarded as a bunch of procedures which when understood and learnt allow the researcher to analyse language and other forms of 'textual material'. This fails to acknowledge that the metaphysical assumptions of the discourse analyst and most other modern qualitative researchers are very different from those of most mainstream psychology. That is qualitative research is a different approach from knowledge and has very different ideas about what can be achieved through research. Although it is fair to say that during the history of modern psychology some qualitative data collection methods, such as in-depth interviewing and participant observation, have been available to psychologists, relatively formal qualitative data *analysis* methods, such as Grounded Theory, conversation analysis and interpretative phenomenological analysis, have only emerged with any force in psychology since the mid-1980s. So what is essentially new in qualitative research in psychology is the means of analysis not the type of data itself.

Psychology is typically ascribed the description 'positivist' in books on qualitative methods in psychology. However, the term positivism is used in a pejorative and dismissive way in these contexts. Actually, the word is extremely difficult to define and is not consistently employed by authors. Its origins are in the writings of the French sociologist Auguste Comte (1798–1857) (Comte, 1975). Essentially, positivism is the third historical stage through which all disciplines and areas of human knowledge pass or progress. The first stage is when knowledge is based on religion and is established through religious authority; the second stage is based on thought and rationality; and the final stage is essentially the scientific or positivist stage. As used in the qualitative writings, positivism is attributed the following characteristics, amongst others:

- *Realism*: the idea that things in the world are real in the sense that they exist independently of human thought.
- *Reductionist*: rather than take a 'global' view of what is being studied, the hope is to transform observations into something more fundamental – such as by explaining psychological processes in terms of physiological ones.
- *Universalistic*: essentially this means that theories and principles are applicable to all humanity irrespective of where in the world they are located geographically, socially and culturally. This is the idea that psychology can develop general 'laws' which apply irrespective of other considerations.

These may be seen as part of the 'received' view of science in psychology. Probably most psychologists recognise in this some of the characteristics of previous generations of psychologists from the earlier parts of the twentieth century. Nevertheless, it is doubtful that many, if any, quantitative psychologists currently share most of these ideas. It is clearly a caricature employed by qualitative researchers in psychology to define what they are not. So the characteristics of this straw-man quantitative psychologist provide part of the definition of what qualitative researchers are. In a sense, this diverts attention from a major issue – that is, how do we define just what qualitative methods in psychology are? The answer to this is quite elusive since qualitative researchers do not subscribe to a single set of beliefs any more than most mainstream psychologists share the same assumptions about quantitative methods.

However, the view of science held within modern qualitative psychology that science is socially constructed by people who:

- cannot observe directly the 'real' world;
- impose a particular view about the nature of things through science;
- demonstrate only low levels of consensus about the appropriate ways studying the world;
- act collectively as part of a social system which is central to the enterpr known as science.

Stated as directly as this, it is apparent that the view of science from qualitative perspective is very different from that putatively held by the quanti tive researcher. Despite this, the distinctive features of qualitative research psychology are not easily identified. There is no criterion which, without f would distinguish qualitative research from quantitative research. Neverthele broadly speaking, qualitative research may be described as having the follow characteristics (Denzin and Lincoln, 2000; also Bryman, 2004):

- Qualitative research generally rejects hypothesis testing approaches in fav of seeking theory and concepts which 'emerge' out of qualitative data.
- The relationship between the researcher and the researched is compa tively close in qualitative research. Sometimes it is difficult to distingu the researcher from the researched. Qualitative researchers tend to themselves as 'insiders' in terms of the subject of their studies. So it is uncommon to find qualitative research in which the researcher co-operat say, with practitioners to jointly engage in research.
- Qualitative research employs relatively unstructured strategies for carry out research.
- Qualitative researchers use rich and deep textual data rather than the h statistically reliable and valid data which is the preference of the quanti tive researcher. Qualitative researchers assume that a fixed reality does exist and that reality is something constructed by the individual in a soc context.
- The qualitative researcher rejects positivistic approaches and reflects postmodern sensibility.
- Qualitative researchers are concerned to obtain the individual's perspecti They also stress the ideographic approach in which individuals studied as individuals and not merely in comparison to each oth (nomothetic).

Defining some of these concepts is not easy. In particular, quite what 'po modern' is other than a step on from Comte's positivism is not clear. Even suggestion that qualitative researchers reject the idea of a fixed reality (realis fails to capture the range or variety of positions within this amongst qualitat researchers. What can be said, however, is that the above characteristics qualitative research are reflected in varying degrees in the main qualitative research methods. For example the anti-realist stance that there is no single reality results in an emphasis on the variety of different viewpoints that individuals have on aspects of their experience. Thus, rather than seek out a consensual viewpoint on aspects of experience, the qualitative literature tends to celebrate the variety of perspectives. One consequence of this is that qualitative researchers are much more likely to present a 'picture' of an individual than quantitative researchers ever do.

Figure 7.1 provides a little more historical detail on the major qualitative data collection and data analysis methods. See Howitt (2010) for details.

The research question in qualitative research and how it is 'framed'

Deciding whether qualitative methods are appropriate

According to Howitt and Cramer (2011), there are a number of circumstances in which qualitative methods might be employed:

* where there is a paucity or lack of research into a particular research topic;
* where the researcher feels it important to understand something in the complexity of its natural setting;
* when it is difficult to find clarity about appropriate research questions and the key theoretical issues in connection with a particular research topic;
* where the research question involves issues to do with the complex use of language in a social context;
* where here the use of highly structured materials, for example questionnaires, may deter individuals from participating in the research;
* where the researcher has studied qualitative research methods in sufficient detail that they understand what qualitative methods can contribute.

Of course, this list tends to emphasise the exploratory role of qualitative methods in research where hypothesis-testing strategies cannot be employed satisfactorily. However, this dichotomises research into the exploratory and the deductive in a way which does not completely reflect the nature of research in modern psychology. It is probably somewhat better to suggest that qualitative research methods are best employed when data collection cannot be pre-structured and, consequently, the data that is collected is rich, complex and descriptive. But the choice between qualitative and quantitative research methods involves such differences in the basic precepts employed by the researcher that this seems a little inadequate. Qualitative and quantitative research are built on such different principles that the choice will rarely be a difficult one to make. At the same time, it has to be acknowledged that some researchers intrinsically reject one or other of the methods or, at least, have difficulty in understanding the relevance or value of, say, qualitative methods or quantitative methods. The difference between

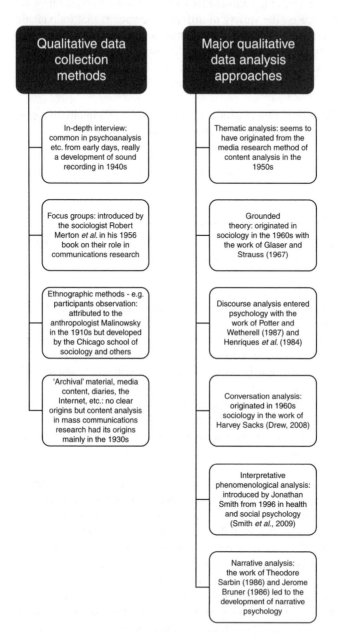

Qualitative data collection methods

In-depth interview: common in psychoanalysis etc. from early days, really a development of sound recording in 1940s

Focus groups: introduced by the sociologist Robert Merton *et al.* in his 1956 book on their role in communications research

Ethnographic methods - e.g. participants observation: attributed to the anthropologist Malinowsky in the 1910s but developed by the Chicago school of sociology and others

'Archival' material, media content, diaries, the Internet, etc.: no clear origins but content analysis in mass communications research had its origins mainly in the 1930s

Major qualitative data analysis approaches

Thematic analysis: seems to have originated from the media research method of content analysis in the 1950s

Grounded theory: originated in sociology in the 1960s with the work of Glaser and Strauss (1967)

Discourse analysis entered psychology with the work of Potter and Wetherell (1987) and Henriques *et al.* (1984)

Conversation analysis: originated in 1960s sociology in the work of Harvey Sacks (Drew, 2008)

Interpretative phenomenological analysis: introduced by Jonathan Smith from 1996 in health and social psychology (Smith *et al.*, 2009)

Narrative analysis: the work of Theodore Sarbin (1986) and Jerome Bruner (1986) led to the development of narrative psychology

Figure 7.1 Different qualitative data collection methods and qualitative data analysis methods set in their historical context.

qualitative and quantitative methods in psychology raises fundamental questions about what psychological research should be. But at a simple level, research involving rich textual data calls for qualitative analysis in most cases, though quantitative analysis is always a possibility for this. Research involving data in a numerical form is not a candidate for qualitative analysis.

Sometimes the situation is presented as if there are two types of researcher – the qualitative researcher and the quantitative researcher. Such a suggestion is probably much more common in psychology than other disciplines where researchers routinely shift from qualitative to quantitative methods and vice versa. Qualitative methods, effectively, are much more recent introductions into psychology and, perhaps, their use is not quite so routinised as in other disciplines. As a consequence, the demarcation between the two appears stronger in psychology.

The loosely framed research questions addressed using qualitative research reflect its exploratory nature compared to the often carefully structured and focused quantitative perspective. In practice this often amounts to the difference between well-explored research areas and ones where little or no previous research is available. Of course, research questions in quantitative research are seen as being built on the outcomes of earlier research. Some qualitative research methods actively eschew this on the grounds that the use of findings from previous research predetermines in various ways the new analysis. Qualitative researchers using Glaser's approach to Grounded Theory would adopt this view as also do many conversation analysts.

Deciding which qualitative method to use

It is too easy to regard different sorts of qualitative methods as fundamentally similar in their basic assumptions. This is far from the truth and the different qualitative research methods address different sorts of research questions. Conversation analysis, for example, is about studying how people go about the process of conversation and, as such, is not generally regarded as suitable for studying in-depth interviews. Equally, it has to be understood that qualitative research methods are not simply another way of addressing the same research questions that quantitative methods are geared towards. Qualitative researchers simply do not sing from the same hymn sheet as quantitative researchers. For example Jonathan Potter (who is a leading figure in discourse analytic research) posed the question of whether discourse analysis provides an answer to any psychological research question. He answered his own question in the following way:

> One of the mistakes that people sometimes make … is to treat discourse analysis as a method that can simply be plugged into a predefined question: for example, 'I am interested in the factors that cause people to smoke: should I use an observational study, an experimental simulation, or discourse analysis?' What this misses is, first, that discourse analysis is not just a

method but a whole perspective on social life and research into it, and, second, that all research methods involve a range of theoretical assumptions. (Potter, 1996, p. 130)

And in a later publication, Potter put the issue more graphically: 'To attempt to ask a question formulated in more traditional terms ('what are the factors that lead to condom use amongst HIV+ gay males') and then use discourse analytic methods to answer it is a recipe for incoherence' (Potter, 2004, p. 607).

This means that researchers cannot simply use a particular qualitative data analysis method to address a particular psychological research question without understanding just what sorts of question that qualitative method is capable of dealing with. We tend to overlook that psychology is so dominated by quantitative research methods that psychologists routinely think quantitatively. In contrast, a qualitative method such as discourse analysis is probably just a name to most psychologists. Discourse analysis is a way of analysing textual material but it is a method which has its own epistemological foundations and a well-developed theoretical base for understanding and studying language as social action. Unless one's research question fundamentally is one about how certain ends are achieved using language then discourse analysis should not be the method of choice. In other words, one is buying into a great deal of theory when a particular qualitative method is adopted.

So in order to understand just what sort of research questions can be addressed by qualitative research methods depends as much on the research method as the nature of the question. The researcher needs to understand a variety of qualitative research methods thoroughly in order to make appropriate choices. The following briefly explains the major focus of the main qualitative data analysis methods used in psychology:

- *Conversation analysis* studies the 'rules' and principles which govern everyday conversation. See Kitzinger and Frith (1999) for a forensic example.
- *Discourse analysis* studies the ways in which language can be seen as social action achieving outcomes. See Benneworth (2006) for a forensic example.
- *Narrative analysis* attempts to understand the storied nature of human experience and the self. See Medlicott (2010) for a forensic example.
- *Interpretative phenomenological analysis* studies how major life events such as illness are experienced. See Meek (2007) for a forensic example.
- *Thematic analysis* attempts to organise the content of textual material into major themes. See Palasinki (2009) for a forensic example.
- *Grounded Theory* is a form of analysis (and to some extent a data collection strategy) which includes a range of methods of generating theory or analysis which closely fits to the data. See Nee (2010) for a forensic example.

It is, of course, very difficult to see what these different approaches to qualitative research in psychology have in common on the face of things. They all involve the use of meaningful, textual data but, apart from that, they are very different. Quite evidently, one would need to dig deeper and understand more about each of the methods before one could confidently make decisions about their use. Indeed, the first four qualitative methods (discourse analysis, conversation analysis, narrative analysis and interpretative phenomenological analysis) can best be seen as very specific areas of research and theory rather than generally applicable methods to psychology. Thematic analysis and Grounded Theory are different in that they are applicable irrespective of the nature of the content to be analysed.

If we consider the major data collection methods used in qualitative research (in-depth interviews, focus groups, participant observation and archival materials) then each of these probably could be used with any of the above data analysis methods in some circumstances – but depending on what the researcher wants to achieve. For example, imagine that the researcher had data in the form of tape recordings of therapeutic interviews between counsellors and their clients. These data clearly could be analysed using thematic analysis which would yield a number of major themes which effectively describe the major content areas of the interviews. On the other hand, these same interviews could be analysed as conversation using conversation analysis. In this case, the researcher might study the ways in which the counsellors brought the therapeutic interview to a close. These are very different ways of analysing the same data.

It is probably helpful here to point out a major difference in qualitative and quantitative research. Quantitative research tends to load the formulation of questions and hypotheses prior to data collection. Usually, these are stimulated by a review of the existing research literature on a topic which then guides what data will be collected. In contrast, qualitative research tends to delay detailed formulation of research questions until after the data have been collected and hypotheses are unlikely to be employed. As a consequence, initially research questions in qualitative research are very loosely framed and may seem to be little more than the identification of topic of research which might prove fruitful. This may appear to be somewhat casual compared to the precision and focus with which quantitative researchers present their hypotheses and so forth.

Design principles and issues

Design principles and issues in qualitative research are radically different in qualitative research from those employed in mainstream quantitative research in psychology. So much so that the qualitative study may seem to verge on the lackadaisical or sloppy to mainstream researchers used to detailed pre-planning prior to data collection and, perhaps, extensive pre-testing of measuring instruments. This does not mean that, in comparison, qualitative methods lack rigour but simply that the structuring of a study tends to fall mainly after data has been collected rather than before. The reasons for this partly lie in the insistence of some qualitative researchers that the analysis should not be predetermined by the existing literature at all – that the role of the literature review is for comparative purposes *after* the analysis is completed.

Richness of data

Another major reason for the relative unstructured data collection methods in qualitative research is the desire to obtain extensive, dense, detailed, rich data rather than carefully focused data to answer focused research questions or even test hypotheses. Structured data and rich data are largely incompatible objectives. This desire of 'rich' data quite clearly means that most of the data collected in the typical quantitative study is inappropriate for a qualitative analysis. The most basic reason for this is that quantitative data is just that – that is, intended to be expressed in terms of numbers. Probably the second most important reason is that the pre-structuring of data collection denies the researcher this required 'richness'. So the question that the qualitative psychologist must ask themselves is just how to ensure that any data they collect achieves the required 'richness'.

In some areas of qualitative research, this is relatively easy. For the conversation analyst the requirement is simply that the data should be a recording of real-life conversation between, essentially, ordinary conversationalists (Liddicoat, 2007). The conversation may be from formal or informal sources so telephone calls to an emergency service and chatter over the back fence are equally viable just so long as there is no or minimal impact from the researcher. Equally, conversation between a counselling psychologist and their client so long as it is recorded as part of a routine therapy session is perfectly acceptable. However, interviews between a researcher and participant set up for research purposes would not be regarded as appropriate for most purposes. The situation is too structured for research purposes and subject to different rules of interaction to count as normal conversation. Even within these strictures, the quantitative psychologist may have difficulty with the mundane nature of acceptable data for conversation analysis. The quantitative researcher is not generally tuned into trying to understand the routine, normal and everyday features of human activity. It is much more likely that they will dwell on relatively unusual circumstances such as mental illness, crises, where things go wrong, abnormalities and so forth. Conversation analysis comes out of a very different intellectual tradition in which the emphasis is much more on the minutiae of social life. For that reason, the data used by conversation analysts often may appear to be mind-numbingly ordinary and trivial. However, what quantitative researchers need to appreciate is the extraordinary analyses which can emerge out of what, to the untrained eye, seems to be merely dull. Another way of putting this is to point out the failures of mainstream psychology to develop our understanding of ordinary life rather than things which are out of the ordinary.

Another approach to ensuring rich data for analytic purposes is to ensure that conventional constraints on data collection are avoided. So ethnographic methods (participant observation) tackles the richness question by encouraging the collection of a wide variety of data from the situation being studied. Although the fieldnotes of the researcher are an important source, the researcher will seek other data sources such as private photographs and documents, interview data with important sources, documents such as newspaper articles and biographical information on the participants in the study. The picture, then, is as full as the researcher can make it. Similarly, the use of focus groups in qualitative research can be seen as a way of enriching the data in certain ways. Focus groups are a form of group interview which encourages the dynamics of social interaction in order to add the interactive component to the data obtained. It is not regarded as a quicker or simpler way of collecting interview data.

So richness and appropriateness of the data is a primary consideration when planning a qualitative research study. So one finds that qualitative studies may be carried out on just one participant especially one who can provide the rich data that qualitative researchers seek. The qualitative researcher often goes about sampling in a way which maximises the richness and quality of the data and its analysis and the representativeness of the participants in the research is not regarded as important. The concept of theoretical sampling is common in qualitative research and is drawn from Glaser and Strauss's Grounded Theory. It refers to the process by which a qualitative researcher chooses new cases or even research locations in ways which are likely to push and challenge the analysis as it has developed at a particular stage of the research. So in quantitative research, the representativeness of the sample of a population is a key objective but many qualitative researchers would reject this entirely in favour of an approach to sampling which is about testing the analysis. So ideas which the researcher starts to develop about the role of families in the experience of prison life among those who have partners and families might be tested and examined critically by extending the sample to include offenders who have been divorced while in prison, for example. Theoretical sampling is a form of purposive sampling which seeks to improve the quality of the theory and analytic ideas which are being developed during the course of the research though it is a concept which sometimes is applied to the planning of data collection at the start of the research. So theoretical sampling has as its primary purpose the testing and the elaboration of theory as it is developing during the course of the research and, in particular, the analysis process. The use of traditional research methods concepts is difficult here because in Grounded Theory data collection and data analysis are mutually interactive processes and not the distinct stages that mainstream quantitative research holds them to be. The areas which are sampled are the ones which are particularly pertinent to the analytic developments at a particular point in time. Thus sampling in qualitative research can deliberately seek out the atypical or the difficult case as a way of interrogating and testing theoretical developments. In quantitative research, such atypical or difficult cases tend to be dismissed as outliers and not part of what is to be understood.

Grounded Theory, even where it is not acknowledged, has had an important influence on most methods of qualitative data analysis. For example, in interpretative phenomenological analysis it is common to collect interview data from just a small number of participants. Just one of these interviews is then subjected to an analysis. Only when this is complete does the researcher then move on to another of the interviews which may be analysed independently initially but then comparatively. In other words, in qualitative research the emphasis is much more on testing the analysis than the data.

There is another facet to rich data which is fairly commonly found in qualitative research. That is, contextualising data gathered from a variety of sources is included in qualitative research reports. In other words, it is more common in qualitative research to include information about the individual participant's characteristics. Sometimes, for example, one finds tables which list key characteristics of each participant. Other qualitative research may include extensive biographic detail of the participants.

How much data to collect?

In mainstream psychology the aim generally is to collect data from enough participants so that important trends in the data are shown to be statistically significant which is the gold standard or acid test for quantitative research. Sample sizes should be sufficiently large to ensure this and it is frowned upon to use small numbers of participants because the data are insufficient to allow this. Specialised areas of statistics such as power analysis have been developed to allow researchers to obtain the optimum balance between obtaining statistical significance and economical sample sizes. No such criteria apply in qualitative methods in psychology, of course, so at what point does the qualitative researcher stop collecting data? It has to be said that some, if not all, qualitative researchers are happy presenting the analysis of a single case such as a single interview. This is common in interpretative phenomenological analysis, narrative analysis and conversation analysis. In the latter case, a very short sequence of conversation may be all that is studied. Quite simply, this is satisfactory in the qualitative ethos because of the richness of the analysis which accompanies what in quantitative terms would probably be seen as woefully inadequate amounts of data. The qualitative methods literature, nevertheless, tends to dwell on the idea of theoretical saturation (sometimes just referred to as 'saturation') which again stresses the interactive nature of the relationship between data and analysis in qualitative research. Theoretical saturation refers to the point in the analysis when nothing new is being learnt from additional data – that is, the analysis to that point is not challenged or added to in any way by additional cases. For the qualitative researcher, this is the point when data collection can sensibly be abandoned. This is only possible when data collection is closely linked to data analysis which is not the case in quantitative research. In quantitative research, at least in its classical formulation, data collection is complete when sufficient data have been gathered to allow the null hypothesis to be falsified. However, these things are specified in advance of the data being collected, they are not consequent on what emerges from the data.

The role of the researcher in qualitative research

One design principle in qualitative research is that the researcher has to be responsible for the analysis of their data. In quantitative research, it would not be surprising or unusual to find that the researcher farms out aspects of the data collection and data analysis to other people. Employing interviewers and statistics specialists would not be an uncommon or an unacceptable strategy. This is possible because the input of the researcher in quantitative research is overwhelmingly at the planning stage which means that there is flexibility to use hired hands for the routine interviewing, coding and similar tasks and number crunching specialists. Qualitative research, almost by definition, does not involve such detailed pre-structuring and planning. There is generally a much more intuitive feel to the data collection process which depends on the skills of the researcher at conducting interviews or running focus groups and the researcher's resourcefulness and adaptability while seeking the richest data possible. This does not mean that all qualitative research is conducted throughout by the researcher though it is most certainly the ideal expressed in the qualitative research literature. The immersion of the researcher in the data collection process allows for flexibility (and regrouping if necessary) but, more importantly, it is an important step towards achieving the close familiarity with the data to enable the analysis to proceed. The quantitative researcher does not generally aim for this familiarity since the essential nature of the data has been predetermined and pre-structured in the planning process. Although quantitative research can involve data exploration, more generally the task is to test one's prior ideas against the data.

Data familiarisation is also achieved through the slow and laborious process of data transcription. Data in the form of sound recording (and video) is almost invariable turned into a transcript which is the basis of almost all qualitative data analysis. Transcripts range quite considerably in what is transcribed from the recording. Simple secretarial or playscript transcripts are simply the words which are said and who says them. A great deal is left out of these. Other transcription methods attempt to include much more than the words which are said – for example the tone, style, pitch, intensity and so forth may be included as well as things such as overlapping speech. The most familiar transcription method of this sort is that developed by Gail Jefferson which is virtually mandatory in conversation analysis studies and some forms of discourse analysis (see Jefferson, 2010, for examples of her work and details of her transcription method). If you have not seen a Jefferson-style transcription before, the following is from Benneworth (2004) and is part of one of her detailed transcriptions of police interviews with paedophiles. This section concerns pornographic pictures:

```
370 DC:    So you felt confident about showing them to (.)
371        Lucy whereas you wouldn't have shown them to
```

372   [your wife].
373 Susp: [yeah I was] I was (3.8) s:exually (0.8) umm
374   (4.0) unconfident anymore about sex and Lucy
375   showing an interest in me and that was
376   flattering in itself and.hhh cos there was no
377   sexual relationships with my wife.

Apart from the words said, this transcription system includes overlaps in speech (denoted by words in square brackets []), pauses denoted by numbers of seconds in brackets (3.8) and extended sounds as in s:exually. The system is complex and no more than a brief illustration can be given here.

Estimates vary greatly but probably ten hours of transcription time is needed for every hour of recording transcribed. However, data familiarisation is an inevitable by-product of the effort devoted to transcription. Where transcription is not involved, the researcher will need to read and reread the text to achieve the same degree of familiarity. There is no clear end-point for data familiarisation since the qualitative researcher will refer back on numerous occasions during the analysis to the transcript or even the original recording from which the transcript was made. Fidelity to the original source is regarded as very important in qualitative research and for this reason the notes made by interviewers during an interview would be regarded as suspect but also greatly lacking in detail and impossible to verify against the data.

Whereas the researcher in quantitative research is regarded as essentially detached, objective and, perhaps, clinical, the researcher in qualitative research is regarded as being involved personally in the research process and, thus, experiences emotions, has thoughts, has preferences and so forth. For this reason, qualitative research reports frequently contain a great deal of subjective material about how the researcher felt and reacted. The qualitative researcher may well keep a diary or notes about their experiences. So a qualitative researcher interviewing a sex offender or anyone about a distressing topic ought to be aware of their thoughts and feelings and the difficulties of the research situation. This would be regarded as important data and relevant to the write-up of the research. It is not regarded as a nuisance to be ignored and smoothed out of the final report. Furthermore, the qualitative researcher should anticipate that there are likely to be difficulties in their research and take steps to deal with issues consequent to the researcher. For example discussing one's interviews with a supervisor, peers or even a close friend if this is ethically possible can be built into the process. Team work might be the ideal way of dealing with such issues. This may also have pay-offs in terms of the analysis.

Of course, the quality of qualitative research will depend, in part, on the rigour with which the analytic stages are carried out but, equally, the training and experience of the analyst contributes to the quality of the study. This is true of all research, quantitative and qualitative, and need not be dwelt on here. Insight and inspiration are among the less tangible factors involved.

Constant comparison

One fundamental characteristic of nearly all qualitative data analysis is constant comparison. Essentially, this is the process of continual checking of the analysis against the data, the data against itself and the analysis against itself – and eventually the analysis against other similar analyses. Generally, the most common form of constant comparison involves checking the analysis against the data. There are no rules governing when this occurs and it is typical of qualitative analysis that the analysis is not deemed finished until the report of the study is finalised. Many writers on qualitative methods in psychology stress the importance of deviant cases as a stimulus to the greater refinement of the analysis. So unlike quantitative research in psychology where the focus is on the 'reliable' variance in the data, the qualitative researcher seeks to understand all of the data so far as it is relevant to the topic of the study. Of course, not all research reaches this high ideal but this principle can serve to guide the qualitative researcher in terms of how far to push the analysis.

Coding

The term 'coding' is virtually universal in qualitative data analysis of all sorts with the possible exception of conversation analysis. This is not quite the unitary concept that it appears to be at first and it is used in a number of different senses. Some discourse analysts use the term for the process of collecting together examples of particular discursive practices which attract the researcher's interest. However, in thematic analysis, Grounded Theory and interpretative phenomenological analysis it has a somewhat different meaning. In each of these cases it refers to the development of interpretative categories which are increasingly generally applicable as the analysis proceeds. Grounded Theory, for example, has several different types of coding – e.g. in vivo coding, axial coding, open coding and selective coding which differ basically in terms of the level of generality involved. Grounded Theory is complex and a little incoherent so anyone wishing to know more about the different methods of coding involved should consult a more specialised source (e.g. Henwood and Pidgeon, 2003; Payne, 2007).

There is nothing magical about the development of coding categories – it is all down to the intellectual sweat of the researcher. Usually coding proceeds by taking a line of data at a time and re-expressing that line in a new way. This is more-or-less a process of providing a somewhat more abstract summary of what the line contains. Line lengths are largely arbitrary and there is no reason why several lines cannot be coded rather than a single line. Unfortunately, published examples of coding are rare and there is a tendency to mystify the process. However, if we take the first line of the transcribed snippet above then the first line 'So you felt confident about showing them to (.)' might be coded 'showing child porn unproblematic'. This is almost simply what the offender said put in different words. The point is that each line has been processed and an attempt has been made to turn the raw data into something more abstract. The method of constant comparison is employed to compare these individual codings one with another in order to consolidate them into the same coding category wherever this is appropriate. It is not the expectation in qualitative research that different researchers analysing the same data will come up with largely identical analyses. Postmodernism celebrates the variety of perspectives on the world and this applies as much to analysts as participants in research.

Qualitative researchers use a number of different analysis aids varying from the use of computer software programs such as NVivo to sorting elements of the data using extracts written on postcards. Writing a sort of diary (memos) of ideas which strike the researcher as he or she proceeds through the analysis is particularly emphasised in the Grounded Theory approach. Mind-maps trying to link different elements of the data conceptually or any other table or chart may be employed as a resource. These basically provide a more systematic approach to the processing of data to highlight issues.

Presentation of findings

There is one design feature in virtually all qualitative research which rarely, if ever, is to be found in the typical quantitative psychology study. Qualitative researchers typically give substance to their analyses by providing illustrative quotations from their data. Sometimes this is accompanied by more detail about individual participants in the research than characteristically appears in quantitative research reports. All of this is part of a more contextualised approach to research among qualitative researchers. One problem with illustrative quotes from the quantitative point of view is the question of representativeness. This is very much a quantitative perspective in itself and one which qualitative researchers with their emphasis of the multiplicity of perspectives on reality tend not to dwell upon for obvious reasons. With this in mind, it becomes less important for the examples to be representative and more important that they are illustrative of the analysis. Hence, when it comes to selecting examples their fit to the analysis is generally presented as the most crucial thing. The illustrative quotation is also about the validity of the analysis. The whole question of validity in qualitative research is mainly regarded as a matter of the validity of the analysis and not the validity of the data which, from a postmodern perspective is a somewhat misconstrued idea. Since there are multiple perspectives on reality according to the qualitative viewpoint, it is meaningless to apply ideas about validity derived from the quantitative approach which often implies (if not assumes) that there is a fixed reality which is tapped through research. As a consequence, the idea of triangulation is frequently mentioned in discussions of the validity of qualitative methods, though it is far more difficult to find triangulation employed. Triangulation is the procedure by which different data sources or analytic procedures are compared to see whether they generate similar outcomes. This is common in quantitative research. The status of triangulation in qualitative research is undermined by the assumption of multiple realities.

However, researchers coming to qualitative methods from a quantitative base may find traditional ideas about reliability and validity (including triangulation) useful in relation to their work. Similar comments would apply to issues such as inter-rater reliability, which is very much a quantitative approach rather than a qualitative one. The judgement has to be one of whether agreement between raters is an important criterion in individual cases rather than the variety of perspectives which would be the key thing from a pure postmodern qualitative perspective. Again, questions of the transferability of findings from a qualitative study to other contexts are less important in the qualitative rather than the quantitative perspective. Typically, qualitative researchers will compare the details of their analysis with those of other analysts but without accepting the quantitative viewpoint that analytic differences indicate methodological flaws rather than the diversity of versions of reality.

Ethics

The ethical status of qualitative research is complex. There is a prospect, in qualitative research, of violating ethical principles due, largely, to the detail which is provided about participants in research which may make them vulnerable or exposed. Qualitative researchers present their analyses in considerable depth and, not infrequently, adopt a case study approach. Each of these may provide sufficient information, especially in notorious forensic cases, by which the reader may identify the participant. To some extent, such problems may be reduced by anonymising the information provided, but there are distinct limits to the effectiveness of this. Furthermore, in the course, say, of an in-depth interview the participant may introduce information about new crimes which may need to be reported to the prison authorities because of the 'contract' of the researcher with the organisation which permits the research. Furthermore, data which are not collected in an anonymised form are subject to data protection legislation which requires a number of additional safeguards to protect the data from inappropriate scrutiny. The preference of some qualitative researchers for recorded interviews may enhance the risk to the participants of being identified.

Figure 7.2 summarises some key features of carrying out qualitative research.

The types of data analysis methods

Howitt (2010) distinguishes between data collection and data analysis methods in qualitative research. This simple distinction is important since it makes clear that data analysis is less dependent on the data collection method in qualitative research than is the case in quantitative research where the way in which data are collected strongly determines the method of analysis. In qualitative research, the data collected tend to have been obtained in a limited number of ways though there is more variety in the data analysis method than for its collection. The one overriding requirement for data in qualitative research is that they consist of extensive, rich, detailed, textual material such as in-depth interviews, focus group

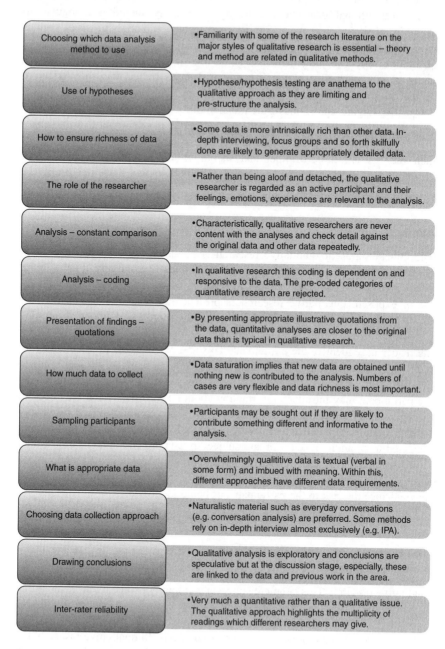

Figure 7.2 Key aspects of qualitative research methods.

interviews, field notes, recordings of natural conversation and more archival material such as materials taken from the media, the internet, diaries and such sources. These can all be described as text which is the term used in qualitative research to refer to any data rich in meaning. There is no reason why this has to be language data but it usually is in qualitative psychology. Visual data such as video can be used, therefore, so long as they meet the requirement of being rich in meaning, though to date visual data are fairly uncommon in qualitative psychology.

Different types of qualitative data analysis have more affinity for certain sorts of data collection methods than others. Not all data analysis methods are equally suitable for every data collection method. Figure 7.3 gives some basic indications of the relation between data and data analysis in qualitative methods. As can be

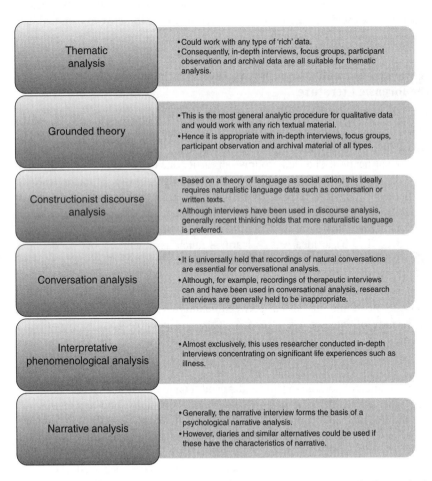

Figure 7.3 The relation between data and data analysis for the major qualitative methods used in qualitative psychology.

seen, some analysis methods are fairly generic such as Grounded Theory
thematic analysis. Other analysis methods require particular types of data.
example conversation analysis specifically requires recordings of naturali
conversation and tends to eschew the use, say, of in-depth interviews des
some authorities claiming that these are conversational in nature. The prefe
data are not, in this case, a particular sort of content but any sort of conten
long as it is recording of natural conversation. Quite different is the case
narrative analysis which requires data which are detailed in terms of hav
a narrative structure linking life experiences, for example, to personality and s
Suitable narrative accounts could emerge in everyday conversation and in-de
interviews – or even from archival material such a diaries or autobiograph
Once again, the nature of the content of the data is more important than any o
characteristic. None of this is self-evident and researchers need a somew
sophisticated understanding of different qualitative data analysis methods
order to make sense of the intricacies of the relationship between data and c
analysis in qualitative research.

A worked example of qualitative research from
the forensic literature

A relevant example from the forensic literature is Sheldon and Howitt (20(
This is a study of internet sex offenders compared with contact sex offend
Unusually, the study mixes together elements of the qualitative methodol
with quantification. The study follows an earlier one by Howitt (1995). Altho
it is difficult to believe given the copious amounts of sex offender resea
available nowadays, at this time there was not a great deal of published resea
which attempted to understand paedophile behaviour. So this study adop
the qualitative tactic of in-depth interviews with a number of paedopl
offenders. The basic idea was to learn as much as possible about paedoph
and their behaviour from as wide a perspective as possible. This study adop
a fairly generic qualitative approach rather than any of the qualitative anal
methods discussed in this chapter. In contrast, Sheldon and Howitt (20
chose to move into the 'space' between qualitative and quantitative methods
their study of internet sex offenders. This was possible because quantitat
research into sex offending had made enormous strides in the years betw
the two studies. Much of this research is discussed in Ward *et al.* (2005). Hav
this research available meant that more focused comparisons could be m
between internet pornography offenders and 'conventional' contact paedophi
The fundamental strategy of the research was to combine both qualitative
quantitative data collection methods. The qualitative data was based on in-de
interviews which, although involving a standard basic structure, allowed
exploration of matters which arose spontaneously in the interviews. The quanti
tive data collection was based on structured questionnaires designed to meas
such concepts as sexual fantasy and cognitive distortions. The quantitat
data were collected before the in-depth interviews and were used, if releva

during the interviews. In other words, there was an opportunity to interrogate quantitative data qualitatively.

Of course, in many ways this then is not typical of the vast majority of qualitative research in psychology which positively eschews the use of quantification. On the other hand, the linking of qualitative and quantitative research constructively in the same study is, arguably, one way of building on the strengths of the two approaches. For the qualitative data, the analysis strategy was based on thematic analysis. Quite clearly approaches such as discourse analysis and conversation analysis were not appropriate. One reason for this was that the researchers were not interested in the interviews as conversation and another was that research interviews tend to be seen as inappropriate sources of data for these qualitative analysis methods. Interpretative phenomenological analysis and narrative analysis would be possible methods for analysing the interview data since they contain both descriptions of how significant life events are experienced as well as narrative accounts of the offenders' lives. Despite this, the researchers had no interest in 'buying into' the theory associated with these two approaches to qualitative data analysis. Furthermore, the study involved many more participants than would be normally the case with interpretative phenomenological analysis and narrative analysis. Both of these methods of qualitative analysis employ procedures to help identify major themes and subthemes in interviews. The researchers actually chose to use thematic analysis since this is less dependent on the availability of pre-existing theory and suited to larger studies. Grounded Theory was not employed as the data collection approach was not directed towards testing ideas as they emerged during the course of the study.

The qualitative analysis was not averse to quantification and some effort was made to ensure that the themes (or codes) developed during the thematic analysis were defined well enough to allow some quantitative analysis of the data. This was as simple as basic frequency counts of the occurrence of each theme but also involved, on occasion, the testing of relationships based on the qualitative themes. Again, this is not typical of most qualitative research. It does, of course, require that the analysis is sufficiently rigorous that what participants have to say can be reasonably objectively coded. The study was firmly qualitative in terms of being exploratory about topics which are poorly understood in the sex offender research literature. So much of the data collection used relatively unstructured questioning that generated the sort of rich, detailed 'textual' data which is favoured by qualitative researchers. At the same time, the researchers were reluctant to 'reinvent the wheel' for topics which have been well-developed by researchers.

Table 7.1 gives more information about the study and how it can be perceived from the perspective of qualitative research.

Evaluation of qualitative methods

It is a basic truism that qualitative research does not replace quantitative research but, rather, supplements it and provides a radically different perspective on

Table 7.1 Some key issues concerning qualitative methods in the Sheldon and Howitt (2007) research

Issue	How dealt with	Relevance to qualitative methods
How was the hypothesis/ research question framed and why?	The research interest grew out of the observation that offenders who used the internet were becoming clients of the probation service. How do they use the internet and are there differences between these offenders and regular contact offenders? Thus the exploratory emphasis of qualitative research (as opposed to hypothesis testing) characterised the research from the start.	The research used both qualitative and quantitative approaches. Comparisons between different types of offenders and statistical methods such as factor analysis are decidedly quantitative in tone but included in their analysis. Simple counts of qualitative codes were feasible and were employed to enhance the rigour of the study.
How were participants sampled?	Like much qualitative research, no attempt was made to randomly sample from the population in question. At the time of the research, the numbers of offenders convicted of internet sexual offences were small. However, attempts were made to recruit as widely as possible, though the extent of co-operation by probation and prison organisations restricted this.	A total of 51 participants took part. Although basically adequate for a quantitative study, the number of participants was comparatively large in terms of the typical qualitative study. The advantage of the larger sample size was that it permitted the closer integration of the quantitative and qualitative approaches.
How were participants recruited?	Where an organisation's co-operation was obtained, key contacts in the organisation 'recruited' participants through various forms of advertising, including a prison 'TV channel'.	Although ideally participants for the study would be chosen so that all types of sex offender were included, the decision of some institutions not to take part might limit the data in significant but unknowable ways. There was no opportunity to optimise the data in the light of trends identified early in the analysis.
What ethical considerations were involved?	Potentially the study might reveal identificatory information despite anonymisation of any interview excerpts presented. However, quotations from the data were brief and many different offenders were quoted, reducing potential difficulties.	Until data is fully anonymised, it has to be stored and used within the restrictions of the Data Protection Act (1998).
What was the role of the researcher?	The researcher carried out all of the stages including interviewing and transcription personally in order to maximise data familiarity.	Unlike much qualitative research, the role of the researcher in this study was relatively distanced with respect to the participants and there was no joint development of the research as one would expect given the subject matter of the study.

What form of transcription was employed?	All interviews were recorded and transcribed, as encouraged in qualitative research, by the interviewer. The transcription focused on the words used and many of the features of Jefferson transcription such as overlapping speech and pauses were omitted. The words stressed by the speaker and implied punctuation were recorded. No tidying up of errors etc. was employed.
	The study did not concentrate on language as such but on the events described and experienced by the offender. As a consequence, the finely detailed analysis of spoken language used in much qualitative research was of no interest.
Why was thematic analysis chosen?	Unlike some other forms of qualitative data analysis, thematic analysis does not link directly to an established body of research literature. The only other qualitative research method with this characteristic would be grounded theory, which could have been used as an alternative. Thematic analysis is a set of procedures for developing a number of codes or themes to summarise important aspects of the data.
	Although thematic analysis primarily develops a set of codes or themes, this does not preclude the development of more general theoretical arguments based on the data. This was done in this study, thereby drawing similarities with grounded theory. For example, the use of a wide variety of data sources including quantitative ones is redolent of grounded theory. However, grounded theory tends to adopt special procedures in terms of sampling especially which were not used in this case.
How were the data coded?	Some parts of the analysis were pre-coded in ways similar to quantitative analysis. However, this was not possible or desirable for the vast bulk of the semi-structured interview data. For this, three coding stages were used: 1) first level descriptive coding which briefly summarised literally a line or two of the transcript; 2) second level coding took the descriptive codes to a more interpretative level which imposed a degree of meaning to the descriptions; and 3) third level thematic coding which, for this study, drew on existing theory as well as the interpretative codes developed from the data.
	Quite clearly the analysis in this study does not represent the purest form of qualitative analysis though this, in general, probably typifies modern qualitative research. There was no attempt to carry out the analysis ignorant of theory in the field of sex offending but, at the same time, the research did not simply dredge for examples of pre-existing categories or themes in the data. Inevitably, though, there was some overlap.
How were the findings presented?	The findings of this study were presented in a wide variety of forms. Material which could be presented in a quantified form was presented much as it would be in any quantitative study. Nevertheless, much of the analysis was qualitative in nature. Primarily this was presented using illustrative quotations from a variety of participants although frequencies were presented wherever possible. Definitions of the themes identified were given when appropriate.
	In terms of the qualitative material, the findings illustrated the major themes which were developed in the analysis. Obviously, given the substantial numbers of participants, it was not possible to provide an in-depth view of each of them though the illustrative quotations came from a wide range of participants. Nevertheless, like most qualitative research, the study was able to contextualise the findings much more effectively than in most quantitative research.

psychology. It is important to regard qualitative research as a method in its own right and not merely a preliminary to research prior to quantification. Indeed, qualitative research can be used to provide substance to quantitative findings. However, these alone fail to appreciate the developments at both the theoretical and analytic levels which have characterised the growth in qualitative methods in psychology during the last three decades, especially. The strengths of qualitative research lie in its radically different epistemological foundations from those of quantitative methods; by the same token, the weaknesses of qualitative methods are the consequence of the same epistemological roots. It is probably incorrect to assume that the strengths of qualitative methods simply cancel out the weaknesses of quantitative methods. The failings of quantitative methods cannot, somehow, be compensated for by qualitative methods and vice versa. For example, it is not possible to use qualitative methods to answer questions of causality where a quantitative method has failed to do so. Similarly, it is not always possible to turn a qualitative analysis into a quantitative one simply by attempting to quantify the major features of the qualitative analysis.

At this stage of the development of qualitative research methods in psychology it is more important to appreciate that by adopting a qualitative approach to your research then you are buying into not just a different way of doing research but a whole different perception of what research should be about. So qualitative methods cannot be adopted by mainstream psychology researchers without considerable efforts being made to understand not only the point of qualitative data collection methods but also the analytic procedures involved and, often, the considerable caucus of theoretical work which has been built up in a particular field of qualitative research. Qualitative methods pose a considerable challenge to all psychologists since they demand a revision of the ways in which research questions are asked and addressed.

Future directions

Qualitative methods have become increasingly popular in a number of areas of social research. While it is not possible to argue that qualitative methods have made big inroads into forensic research, as yet, there is at least one review of the contribution of qualitative methods to forensic research (Bannister, 2008). One of their big advantages is that they produce analyses which are expressed in ways which users of research can readily understand. The participants in research are the primary source of ideas that eventually become part of the concepts which the researcher generates as part of the analysis. The ability of the qualitative researcher to relate their analyses back to the words which their participants use makes qualitative research especially pertinent to policy and decision makers.

In this chapter we have seen the range of qualitative research methods which have been developed in qualitative psychology. Many of these have applications in forensic psychology, and more to the point their use would enrich the discipline. It hardly needs to be said that forensic psychology has achieved remarkable progress in the last two or three decades because of its achievements in terms of helping to provide solutions to problems for the criminal justice system, such as those associated with eyewitness testimony, interviewing, crime scene analysis and so forth. Some of these are also worthy candidates for qualitative approaches, especially given their fundamentally textual nature. For example does an interviewee who is lying use different conversational devices during police interviews?

More generally, there is a case for the use of qualitative research methods as an exploratory tool more generally in forensic psychology. While it is not unknown for forensic psychologists to carry out pilot work of various sorts as a preliminary to their research studies, what is being proposed here is that qualitative analysis methods provide a more systematic form of analysis. Because of the general nature of qualitative research with its emphasis on giving a voice to the research participants, inevitably the use of qualitative research methods with offenders and forensic patients would bring with it the challenge of how to present their perspectives in the context of forensic psychology. Furthermore, how influential the qualitative approach would be depends to an extent on its acceptability to policy makers. It is notable the extent to which qualitative research in other areas of psychological research has proven acceptable to policy makers.

Acknowledgements

Thank you to those who read and commented on the draft chapter – especially Jennifer Gallagher whose perspective was particularly valuable. None of you should feel too guilty. Just a little bit.

Recommended texts

Howitt, D. (2010). *Introduction to qualitative methods in psychology*. Harlow: Pearson Education.
Smith, J. (Ed) (2008). *Qualitative psychology: A practical guide to research methods*. 2nd edn. London: Sage.
Willig, C. (2008). *Introducing qualitative research in psychology*. 2nd edn. Maidenhead: Open University Press.

General reading on qualitative methods including web resources

Antaki, C. (2002). An introductory tutorial in conversation analysis. Online at Antaki, C. (n.d.) An introductory tutorial on conversation analysis. Available from www-staff. lboro.ac.uk/~sscal/ (accessed 17/3/10).
Arribas-Ayllon, M. and Walkerdine, V. (2008). Foucauldian discourse analysis. In C. Willig and W. Stainton-Rogers (Eds). *The Sage handbook of qualitative psychology* (pp. 91–108). Los Angeles, CA: Sage.

Ashworth, P. (2008). Conceptual foundations of qualitative psychology. In J. A. Smith (Ed). *Qualitative psychology: a practical guide to research method* (pp. 4–25). 2nd edn. London: Sage.

Birkbeck College, University of London (2009). Interpretative phenomenological analysis. Available from www.ipa.bbk.ac.uk/references (accessed 16/3/10).

Braun, V. and Clarke, V. (2006). Using thematic analysis in psychology. *Qualitative Research in Psychology*, 3: 77–101.

Dawson, S. and Manderson, L. (n.d.) A manual for the use of focus groups. Available from www.unu.edu/unupress/food2/UIN03E/UIN03E00.HTM (accessed 16/3/10).

Eatough, V. and Smith, J. A. (2008). Interpretative phenomenological analysis. In C. Willig and W. Stainton-Rogers (Eds). *The Sage handbook of qualitative psychology* (pp. 179–94). Los Angeles: Sage.

Henwood, K. and Pidgeon, N. (2003). Grounded theory in psychological research. In P. M. Camic, J. E. Rhodes and L. Yardley (Eds). *Qualitative research in psychology: expanding perspectives in methodology and design* (pp. 131–56). Washington, DC: American Psychological Association.

Krueger, R. A. and Casey, M. A. (2009). *Focus groups*. 4th edn. Thousand Oaks, CA: Sage.

Murray, M. (2008). Narrative psychology. In J. A. Smith (Ed). *Qualitative psychology: a practical guide to research methods* (pp. 111–32). 2nd edn. London: Sage.

O'Reilly, K. (2009). *Key concepts in ethnography*. London: Sage.

Penn Anthropology (n.d.). How to do ethnographic research: a simplified guide. Available from www.sas.upenn.edu/anthro/anthro/cpiamethods (accessed 16/3/10).

Potter, J. and Hepburn, A. Transcription. Available from www-staff.lboro.ac.uk/~ssjap/transcription/transcription.htm (accessed 16/3/10).

Riessman, C. K. (n.d.). Narrative analysis. Available from http://eprints.hud.ac.uk/4920/2/Chapter_1–Catherine_Kohler_Riessman.pdf (accessed 16/3/10).

Ten Have, P. (2007). *Doing conversation analysis: a practical guide*. London: Sage.

Wiggins, S., and Potter, J. (2008). Discursive psychology. In C. Willig and W. Stainton-Rogers (Eds). *The Sage handbook of qualitative psychology* (pp. 73–90). Los Angeles, CA: Sage.

References

Bannister, P. (2008). Forensic psychology. In C. Willig and W. Stainton-Rogers (Eds). *The Sage handbook of qualitative research in psychology* (pp. 505–23). London: Sage.

Benneworth, K. (2004). A discursive analysis of police interviews with suspected paedophiles. Doctoral dissertation (Loughborough University, England).

—— (2006). Repertoires of paedophilia: conflicting descriptions of adult–child sexual relationships in the investigative interview. *The International Journal of Speech, Language and the Law*, 13(2): 190–211.

Bruner, J. (1986). *Actual minds, possible worlds*. Cambridge, MA: Harvard University Press.

Bryman, A. (2004). *Social research methods*. 2nd edn. Oxford: Oxford University Press.

Comte, A. (1975). *Auguste Comte and positivism: the essential writings*. G. Lenzzer (Ed). Chicago, Illinois: University of Illinois Press.

Denzin, N. K. and Lincoln, Y. S. E. (2000). Introduction: the discipline and practice of qualitative research. In N. K. Denzin and Y. S. E. Lincoln (Eds). *The Sage handbook of qualitative research* pp. 1–28. 2nd edn. Thousand Oaks, CA: Sage.

Drew, P. (2008). Conversation analysis. In J. A. Smith (Ed). *Qualitative psychology: a practical guide to research methods* (pp.133–59). 2nd edn. London: Sage.

Glaser, B. G. and Strauss, A. L. (1967). *Discovery of Grounded Theory: strategies for qualitative research*. New York: Aldine de Gruyter.

Henriques, J., Hollway, W., Urwin, C., Venn, C. and Walkerdine, V. (1984). *Changing the subject: psychology, social regulation and subjectivity*. London: Methuen.

Henwood, K. and Pidgeon, N. (2003). Grounded theory in psychological research. In P. M. Camic, J. E. Rhodes and L. Yardley (Eds). *Qualitative research in psychology: expanding perspectives in methodology and design* (pp. 131–56). Washington, DC: American Psychological Association.

Howitt, D. (1995). *Paedophiles and sexual offences against children*. Chichester: Wiley.

—— (2009). *Introduction to forensic and criminal psychology*. Harlow: Pearson Education.

—— (2010). *Introduction to qualitative methods in psychology*. Harlow: Pearson Education.

Howitt, D. and Cramer, D. (2011). *Introduction to research methods in psychology*. 3rd edn. Harlow: Pearson Education.

Jefferson, G. (2010). Born to transcribe Watergate. Available from www.gail-jefferson. com/ legacy.html (accessed 2/6/10).

Kitzinger, C. and Frith, H. (1999). Just say no? The use of conversation analysis in developing a feminist perspective on sexual refusal. *Discourse and Society*, 10(3): 293–316.

Liddicoat, A. J. (2007). *An introduction to conversation analysis*. London: Continuum.

Medlicott, D. Narratives of memory, identity and place in male prisoners. Available from www2.hud.ac.uk/hhs/nme/books/2004/Chapter_10_Diana_Medlicott.pdf (accessed 4/6/10).

Meek, R. (2007). The experiences of a young gypsy-traveller in the transition from custody to community: an interpretative phenomenological analysis. *Legal and Criminological Psychology*, 1: 133–48.

Merton, R. K., Fiske, M. and Kendall, P. L. (1956). *The focused interview: a manual of problems and procedures*. Glencoe, Illinois: The Free Press.

Nee, C. (2010). Research on residential burglary: ways of improving validity and participants' recall when gathering data. In W. Bernasco (Ed). *Offenders on offending: learning about crime from criminals*. Devon: Willan Press.

Palasinki, M. (2009). Testing assumptions about naivety in insurance fraud. *Psychology, Crime & Law*, 15(6): 547–53.

Payne, S. (2007). Grounded theory. In E. Lyons and A. Coyle (Eds). *Analysing qualitative data in psychology* (pp. 65–86). London: Sage.

Potter, J. (1996). Discourse analysis and constructionist approaches: theoretical background. In J. E. Richardson (Ed). *Handbook of qualitative research methods for psychology and the social sciences* (pp. 125–40). Leicester: British Psychological Society.

—— (2004). Discourse analysis. In M. Hardy and A. Bryman (Eds). *Handbook of data analysis* (pp. 607–24). London: Sage.

Potter, J. and Wetherell, M. (1987). *Discourse and social psychology: beyond attitudes and behaviour*. London: Sage.

Sarbin, T. R. (1986). The narrative as a root metaphor for psychology. In T. R. Sarbin (Ed). *Narrative psychology: the storied nature of human conduct* (pp. 3–21). New York: Praeger.

Sheldon, K. and Howitt, D. (2007). *Sex offenders and the internet.* Chichester: Wiley.

Smith, J. A., Larkin, M. and Flowers, P. (2009). *Interpretative phenomenological analysis: theory, method and research: understanding method and application.* London: Sage.

Ward, T., Polaschek, D. L. L. and Beech, A. (2005). *Theories of sexual offending.* Chichester: Wiley.

Part IV
Assessing individual change

8 Single case methodologies

Jason Davies and Kerry Sheldon

Introduction

Evaluation and research at the individual level has a long history that can be traced back to individual case description and case studies. However, these descriptive accounts of change, whilst useful for debate, have many limitations. A more robust form of individual level investigation is the rigorous assessment of individual change over time in the form of the single case experimental design (SCED) also referred to as time series design. In contrast to group based designs and randomised controlled trials (see Chapters 11 and 14), the strength of the SCED lies in the ability to answer research and evaluation questions concerning the extent and nature of individual change. Indeed, as outlined by Davies (2010), group based research focuses upon the question 'what might work for this *type of need*', whereas approaches such as SCED address the question 'has change taken place in *this individual*?'.

Single case experimental designs are ideal for answering research questions that aim to explore clinical treatment outcomes i.e. 'the effectiveness of an intervention when provided to one or more individuals'. Traditionally, SCED has also been used as a rigorous approach to providing 'proof of principle' when novel interventions are being developed. This approach is particularly useful when group based designs are unfeasible, for example when there is a lack of a sufficiently large homogeneous group to treat, or when evidence indicates that a treatment could have value and the researcher is concerned whether it will work for a specific individual. In many clinical settings this approach is one of necessity as often the number of service recipients is too small to allow meaningful groups to be formed. An example of many of these points is provided by Adkins *et al.* (2010) with regard to mindfulness practice with individuals with intellectual disabilities. However, SCED approaches have been argued for because they can be used to reveal not only the efficacy of an intervention but also the process of change, providing an inexpensive yet scientifically valid approach (Smith, Handler and Nash, 2010).

It is important to note that the differences between the characteristics of group members are frequently overlooked in forensic settings in order to facilitate the aggregation of individuals into groups. Therefore, many studies are based on

pseudo-homogeneous groups that hide the multitude of differences that may e
between and within groups. This is particularly important to appreciate w
statistical differences are not found or are reported to be small. The importa
of idiographic (single case) research and its scientific merit has been reinfor
for the development of psychological science in general (Barlow and Nc
2009); for specific areas of intervention (e.g. self injurious and suicidal beh
iours; Rizvi and Nock, 2008); and for forensic and personality disorder serv
(Davies *et al.*, 2007). However, it is worth noting that SCED is an under-utili
approach in forensic settings.

The decision to undertake SCED must be taken early in the research/evalua
process as the nature and investment required for data collection is very diffe
from that required by other designs. Although SCED can be used for deta
assessment (e.g. functional assessment; Ivanoff and Schmitt III, 2010)
chapter will focus on their use for assessing change over time in the contex
an intervention being applied. Many excellent texts exist which provide detai
using this approach. One of the most systematic and accessible is that of Blo
Fischer and Orme (2006).

In mental health settings, time series approaches originated in behavio
research and have a long history of being used to develop clinical treatr
approaches and to assess the nature and extent of change (e.g. Bloom *et al.*, 2(
Turpin, 2001; Long and Hollin, 1995). The paradigm uses repeated measuren
over time to create a pool of data to be analysed. The data are gathered at reg
time intervals (hence the name time series) which is commonly hourly, dail
weekly. Often, this data will be accompanied by the use of pre–post psychome
testing especially in situations where the impact of an intervention is b
assessed (see Davies, 2010). Methods for estimating the quality and rigo
single case studies have been outlined (Logan *et al.*, 2008) and include 14 q
tions against which to review published research.

Basic principles of single case designs

Many designs are used within the single case framework; however, all follow
same logic – that is measurement covering more than one phase. In the most b
form of this approach the two phases are known as *baseline* (the period before
treatment is introduced) which is denoted by an A, and *intervention* whic
denoted by a B. Sometimes this design will also incorporate a period of follow
during which the 'lasting effects' of the intervention can be tested. This is sir
referred to as A, B with follow-up. The case study later in the chapter (and Fig
8.4) show such a design. There are many examples of this design in the litera
such as Smith, Handler and Nash (2010) who used this design to investigate
impact of therapeutic assessment with three boys with oppositional defiant di
der and their families. In this study the authors identified five or six variable
conjunction with each family to be recorded on a daily basis. These were spe
to each individual child. Recordings were made for at least 10 days prior to tr
ment (baseline); during the nine weeks of treatment and at a follow-up p

which occurred at least 60 days after the intervention ceased. Unlike classical experimental/control group designs in which the comparison is between groups, single system designs involve a comparison between time periods for the same individual. The underlying assumption is that if the intervention had not occurred, the pattern of events occurring during the baseline is likely to have continued to occur as before.

Although most psychological interventions are not reversible (i.e. they cannot be completely removed or undone), where interventions can be taken away with the expectation that the individual would return to their pre-intervention state without them (as in the case of the withdrawal of many medications or with some environmental or contingency management programmes) the design would be described as an ABA design. An example of such a design is presented by Freeman *et al.* (2010) who used this design to test the impact of an exercise programme on balance and mobility in individuals with multiple sclerosis. In their study the same measures were made weekly over a four-week baseline period, eight weeks of intervention and four weeks of withdrawal. An important consideration in ABA designs is the 'absolute' extent to which the withdrawal or reversal is achieved. For example in the Freeman *et al.* study, careful checking would be necessary to ensure that all individuals followed the instruction to cease home exercise (especially if they believed it had made a difference to their functioning). Where more than one intervention is studied, different interventions are given different letters (C, D and so on). An example of this would be a baseline (A) followed by the introduction of mindfulness (B), followed by a cognitive intervention (C) and finally a family intervention (D).

Regardless of the design, data should be collected for a period of time long enough to be useful for the assessment and evaluation of progress (Bloom *et al.*, 2006), and should be guided by whatever realistic or ethical concerns you may have about a given case (i.e. regarding withholding treatment) (Barlow *et al*, 2009). The baseline should contain, as an absolute minimum, three time points, although typically phases will contain three or more times this number (Bloom *et al.*, 2006). It is likely that the number of data points necessary will vary from case to case and even the type of data recording method used will affect the length of baseline.

One important practical issue in collecting baseline data is to try to account for systematic variance which may be present. By way of example, if data are being collected daily it is helpful to collect data across at least one full week (i.e. seven consecutive days so that each day has been sampled once). This way pre-existing variations such as those between week days and weekend days may be noted from the start and the typical pattern of occurrence of the problem may be shown. In an ideal world the baseline would be continued until the researcher could confidently predict the subsequent data points from those that they already have (i.e. the baseline is stable). However, this is not always practical so variability can be managed in a variety of ways such as averaging the data (Kazdin, 1982). Bloom, Fischer and Orme (2006) provide a summary of commonly seen baseline patterns.

When using single systems design it is important to be clear and precise in defining your interventions (Bloom *et al.*, 2006). However, this can seem difficult as some would argue that anything a clinician does could be deemed as helpful to a client or patient. In order to address this, Bloom *et al.* (2006) suggest that, at the broadest level, intervention is what the clinician does in a planned way to change a target behaviour or problem. Therefore it is the formal, planned and systematic nature of intervention that distinguishes it from a baseline or assessment period. Furthermore, as single case designs become more involved there are factors which complicate their analysis including carry-over effects (where the effects of one phase carry over to another phase) and the order of presentation of interventions (which may have a causal impact), and there may be occasions when there are incomplete data in the baseline and/or intervention periods. Bloom *et al.* (2006) describe these in detail and offer some solutions. For example, in terms of the order of the interventions being presented you may not be able to tell whether the effects of one intervention built on the effects of a prior one, nor whether the outcome would have been different had the interventions being presented in a different order. One solution may be to randomise the order of the presentation across several individuals so that this could be tested.

It is important to seek to use multiple measures in the design and where possible these should be from different sources (e.g. self-report, observer report). However, careful selection of measures is needed if one or more are not to be redundant (i.e. when two measures sample the same or highly related constructs). Where a client has more than one problem, where there is more than one client being treated or where the problems occur in more than one setting, a multiple baseline design can be utilised. A non-forensic example of a multiple baseline study across individuals and across 'settings' (meal times) is provided by Powers *et al.* (2006), whilst Adkins *et al.* (2010) provide an example across three individuals who present with maladaptive behaviours. The multiple baseline design allows us to investigate the specificity of the intervention (more than one problem, more than one setting) and the generalisability of the intervention (more than one client). Typically, multiple baselines involve obtaining a baseline on two or more targets (e.g. problems, people or situations) and then introducing an intervention to the first target whilst still recording information on the others. Once a predetermined level of change is obtained on the first target, an intervention is applied to the second target and so on. The idea of multiple baselines is that they demonstrate control over the targets and show that changes only occur when the intervention has been applied. There are many other designs and design permutations which can be used such as multiple-target designs, cross-over and constant time-series designs; interested researchers should consult Bloom, Fischer and Orme (2006) for details.

The starting point for most SCED is a formulation of the problem being addressed (see Sturmey, 2010 for a discussion of case formulation in forensic psychology). Case formulation is a generic clinical skill that draws out key features of a case to guide the selection of the most effective treatment for each specific person. It is considered 'a hypothesis about the causes, precipitants and maintaining influences of a person's psychological, interpersonal and behavioural problems' (Eells, 2007, p. 4) The formulation should detail what *needs* to change (e.g. in forensic settings the needs/risks that need to be managed in order for an individual to be released/discharged) and what is *expected* to change based on the researchers' understanding of the individual, the problems being addressed, the evidence from the literature and the researchers'/clinicians' knowledge. In forensic contexts examples for the focus of change measurement might include offence paralleling behaviours (see Davies *et al.*, 2010); aggression (see Gresswell and Hollin's (1992) formulation of the development of multiple murder and Daffern *et al.*'s (2007) formulations of a violent offender's behaviour); substance use; sexually inappropriate behaviour (see Drake and Ward (2003) for a pathway model of sexual offending); suicide and self-harm (Sturmey, 2010); PTSD symptoms; anxiety; depression; and relationship-related problems. The exact focus and the method of measurement will be dictated by the individual formulation.

Data collection

Data can be gathered from a wide variety of sources such as self-report, observer report and physical measurement (see Davies, 2010 for examples in forensic settings). Regardless of the approach to measurement, it is vital that the recording of data follows a regular time period i.e. if measurement is daily then each day would be expected to have data recorded for it. One common error experienced by people using this approach for the first time is the temptation to use the occurrence of an event as the trigger for recording data rather than a time interval. Using the time trigger ensures that each period (e.g. hour, day, week) has been fully considered for the presence or absence of the phenomenon being studied. This is essential for the analysis and reporting of data and importantly to ensure that the absence of the phenomena under scrutiny is recorded. An important consideration with all measurement is to achieve a balance between quantity, quality and ease. Specifically, in SCED, ensuring that data collection does not become overwhelming or a burden for the patient, family or staff is an important aspect of this.

Deciding upon and where necessary constructing an appropriate measurement/recording tool requires careful consideration. Discussion relating to outcomes measurement in general and in relation to selecting appropriate outcome measures (including psychometric measures) are provided by authors such as Ogles, Lambert and Fields (2002); Sperry, Brill, Howard and Grissom (1996); Ogles, Lambert and Masters (1996); Ottenbacher (1986); Lambert (1994); Newman and Ciarlo (1994) and Bloom, Fischer and Orme (2006). Guides on specific measures such as goal attainment scaling (Kiresuk *et al.*, 1994); process measurement (e.g. Ogles *et al.*, 1996) and individualised rating scales (Bloom *et al.*, 2006; Chapter 6) exist, however; examples can be found in most published examples of this approach. For the purposes of this chapter, we will focus on the most widely used method – individualised rating scales.

Individualised rating scales

Individualised rating scales can be used as a way of measuring a target behavi
or problem, designed specifically for a given individual. These often forr
component part of a diary or recording log (see page 168). Rating scales are ty
cally devised so that a person rates each target behaviour or problem (one s
per problem) along relatively subjective dimensions; for example how *inte*
something is, how *satisfied* they are with something, how *severe* something
how *important* something is, or how *serious* something is. Although ratings r
be binary (i.e. features rated as present or absent) usually the rating scale
several points (e.g. from 0–5). Each point on the scale should be anchored b
clear description of the problem or behaviour being measured. Often this
include specific behavioural or physiological manifestations of the probl
Whilst the therapist, researcher and individual are free to determine the num
of rating points, it should be borne in mind that most people find clearly discr
inating more than seven points on a scale difficult resulting in a loss of precisi
In the authors' experience a six point scale (from 0–5) is adequate for most s
ations. Figure 8.1 shows an example of an individualised rating scale. Whene
rating scales are employed in SCED, regular checks are needed to ensure t
there is consistency in scale use over time.

Individualised rating scales usually rely on recording frequency, duration
severity information:

- how often something occurs (frequency) – most useful when the goal is
  increase or decrease the number of times an event occurs, e.g. the num
  of times an individual attends therapy, number of fights during inc
  ceration, number of positive self-statements or number of homework ta
  completed;
- how long an event lasts (duration) – most useful when the goal is to incre
  or decrease the length of time an event lasts, e.g. time spent in seclusion, ti
  spent in obsessive thinking, periods of feeling depressed and so on;

Amount of anxiety you feel				
0	1	2	3	4
Little or no anxiety 'I feel absolutely calm'	Some anxiety	Moderate anxiety 'I feel nervous but can manage it'	Strong anxiety	Intense anxiety 'Palms are sweaty, heart is racing, I feel scared'

Figure 8.1 Example of an individualised rating scale.

- how extreme is the event (intensity) – useful when the focus of the intervention is to increase or decrease the intensity of an event, e.g. the level of self-harm, degree of aggression, degree of relaxation.

Behavioural observation

Behavioural observation is a specific form of individualised rating and is a widely used data collection approach as behaviours are often the most direct expression of an individual's concerns or problems. The behaviour can be recorded by the person in question (self-monitoring) or by someone else such as a peer or staff member (observer report). For all observational data, the behaviour needs to be predetermined, clearly defined and have a clear beginning and end point.

With all behavioural observations there are some basic principles to follow:

1 The target behaviour needs to be turned into units of behaviour that can be observed and counted.
2 Decide how many behaviours to record; being mindful of what is feasible and can be recorded reliably.
3 Decide who should collect the data – the client/patient/offender, the researcher, independent observer or a relevant other.
4 Decide when and where to record. Do you want to observe each occurrence of target behaviour every time it occurs (continuous recording) or do you want to gather a snapshot of the target behaviours for a sample of clients, situations or times (sampling recording)? Either way the key is to obtain a representative picture of the occurrence of the behaviour. A number of sampling approaches can be used and interested readers should consult Bloom *et al.* (2006) for details of these.
5 Train the observer. The behaviour needs to be clearly defined and the observer needs to know when, where and for how long to observe the behaviour. Sometimes it is necessary for the rater to practise making observations until they are able to do so accurately. This step needs to be revisited from time to time to minimise 'rater drift' i.e. to ensure the scale is being used consistently over time (and where relevant across raters). Importantly, if the measure is designed for use by practitioners, relevant others or independent observers for obtaining information about observable events you should test, or look, for evidence of 'inter-observer reliability' (the consistency with which different observers observe or rate the same behaviour). Different observers should independently observe and record the same behaviours where practically possible. Inter-observer reliability is usually recorded as some type of percentage of agreement. Generally, 80 per cent or above (or .80 if not converted to percentages) is considered 'good' (Bloom *et al.* 2006).

Diary or log

The most common method of data recording device is the self-report or observer report diary. These are typically divided into the time periods being reported (as rows) and the phenomenon being rated (as columns). Self-report data will often be based on event reporting (e.g. went to the gym – yes, no) and experience reporting (e.g. level of distress) and individualised rating scales. In principle anything that can be quantified in some way can provide data. Recording should include features that are expected to increase and decrease over the course of treatment and factors that are expected to be unaffected by the intervention. Figure 8.2 is an example of a self-report diary extract. For this service user, his treatment targets included, amongst others, a reduction in feelings of anger and being easily influenced by others, such as peers, but also an increase in assertiveness skills. The latter included elements of non-verbal assertiveness, especially increasing appropriate eye contact. The treatment targets (behaviours) were labelled on the patient's diary card and the individual provided daily behavioural recordings based on a Likert scale (0, 1, 2). These ratings were developed

Treatment targets	Feeling angry	Feeling easily influenced by my peers	Assertiveness skills – eye contact
Rating scale	Rate from 0, 1, 2	Rate from 0, 1, 2	Rate from 0, 1, 2
Behaviours, thoughts, feelings and physical signs related to the treatment target.	0 = Not at all angry, calm, relaxed, heart beating slowly, I am not shaking, I am thinking calm thoughts	0 = I do not feel easily influenced by my peers, I am happy to say no, I don't care if a person doesn't like me	2 = I feel confident and I am looking directly at the other person while I am speaking almost all of the time
	1 = Slightly angry, irritated, feel a little hot, I feel impatient, 'are they doing that on purpose?'	1 = I struggle between not wanting to go along with it but thinking I can't say no, I feel a bit energetic	1 = I feel a bit shy but I do sometimes look right at the person when I am talking to them
	2 = I feel very angry, my heart is beating fast, I am shaking, fast moving thoughts, I am going to lose it, I am going to hit someone	2 = I feel easily influenced by others, I want to be liked by others, I feel dangerous when I am with my friends, I want to stand out as dangerous, I feel full of energy, I don't want to lose face	0 = I feel aware of myself and when I talk to people I cannot look at them at all or I look at the floor, or I look to the side
Monday 4th October	0	0	2
Tuesday 5th October	0	0	2
Wednesday 6th October	2	0	0
Thursday 7th October	2	0	2
Friday 8th October	0	2	0
Saturday 9th October	0	2	0
Sunday 10th October	0	2	0

Figure 8.2 Self-report diary extract.

	Patient: John	8th October 2010	
Time	Incident/event	Anxiety scale	Reaction
8 am	Breakfast	4	None
10.30 am	Group therapy	8	Feel scared
2 pm	Individual therapy	6	Irritable, things annoying me

Anxiety scale: 0 is not anxious at all, 5 is moderately anxious and 10 is very anxious.

Figure 8.3 Self-report diary extract showing both qualitative and quantitative data.

between the therapist and service user and defined specific behaviours, thoughts or physiological manifestations that reflected 0, 1 and 2 on the Likert scale. This helped ensure consistent recording. These daily rated variables were also used for discussion during individual therapy where concerns are noted.

Diaries can also be used to collect a broad range of qualitative and quantitative information (as shown in Figure 8.3). This might include the antecedents and consequences of a behaviour. The difficulty here is the problem of knowing whether these are true reactions or whether they are pre-emptive, i.e. they precede the event either in an anticipated way or some other way. You may be able to include space for recording the antecedents and consequences into the recording forms by simply adding column(s). Collecting an array of data such as this can allow the relationship between events, behaviours or other factors to be explored. Bloom *et al.* (2006) describe a number of diaries, logs or journals that can be kept by a client to record unique qualitative or quantitative dimensions surrounding their problems, including intensity and frequency. Client diaries and logs can also be adapted to be used by practitioners in much the same way as a client diary or log. However, as with all data collection within the SCED paradigm, recording needs to be made before and after the intervention is in place.

It should also be noted that the act of measuring may itself cause change in behaviour. This is for a number of reasons. First, asking someone about their behaviour might cause them to re-examine and change that behaviour. Second, individuals may unintentionally alter their behaviour, which in turn affects recording. Third, people may intentionally distort their recording in order to present themselves in a different light. Fourth, as individuals become more familiar with the measurement they may take less care over recording or be less motivated to make accurate ratings. There are a number of ways to try to manage these problems:

1   Ensure clear instructions are given to the individual(s) who is completing the measure and emphasise the importance of accurate recording.

2   Use multiple measures of the target behaviours including where possible measures from different people, e.g. self, therapist, prison officer, family member. This can help maximise and verify the reliability and validity of the diary or log.

3   Consider the use of supplementary unobtrusive measures. Bloom *et al.* (2006) argue that unobtrusive measures are mostly suited as secondary sources of data. Examples include contemporary records (e.g. file entries, adjudications); indirect data (e.g. repair costs as an indicator of criminal damage); physical data (e.g. number of cigarette ends left in an ashtray as evidence of smoking level); or unobtrusive observations (e.g. proximity of family members during a therapy session as an indicator of their feelings towards each other).

Standardised questionnaires

Occasionally SCED will only use standardised self-report (psychometric) measures/questionnaires. An example of this approach is a single case series reported by Nordahl and Nysaeter (2005) who used this method to evaluate schema therapy in six individuals. In their study, measures such as the Beck Depression Inventory (Beck *et al.*, 1961) and the Inventory of Interpersonal Problems (Horowitz *et al.*, 1988) were used on three occasions during a 10 week baseline at the start, twice during and at the end of treatment and a follow up 12–16 months after treatment ended.

When choosing a standardised questionnaire it is important that there are some data concerning its reliability and its validity although the quality and quantity of this information will differ considerably between measures. This will be considered in the next section.

There are a number of further important considerations when selecting a questionnaire. As single case design requires repeated measurement over time the ease with which a questionnaire can be used is important. A client may become bored filling out a long 200-item questionnaire week after week. This is not just a problem with questionnaires, asking someone to complete a daily diary requires time, effort and motivation. The time it takes to score and interpret the measure is another important consideration. Bloom *et al.* (2006, p. 218) argue that the measurement also needs to enhance the intervention process in some way and that there are a number of questions that you should ask when selecting a questionnaire, including: will it help determine whether a target behaviour is improving or deteriorating?; will it help determine what may be affecting or maintaining the target?; will it determine whether a client is in need of an intervention?; and will it help identify the most effective intervention for the client?. They emphasise that although a single questionnaire is unlikely to answer all of these questions, if the answer to most of them is no then you should reconsider the use of that particular psychometric questionnaire.

Reliability and validity

As with other forms of quantitative research, the reliability and validity of measurement must be carefully considered. Reliability is concerned with whether the measure(s) produces consistent results when the same entities are measured at different times under different conditions, whilst validity is concerned with whether or not the measure assesses what it claims to measure. In SCED, the reliability of the measures used can be enhanced by a) using well-researched and evidenced psychometric measures whenever possible; b) having clear anchor points for all rating scale measures; and c) reviewing the inter-rater reliability between observers. In order to increase the confidence a researcher can have in the causal explanations they use (i.e. that this intervention caused this change) data should be collected in areas which are not expected to change.

Validity in SCED is often considered in terms of other factors which might account for any changes observed (often termed 'threats to validity'). Widely discussed threats include 'maturation' – the natural course of change over time; 'testing' – the impact of measurement and monitoring, e.g. diary keeping as an intervention rather than a benign assessment; and 'regression to the mean' – the tendency for extreme responses to be less extreme on repeat measurement (Davies, 2010). Although these are discussed extensively elsewhere (e.g. Turpin, 2001; Bloom *et al.*, 2006), simple ways to minimise their impact is to use multiple measures and to record all known intended and incidental interventions and life events (e.g. new relationships; gaining employment) which might themselves provide alternative explanations for the changes observed (Davies 2010). Investigation of whether the effects observed generalise (to other settings, or in other individuals) can add further weight to the causal explanations formed. Researchers using this approach should see Davies (2010), Turpin (2001) and Bloom *et al.* (2006) for further consideration of reliability and 'threats to validity' and their management.

When using psychometric measures, attention should be paid to the reported psychometric properties of the tool. In terms of reliability these can include the internal consistency of the questionnaire. Cronbach's alphas are generally assumed to reflect inter-item consistency of a scale (although there is debate about this, see Boyle (1991); Field (2009) also gives some advice on interpreting Cronbach's alpha). Other methods of reliability include 'split-half' reliability (see Cortina (1993) for more details); test-retest reliability (the stability of the responses to the questionnaire over time; this is especially important in single case designs as the questionnaire or measure is being repeated over baseline and intervention periods); and where appropriate inter-rater reliability (how consistent the information is provided by different observers or raters) should be considered. Such reliability information can be found in the questionnaire manual, from previous literature or from the author(s) of the measure. As a general rule a reliability of .80 or higher is considered 'good' (Field, 2009), although alphas of .70 are generally acceptable and for research .60 has been used (Fritzon and Miller, 2010). Manuals should also be consulted to check whether the test designer has any comments on the minimum time that should be allowed to elapse between administrations.

Various forms of validity may be reported by test developers in relation to psychometric assessments. These include 'face validity' – does your assessment measure what its name implies?; 'content validity' – do the items represent all the areas that appear relevant to the domain being assessed?; and 'convergent and divergent validity' – does the measure correlate with established measures of the same construct (to an expected degree) but not with measures of unrelated constructs? Again, such information can be obtained from past literature or the assessment manual.

Data analysis and reporting

Analysing single case data typically involves the use of visual presentation using graphs and statistical and clinical significance testing. Presenting and analysing data visually requires the researcher to use a number of standardised techniques. These have developed over time and help ensure that the data is presented in ways in which distortion and bias are minimised and the researcher is aided, as much as is possible, to make their interpretations. As with all other research, however, the researcher's interpretation skills are an essential component of the process. Some of the important characteristics of visual presentation of results have been outlined (e.g. Morley and Adams, 1991, Bloom *et al.*, 2006 and Davies, 2010) and a discussion of the use of visual and statistical analyses in simple single case designs is provided by Brossart *et al.* (2006). Presenting data in graphical form is a very powerful way to report data and is generally considered to be the first step in data analysis and reporting. Given the impact a graph can have in terms of influencing the reader (a picture being worth a thousand words), it is incumbent upon the researcher to ensure that the graph is presented clearly and professionally. In order to support this there are a number of conventions typically used such as the use of a line graph with a clear title and detailed axes; time presented along the x axis; phases clearly marked; and presenting a limited number of factors per graph. One technique for minimising potential bias and distortion of the data is to ensure that the scale on the y axis is appropriate, i.e. that it covers the full range of the rating used. Features such as trend lines, annotations and summary scores can all be used to help clarify the presentation of the data. Box 8.1a presents a case example and describes how the techniques discussed in this chapter have been applied, including graphical presentation of data.

Statistical analysis can be particularly helpful when the data contain large variance or when it is important to determine whether a change is statistically significant. Traditionally, researchers using SCED employ mean difference statistics (e.g. t-test) to compare phases of the design (e.g. baseline with intervention). The time series nature of single case designs introduces a confound known as serial dependency that can cause problems for the assumptions underlying the statistical tests generally used. In general terms, serial dependency concerns the

BOX 8.1a

A case study example

Overview

The case study involves Robin, a patient resident in a high security setting. He has received a diagnosis of both antisocial and borderline personality disorders. Since entering into the unit, Robin has engaged in violent behaviour such as punching, kicking and vandalism towards others/objects, name calling and making verbal threats. He reported high levels of anxiety and symptoms such as ruminative worry, subjective feelings of apprehension and physical signs of tension and stress. He also reported dissociative experiences such as reliving the past vividly, staring blankly at objects for some time, finding evidence of doing something but not remembering doing it and missing parts of a conversation. Dialectical behaviour therapy treatment (DBT) (Linehan, 2003) was recommended as a beneficial treatment to assist him in recognising and managing his anger and to enable him to cope with emotional and interpersonal experiences (see Tennant (2010) for a discussion of how DBT can be used in male forensic in-patient settings).

Measurement of change

Measurement of change was based on three sources of information

1   Daily self-recording of the frequency of angry thoughts and urges.
2   Staff observations of the frequency of name calling, verbal threats, shouting and aggressive behaviours such as physical assault. These are recorded by trained staff on standard hospital incident forms.
3   Psychometric measures:

   (a) State-Trait Anger Inventory-2 (STAXI-2) (Spielberger, 1999). This assessment measures state and trait anger and how the person manages their anger.
   (b) The Dissociative Experiences Scale (DES; Bernstein and Putnam, 1986). This is a self-assessment questionnaire that measures dissociative symptoms and experiences. Higher scores are more problematic.
   (c) The Beck Hopelessness Questionnaire (BHI; Beck and Stree, 1988). This is designed to measure three major aspects of hopelessness: feelings about the future, loss of motivation and expectations. Higher scores are more problematic.

(d)   The Personality Assessment Inventory (PAI; Morey, 1991). The PAI is a test of personality and psychopathology designed to provide information on critical service-user variables in behavioural healthcare settings. Higher scores are more problematic.

The psychometric measures were chosen as they are part of the high security setting's routine clinical assessment and there are both functional[2] and dysfunctional[3] norms available.

Predictions of change

Prior to starting DBT, the clinical team predicted that changes would be recorded as:

1   A reduction in levels of anxiety, as measured by the anxiety (ANX) scale of the Personality Assessment Inventory.
2   A reduction in his expression of anger as measured by the anger expression out scale (AX-O) of the STAXI measure. This scale measures the expression of anger in aggressive behaviour directed at others or objects.
3   A reduction in the frequency of angry thoughts and urges per day.
4   A reduction in the number of aggressive behaviours, e.g. name calling, shouting, physical assaults, verbal threats etc.
5   A reduction in dissociative experiences, as measured by the DES.
6   An increase in the number of skills used to cope with angry thoughts and urges.

The prediction was that if DBT was successful it should specifically target anger, aggressive behaviour, anxiety and dissociative experiences without specifically changing other factors such as hopelessness.

Has change occurred?

Daily ratings

The first method for analysing the data was simply a review of the raw data – in other words, looking at whether the behavioural frequency of angry thoughts and urges decreased over time. First we will concentrate on baseline to treatment data. Figure 8.4 shows that over the ten months of available data (five months prior to treatment and five months during treatment) the average number of angry thoughts recorded by the patient shows a downward trend. The insertion of trend lines also helps to identify changes that have occurred. The trend lines show a reduction in anger during the treatment phase that would not have been expected if no

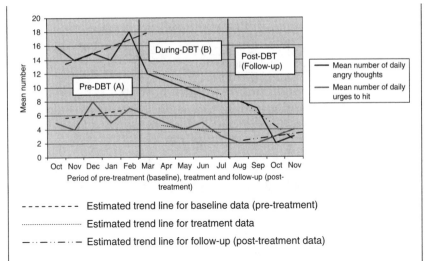

- - - - - - - - - Estimated trend line for baseline data (pre-treatment)

.... Estimated trend line for treatment data

— ·· — ·· — ·· — Estimated trend line for follow-up (post-treatment data)

Figure 8.4 Basic graph showing average number of daily angry thoughts and urges to hit prior to, during and post intervention.

treatment had been provided (this can be estimated by extending the baseline trend line). There was a small reduction in the number of urges to hit from baseline to treatment. The baseline average for angry thoughts is 15.4, and for urges it is 5.8. The treatment average for angry thoughts is 10, and for urges it is 4.6. Post-treatment average of angry thoughts is 5, and for urges it is 2.75.

Simultaneously, there was an increase in the number of DBT skills used from baseline to treatment, as shown by Figure 8.5. The baseline average for daily skill use is 0.6. The treatment average for daily skill use is 2.2. The post-treatment average for daily skill use is 2.5.

Observer reports

Over the ten months of available data there were incidents of name calling, verbal threats, shouting and aggressive behaviours including two serious physical assaults; all of which occurred during the pre-treatment phase. During the intervention phase, incidents had reduced to zero.

Psychometric change

STAXI-2 – decrease on the AX-O scale.
PAI – decrease on the ANX scale.
DES – decrease on the overall scale.
BHI – no change on the hopelessness scale.

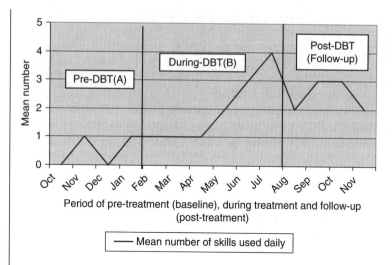

Figure 8.5 Basic graph showing average number of daily skills used prior to, during and post intervention.

Summary

Based on the data reported above, it would seem that Robin has changed in a number of areas measured across all three modes of measurement used (psychometrics, daily self-report and observer reports).

See Sheldon and Tennant (2009) for further related case study examples.

relationship between data points and can be assessed using autocorrelation statistics. Many resources exist which detail statistical approaches to single case data. Morley and Adams (1989) provide a helpful summary. When trying out this approach, it can be beneficial to identify a person who can support you to explore the method fully.

In addition, dedicated single case analysis packages exist (e.g. SINGWIN, Bloom *et al.*, 2006); however standard packages such as Microsoft Excel and SPSS can also be used for single case data analysis.

Clinical significance

Clinical significance/relevance is the ultimate test of individual change especially in forensic settings. Clinically meaningful change concerns the clinical impact and practical meaning of recorded change and can be assessed in a broad range of ways. A very readable review of the methods and approaches to clinical significance is provided by Ogles, Lunnen and Bonesteel (2001). They highlight the use of approaches such as assessing the magnitude of change and considering the social validity of change (i.e. does the therapist, client or others consider the amount of change significant) for addressing this. The social validity of change can be included in all applications of SCED; however, the magnitude of change is most commonly assessed when psychometric measures have been used as part of the design. These techniques will be briefly considered next.

Social validity of change

Social validity generally concerns the subjective views of others in relation to change. This might include descriptive accounts of what has changed and by how much but may also be concrete evidence of what impact a change has had on someone's life and whether people think that more change is possible (or desirable). In forensic settings there are also formal sources of social validity such as parole boards and mental health review tribunals which will provide a view on the extent and impact of changes made.

Assessing the magnitude of change

Determining the magnitude of change requires the researcher to assess two components – whether the change is a) statistically reliable and b) clinically significant. The most widely used technique for assessing the statistical reliability of change is the Reliable Change Index (RCI; Jacobson and Truax, 1991). The RCI is an assessment of whether or not the observed change over time is greater than the change that would be expected due to the unreliability of the measure (Wise, 2004). There are online calculators available to help with this, including www.psyctc.org/stats/rcsc1.htm and www.leeds.ac.uk/lihs/psyciatry/courses/dclin/completed_research/RCI_Tramline_Display/RCI_main_page.html.

For those of you who wish to calculate the RCI by hand, the RCI formula is:

$$\frac{\text{(Post-intervention score} - \text{Pre-intervention score)}}{\text{Standard difference.}}$$

Standard difference can be calculated by:

$$\sqrt{2}\left(\text{Standard error}\right)^2$$

Standard error is calculated as follows =

$$s_1 \sqrt{1 - r} \; xxx$$

where *r xxx* is the test-retest reliability or alpha of the measure and s_1 is the standard deviation of the control, normal or pre-treatment group.

Such information should be readily available in test manuals and in previously published research. Evans (1998) recommends using alpha values for the measure, preferably from the same population you are researching or from a similar population.

Pre–post change is significant at $p < .05$ if the RCI (the number you calculate) is *greater* than 1.96 (see Collie *et al.*, 2003). If the reliable change index is a minus figure then this indicates the person has deteriorated. If we want to test for a significance level of $p < .01$ (in other words if we want to be 99 per cent confident that the change is a reliable one) then we need an RCI that is *above or equal to* 2.58. The RCI will allow you to conclude that changes are not due to measurement error and unlikely to be due to regression to the mean; however, it cannot tell you what caused the change. One example of the use of RCI information to supplement other analysis is found in Kellett (2007). This study, which explores the use of cognitive analytic therapy with an individual with histrionic personality disorder, also shows the use of this design to investigate the process of change and provides an example of many of the features of SCED, for example its role in novel interventions and the role of formulation in the design.

To determine the clinical significance of change a number of approaches have been advocated (see Atkins *et al.*, (2005) for a discussion on the most widely considered clinical significance methods). Jacobson, Follette and Revenstorf (1984) offer three different ways of working out the clinical significance:

- Method A – has the person moved more than 2 standard deviations from the mean for the 'problem' group? (conservative)
- Method B – has the person moved to within 2 standard deviations of the mean for the 'normal' population? (lenient)
- Method C – has the person moved to the 'normal' side of the point halfway between the above?

Jacobson and Truax (1991) offer an equation for calculating Method C:

$$\frac{(SD^1)(Mean^2) + (SD^2)(Mean^1)}{SD^1 + SD^2}$$

$Mean^1$ and SD^1 are the mean and the standard deviation from a functional group (e.g. non-mentally ill, controls, students, non-offenders etc.) and $Mean^2$ and SD^2 are the mean and the standard deviation from a dysfunctional group (e.g. offenders, mentally ill, high risk offenders etc.). These can be obtained from the measure's manual (should it have one) or from previous literature (see Box 8.2 for key information required for calculating the Clinical Significance of Change). What this formula allows you to do is to calculate the score that a patient's

Box 8.2

Key information required for calculating Clinical Significance of Change

Prior to starting ensure you have the following information:

1   norms (means and standard deviations from a functional and dysfunctional sample*);
2   the individual's (offender, patients, client etc.) pre-score and post-score on the measure;
3   know whether high scores on the measure indicate improvement or deterioration*;
4   test-retest reliability value or alpha coefficient for the measure.

  * This information may be found in the measures manual, or else from previous literature.

post-treatment score must cross for change to be considered clinically significant (the cut-off between dysfunctional and functional responding). For example, a patient scores 50 prior to treatment and subsequently scores 20 post-treatment on a measure of depression, furthermore the measure is negatively tuned (i.e. higher score = worse). The cut-off point between dysfunctional and functional responding (as calculated by the formula) is 22, therefore the individual needs to score 22 or less to be deemed as clinically changed (i.e. less depressed), which he has. Alternatively, there are online calculators available to help you calculate the clinical significance of change, for example www.psyctc.org/stats/rcsc2.htm.

Using pre-determined thresholds to determine change (e.g. number of standard deviations of change; score needed to be reached) is also important; however, careful consideration and justification of the thresholds used should be provided (Davies, 2010).

In cases where the Reliable Change Index is significant but the client has not crossed the clinical threshold set then the individual is deemed to have improved (or deteriorated). If both reliable change and clinical significance are reported in the desired direction, then the client is deemed to have recovered (Jacobson *et al.*, 1999). When using this in practice there are additional questions that should be asked such as whether the change was uniform over time; did the individual improve in the critical area(s); and, did change occur in other scales? Box 8.1b continues with the case example. It shows how the clinical significance of change and the RCI can be applied to the psychometric data and explores whether the changes observed in our case study are significant, meaningful, relevant and stable over time.

Box 8.1b

A case study example continued

Are the changes statistically significant/reliable?

Returning to our example of Robin, the service user made quantifiable changes in a number of key areas. The next step was to establish whether the changes which occurred were *significant*, *meaningful* and *relevant*. To consider whether the changes were worthy of consideration (i.e. significant and not simply the result of random fluctuations or error) both the clinical significance of change and the reliable change index were calculated using the internet calculators as reported above. Table 8.1 summarises the results.

Table 8.1 Pre- and post-treatment scores; clinical significance and reliable change for case example

	Pre-DBT	Post-DBT	Clinical significance threshold	Clinical significance	Reliable change criterion
PAI – Anxiety[1]	38	25	21.34	No	14.89
STAXI-2 – AX-O[2]	29	14	15.54	Yes	5.16*
DES [3]	32.5	10	14.75	Yes	18.01*

Notes:

1 Anxiety Scale – clinical sample and census matched normal sample test data.
2 Anger Expression Scale – male psychiatric patients and normal non-psychiatric adults test data.
3 Dissociative Experiences Scale – personality disordered patients and community non-PD adult test data.
* Change is reliable because there is a drop/reduction which is greater than the reliable change criterion calculated.

Are the changes clinically meaningful?

The AX-O scale of the STAXI measure fell below the clinical threshold; so too did the service user's score on the dissociative experiences measure. These changes were also statistically reliable. Changes in anxiety levels (e.g. ruminative worry, subjective feelings of apprehension and physical signs of tension and stress) showed a decrease, but the change was not clinically meaningful or statistically reliable.

For the self-report data means were calculated. The average number of recorded daily angry thoughts showed a change of 5.4 points (mean during baseline = 15.4; mean during treatment = 10). Urges to hit decreased by just over 1 point from baseline to treatment (mean during baseline = 5.5; mean during treatment = 4.6). From baseline to treatment the mean score on the daily ratings for the number of strategies used showed an increase of 1.6 points (mean during baseline = 0.6; mean during treatment = 2.2).

The observer report data showed that during the baseline there were 11 incidents of name calling, verbal threats, shouting and aggressive behaviours including two serious physical assaults, but there were none during the treatment phase.

Are the changes relevant?

The results in Table 8.1 indicate that the service user showed changes in the desired direction on two of the psychometric scales (anger expression and dissociative experiences). The change in daily self-report data also showed expected changes. The increase in skills use suggested skills acquisition related to the treatment content. The positive changes in observer reports were also consistent with the treatment goals.

Is the change stable over time?

Of course whether or not changes are maintained over time is a major issue for clinicians and decision makers. Davies, Jones and Howells (2010) argue that once stability over time has been secured it may be possible to explore the generalisability of the change to different contexts and situations which may be both familiar and unfamiliar to the individual. They argue that there may be opportunities to explore the stability of these changes over time by returning back to the original case formulation and predicting those factors which might support or reverse any changes noted. These might include internal factors, such as stress or coping, and external factors such as their social network or the environment. In this case study, whether the changes were maintained over time was simply tested by continuing some of the key variables during a period of time when the treatment had ceased. This provided a test of stability over time. For this case study angry thoughts reduced from treatment to post-treatment by a further 5 points. Similarly, the mean number of strategies used, which had showed an increase from baseline to treatment, was maintained at an average of 2.5 skills per day. Although there was an average small decrease in urges to hit from baseline to treatment, a larger decrease was maintained from treatment to post-treatment (overall average decrease of 3 points from baseline to post-treatment). Administration of the psychometrics measures, repeated four months after treatment had ceased, showed further reductions in the AX-O (treatment stage = 14; follow-up = 13) and the anxiety scales (treatment = 25; follow-up period = 7), whilst the dissociative scale remained at the same level as it was at the last time of measurement (final week of treatment). The anxiety scale decrease from pre-treatment to follow-up is now clinically significant and statistically reliable.

Stability of change could also be tested when the individual is introduced to new settings or contexts (e.g. move to a new unit or ward, or the introduction of different staff on the ward) or is experiencing new emotional states. There were no observed incidents of physical aggression, verbal threats, name calling or shouting during the treatment phase. There were two incidents of name calling and shouting occurring at the beginning of the follow-up period. This coincided with Robin commencing a violence reduction programme where intense emotional states are explored. There were no further observed incidents of physical aggression, verbal threats, name calling or shouting.

Again, care must be taken to ensure that consistency in measurement is maintained, such as by training observers. If you end the measurement at the end of the intervention it is possible to conclude that an intervention is successful or unsuccessful when the reverse is true, or that relationships between other key variables are missed over time.

What caused the change?

One important question is the extent to which the changes noted are a result of the intervention. There are many factors which can influence change other than treatment, such as the ward atmosphere, medication, biofeedback and even other individuals. Measurement, and where possible management, of these factors need to take place if *cause for the change* is to be shown. In this case study in order to increase the clinician's confidence in their findings (i.e. that DBT caused this change) data were collected in areas which were not expected to change i.e. hopelessness and indeed no change in scores was found. In addition, a systematic note was made of all other events, experiences and interventions (intentional and unintentional) which might themselves provide alternative explanations for the changes observed (e.g. changes in relationships, move to another ward/unit, anniversary of a significant event). It was found that after the introduction of DBT treatment the patient was prescribed quetiapine (an anti-psychotic drug) and there was a move to another ward. Both these events open up the possibility of several alternative interpretations of what caused the change including the possibility that the medication may have allowed Robin to become more stable and more receptive to treatment. Another way the clinicians may have strengthened the confidence in their findings, and thus the cause and effect link, would be to review change across a number of individuals completing DBT to identify common patterns and thus draw aggregate conclusions about the cause of change.

Group level analysis

SCED can be used to provide group data. A number of methods have been outlined for achieving this including hierarchical linear models (Van den Noortgate and Onghena, 2007) and other statistical approaches (Shadish and Rindskopf, 2007) as well as simple techniques such as averaged scores as used in published studies (e.g. Powers *et al.*, 2006). Further examination of the techniques for group level reporting of single case data is outside the scope of this chapter; however, the sources listed here form one starting point for interested readers.

Strengths and limitations of SCED in forensic practice

As we have seen throughout this chapter, the principal strength of SCED is in allowing change to be examined at the individual or small group level; something that cannot be robustly achieved with the methods widely used in outcome research which report findings based on groups of individuals. The use of the individual as their own comparison (baseline) allows conclusions about the degree and type of change to be reached; this is not possible with other methods. In addition, this approach can be designed to investigate the level of change produced by specific components of an intervention and to quantify 'deterioration' (i.e. an increase in the problem being monitored). Such negative effects of interventions are often lost or overlooked in group designs when the overall effectiveness is positive. The approach also demands that the researcher gives careful thought to the limitations of measurement and the multitude of other explanations that may account for change. Group designs (e.g. RCT approaches) make assumptions, in our opinion naively, that such issues (and others) can be 'managed' by the design. Using SCED demands a good understanding of measurement and design issues. A final strength is that this approach is almost always used in real-world settings and thus it gives us information on actual practice as it is conducted under the usual constrains of the practice setting.

Despite these strengths there are limitations of which the practitioner and researcher should be mindful. This approach requires the researcher to consider quantitative data in ways which may be unfamiliar. Although most individuals who have received research training at undergraduate level or above will have been exposed to quantitative (group and large *n*) designs and qualitative approaches, it is common that exposure to SCED may have been absent or very limited. Thus individuals may lack skills and confidence to use this approach. Second, SCED deals with the issues of reliability and validity in ways which differ from other quantitative approaches. For example the focus on internal validity and understanding threats to validity represents a shift from the more familiar attention to external validity (i.e. generalisability) which is at the heart of most large scale research. Generalisability can be achieved (across problems; across settings and across individuals); however, this requires effort and planning. Third, analysis generally makes use of graphical and statistical approaches that researchers are often not trained in. Issues such as serial dependency can compound the unfamiliarity of approach. Fourth, SCED allows flexibility and adaptations to be made to the design and data collection when necessary. Although practitioners will generally feel comfortable with the practical nature of this, many researchers consider this to be very problematic. Fifth, there is much debate about the utility and application of methods, which can cause confusion.

Summary

Measuring change at the individual level requires careful planning at each stage of the study. This includes creating a formulation of change; selecting appropriate measures; and using (wherever possible) multiple approaches to measurement, ensuring repeated measurement over time and where possible measurement across settings. Within these parameters, single case experimental designs provide a robust methodology for assessing change in individuals by comparing data from multiple time points, typically before an intervention was applied to data from during and after the treatment has been delivered. Single case methods can be used with any type of intervention e.g. pharmacological, psychological, social or environmental, and are capable of using data for a multitude of sources. Taking steps to address common 'threats to validity' is critical; however, when single case and other idiographic approaches are employed appropriately 'the flexibility and efficacy of these designs make them ideally suited for use by psychological scientists, clinicians and students alike, given that they ... can provide strong evidence of causal relations between variables' (Barlow and Nock, 2009, p. 20). Authors also argue that showing patients or offenders a copy of their progress to be very motivating and engaging (Sheldon and Tennant, 2009).

Further resources

A number of helpful texts and articles exist for the researcher or practitioner wishing to utilise this approach:

Bloom, M., Fischer, J. and Orme, J. G. (2006). *Evaluating practice: guidelines for the accountable professional.* 5th edn. Boston: Allyn & Bacon. A very detailed and accessible text providing a detailed account of SCED. An analysis package (SINGWIN) in included with the text.

Davies, J. (2010). An individual approach to assessing change. In N. Gordon and P. Willmot (Eds). *Working positively with personality disorder in secure settings: a practitioner's perspective.* Chichester: Wiley & Sons. A useful summary of a wide range of individual change methods.

Davies, J., Jones, L. and Howells, K. (2010). Evaluating individual change in forensic settings. In M. Daffern, L. F. Jones, and J. Shine (Eds). *Offence paralleling behaviour: a case formulation approach to offender assessment and intervention.* Chichester: Wiley & Sons. This is a very useful chapter for understanding the use of idiographic approaches for assessing change in the context of forensic settings.

Evans, C., Margison, F. and Barkham, M. (1998). The contribution of reliable and clinically significant change methods to evidence-based mental health. *Evidence Based Mental Health,* 1: 70–2. This is a very readable introduction.

Wilson, S. L. (1995). Single case experimental designs. In Glynis M. Breakwell, Sean Hammond and Chris Fife-Schaw (Eds). *Research methods in psychology.* London: Sage. A succinct introduction to the main features of the approach.

Notes

1 The term event is used to include behaviour, affect, cognition, social interaction and physiological experience.
2 Functional refers to a sample of participants which are deemed 'normal', 'non-problematic'.
3 Dysfunctional refers to a sample of participants which are deemed 'abnormal' or 'problematic'.

References

Atkins, D. C., Bedics, J. D., McGlinchey, J. B. and Beauchaine, T. P. (2005). Assessing clinical significance: does it matter which method we use? *Journal of Consulting and Clinical Psychology,* 73(5): 982–9.

Adkins, A. D., Singh, A. N., Winton, A. S. W., McKeegan, G. F. and Singh, J. (2010). Using a mindfulness-based procedure in the community: translating research into practice. *Journal of Child and Family Studies,* 19: 175–83.

Barlow, D. H. and Nock, M. K. (2009). Why can't we be more idiographic in our research? *Perspectives on Psychological Science,* 4(1): 19–21.

Barlow, D., Nock, M. and Hersen, M. (2009). *Single case experimental designs: strategies for studying behavior for change.* Boston: Allyn & Bacon.

Beck, A. T and Stree, R. A. (1988). *Manual for the Beck Hopelessness Scale.* San Antonio, TX: Psychological Corporation.

Beck, A. T., Ward, C. H., Mendelson, M., Mock, J. E. and Erbaugh, J. K. (1961). An inventory for measuring depression. *Archives of General Psychiatry,* 4: 561–71.

Bernstein, E. M. and Putnam, F. W. (1986). Development, reliability, and validity of a dissociation scale. *The Journal of Nervous and Mental Disease,* 174(12): 727–34.

Bloom, M., Fischer, J. and Orme, J. G. (2006). *Evaluating practice: guidelines for the accountable professional.* 5th edn. Boston: Allyn & Bacon.

Boyle, G. (1991). Does item homogeneity indicate internal consistency or item redundancy in psychometric scales? *Personality and Individual Differences,* 12: 291–4.

Brossart, D. F., Parker, R. L., Olson, E. A. and Mahadevan, L. (2006). The relationship between visual analysis and five statistical analyses in a simple AB single-case research design. *Behavior Modification*, 30(5): 531–63.

Collie, A., Maruff, P., McStephen, M. and Darby, D. (2003). Are reliable change (RC) calculations appropriate for determining the extent of clinical change in concussed athletes? *British Journal of Sports Medicine*, 37: 370–6.

Cortina, J. M. (1993). What is coefficient alpha? An examination of theory and applications. *Journal of Applied Psychology*, 78: 98–104.

Daffern, M., Jones, L., Howells, K., Shine, J., Mikton, C. and Tunbridge, V. (2007). Editorial. Redefining the definition of offence paralleling behaviour. *Criminal Behaviour and Mental Health*, 17: 265–73.

Davies, J. (2010). An individual approach to assessing change. In N. Gordon and P. Willmot (Eds). *Working positively with personality disorder in secure settings: a practitioner's perspective.* Chichester: Wiley & Sons.

Davies, J., Howells, K. and Jones, L. (2007). Using single case approaches in personality disorder and forensic services. *Journal of Forensic Psychiatry and Psychology*, 18(3): 353–67.

Davies, J., Jones, L. and Howells, K. (2010). Evaluating individual change in forensic settings. In M. Daffern, L. F. Jones, and J. Shine (Eds). *Offence paralleling behaviour: a case formulation approach to offender assessment and intervention.* Chichester: Wiley & Sons.

Drake, C. R. and Ward, T. (2003). Treatment models for sex offenders: a move toward a formulation-based approach. In T. Ward, D. R. Laws and S. M. Hudson (Eds). *Sexual deviance: issues and controversies* (pp. 226–43). Thousand Oaks, CA: Sage.

Eells, T. D. (2007). History and current states of psychotherapy case formulation. In T. D. Eells (Ed). *Handbook of psychotherapy case formulation*, 2nd edn. New York: Guilford Press.

Evans, C. (1998). Reliable and clinically significant change. *Psychology, psychotherapy, consultancy and training in the community*. Available from www.psyctc.org/stats/rcsc.htm (accessed 24/1/11).

Evans, C., Margison, F. and Barkham, M. (1998). The contribution of reliable and clinically significant change methods to evidence-based mental health. *Evidence Based Mental Health*, 1: 70–2.

Field, A. (2009). *Discovering statistics using SPSS*. 3rd edn. London: Sage.

Freeman, J. A., Gear, M., Pauli, A., Cowan, P., Finnigan, C., Hunter, H., Mobberley, C., Nock, A., Sims, R. and Thain, J. (2010). The effect of core stability training on balance and mobility in ambulant individuals with multiple sclerosis: a multi-centre series of single case studies. *Multiple Sclerosis*, 16(11): 1377–84.

Fritzon, K. and Miller, S. (2010). Functional consistency in female forensic psychiatric patients: an action system theory approach. In M. Daffern, L. F. Jones and J. Shine (Eds). *Offence paralleling behaviour: a case formulation approach to offender assessment and intervention.* Chichester: Wiley & Sons.

Gresswell, D. M. and Hollin, C. R. (1992). Toward a new methodology of making sense of case material: an illustrative case involving attempted multiple murder. *Clinical Behaviour and Mental Health*, 2: 329–41.

Horowitz, L. M., Rosenberg, S. E., Baer, B. A., Ureno, G. and Villasenor, V. S. (1988). Inventory of interpersonal problems: psychometric properties and clinical applications. *Journal of Consulting and Clinical Psychology*, 56: 885–92.

Ivanoff, A. and Schmidt III, H. (2010). Functional assessment in forensic settings: a valuable tool for preventing and treating egregious behavior. *Journal of Cognitive Psychotherapy*, 24(2): 81–91.

Jacobson, N. S., Follete, W. C., and Revenstorf, D. (1984). Psychotherapy outcome research: methods for reporting variability and evaluating clinical significance. *Behaviour Therapy*, 15: 336–52.

Jacobson, N. S. and Truax, P. (1991). Clinical significance: a statistical approach to defining meaningful change in psychotherapy research. *Journal of Consulting and Clinical Psychology*, 59: 12–19.

Jacobson, N. S., Roberts, L. J., Berns, S. B. and McGlinchey, J. B. (1999). Methods for defining and determining the clinical significance of treatment effects: description, application, and alternatives. *Journal of Consulting and Clinical Psychology*, 67: 300–7.

Kazdin, A.E. (1982). *Single-case research designs: Methods for clinical and applied settings*. New York: Oxford Press.

Kellett, S. (2007). A time series evaluation of the treatment of histrionic personality disorder with cognitive analytic therapy. *Psychology and Psychotherapy: Theory, Research and Practice*, 80: 389–405.

Kiresuk, T. J., Smith, A. and Cardillo, J. E. (Eds) (1994). *Goal attainment scaling*. New Jersey: Lawrence Erlbaum Associates.

Lambert, M. J. (1994). Use of psychological tests for outcome assessment. In Mark E. Maruish (Ed.) *The use of psychological testing for treatment planning and outcome assessment*. New Jersey: Lawrence Erlbaum Associates.

Linehan M. M. (2003). *Cognitive behavioural treatment of borderline personality disorder*. New York: Guilford Press.

Logan, L. R., Hickman, R. R., Harris, S. R. and Heriza, C. B. (2008). Single-subject research design: recommendations for levels of evidence and quality rating. *Developmental Medicine and Child Neurology*, 50: 99–103.

Long, C. G. and Hollin, C. R. (1995). Single-case design: a critique of methodology and analysis of recent trends. *Clinical Psychology and Psychotherapy*, 2: 177–91.

Morey, L. C. (1991). *The Personality Assessment Inventory professional manual*. Odessa, FL: Psychological Assessment Resources.

Morley, S. and Adams, M. (1991). Graphical analysis of single-case time-series data. *British Journal of Clinical Psychology*, 30(2): 97–115.

Morley, S. and Adams, M. (1989). Some simple statistical tests for exploring single-case time-series data. *British Journal of Clinical Psychology*, 28: 1–18.

—— (1991). Graphical analysis of single-case time series data. *British Journal of Clinical Psychology*, 30: 97–115.

Newman, F. L and Ciarlo, J. A. (1994). Criteria for selecting psychological instruments for treatment outcome assessment. In Maruish, M.E. *The Use of Psychological Testing for Treatment Planning and Outcome Assessment*. New Jersey: Lawrence Erlbaum Associates.

Nordahl, H. M. and Nysaeter, T. E. (2005). Schema therapy for patients with borderline personality disorder: a single case series. *Journal of Behavior Therapy and Experimental Psychiatry*, 36: 254–264.

Ogles, B. M., Lambert, M. J. and Masters, K. S. (1996). *Assessing outcome in clinical practice*. Boston: Allyn and Bacon.

Ogles, B. M., Lambert, M. J. and Fields, S. A. (2002). *Essentials of outcome assessment*. New York: John Wiley & Sons.

Ogles, B. M., Lunnen, K. M. and Bonesteel, K. (2001). Clinical significance: history, application, and current practice. *Clinical Psychology Review*, 21: 421–46.

Ottenbacher, K. J. (1986). *Evaluating clinical change*. Baltimore: Williams & Wilkins.

Powers, S. W., Piazza-Waggoner, C., Jones, J. S., Ferguson, K. S., Daines, C. and Acton, J. D. (2006). Examining clinical trial results with single-subject analysis: an example involving behavioural and nutrition treatment for young children with cystic fibrosis. *Journal of Pediatric Psychology*, 31(6): 574–81.

Rizvi, S. L., and Nock, M. K. (2008). Single-case experimental designs for the evaluation of treatments for self-injurious and suicidal behaviors. *Suicide and Life-Threatening Behavior*, 38(5): 498–602.

Shadish, W.R. and Rindskopf, D. M. (2007). Methods for evidence-based practice: quantitative synthesis of single-subject designs. *New Directions for Research*, 113: 95–109.

Sheldon, K. and Tennant, A. (2009). Using dialectical behaviour therapy with forensic personality disorder patients: some preliminary findings on the use of single case methodologies. The British and Irish Group for the Study of Personality Disorder (BIGSPD). Annual Conference, Dublin, 2–4 March.

Smith, J. D., Handler, L. and Nash, M. R. (2010). Therapeutic assessment for pre-adolescent boys with oppositional defiant disorder: a replicated single-case time-series design. *Psychological Assessment*, 22(3): 593–602.

Sperry, L., Brill, P., Howard, K. I., and Grissom, G. (1996). *Treatment outcomes in psychotherapy and psychiatric interventions*. New York: Brunner/Mazel.

Spielberger, C. D. (1999). *STAXI-2: State-Trait Anger Expression Inventory-2 professional manual*. Lutz, FL: Psychological Assessment Resources.

Sturmey, P. (2010). Case formulation in forensic psychology. In M. Daffern, L. F. Jones, and J. Shine (Eds). *Offence paralleling behaviour: a case formulation approach to offender assessment and intervention* (pp. 25–51). Chichester: Wiley & Sons.

Tennant, A. (2010). Dialectical behaviour therapy targeting violent behaviour in a male forensic in-patient setting. In A. Tennant and K. Howells (Eds). *Using time not doing time: a practitioner's perspective of personality disorder and risk* (pp. 63–80). Chichester: Wiley & Sons.

Turpin, G. (2001). Single case methodology and psychotherapy evaluation: from research to practice. In C. Mace, S. Moorey and B. Roberts (Eds). *Evidence in the psychological therapies: a critical guide for practitioners* (pp. 91–113). Hove, UK: Brunner-Routledge.

Van den Noortgate, W. and Onghena, P. (2007). The aggregation of single-case results using hierarchical linear models. *The Behavior Analyst Today*, 8(2): 52–75.

Wise, E. A. (2004). Methods for analyzing psychotherapy outcomes: a review for clinical significance, reliable change, and recommendations for future directions. *Journal of Personality Assessment*, 82: 50–9.

9 The idiographic measurement of change

Sean Hammond

The present chapter represents an enlargement and adaptation of a didactic paper presented by the author in another place (Hammond and O'Rourke, 2007).

Introduction

Almost all intervention programmes seek to facilitate change of some sort. Indeed, a therapeutic intervention that failed to induce change might reasonably be considered irrelevant and unjustified. Therapeutic interventions in clinical forensic settings are largely aimed at improving or changing mental health status while enabling clients to acquire prosocial skills and reduce risk. This typically involves targeting behavioural deficits and cognitive processes (Marshall *et al.*, 1998). Therapeutic procedures exist to facilitate these changes in client functioning and there is some reason for cautious optimism in their efficacy (McGuire, 1995; Blackburn, 1998; Bateman and Fonagy, 2000; Warren *et al.*, 2003; Huchzermeier *et al.*, 2006; Nadorta *et al.*, 2009).

The measurement of change underpins the process of programme evaluation and, in essence, the problem is a simple one. The researcher needs only to take a measurement before the intervention begins and then again afterwards. Change may then be viewed as the discrepancy between the two measures. This simple principle serves as the basis for most randomised controlled trials of therapeutic interventions. Participants are randomly allocated to two groups, treatment and control. One group receives the therapeutic intervention and the other does not. Measures are taken from each participant prior to the intervention applied to the treatment group. Following the intervention, measures are again taken from all participants in both groups. The logic of this approach is that, if the characteristics being measured are influenced by the intervention, the scores obtained in the treatment group will change in a predictable and consistent fashion between time 1 and time 2 while there will be no such change for the control group. If both groups show a similar pattern of change then this cannot be ascribed to the therapeutic intervention.

The issues addressed by treatment are often multifaceted and varied, for example treatment may involve such targets as self-concept, victim empathy, impulse control and other clinical disorders such as post-traumatic stress disorder as well as taking into account idiosyncratic contextual factors. For this reason the evaluation of therapeutic interventions using some form of aggregated global measure such as long-term recidivism or mental health status, while ultimately informative, cannot provide much detail concerning the utility of the treatment in question upon the individual client.

In addition to trying to identify a client's degree of change over treatment, it is also useful to explore the process of treatment (Howard *et al.*, 1996; Pfafflin *et al.*, 2005). Within the general psychotherapy literature there has been much work on identifying the factors that promote change (Greenberg and Pinsof, 1986; Grawe, 1997) and there is a sense that research in this area needs to reflect the 'real world of therapy practice' (Goldfried and Wolfe, 1996). The implication here is that the therapeutic context leads naturally to an idiographic focus in which individual change takes on a primary importance.

Statistical methods employed for evaluating change are many and varied (Tate and Hokanson, 1993; Overall and Tonidandel, 2002; Steyer *et al.*, 1997; Croon *et al.*, 2000; Spiel and Glueck, 1998; Gesch *et al.*, 2001; Lane and Zelinski, 2003) and have potential relevance to the evaluation of change in forensic settings. However, they nearly all operate on the level of group differentiation. While this orientation is appropriate when the treatment itself is the unit of analysis and clients are viewed as essentially homogeneous, it is not helpful when the focus is upon individual change. For example the assumption of homogeneous client groups is often difficult to justify with personality disordered clients (Farrington and Jolliffe, 2002).

One difficulty with the 'group level' feature of statistical analysis is that clinicians may become disillusioned with the aggregation of data in order to facilitate statistical analyses pertinent to their individual cases (Fishman, 2002). Unfortunately, many researchers hold that these aggregated forms of statistical analysis are fundamental to actuarial practice. This has led to a rejection of the scientific method among many therapists to be replaced by a more client-centred or experiential approach. It is my contention that an idiographic orientation does not preclude actuarial science and that there exists ample objective means to properly evaluate treatment that utilise the richness of idiographic context as well as the objective and structured advantages of statistical analysis.

None of these techniques are new but they are not widely used. In this chapter I propose to demonstrate how objective techniques for evaluating change can be applied to the idiographic context. Furthermore, I wish to demonstrate how qualitative data, when properly structured, can provide a good basis for and actuarial assessment of change. In so doing, I imagine that I will be pushing against an open door for many clinical practitioners. Nevertheless, despite the fact that the techniques I will describe have been around for many years they are largely ignored in the scientific literature (Fortune and Hutson, 1984).

Clinical assessment is predominantly performed in an idiographic context, since judgements and decisions made on the basis of the assessment are individualistic and pertain directly to the client's own idiosyncratic needs and characteristics (Farmer and Nelson-Gray, 1999). Nevertheless, it is typical to apply norm-based psychometry to provide standards against which an individual's performance or behaviour can be judged. Much research of ongoing treatment efficacy relies upon repeated application of psychometric tests in order to gauge the manner and degree of change exhibited by clients (Chiesa and Fonagy, 2000). Objective tests, whether they are performance measures or based on self-report, are largely norm-referenced. This approach explicitly excludes the idiosyncratic nature of the client and their context (Quayle and Moore, 1998).

Psychometric indices of change

Before describing the structured idiographic approach, I wish to take a look at a useful and widely used strategy for identifying individual change that utilises normative information but still provides an idiographic focus. I will also attempt to highlight some of its limitations.

Typically, psychologists have approached the challenge of assessing individual change by taking measures prior to, and following, a specific intervention. The two measures are then compared to examine the differences between them. This difference is considered to represent the degree of change that has occurred. This appears to be a simple and direct approach to the problem, but unfortunately a change in a test score does not guarantee 'true' psychological change. The reason for this is that every psychological measure contains error and is prone to overestimate or underestimate unpredictably. This instability of the test score can be such that it will invalidate simple before and after comparisons. One way in which we identify the stability of our measure is to establish the reliability of the test using a large representative or 'normative' sample. This essentially relies on the assumption that when scores are aggregated across a large sample the estimation error should partial itself out.

It is important to be able to demonstrate that the test scores do not change appreciably over time. Thus, the particular form of reliability we are concerned with is derived from a test-retest design since this is the estimate that relates to the temporal stability of the test. Only tests with good levels of test-retest reliability are appropriate for evaluating change.

The degree of error or instability in the test score is identified as the standard error of measurement (SEM). This is estimated using normative information that has already been gathered for the psychometric measure in question. The parameters needed are the standard deviation of the test score and its test-retest reliability coefficient. The SEM can then be calculated using the following formula:

SEM = Standard Error of Measurement
σ_o = Standard deviation of the observed test score
r_{tt} = Test-retest reliability coefficient

A variety of techniques have been proposed to use these norm based parameters in order to evaluate the reliability of the observed change in scores

(Jacobson and Truax, 1991; Mellenbergh and Van den Brink, 1998; Wise, 2004; Bauer, Lambert and Nielson, 2004) and these have become known as reliable change indices (RCI). One general formula for evaluating individual change, used by Lord and Novick (1968), is as follows:

$$z = \frac{x_1 - x_2}{SEM\sqrt{2}} = RCI$$

Where:

x_1 is the score at time 1
x_2 is the score at time 2
z is normally distributed with a mean of zero and s.d. of one.

This formula may also be expressed as:

$$z = \frac{x_1 - x_2}{\sqrt{2(SEM)^2}} = RCI$$

This is the form in which it is presented by Jacobson and Truax. The denominator in both cases is an estimate of the standard error of difference and there have been a number of suggested improvements on the basic model (Maassen, 2004; Evans *et al.*, 1998; Parsons *et al.*, 2009). However, although they rely on slightly different underlying assumptions (Atkins *et al.*, 2005), these modifications do not appear to appreciably alter the basic result (Temkin, 2004).

Thus, by use of normative information for a given psychometric test, it becomes possible to identify the degree of reliable change between two administrations of that test for any individual. Nevertheless, there remains a number of limitations to this approach.

In order to demonstrate the simplicity of the technique and also to highlight some of its limitations a hypothetical example is provided in Box 9.1. Here Mr A and Mr B have both been tested on a ten-item test. Items are answered true or false. Consistent with typical practice, a 'true' response is given a numerical code of '1' and 'false' is coded '0'. The total score is the sum of the 'true' responses. Here we see that Mr A has a score of 7 at time 1 but at time 2 his score has dropped to 3. Mr B, on the other hand has an identical score (5) at time 1 to that at time 2. The norms for this hypothetical test are found in the hypothetical test manual. We are particularly interested in the SD (2.1) and the test-retest reliability estimate (0.85).

By using the formula above we find that the RCI for Mr A is 3.51 and that for Mr B is 0.00. As this value can be treated as a normal deviate, we now know that Mr A has manifested statistically significant change while Mr B has not.

Box 9.1 **Example of two cases scoring on a hypothetical ten-item test**

	Mr A		Mr B	
	Time 1	*Time 2*	*Time 1*	*Time 2*
	1	1	1	0
	1	1	0	1
	0	1	1	0
	1	0	0	1
	0	0	1	0
	1	0	0	1
	1	0	1	0
	0	0	0	1
	1	0	1	0
	1	0	0	1
	7	3	5	5

Norms for the test score

Mean = 4.2, SD = 2.1, Test-retest reliability (r_{tt}) = 0.85

$$SEM = SD \times \sqrt{(1 - r_{tt})} = 2.1 \times \sqrt{1 - 0.85} = 2.1 \times 0.387 = 0.81$$

$$SE_{dif} = SEM \sqrt{2} = 0.81 \times 1.41 = 1.14$$

Mr A   Mr B

$$RCI_A = \frac{x_1 - x_2}{SE_{dif}} = \frac{4}{1.14} = 3.51 \qquad RCI_B = \frac{x_1 - x_2}{SE_{dif}} = \frac{0}{1.14} = 0.00$$

The most glaring limitation of this procedure is that it is only concerned with the aggregated test score and this can mask significant changes in the client's response profile. For example Mr B shows no change whatsoever (RCI = 0) but if we look at the profile of item responses we can easily see that every one of his answers has changed. It is arguable that Mr B has changed more than Mr A because ten of his answers have changed while only six of Mr A's have. This is missed because our only unit of analysis is the aggregated test score.

In addition, RCI measures are based upon the principles of classical test theory which itself is founded upon the assumption that measurement error is random. However, in many of the non-compliant cases that are encountered in a forensic setting we would expect a confounding of the test score due to dissembling or defensive responding to the test items (Lanyon, 2001; Resnick, 1988). Thus, substantial parts of the measurement error may be systematic rather than random.

A further limitation is that the method assumes that there exists a valid normative data set from which to draw the requisite parameters. Many tests in common usage lack this information, especially those developed in different countries from the target sample where the normative base may be culturally or linguistically inappropriate. The forensic population is relatively small and it may not be possible to find data that represent the particular client group to which the case under scrutiny belongs. Thus, the number of tests that lend themselves to these individual analyses is greatly limited.

Finally, an obvious limitation is that of ceiling or floor effects in the estimation of change. Clearly, if an individual had a very high score at time 1 it would be easier for their score to decrease than someone who started with a medium score. In fact, each individual should have a unique SEM that reflects their own score level but the use of classical test theory means that the SEM is a function of the test and not of the individual (Mellenbergh and Van den Brink, 1998). For this reason it is most accurate around the mean and loses accuracy as the scores move to the extremes. Thus, tests used in forensic settings (for example anger measures used to evaluate anger management programmes) where the score may be expected to deviate from the norm may provide misleading results usually by underestimating the degree of reliable change.

The take home message here is that there will be cases where the true picture of individual change is masked by test score aggregation and it may be necessary to move away from total dependence on the test score in order to gain a truly individualised assessment of change. Fortunately, methods for comparing profiles do naturally emerge from item response theory (Fischer and Molenaar, 1995; Spiel and Gluek, 1998) and may prove applicable as a means of evaluating change. However, these techniques also impose assumptions and models that need to be verified with large normative samples. The reader is referred to Mellenberg and Van den Brink (1998) for an excellent and accessible review of alternative psychometric approaches to measuring individual change.

However, a final and critical limitation of these psychometric approaches to individual change is that they are constrained by the availability of relevant measures. The implication is that individual change can only be assessed along prescribed and tightly defined dimensions. Furthermore, the meaning of these dimensions is held constant across individuals. This is a risky assumption as demonstrated in the area of depression (Hammond, 1995a) where depressed clients appear to manifest more qualitatively discrete responses to the Beck Depression Inventory than healthy normative respondents. In addition, there are areas relevant to the assessment of violent and troubled clients that do not lend themselves to a simple trait-like conceptualisation. These might include motivational and situational factors as well as idiosyncratic construal systems. In order to obtain a full picture of the degree of individual change, it is necessary to tap into the idiosyncratic manner in which a given client construes the world and this cannot be explored effectively using standard normative methods.

The structured idiographic approach

There are a number of important aspects of a client that may best be explored in an idiographic manner. For example, the family dynamics of one individual will be qualitatively different from those of another simply because the size, structure and quality of interactions will vary according to the individual case. No individual will have exactly the same familial experiences. Similar arguments can be made when exploring, for example, mental health status, social supports, functional analyses of criminal behaviour and the underlying structure and function of fantasies.

A well-used and effective means of tapping into the unique experience and construal system of individual clients is the repertory grid (Beail, 1985; Houston, 1998; Bell, 1988). The repertory grid works on the principle that a person's state is defined by the constructs they use to construe the contextual elements of their world. Using a form of interview, the elements and constructs that define the area of construing under investigation are extracted by the assessor. The constructs are generally defined in bi-polar terms. These are then formulated into a unique and idiosyncratic grid, enabling the participant to judge each element on each construct using a pre-specified response range. This technique is the methodological component of personal construct theory (PCT: Kelly, 1955) and while it is true that the technique used in conjunction with a PCT framework can produce great insight in offender work (Houston, 1998), the technique itself is not bound to Kelly's original theoretical model.

Many clinical practitioners are daunted by statistical formulae and it is important to state here that the techniques we are describing apply geometry and algebra rather than statistics as an objective base. Statistical reasoning implies a probabilistic approach based upon generalisation from sample data. In the case of the idiographic techniques we are describing, the approach is more structural and relies instead upon co-ordinate geometry to provide interpretable results. While this will not necessarily placate the statistic-phobes among you, the important message is that the results of these assessments rely upon graphical presentations of maps rather more than numbers.

The grid is essentially a tailormade questionnaire that has relevance only to the client being assessed. There are a number of strategies for analysing data in order to summarise and interpret the pattern of connections exposed by the grid (Bell, 1988). However, at the heart of them all is the mathematical operation of singular value decomposition (SVD) of the grid matrix. This can be represented in formal matrix algebra as:

$$A = \Lambda \Psi \Omega$$

A = Matrix of element × construct connections
Λ = Spatial co-ordinate (map) matrix for elements
Ψ = Eigen value (variance) vector
Ω = Spatial co-ordinate (map) matrix of constructs

Repertory grid programmes all utilise this convention in one way or another in order to obtain spatial map co-ordinates for the elements and for the constructs. Terms often used are principal components, principal axes, principal coordinates, biplot, dual scaling or correspondence analysis, but they all describe essentially the same process. The resulting graphical representation of the client's construal system is one of the greatest advantages of this technique as it demonstrates in spatial terms how the individual structures their own psychological space.

Thus the repertory grid approach has the distinct advantage of providing a highly structured procedure for tapping into the unique idiosyncratic world of the client. It is also an extremely flexible technique and may be readily applied to the analysis of change (Winter, 2003; Koch, 1983; Houston, 1998).

Nevertheless, there is a major limitation to the method. The response format is imposed upon the client and must be common to all constructs. This limits the choice of constructs that the client can use. It is very likely, for example, that clients will have a variety of levels for categorising elements. Thus the construct 'friendly' may be categorisable in an ordered manner ranging from 'very' to 'not at all' while other important constructs may be purely nominal, such as 'where I interact with this person' (i.e. 'work', 'family', 'social', 'on the bus'). The repertory grid cannot accommodate both of these constructs within the same grid.

A technique that generalises the grid approach for multiple formats is the multiple card sort procedure. This technique has been used over many years in a number of contexts (Coxon, 1999) but its clinical use owes most to the description found in Canter, Brown and Groat (1985). This is an idiographic approach used to access individual classification systems involving attitudes, values, beliefs, representations and knowledge. The use of multiple card sorting (MCS) has been largely pioneered by David Canter and his colleagues (Wilson and Canter, 1993; Canter and King, 1996; Scott and Canter, 1997; Brown *et al.*, 2004).

MCS is similar in principle to the repertory grid approach and its rationale was initially grounded on the premises of personal construct theory. However, MCS has been advanced to challenge and test Kelly's assumption of the bipolarity of constructs. The underlying supposition of MCS is that

> the ability to function in the world relates closely to the ability to form categories and to construct systems of classification by which non-identical stimuli can be treated as equivalent ... Thus, an understanding of the categories people use and how they assign concepts to those categories is one of the central clues to the understanding of human behaviour.
>
> (Canter *et al.*, 1985, p. 79)

In addition, to its greater generality a further advantage of the multiple card sort procedure over that of the repertory grid is that it is simple to apply and is far less time consuming. While the principal interest is on the graphical representation of clients' construal systems, there is no loss of mathematical sophistication and equivalent measures are available for both techniques.

Administering a multiple card sort

The MCS procedure is extremely adaptive and can be conducted in either a structured or an unstructured manner. The following is the method of administration most frequently used by clinicians and researchers.

First, the client is invited to select a number of 'elements' to include in the sorting procedure. Elements are selected to have personal relevance to the domain in question; they can be people, places, images, fantasies and so on. It is entirely up to the client who or what they choose to include. The only stipulation is that the elements represent the domain in which construing is to be investigated. Thus, if the domain in question relates to the client's relating to others, the elements chosen may represent important people within the client's social world. Additional elements such as 'self' or 'self as child' may be added by the assessor. Each element is then written on a card and placed in front of the client. These cards form the basis of the sorting procedure.

The client is then asked to arrange, or group, the cards (elements) in any way they wish. There are no restrictions on the number of groups that can be formed or the number of cards placed in each group. The assessor takes a record of the cards in each grouping and then invites the client to arrange the cards again, using a different construct. This procedure is repeated until the client feels that all the possible groupings have been exhausted. Alternatively, the assessor can place an upper limit on the number of constructs used in the sort.

It is possible to impose a degree of structure on the MCS method. Structured card sorts involve the investigator predefining the elements, constructs or categories to be used by the client. For example the investigator may have a particular interest in the client's family and ask that the elements include themselves and the members of their immediate family. Alternatively, the investigator may choose a collection of predefined constructs or themes that the client is then required to use in sorting the cards. The structured method may be useful for investigators who want to focus the client on a specific conceptual system or who want to improve comparability between different sorts. However, careful consideration needs to be given to choosing elements and constructs. Indeed constraining the process too tightly has the potential to confine or restrict the participant, or to impose an unfamiliar or meaningless structure on their subjective reality. There are eight possible designs with MCS depending on the levels of constraint imposed on the data elicitation process. These are indicated in Table 9.1, where it should be apparent that at one extreme it is possible to identify an essentially normative design and at the other is a purely idiographic design.

Because of the fact that the response categories can now vary, the analysis of MCS data poses some fairly unique challenges over those used for the analysis of repertory grids. The variety of analytic techniques available to MCS users is

Table 9.1 Eight MCS designs by constraining idiographic expression

	Categories provided		Categories free	
	Constructs provided	Constructs free	Constructs provided	Constructs free
Elements provided	Pure Normative	X	X	X
Elements free	X	X	X	Pure Idiographic

well reviewed in Coxon (1999) but one very tractable method is known as Multiple Scalogram Analysis (or Multiple Structuple Analysis; MSA). The procedure was developed by Lingoes (1968) based upon the seminal work of Guttman (1950) on the principal components of scales. The purpose of the analysis is to map the cards (or elements) into a meaningful space defined by the sorts (or constructs) by which they are construed. The regions in the resulting map are then informed by partitions defined by the categories used. This may sound rather complex but the following example should provide a clearer insight.

Briefly, the MSA technique conceptualises a three-way data matrix (X) to represent the observed card sort table. This is known as the characteristic function and the elements of this matrix are identified as x_{ijk} and are recorded as 1 or 0. Thus, $x_{ijk} = 1$ if card i is placed in category k within sort j and zero otherwise. In this way the data may be viewed as a multi-category generalisation of the dichotomous situation from which Guttman derived his original scalogram measurement model, hence the term Multiple Scalogram Analysis.

In principle, Lingoes (1968) uses the characteristic function to generate a card by card association matrix that is simply the number of times a pair of cards have shared a similar category in the sorting process. This matrix is then subjected to an SVD analysis. The procedure does not end there, however, since the coordinates are then transformed such that all cards within a given category will be positioned in contiguous space. This requires that the boundaries defining the regions in the space are identified. This is done in an iterative manner, applying a loss function that allows the resulting co-ordinate space to reflect closely the observed characteristic function of the data. The technical detail of the method is found in Lingoes (1968) and less technical treatments can be found in Zvulun (1978) and Wilson (2000), the latter of which is particularly accessible. The MSA method, because of its generality, can be used on a wide variety of data sets and although we describe it here in relation to MCS it may also be used on repertory grids.

An example is presented in Table 9.2. This is taken from a study on the viability of MCS for the assessment of sexual fantasy (Kelly, 2002). Cards were selected from the Abel and Becker fantasy card sorting protocols. The participant reported in Table 2 carried out 4 sorts. In the first she classified the cards according to how arousing she found each scenario. In the second, the construct used was based on whether the card represented acceptable behaviour. She then sorted the cards from the perspective of a male and used the construct '*acceptable*', and

Table 9.2 The card sort table of one case using 16 cards (elements) and 4 sorts (constructs)

	Own perspective		Male	Old man
	Arousing	Acceptable	Acceptable	Arousing
1 Voyeuristic	2	3	3	3
2 Masochistic	1	1	3	3
3 Voyeuristic	3	3	3	3
4 Transvestism	2	2	1	2
9 Homosexual	2	3	1	1
10 Voyeuristic	2	2	3	3
12 Heterosexual	3	3	2	3
13 Heterosexual	1	2	1	2
14 Heterosexual	1	2	1	1
15 Heterosexual	1	2	1	3
16 Heterosexual	1	1	2	3

1 = Not arousing   1 = Not acceptable
2 = Arousing   2 = Acceptable
3 = Very arousing   3 = Very acceptable

finally she sorted the cards according to '*arousal*' from what she perceived to be an old man's perspective. It is possible that her use of a male perspective in sorting the cards reflects a distancing strategy but that is not an emphasis that we will address here. In each case this participant chose to use three ordinal categories for her sorts although she was free to use whatever categorisation scheme she wanted. In Figure 9.1 the resulting plot from the MSA is presented. Alongside the main plot are the partitions defined by the sort categories.

From the main plot it is clear that the homosexual and heterosexual fantasies have been discriminated despite the fact that this was not an explicit sorting theme. Thus, orientation may be viewed as an implicit construct for this particular case. Also voyeuristic themes have been integrated within the heterosexual region while transvestism appears to be more closely associated with homosexual themes. We also note that the masochistic fantasies are regionally separated.

Interpretation of the MSA plot is a largely qualitative exercise and may involve the insights of the clients themselves. However, the fact that the space may be partitioned by the categories used by the clients during their sorting provides a clear aid in regional interpretation that is not present in the standard principal component method of the repertory grid. A useful source for the interpretation of such analyses is provided in Wilson (2000).

The evaluation of change

The use of MCS or repertory grid provides a useful snapshot of the client's current construal of the elements in question. In order to evaluate change, of course, the process must be repeated a number of times and the resulting

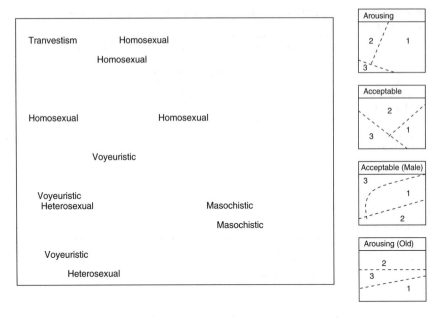

Figure 9.1 MSA plot of multiple card sort in Table 2.

structures compared. This provides a challenge because change cannot be readily summarised by the comparison of simple numeric scores. The procedure proposed here incorporates a qualitative and a quantitative amalgam.

In order for change to be evaluated it is important that some aspects of the procedure remain common to each administration of the task. Typically, the elements identified in the first administration remain fixed for each subsequent test. In this case, the client's choice of sorting constructs might be examined to see whether these have changed in quality or quantity. In Kelly's (2002) study her 14 participants repeated the card sort procedure three times over a three-month period. In Figure 9.2 the three MSA solutions are presented for a male participant. The degree of change over the three-month period is observable from the movement of the cards (elements) relative to each other across the three plots.

In order to compare an individual's plots resulting from a number of MSA analyses it is important to recognise a number of arbitrary features of the analysis. Firstly, the map co-ordinates generated by the programs have an arbitrary orientation. In other words the map resulting from the second administration of a multiple sorting assessment may be very similar to the first but be upside down or otherwise rotated and this may make direct comparison between the solutions awkward to interpret. In addition, it is quite possible that one solution is transposed into a mirror image of the other. Mathematically, these variations between solutions are not a problem because they do not affect the relative distance of each point in space from another. However, they do make the

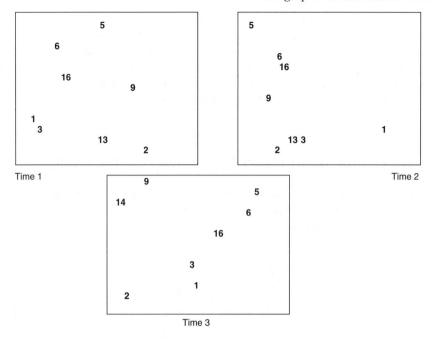

Time 1   Time 2

Time 3

Figure 9.2 Three MSA solutions of the same participant taken one month apart.

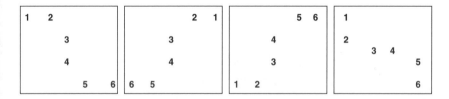

Figure 9.3 Four identical structures distinguished by rotation and translation while the relative distances between points remain identical.

interpretation of change difficult. An example of four identical structures confounded by rotation and transposition is presented in Figure 9.3.

Another issue with the direct comparison of spatial maps is that objective criteria for describing the degree of change are hard to establish. It is one thing to observe that a particular pattern has changed shape or that one element or card has moved across the space, but quite another to quantify that movement. One approach, originally proposed by Banister and Fransella (1967) for assessing the stability of repertory grids, was to identify the correlation matrix between the elements for each of the two administrations and then to calculate a correlation between the two matrices. This was done by taking the lower triangle of each correlation matrix and turning them into two vectors which were then correlated using a rank order procedure. However, MCS does not afford such correlation matrices. In Box 9.2 we demonstrate how, using the standardised co-ordinates from the plots, it is possible to generate a matrix of inter-element distances. This is a simple application of Pythagoras' theorem because the distance between any two points in space can be defined if their coordinates are known by conceiving a right-angled triangle in which the distance is viewed as the hypotenuse.

***Box 9.2* Deriving inter-element distances from a two-dimensional plot**

Let us suppose that the results of a MCS of four cards, A, B, C and D, have been carried out and the resulting plot is shown to the right. The co-ordinates for each card are as follows:

A	4	4
B	2	3
C	3	1
D	1	2

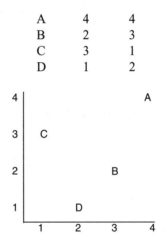

Now let us assume that we wish to calculate the distance between cards A and B. Using Pythagoras' Theorem we know that the square of the hypotenuse equals the sum of the squares of the two other sides, so we need to create a right angle triangle such that AB is the hypotenuse.

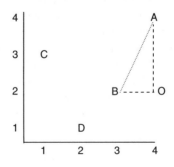

Finding O, we can now easily calculate the squared distance between A and B (d_{AB}) as follows:

$$AB = BO^2 + AO^2 = 1^2 + 2^2 = 5$$

Given that we know the co-ordinates (x_x and x_y) for each card the formula can be expressed more generally as:

$$d_{ij} = (x_{i1} - x_{j1})^2 + (x_{i2} - x_{j2})^2 = \sum_{k=1}^{ND} (x_{ik} - x_{jk})^2$$

The expression on the far right describes the situation with ND dimensions.

The reader should now be able to verify that the distances between all the cards can be shown in the distance matrix below above the diagonal. Since these represent the square of the hypotenuse it is conventional to take the square-root of this value to represent the true distance (below the diagonal).

	A	B	C	D
A	0.00	5.00	10.00	13.00
B	2.24	0.00	5.00	1.00
C	3.16	2.24	0.00	5.00
D	3.60	1.00	2.24	0.00

Once the d-matrices are generated it is quite legitimate to follow Bannister and Fransella's example and compute rank-order correlations between two solutions.

This approach, while a bit tedious, is readily performed by hand. The tedium can be alleviated by writing a little program to do the mundane math (see Box 9.3). The result of such an analysis is to provide a numerical value indicating how similar the two plots are.

A second strategy is rather more complex but has the advantage of providing an index of the reliability of change. This may be viewed as analogous to classical test theory which can be expressed formally as:

$$T = O + E$$

where O is the observed score derived from a psychometric test, E is an error term and T is the 'true' score. Extrapolating to co-ordinate structures rather than single

---

Box 9.3 A simple Pascal listing to generate distance from an ND-dimensional set of co-ordinates

```
// NC = N of cards (Input)
// ND = N of dimensions (usually 2) (Input)
// x[NC,ND] = matrix of coordinates (Input)
// d[NC,NC] = matrix of distances between cards

for i:=1 to NC do
begin
        for j:=1 to NC do
        begin
                d[i,j]:=0;
                for k:=1 to ND do
                begin
                        d[i,j]:=d[i,j]+sqr(x[i,k]–x[j,k]);
                end;
                d[i,j]:=sqrt(d[i,j]);
        end;
end;
```

---

test scores we might present a similar model for structured idiographic assessments as:

$$T = O_i + E$$

where O_i is the observed structure at time i, E is a matrix representing error in the placement of points and T is the 'true' structure. In fact it is a little more complicated than this because we have to control for the rotational and transpositional arbitrariness. This is done by introducing the following:

$$sTR_i = O_i + E$$

In this expression, R_i is an orthogonal rotation matrix for T into O_i and s is a translation vector. R and s can be readily found using matrix algebra providing T exists, but this is unknown at the moment. However, a method known as generalised procrustean analysis provides the answer (Gower, 1975; Lingoes and Borg, 1978; Commandeur, 1991; Borg and Groenen, 1997). In this analysis an average or 'centroid' configuration is derived in an iterative manner by using one observed configuration as the starting point and cyclically updating it by rotation and translation while keeping the others fixed. There are a number of ways of achieving the 'best' centroid configuration. In Box 9.4 a short computer listing is provided to help the reader grasp one of the simplest and most direct methods.

Applying the analogy of classical test theory where averaging a test score over occasions gives an estimate of the 'true' (T) score, we may treat the centroid configuration as a 'true' structure. Having obtained this centroid (T) we can them employ results from Lingoes and Borg (1978) who identified a measure of common variance between matrices. This measure may be used to estimate the squared correlation between the centroid (T) and the observed structure at time i (O_i) and this may then be interpreted as a reliability coefficient. Thus if a client produces exactly similar structures over time the index of fit will be a perfect 1.0 on each occasion. The degree to which an individual's idiographic structures deviate can be evaluated by examining this measure.

It should be stressed that the centroid is obtained under conditions of rigid rotation and translation. This imposes a model in which the relative distances between the points in space do not vary. More relaxed models are possible and these will inevitably provide better fit. Lingoes and Borg (1978) describe these models in their general procrustean individual differences (PINDIS) approach (see also Commandeur, 1991). However, interesting though these models may prove to be with particular cases, they should be used with caution as it is not

---

***Box 9.4* A simple Pascal listing to generate a centroid co-ordinate solution**

```
// nc = number of configurations
// nd = number of dimensions
// nv = number of elements

// The individual configurations from time 1 to t are stored in a
   3 dimensional array x
// where xijk represents the co-ordinate for element j on dimension
   k for configuration i
// Note that the configurations should all be normed before the
   procedure starts

// Stress is a measure of the overall fit of the configurations to the
   resulting centroid
// Cycle is the number of iterative cycles required to obtain the centroid
// Fiti is a measure of the degree of fit of configuration i to the centroid

// Note: the routine ROTATE is not supplied here. The user should
   insert a standard
// procrustean orthogonal rotation procedure. These normally require
   additional
// routines to carry out singular value decomposition.
```

```
         stress:= 999;
         cycle:= 0;
iterate:   cycle:= cycle + 1;
       r:= 0;
       for j:= 1 to nd do
       begin
         for i:= 1 to nv do
         begin
           r:= r + sqr(d2[i,j]);
           c(i,j):= 0;
         end;
       end;
       s:= 1 - r;
       if abs(stress - s) < 0.000001 then
       begin
         stress:= s;
         for k:= 1 to nc do
         begin
           fit[k]:= 0;
           for i: = 1 to nv do
           begin
             for j:= 1 to nd do
             begin
               a[i,j]:=x[k,i,j];
             end;
           end;
           rotate(nv,nd,a,d);// A standard procrustean orthogonal rotation
           for i:= 1 to nv do
           begin
             for j:= 1 to nd do
             begin
               c[i,j]:=c[i,j]+a[i,j];
               fit[k]:=fit[k]+a[i,j]*d[i,j];
             end;
           end;
         end;
         for i:= 1 to nv do
           for j:= 1 to nd do
             d[i,j]:= c[i,j] / nc;
           end;
         end;
         goto iterate;
       end;
```

always possible to apply psychological meaning to the differential weightings required by them.

In the case of our example a centroid solution is generated from the three solutions in Figure 9.2. We can see that the three solutions are remarkably similar and show little change. This is reflected in fit indices of 0.97, 0.97 and 0.94 for the three solutions respectively. The average of these is 0.96 and this represents the stability of the idiographic structure over a three month period with three monthly measurement points. In fact, a reanalysis of Kelly's data revealed a high degree of stability for all of her 14 participants with stability indices ranging from 0.80 to 0.99. This is despite the fact that participants were free to use different constructs at each assessment point.

Clearly, in a therapeutic intervention it is expected that a degree of change will be observed and this will be expressed in low indices of stability. The point at which change occurs can also be observed by examining the relationships between structures. This can be demonstrated graphically as well as numerically since each configuration can be plotted as a point in space. To demonstrate two cases from Kelly's data are presented scaled and superimposed into two-dimensional space in Figure 9.4. The female participant of table 3 manifested an overall stability of 0.80 while the male participant described above revealed a stability index of 0.96. The points F1, F2 and F3 represent the three MCS administrations from the female case while M1, M2 and M3 represent the male participant.

From here it should be clear that the female has shown the greatest movement and this is reflected in her lower stability index. What is also of interest is that the female participant showed the greatest change between months 2 and 3. Had this been a therapeutic intervention it would be apparent that the major point of

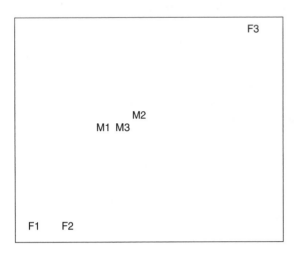

Figure 9.4 Plot of two cases (F and M) showing the relative degree of change over three assessments.

change happened after the second assessment. As this data was not collected over therapy there is no further information that we can utilise to explain the large shift at time 3. In order to interpret the meaning of this change more qualitative analyses would be required in which the changes in regional structure are examined in detail.

Application of structured idiographic methods

In evaluating therapeutic change the practitioner has a number of potential strategies that can be brought to bear. The structured idiographic approach has a number of advantages whether using a repertory grid or a multiple card sort procedure. The primary advantage is that the assessments convey information regarding the construal system of the client and the manner in which the results are presented leaves much room for client involvement in the interpretation. Indeed, the client's interpretation of the emergent maps may prove to be extremely fruitful in the therapy itself as well as enabling the practitioner to gain some clear insight into the degree and nature of any change.

Principally, it is the nature of the change that is the focus of these techniques rather than its degree. For this reason, it is hard to see how such assessments will play out in a court of law where burdens of proof are required, or in a policy making context where aggregated statistical data is largely considered necessary. Nevertheless, the therapeutic context should benefit greatly from the use of structured idiographic methods where the experiential aspects may be couched within a transparent and actuarial framework.

The utility of these techniques relies heavily upon the choice of elements or cards under scrutiny. They are particularly insightful where the cards represent people in the lives of the client (usually including the self at various stages). However, it should be emphasised that the cards can represent anything – fantasy themes, activities, stories or biscuits.

The continuing debate about the treatability of clients classified as having severe antisocial personality disorders places great emphasis upon the notion that treatment can occasion change in such people (Duggan, 2005; Polaschek, 2010). It behoves psychologists working with offenders with personality disorders to utilise the most appropriate and effective means possible to evaluate the changes that therapeutic interventions occasion.

Idiographic change describes the psychological movement observed in an individual client. This is a vital concern, because while group change is relatively easy to assess, it does not help much in decisions relating to individual clients that may impact upon public safety. The heterogeneity of forensic clients is such that a particular treatment may be of huge benefit to one client while having a negligible, or even deleterious, effect on another.

Dangerous clients manifest distorted conceptual systems that may lead to unpredictability and often this distorted thinking is highly idiosyncratic (Abel *et al.*, 1989; Bjørkly, 1997). The MCS procedure is designed to offer a flexible tool for exploring an individual's conceptual system. In so doing, it retains a focus on the subjective, personal and unique construction of meaning. It specifically facilitates the study of the unique categories and constructs the client attributes to the unique elements in his or her world. The analysis of MCS permits the elicitation of in-depth qualitative information while structuring information sufficiently for quantitative systematic analysis (Tanner and Hammond, 1996; Wilson, 2000).

In addition to its potential for accessing the client's construal system, MCS has the potential for demonstrating patterns of change and allowing the development of meaningful hypotheses by examining the structure of the idiographic profiles of the same individual overtime. It allows the clinician to clarify the intermediate processes that have instigated these changes from the juxtaposition of elements within the person's idiographic space.

An important advantage of the MCS approach is that it is empowering for the participant by enabling them to determine both the course and content of the assessment. However, while MCS is less prescriptive than other assessment tools, its outcome is not as easily manipulated by the client as the standard self-report assessment techniques. Such is the complexity of the algebra required to move from the sorts to the spatial solution, it is hard to imagine how a client will be able to produce a desired solution by deliberate design. That said, anomalies in the structures might indicate attempts at obfuscation. Just as with repertory grids, it may be possible to identify distancing tactics in the choice of construct. However, the clarity with which a construct's categories discriminate the space is a good indicator of its relevance to the domain in question. Therefore, the MCS offers a ready way to reveal the obfuscatory choice of unhelpful constructs.

Finally, MCS can be readily integrated into the therapeutic process (Kavatha, 1997), which should encourage greater cohesion between assessment and therapy. It has been used successfully with young offenders with low levels of educational achievement (Murphy, 2005) as well as university students (Hammond, 1995). Because the constructs are elicited during the process of assessment, MCS is generally much quicker to perform than a repertory grid. This makes it a more realistic option for complementing existing assessment batteries.

The typical approach to assessing change by looking at test score differences has an important place in evaluating individual change but it has limitations, some of which are answered by uncoupling the assessment from its norm reference and applying a specifically idiographic approach. This chapter has attempted to introduce a method and model for using a structured idiographic procedure in the assessment of change.

Design and limitations of MCS assessments

The preceding paragraphs may suggest that MCS is a great panacea for forensic assessment of change but it does have limitations. The focus of interest is upon the construal system of the client and observing how this changes over a period of time. It does not lend itself readily to the exploration of changes to traits or competencies and these systems may be best approached using the more conventional psychometric procedures.

A major challenge in setting up an MCS assessment is defining the domain of interest. The social environment is a reasonably straightforward domain since the elements utilised are often people within the clients social world. Things become more complex when the domain is more abstract or tightly focused because the necessary reduction of the domain into constituent elements may become problematic. Because the procedure is designed to tap the individual's own sense of a domain, the assessor cannot be too directive in defining the manner that it is to be reduced. The ecological validity of the elements constituting the domain is dependent upon the individual client's understanding of the constructs in question. Often this means that things must be kept simple and uncomplicated. When elements are physical entities the assessment is generally simple and straightforward, but if they are abstract concepts the burden of abstraction may prove too much for many clients.

Future directions

The MCS procedures described here are still relatively new and merit further research and development. First, the realistic scope of MCS within forensic assessment of change is an area for further work. As mentioned, a most straight-forward use of MCS construal of others and the social mileu. However, MCS promises a wider scope into areas such as fantasy, victimology and therapeutic alliance, all of which merit further research.

The data analytic strategies employed would also benefit from further scrutiny. There are a great many ways that the configurations may be generated, we have advocated the MSA approach here as a good general method, while most repertory grid enthusiasts use a principal components strategy. Comparative analyses of the variety of dimension reducing techniques for MCS data would be a useful addition to the research literature.

The treatment of change advocated here has been to treat time as a facet in a three-dimensional data block (element by dimension by time) and then to apply a procrustean analysis to the two-dimensional (element by dimension) configurations from each time point. There are a number of alternative procedures that might serve to do the job efficiently and informatively. I have carried out comparative analyses that have led me to prefer the procrustean method reported here, but further comparative research would be useful in order to promote the method in clinical and forensic assessment.

Conclusions

The clinician working with violent offenders must take on board a number of highly idiosyncratic elements such as interpersonal dynamics and idiosyncratic and contextual risk factors, as well as distortions in cognition and emotional processing. The MCS approach allows a tailored and authentic assessment of client construal systems to be undertaken. The use of generalised procrustean analyses of multiple MCS assessments provides further detail, allowing for objective measures of change that are informed by qualitative representations of regional shift.

This chapter proposes that idiographic graphical representations of psychological change should complement psychometric test scores in the forensic context. In particular, it is argued that idiographic procedures offer sensitive and precisely targeted assessments. We have attempted to show the way in which a technique like MCS may provide both qualitative and quantitative insights into the change exhibited by a single client. The information returned from this assessment is qualitative but highly structured and may be used to inform treatment planning and evaluation.

Further reading

The MCS procedure advocated in this chapter has not been widely disseminated to date. It is increasingly being used in ergonomics and website evaluation studies but there is still a paucity of published clinical applications. Interested readers are encouraged to acquaint themselves with the general idiographic framework pioneered by George Kelly and his followers, in particular the excellent book by Julia Houston (1998) where its value in the appraisal and treatment of offenders is described.

The more specific utility of card sorting is examined in the work of David Canter and colleagues; Canter, Brown and Groat (1985) is the seminal work in this regard. Of particular interest is Canter (2006) where a synthesis of MCS and PCT is provided. Margaret Wilson (2000) provides an excellent general introduction to the process of interpreting card sort maps and the paper by Zvulun (1978) is recommended to provide a non-technical account of the analysis procedure.

Most of the literature describing the analysis methods derives from the field of multidimensional scaling and the early accounts are particularly recommended for starters (Gower, 1975; Lingoes and Borg, 1978; Commandeur, 1991). An excellent general text is Borg and Groenen (2005); see especially Chapters 20, 21 and 22.

References

Abel, G. G., Gore, D. K., Holland, C. L., Camp, N., Becker, J. V. and Rathner, J. (1989). The measurement of the cognitive distortions of child molesters. *Annals of Sex Research*, 2: 135–53.

Atkins, D. C., Bedics, J. D., McGlinchey, J. B. and Beauchaine, T. P. (2005). Assessing clinical significance: does it matter which method we use? *Journal of Consulting and Clinical Psychology*, 73 (5): 982–9.

Bannister, D. and Fransella, F. (1967). *A grid test of schizophrenic thought disorder: a standard clinical test*. Barnstaple: Psychological Test Publications.

Bateman, A. W. and Fonagy, P. (2000). Effectiveness of psychotherapeutic treatment of personality disorder. *British Journal of Psychiatry*, 177: 138–43.

Bauer, S., Lambert, M. J., and Nielsen, S. L. (2004). Clinical significance methods: a comparison of statistical techniques. *Journal of Personality Assessment*, 82: 60–70.

Beail, N. (1985). *Repertory grid technique and personal constructs: applications in clinical and educational settings.* London: Groom Heim.

Bell, R. C. (1988). The analysis of repertory grid data. *International Journal of Personal Construct Psychology*, 1: 101–18.

Bjørkly, S. (1997). Clinical assessment of dangerousness in psychotic patients: some risk indicators and pitfalls. *Aggression and Violent Behavior*, 2(2): 167–78.

Blackburn, R. (1998). Treatability of personality disorders: Paper submitted to the committee of inquiry into the Personality Disorder Unit, Ashworth Special Hospital.

Borg, I. and Groenen, P. (1997). *Modern multidimensional scaling: theory and applications.* New York: Springer.

Borg, I. and Groenen, P. (2005). *Modern multidimensional scaling: theory and applications.* Springer, Second edn.

Brown, J., Fritzon, K., Miller, S. and Sees C. (2004). HMP Dovegate therapeutic community: the evaluation of treatment outcome in relation to reconviction, social re-integration and psychological change: progress report. Forensic Psychology Unit: University of Surrey.

Canter, D. (2006). Doing psychology that counts: George Kelly's influence. *Personal Construct Theory and Practice*, 4: 27–38.

Canter, D. and King, K. (1996). Ward development project. *Psychology in Action*, 5: 239–55.

Canter, D., Brown, J. and Groat, L. (1985). A multiple sorting procedure for studying conceptual systems. In M. Brenner, J. Brown and D. Canter (Eds). *The research interview: uses and approaches.* London: Academic Press.

Chiesa, M. and Fonagy, P. (2000). Cassel personality disorder study. Methodology and treatment effects. *British Journal of Psychiatry*, 176: 485–91.

Commandeur, J. J. F. (1991). *Matching configurations.* Leiden: DSWO Press.

Coxon, A. P. M. (1999). *Sorting data: collection and analysis.* Thousand Oaks, CA: Sage.

Croon, M. A., Bergsma, W. and Hagenaars, J. A. (2000). Analyzing change in categorical variables by generalized log-linear models. *Sociological Methods & Research*, 29: 195–229.

Duggan, C. (2005). Treatment of severe personality disorder. *Psychiatry*, 4(3): 26–8.

Evans, C., Margison, F. and Barkham, M. (1998). The contribution of reliable and clinically significant change methods to evidence-based mental health. *Evidence Based Mental Health*, 1: 70–2.

Farmer, R. F. and Nelson-Gray, R. O. (1999). Functional analysis and response covariation in the assessment of personality disorders: a reply to Staats and to Bissett and Hayes Behaviour. *Behaviour Research and Therapy*, 37: 385–94.

Farrington, D. P. and Jolliffe, D. (2002). *A feasibility study into using a randomised controlled trial to evaluate treatment pilots at HMP Whitemoor.* London: Home Office Report 14/02.

Fischer, G. H. and Molenaar, I. W. (1995). *Rasch models: foundations, recent developments and applications.* New York: Springer.

Fishman, D. B. (2002). From single case to database: a new method for enhancing psychotherapy, forensic, and other psychological practice. *Applied & Preventive Psychology*, 10: 275–304.

Fortune, J. C. and Hutson, B. A. (1984). Selecting models for measuring change when true experimental conditions do not exist. *Journal of Educational Research*, 77(4): 197–206.

Gesch, C. B., Hammond, S. M., Hampson, S. E., Eves, A. and Crowder, M. J. (2001). Influence of supplementary vitamins, minerals and essential fatty acids on the antisocial behaviour of young adult prisoners: randomised, placebo-controlled trial. *British Journal of Psychiatry*, 181: 22–8.

Goldfried, M. R. and Wolfe, B. E. (1996). Psychotherapy practice and research: repairing a strained alliance. *American Psychologist*, 51: 1,007–16.

Gower, J. (1975). Generalised procrustes analysis. *Psychometrika*, 40: 33–51.

Grawe, K. (1997). Research-informed psychotherapy. *Psychotherapy Research*, 7: 1–19.

Greenberg, L. S. and Pinsof, W. M. (1986). *The psychotherapeutic process: a research handbook*. New York: Guilford Press.

Guttman, L. (1950). The principal components of scale analysis. In S. A. Stouffer (Ed) *Measurement and prediction*. Princeton: Princeton University Press.

Hammond, S. M. (1995a). An IRT investigation of test bias in the beck depression inventory. *European Journal of Psychological Assessment*, 11: 14–21.

—— (1995b). Methods for the normative analysis of idiographic space. Paper presented at the biannual conference of the European Association of Psychological Assessment. Trier.

Hammond, S. M. and O'Rourke, M. M. (2007). Measurement of individual change: a didactic account of an idiographic approach. *Psychology, Crime and Law*, 5: 100–14.

Houston, J. (1998). *Making sense with offenders: personal constructs, therapy and change*. Chichester: Wiley.

Howard, K. I., Moras, K., Brill, P. L., Martinovich, Z. and Lutz, W. (1996). Evaluation psychotherapy: efficacy, effectiveness and patient progress. *American Psychologist*, 51: 1,059–64.

Huchzermeier, C., Bruß, E., Godt, N. and Aldenhoff, J. (2006). Kiel psychotherapy project for violent offenders: towards empirically based forensic next term psychotherapy – disturbance profiles and risk of recidivism among incarcerated offenders in a German prison. *Journal of Clinical Forensic Medicine*, 13(2): 72–9.

Jacobson, N. S. and Truax, P. (1991). Clinical significance: a statistical approach to defining meaningful change in psychotherapy research. *Journal of Consulting and Clinical Psychology*, 59: 12–19.

Kavatha, E. (1997). A scientist-practitioner approach to psychological assessment: an evaluation of multiple card sort procedure as an assessment technique used by counselling psychologists. Doctoral thesis. Department of Psychology: University of Surrey.

Kelly, A. (2002). An investigation into the viability of multiple card sorting in the assessment of sexual fantasy. Dissertation. Department of Applied Psychology: University College, Cork.

Kelly, G. A. (1955). *The psychology of personal constructs*. London: Routledge.

Koch, H. C. H. (1983). Changes in personal construing in three psychotherapy groups and a control group. *British Journal of Medical Psychology*, 56: 245–54.

Lane, C. J. and Zelinski, E. M. (2003). Longitudinal hierarchical linear models of the memory functioning questionnaire. *Psychology and Aging*, 18: 38–53.

Lanyon, R. I. (2001). Dimensions of self-serving misrepresentation in forensic assessment. *Journal of Personality Assessment*, 76: 169–79.

Lingoes, J. C. (1968). The multivariate analysis of qualitative data. *Multivariate Behavioral Research*, 3: 61–94.

Lingoes, J. C. and Borg, I. (1978). A direct approach to individual differences scaling using increasingly complex transformations. *Psychometrika*, 43: 491–519.

Lord, F. and Novick, M. R. (1968). *Statistical theories of mental test scores.* Reading, MA: Addison-Wesley.

Marshall, W. L., Fernandez, Y. M., Hudson, S. M. and Ward, T. (1998). *Sourcebook of treatment programs for sexual offenders.* New York: Plenum.

Maassen, G. H. (2004). The standard error in the Jacobson and Truax Reliable Change Index: the classical approach to the assessment of reliable change. *Journal of the International Neuropsychological Society*, 10: 888–93.

McGuire, J. (1995). *What works: reducing reoffending.* Chichester: Wiley.

Mellenbergh, G. J. and Van den Brink, W. P. (1998). The measurement of individual change. *Psychological Methods*, 3: 470–85.

Murphy, S. (2005). Evaluation of a small scale Irish probation service offender intervention initiative. Forensic master's dissertation. Department of Applied Psychology: University College, Cork.

Nadorta, M., van Dycka, R., Smita, J. H., Giesen-Bloob, J., Eikelenbooma, M., Wensingc, M., Spinhovend, P., Dirksene, C., Bleeckeb, J., van Milligena, B., van Vreeswijkf, M. and Arntzb, A. (2009). Three preparatory studies for promoting implementation of outpatient schema therapy for borderline personality disorder in general mental health care. *Behaviour Research and Therapy*, 47(11): 938–45.

Overall, J. E. and Tonidandel, S. (2002). Measuring change in controlled longitudinal studies. *British Journal of Mathematical and Statistical Psychology*, 55: 109–24.

Parsons T. D., Notebaert, A. J., Shields, E. W. and Guskiewicz, K. M. (2009). Application of reliable change indices to computerized neuropsychological measures of concussion. *International Journal of Neuroscience*, 119: 492–507.

Pfafflin, F., Bohmer, M., Cornehl, S. and Mergenthaler, E. (2005). What happens in therapy with sexual offenders? A model of process research. *Sexual Abuse: A Journal of Research and Treatment*, 17: 141–51.

Polaschek, D. L. L. (2010). Many sizes fit all: a preliminary framework for conceptualizing the development and provision of cognitive-behavioral rehabilitation programs for offenders. *Aggression and Violent Behavior*, doi: 10.1016/j.avb.2010.10.002.

Quayle, M. and Moore, E. (1998). Evaluating the impact of structured groupwork with men in a high security hospital. *Criminal Behaviour and Mental Health*, 8: 77–92.

Resnick, P. (1988). Malingering of posttraumatic disorders. In R. Rogers (Ed). *Clinical assessment of malingering and deception* (pp. 84–107). New York: Guilford.

Scott, M. J. and Canter, D. (1997). Picture or place? A multiple of landscape. *Journal of Environmental Psychology*, 17: 263–81.

Spiel, C. and Glueck, J. (1998). Item response models for assessing change in dichotomous items. *International Journal of Behavioral Development*, 22: 517–36.

Steyer, R., Eid, M. and Schwenkmezger, P. (1997). Modeling true intraindividual change: true change as a latent variable. *Methods of Psychological Research Online*, 2. Available from www.pabst-publishers.de/mpr/ (accessed 25/4/11).

Tanner, S. and Hammond, S. (1996). Shared representations of cancer: a normative evaluation of idiographic data. Paper presented at the British Psychological Society Conference. London.

Tate, R. L. and Hokanson J. E. (1993). Analysing individual status and change with hierarchical linear models: illustration with depression in college students. *Journal of Personality*, 61: 181–206.

Temkin, N. R. (2004). Standard error in the Jacobson and Truax Reliable Change Index: the 'classical approach' leads to poor estimates. *Journal of the International Neuropsychological Society*, 10: 899–901.

Warren, F., Preedy-Fayers, K., McGauley, G., Pickering, A., Norton, K., Geddes, J. R. and Dolan, B. (2003). *Review of treatments for severe personality disorder*. London: Home Office Report 30/03.

Wilson, M. (2000). Structuring qualitative data: Multidimensional Scalogram Analysis. In G. Breakwell, S. Hammond and C. Fife-Schaw (Eds). *Research methods in psychology*. London: Sage Publications.

Wilson, M. and Canter, D. V. (1993). Shared concepts in group decision making: a model for decisions based on qualitative data. *British Journal of Social Psychology*, 32: 159–72.

Winter, D. A. (2003). Repertory grid technique as a psychotherapy research measure. *Psychotherapy Research*, 13: 25–42.

Wise, E. A. (2004). Methods for analyzing psychotherapy outcomes: A review of clinical significance, reliable change and recommendations for future directions. *Journal of Personality Assessment*, 82(1): 50–9.

Zvulun, E. (1978). Multidimensional Scalogram Analysis: the method and its application. In S. Shye (Ed). *Theory construction and data analysis in the behavioral sciences*. San Francisco: Jossey-Bass.

10 Functional analysis

Michael Daffern

Overview

The aim of this chapter is to describe function analytic assessment approaches and provide instruction in techniques for research using functional analysis in applied forensic settings. It also introduces a novel application of functional analytic methodology, experimental functional analysis using offence paralleling behaviour, and describes a range of research tasks that are necessary for validation of this method and for functional analysis more generally. Before proceeding, it is important to note that function analytic assessment approaches are regularly used in forensic settings. There is, however, very little published research using this assessment approach in this context. This is partly because the idiographic approach is the most common application of functional analysis and researchers and clinicians rarely publish case studies. The scarcity of published research on functional analysis is also because there are very few well-validated methods available to develop and test functional analysis. A task for researchers is to remedy this problem by developing reliable and valid methods for conducting both idiographic and nomothetic functional analytic methods. This chapter will begin with a review of functional analysis, and then elucidate its application to offender assessment. An example of function analytic methodology that was developed and used to study aggression in psychiatric inpatients will then be described. Opportunities to use functional analysis and the need to consider experimental functional analyses are provided before the strengths and limitations of functional analysis are described.

Functional analysis

Numerous approaches to the assessment of an individual's presenting problem may be taken, with a distinction often made between structural and functional approaches (Haynes and O'Brien, 1998; Sturmey, 1996; Sturmey *et al.*, 2007). Structural assessment approaches focus on 'nonobservable inferred constructs' (Sturmey *et al.*, 2007, p. 4) or enduring traits within the individual (e.g. historical intrapsychic conflicts) (Bellack and Hersen, 1998). These approaches emphasise the correct classification of the form (topography) of a particular behaviour. By contrast, functional analyses seek to identify the purpose (function) of behaviour. The difference between form and purpose characterises the differences between structural and functional approaches. As an example, two patients may assault a member of staff in an identical manner, by punching them with a closed fist. Based on a topographical analysis, the two acts are identical. However, the purpose of the aggression may vary. One patient may behave aggressively because he is frightened and has learned that when he is aggressive he is taken to seclusion, somewhere where he might feel safe. Based on an assessment of purpose the interventions that are likely to result in a decrease of aggressive behaviour may include teaching the patient assertion skills, addressing his fears, providing safety and not reinforcing his avoidant behaviour (i.e. not secluding him). The second patient may behave aggressively because he is acutely psychotic and believes members of staff poison his food. Improvement of his mental state through pharmacological and cognitive behavioural interventions would be indicated for this individual.

As well as a focus on purpose, functional analyses describe the precise determinants of behaviour, with special emphasis on those that may be modified. This is typically achieved through assessment of the 1) behaviour of interest, 2) distal (predisposing) characteristics, 3) antecedent events, which are important for the initiation of the behaviour, and 4) consequences, which maintain and direct the course of the behaviour of interest. In typical *descriptive* functional analyses (rather than *experimental* functional analyses, in which hypothesised variables are manipulated to examine their influence) the target behaviour (e.g. aggression towards female staff), replacement behaviour (e.g. assertive communication of dissatisfaction) and the consequences maintaining the behaviour are specified in functional terms (Sturmey, 1996). Further, in functional analyses all behaviour is considered to be a consequence of multiple, interacting causal factors; variation in behaviour across settings is expected and explicitly sought. These variations are thought to be a function of important environmental controlling variables. Finally, in functional analyses there is a need to examine not only the determinants that maintain a problem behaviour but also those that maintain the non-occurrence of more adaptive behaviours (e.g. aggression may persist because the individual lacks appropriate anger regulation or assertion).

The key to identifying the precise determinants of behaviour lies in the principle of *adaptation to environment* (i.e. all behaviour is acquired and maintained because it is purposeful and has meaning when considered within the context of the person's limitations, tendencies, skills, values and vulnerabilities). Another key assumption of functional analysis (*aetiological heterogeneity*) is that behaviour is the result of a complex interaction between biological make-up, previous learning history and current situational influences (Haynes and O'Brien, 1998; Lee-Evans, 1994; Sturmey, 1996). Problem behaviours can be seen, therefore, as the result of a failure to learn adaptive behaviours or of learning maladaptive behaviours to satisfy an individual's functional needs. Accordingly, the focus of intervention is to: (1) design an intervention that introduces new controlling variables; and (2) 'to support and increase functionally equivalent alternate behaviours' (Sturmey, 1996, p. 7).

The purpose of function analytic assessment

Functional analysis serves a number of purposes; these include description, classification, measurement, treatment evaluation, assessment of causes, developing hypotheses about the function of behaviour and generating predictions about future behaviour (Sturmey, 2010). Its core purpose, however, is to gather information relevant to planning interventions (Lee-Evans, 1994). In the forensic context functional analysis may help clinicians integrate diverse client information, assist clients understand their own problems, enhance the therapeutic relationship (Eells, 2007, in Sturmey, 2010) and guide treatment.

The focus of functional analysis is varied and includes the study of psychological process (e.g. readiness to participate in treatment), systems (e.g. the purpose of events or activities of psychiatric units or prisons), groups (e.g. aggressive patients, or patients with particular issues like non-adherence) or individuals (e.g. why a particular individual continues to use drugs in prison). When using functional analysis the clinical and research question should be framed in terms of purpose: that is, what purpose does this behaviour serve?

Although functional analysis has demonstrated efficacy in prescribing interventions for other problem behaviours such as self-injury (Iwata *et al.*, 1982), and has been regarded by experts in the field to be a legitimate assessment approach for anger management problems (Howells, 1998), there are very few published studies in forensic settings that have used function analytic methodology. There are a number of published case studies utilising functional analysis for aggressive behavior (Thompson *et al.*, 1998; Kern *et al.*, 1997) and several attempts to conduct function analytic assessments of aggression in psychiatric hospitals (Daffern *et al.*, 2006; Daffern and Howells, 2009; Shepherd and Lavender, 1999) and adolescent secure units (McDougal, 2000). Gresswell and Hollin (1992) have used Multiple Sequential Functional Analysis (MSFA) to study the development of offending behaviour and Daffern (2010) has advocated a structured MSFA to aid violence risk assessments. Clark, Fisher and McDougall (1994) have demonstrated, through functional analysis, that a prisoner's index offence often shows functional equivalence to behaviour in prison. They used this finding to justify the inclusion of prison behaviour when institutional staff were required to make predictions about violent reoffending following release from prison. More recently, Daffern and others (Daffern *et al.*, 2007) have drawn upon functional analysis to refine the Offence Paralleling Behaviour (OPB) framework. This framework was developed to assist clinicians identify behaviour in incarcerated/hospitalised offenders that may parallel offending behaviour in the community. These so-called OPBs can be used to assist treatment or for risk assessment.

Design principles and issues

Although the questions that can be addressed by functional analysis are varied, the idiographic approach is the most common application of functional analysis. Most research and clinical questions using functional analysis have focused on the efficacy of innovative treatments for individuals or the application of routine treatments to individuals or groups with unique problems. Idiographic functional analysis typically utilises *multiple methods* (e.g. behavioural interviewing, behavioural observation, psychophysiological assessment, self-report inventories, self monitoring, informant questionnaires and interviews). It is *multimodal* (e.g. it examines motor, verbal, cognitive, physiological elements of behaviour) and should consider *multiple parameters* of behaviour (rate, severity, duration and onset). As discussed on page 243, function analytic methodology is also applicable to the study of psychological process, groups or individuals. Studies of these other processes should also be multimodal, use multiple methods and consider multiple parameters of behaviour. These design issues are discussed in the following worked example of research using functional analysis.

A descriptive functional analysis of aggression in patients with personality disorder

The following is a description of a study using functional analytic methodology to examine aggression in a psychiatric unit. The patients of this unit were all diagnosed with personality disorder and all were considered to be at a high risk of serious offending. This study is described to show how function analytic methodology can be used to understand the purpose of a problem behaviour (aggressive) exhibited by members of a group (patients with personality disorder living in a high security psychiatric hospital). In this study the function of aggression was assessed using the Assessment and Classification of Function (ACF; Daffern *et al.*, 2006), a structured classification system developed by Daffern, Howells and Ogloff (2006) that may be used to assess the functions of aggression in psychiatric hospitals (see Box 10.1 for information on the development of the ACF).

This study has been published previously (Daffern and Howells, 2009) and readers are advised to consult this paper for more information. The aims of the study were first to examine the functions of aggression in a group of patients with so-called 'severe personality disorder' (determining the functions of aggression at the group level is important for programme development; it indicates what programmes – e.g. anger management – may be usefully provided to this type of patient), and second to ascertain whether the aggression in this group is primarily instrumental, as some scholars of psychopathy have suggested (Cornell *et al.*, 1996; Porter and Woodworth, 2007). Contrary to this proposition, some (e.g. Daffern and Howells, 2007) have argued that certain biases may contaminate the classification of aggressive acts, particularly the aggressive behaviour of patients with personality disorder. Since staff tend to have negative perceptions

Box 10.1 The development of a method – the Assessment and
Classification of Function

There are few guidelines available to assist clinicians in assimilating
assessment data into a functional analysis. No instrument to assist the
discrimination of differently motivated forms of aggression amongst inpatients exists. For this purpose, we (Daffern, Howells and Ogloff, 2006)
developed the Assessment and Classification of Function (ACF). The ACF
helps raters structure their assessments of aggressive behaviour so that a
comprehensive assessment of function may be conducted.

The functions that are assessed by the ACF were derived from the cognitive model of anger developed by Raymond Novaco (1976; 1994), the
instigating mechanisms outlined by Albert Bandura (1977) and the interactions antecedent to aggression identified in previous research on aggression
in psychiatric inpatient units (Powell *et al.*, 1994; Shepherd and Lavender,
1999; Sheridan et al., 1990). Each function contained within the ACF is
investigated and scored as present or absent for each act of aggression.
Whilst a single purpose may initially precede aggression, several purposes
may be achieved, some of which may be unintended and influence the
likelihood of subsequent aggressive behaviour. As such, aggression may
serve several purposes. For example a patient who behaves aggressively
following a demand to attend to an activity may be secluded and therefore
succeed in avoiding the activity. An unintended function may be that the
patient is revered by his peers, who similarly dislike unit-based activities.
The patient may experience an increase in status or receive tangible
rewards, such as cigarettes. Given the possibility of several purposes being
served by one incident, a range of purposes may be identified for each
incident through this classification system.

The ACF ratings are made following separate interviews with the
aggressive patient and staff observers. The interview reviews proximal
(immediate) antecedents to, and consequences of, aggression, as well as
the individual's predisposing personal attributes and limitations. There is
a series of general questions (e.g. What did the patient do during the
incident? Did the patient say anything during the incident?) and then
specific questions relevant to each of the functions being assessed. For
example some of the questions that are asked to determine whether
the purpose was 'demand avoidance' include: Did anybody ask the patient
to do something or to stop doing something prior to the incident? If no,
what is the patient generally expected to do at the time of the incident?
After the staff and patient interviews have been conducted a rating sheet,
containing a list of all possible functions of aggression, is scored (see
Daffern *et al.*, 2006).

Assessing accuracy, reliability and validity

During the development of the ACF a pilot study was conducted to examine the 'quality' of the ACF. In general, the 'quality' of a behavioural observation is determined by three characteristics: accuracy, validity and reliability (Cone, 1998). In 'the psychometrics of behavioural assessment, accuracy and reliability are … the two most important characteristics' (Cone, 1998, p. 33). Accuracy may be defined as 'the extent to which observations are sensitive to objective topographic features and dimensional quantities (i.e., frequency, latency, duration, magnitude) of behaviour' (ibid., p. 29). If an observation of behaviour is the result of the behaviour's occurrence, then the observation can be said to be accurate. To establish accuracy, clear rules and procedures for measuring behaviour are required (ibid.). To achieve accuracy in the assessment of purpose a structured method was developed to assess purpose, the ACF.

If an instrument remains accurate it is said to be reliable. In behavioural assessment, reliability is used to characterise the consistency of observations of behaviour (Cone, 1998). In other words, if comparable scores result from multiple observations, then the scoring system may be considered reliable. When accuracy and reliability cannot be ascertained, the concept of believability may be useful (Johnston and Pennypacker, 1993). Inter-observer agreement is one method of enhancing believability. The intra-class correlation coefficient (Bakeman and Gottman, 1986) may be used to demonstrate inter-observer agreement and believability (Cone, 1998).

To assess the inter-observer agreement of the ACF, Daffern *et al.* (2006) conducted a pilot study in which six clinical psychologists and two clinical psychology doctoral students were provided with a copy of the ACF, and given a presentation describing the rationale for assessing the purpose of aggression and an information sheet regarding the pilot study. They were then given a one-hour lecture on how to score purpose according to the classification system. Ten vignettes consisting of 300-word descriptions of aggressive behaviour perpetrated by patients on a male acute ward within the Thomas Embling Hospital were given for classification. Psychologists and students were requested to read and score each vignette. Results revealed an inter-item correlation coefficient mean of .65, with a minimum of .30. The single measure intra-class correlation coefficient was .64. The average measure intra-class correlation coefficient was .94. These results indicate the ACF has acceptable reliability.

of patients with personality disorder (Lewis and Appleby, 1988), and see their behaviour as controlled (Markham and Trower, 2003), it is possible that the aggressive behaviour of these patients may be vulnerable to misclassification by staff, and may be more frequently (and perhaps inappropriately) considered instrumental acts. Individuals whose problem behaviours are considered to be controlled may be denied help by staff (Daffern and Howells, 2007).

The first stage of this project was to determine whether staff could be engaged to participate. Conducting research in secure facilities is dependent on good working relationships between researchers and treating staff. Numerous briefing sessions were held in which Michael Daffern met with staff to describe the aim of the project and its procedure. As a consequence of these discussions staff committed to the research, which involved staff assisting the research team interview patients on the unit after acts of aggression and then interviewing staff who had observed the aggressive behaviour. Further, staff made suggestions about revising the ACF. The ACF, which had previously been used to study the functions of aggression in patients with mental illness (Daffern *et al.*, 2007b), was amended to include two additional functions: *sensation seeking* and *sexual gratification*. At the time of the study most patients on the unit where the study was conducted were assessed as high scorers on the Psychopathy Checklist-Revised (Hare, 1991). Sensation seeking is a prominent characteristic of the psychopathic personality (Hare, 1991). Sexual gratification was also included as many patients in this unit had a history of sexual offending (see Daffern *et al.*, 2008). The functions assessed by this revised ACF in this study were therefore demand avoidance, force compliance, express anger, reduce tension (catharsis), obtain tangibles, reduce social distance (attention seeking), enhance status or social approval, compliance with instruction, observe suffering, seek sensation and seek sexual gratification.

Following approval to conduct the research by a Human Research Ethics Committee the study began with the researchers inviting all patients in the unit (approximately 45) to participate in the study. Patients were provided information on the study, which would involve interviewing them after any aggressive behaviours and also interviewing staff to obtain information on the purpose of every aggressive act occurring during the course of the study. The aim of the research was described as 'learning about the purposes of aggression in the unit'. After recruitment, Michael Daffern attended the wards three times per week and asked staff whether any of the participants had been aggressive. If so, a nurse who observed the incident was asked, after having the study explained and providing informed consent, to describe the aggressive behaviour according to the staff ACF structured interview schedule. After the staff interview, the aggressive patient was approached and invited to participate in a similar ACF semi-structured interview – provided that the patient was not in seclusion and was able to provide informed consent (determined by ward staff), and staff believed that an approach to participate in the research would not increase the likelihood of further aggression (where this was expected the patient was excluded from the research). Following the interview(s) (there was always a staff member who agreed to participate but sometimes patients did not want to talk about the incident) the various accounts of the aggressive behaviour were considered by Michael Daffern and the functions were rated.

Descriptive statistics were primarily used to analyse data. The percentage of incidents in which each function was evident was recorded. The most striking finding was the multifunctional nature of aggressive behaviour, though most acts of aggression involved the expression of anger (96.96 per cent). The number of functions evident in each of the aggressive behaviours ranged from 2 to 5; the median number of functions was 3 ($M = 3.333$, $SD = 0.854$). The finding that anger expression was common is consistent with the notion that most incidents of aggression are of an angry, aggressive, rather than an instrumental, nature, even for personality disordered patients. Instrumental functions were relatively rare, although they did occur. This finding contradicts previous suggestions that personality disorder is predominantly associated with controlled instrumental acts of aggression. Results of this study have implications for how we understand the aggression of patients with personality disorder and the types of treatments that could be offered to patients in this unit. For example anger management programmes that help patients manage emotional arousal, communicate adaptively, relax and avoid high-risk situations, and modify dysfunctional or distorted beliefs, particularly where these beliefs consist of appraisals of events as malevolent and deliberate, seem appropriate (Daffern *et al.*, 2006).

As a consequence of this study it was possible to compare the profile of functions observed with that reported in a study of aggressive in-patients with mental illness (Daffern *et al.*, 2007b). Such comparison allows for exploration of the relative frequency of different functions of aggression in hospitalised patients with mental illness and hospitalised patients with personality disorder. Results of this comparison suggested that the function of aggression in inpatients with mental illness appears to be more frequently determined by institutional demands and by anger expression co-occurring with demand avoidance and force compliance, whereas the observation of suffering and the attainment of tangible functions are more commonly observed in hospitalised patients with personality disorder.

The main difficulties in conducting the type of applied research on a problem like aggression in psychiatric hospitals are (1) hospitals, including their administrators, clinical leaders and ward staff, need to facilitate the work, and (2) patients can be very wary of acknowledging and describing the antecedents, consequences and details of their actual aggressive behaviour. In both this study and our previous research (Daffern *et al.*, 2007b) patients were occasionally unwilling to sign a consent form, presumably because they feared this might be construed as evidence that they had in fact behaved aggressively. If researchers are to examine the functions of aggressive behaviour then a very real challenge will be to ensure patients are confident that their descriptions of aggressive acts are complete and honest and that they are comfortable that their participation does not result in adverse outcomes for themselves. When the problem behaviour under question is criminal then this will pose problems for researchers who may have both ethical and legal responsibilities, depending on the jurisdiction in which the researcher is working. For studies of criminal behaviour it is necessary that researchers are aware of their legal and ethical responsibilities and that participants are also aware of the same, and it is further recommended that studies of the functions of criminal behaviour occur after the offending behaviour in question has been adjudicated by the courts. Regarding the former issue about co-operation between researchers and hospital administrators and staff, it is important that would-be researchers be transparent and collaborative. Mental health and correctional services are understandably wary of external researchers highlighting problem behaviours and deficits in organisations. However, they are often keen to learn and to improve their services. External researchers must be willing to conduct rigorous research but be prepared to assist mental health and correctional services to improve their functioning by sharing the results of research in a respectful and constructive manner.

Another problem in this study was the occasional varied accounts of aggressive behaviour given by staff and patients. When different accounts of the aggressive behaviour were reported in this study Michael Daffern had to make a decision about the classification of functions based on knowledge of well-known biases in decision making (Tversky and Kahneman, 1974), and attribution, such as the *fundamental attribution error* (Ross, 1977), which must be taken into account by observers when they attempt to classify the reasons for other people's behaviour. Furthermore, the author took a liberal view to classification of function and recorded a function as present if, according to staff or patient, there was evidence that the function was present. The validity of assessments like this is of course open to criticism (see discussion on page 251 on experimental functional analyses). Future research on aggression and its functions might consider critically evaluating the similarity of staff and patient accounts of aggressive behaviour and its functions when using single sources (e.g. a patient or a member of staff) rather than multi-informant assessment. This is particularly important for offenders who are considered to be psychopathic, as this group may have a tendency to highlight environmental (e.g. the influence of other people and their actions) rather than internal causes for their aggressive behaviour (Porter and Woodworth, 2007). Such comparisons are likely to illuminate biases in decision making and attributions as well as the limitations of functional assessment paradigms that rely on single sources of information.

Opportunities for future research

Most functional analyses are *descriptive* rather than *experimental* (Sturmey, 1996). The aforementioned study is an example of a descriptive functional analysis in that the function of aggression was assessed by scrutinising observed behaviour and its purported contingencies. There was no manipulation of environmental variables to test their relationship with aggression. There are two problems with descriptive functional analyses (Sturmey, 1996): 1) it is difficult to verify whether variables that are hypothesised to be activating and maintaining the problem behaviour are indeed exerting influence, and 2) many chronic problems may be maintained by 'relatively thin, intermittent schedules of reinforcement' (p. 15). The former issue is pertinent to all descriptive functional analyses, whereas the latter issue is particularly relevant to forensic practitioners who are often required to conduct assessments (for treatment or release considerations) on individuals who at some point in time have committed a serious yet infrequent criminal behaviour (e.g. rape, murder). Typically, when psychologists are required to conduct these assessments they rely on descriptive functional analyses and attempt to understand the contingencies that caused the rare event and then attempt to understand whether these contingencies remain operative. Rarely are experimental functional analyses conducted.

Experimental functional analysis and offence paralleling behaviour

Experimental functional analysis involves 'the experimental manipulation of variables to demonstrate causal relationships between an independent variable and behavior' (Sturmey, 1996, p. 16). An experimental functional analysis is typically conducted after a descriptive functional analysis has been produced. Given that many descriptive functional analyses are tentative (for the reasons outlined by Sturmey (1996; see page 250) assessors need to consider how they can then conduct relevant experiments to test the contingencies that they hypothesise control the behaviour of interest. For instance an assessor may hypothesise that the aggression of an offender occurs when the offender feels 'taken advantage of', 'abused' or 'insulted'. The offender may have seriously assaulted a car parking attendant when asked to move their car. Several possible controlling variables may be important to this offence and the aggressive act may have numerous functions. First, the individual's emotional and physical state prior to the incident may be important – they may have been tired, frustrated, hungry or in pain. The social situation may also have been important – they may have been in the company of peers and these peers may have resulted in the offender feeling a 'need' to act aggressively so they did not lose face. Alternatively, the peers may have been an audience for the offender to demonstrate their fighting prowess. The function of the aggression may have been to express anger or to prevent deterioration in social status. These are but a few examples of the person, social and environmental variables that could have contributed to the assault.

To ensure comprehensiveness, Howells (1998) has listed the variables that need to be considered when developing a descriptive functional analysis of an individual's aggressive behaviour: (a) frequency, intensity, duration and form of aggression; (b) environmental triggers (including background stressors); (c) cognitive antecedents (including biases in appraisal of events, dysfunctional schemata, underlying beliefs and values supporting aggression); (d) affective antecedents (emotions preceding aggressive acts, e.g. anger or fear); (e) physiological antecedents; (f) coping and self-regulatory skills; (g) personality dispositions (e.g. anger proneness, impulsivity, neuroticism, agreeableness, psychopathy, over-control); (h) mental disorder variables (e.g. mood, brain impairment, delusions, hallucinations); (i) consequences/functions of aggressive acts (i.e. for perpetrator and others, short term and long term, including emotional consequences such as remorse and peer group or institutional reinforcement); (j) buffer factors (e.g. good relationships, family support, achievement or productivity in some area); (k) opportunity factors (e.g. weapons, victim availability, restrictions); and (l) disinhibitors (e.g. alcohol, drugs). Assessors should also be familiar with contemporary models of the behaviour of interest and should consider whether their formulation is consistent with these models. For example, assessors of violent offenders should consider the General Aggression Model (Bushman and Anderson, 2001).

Once the descriptive functional analysis has been completed the next task would be to conduct experiments to determine whether the variables hypothesised to be controlling the offender's aggressive behaviour (according to the descriptive functional analysis) are truly important. Experiments would be developed by using 'analogous' variables that exist within the secure setting. Limited opportunity (e.g. access to weapons, victim availability) and environmental constraints (e.g. rapid intervention from staff) dramatically alter the nature of behaviour within institutions. Against the background of these concerns Jones (1997, 2004) and Daffern and colleagues (Daffern *et al.*, 2007a; Daffern, Howells, Manion, and Tonkin, 2009; Daffern, Jones and Shine, 2010) have developed the Offence Paralleling Behaviour (OPB) framework. According to Daffern and colleagues (2009) OPBs are those behavioural sequences incorporating overt behaviours (that may be muted by environmental factors), appraisals, expectations, beliefs, affects, goals and behavioural scripts, all of which may be influenced by the patient's mental disorder, that are functionally similar to behavioural sequences involved in previous criminal acts. The central premise of the OPB approach is that the behavioural sequences that contribute to offending will manifest inside an institution, albeit in a topographically dissimilar form (Daffern *et al.*, 2007c) so long as the important 'psychologically active' (Mischel, 2004; p. 195) features of a situation, which have significant meaning for the individual, are present. The task for assessors considering experimental functional analyses is to devise experiments that test hypothesised contingencies using available, psychologically meaningful variables.

The use of experimental functional analyses in forensic settings is of course confronted by practical risk-related and ethical issues (e.g. it would not be proper to 'provoke' an offender; such experiments may result in aggression towards others, which may of course have dramatic implications for staff and other residents. Injury may occur and the offender's liberty may be compromised). As such, great care needs to be exercised in 'planning' experiments. The more ethical approach would be to have hypothesised contingencies tested by way of routine activity. For instance, in the case described previously, one experiment may involve asking the offender to undertake some routine activity that they may not enjoy but which is required (e.g. attending a psychotherapy group) when they are (a) on their own, and then (b) in the company of others. An experiment like this would determine whether the presence of peers determines the offender's aggression (all other variables remaining equal). If during the experiment an offender behaved aggressively in response to the demand in front of their peers (all other variables remaining equal) then this experiment would confirm the importance of demands and the presence of peers. The aggression could be considered an OPB.

There are other limitations to this experimental function analytic approach. For instance it may not be possible to introduce and test some potentially important causal variables to the secure setting (e.g. drugs). Where there are variables that are thought to be important but which cannot be tested, then it would be essential to look for opportunistic examples of equivalent behavioural experiments. For instance, when the offender is on leave from the unit do they engage in alcohol or drug use? If so, does alcohol or drug use seem to be related to their problem behaviour? It may also be possible to look for proxies to drug and alcohol use and intoxication. Thomas and Hodge (2010) have introduced the notion of substance use paralleling behaviours. These are behaviours the offender engages in that mimic drug and alcohol use and which may lead to intoxication (e.g. achieving an intoxicated state following consumption of no-alcohol beer, caffeine, coca cola or prescribed medication). It may be possible, should a patient achieve an intoxicated state using substance use paralleling behaviours, to assess the relevance of this state to aggression.

Finally, the use of experimental functional analysis must be subjected to empirical scrutiny. Important tasks in a program of research designed to evaluate this methodology would be:

- tests of the reliability of descriptive functional analyses as these are the basis for the creation of experiments using analogous contingencies within secure settings;
- an assessment of the validity of the paralleling contingencies and the (inter-rater) reliability of the hypothesised analogous contingencies;
- an assessment of the impact of the imposition of these experiments on patients to ensure there are no adverse risk-related or ethical issues arising;
- an assessment of the predictive validity of risk assessments based on experimental functional analyses and comparison of this predictive validity against other well-known risk assessment methods (i.e. actuarial and structured risk assessment instruments);
- treatments informed by experimental functional analyses assessed to determine whether they are more effective than other treatments.

The strengths and limitations of functional analysis

The main strength of functional analysis is its flexibility; it can be applied to any problem, individual, psychological processes or setting. The functional analytic approach is respectful to clients; the principle of adaption to environment emphasises the adaptive nature of the individual's problem behaviour. This has the potential to limit the use of pejorative and simplistic classification of individuals and their behaviour. This is particularly important for clients whose behaviour appears self-limiting, bizarre or harmful to other people. The problems associated with functional analysis include:

- The methods for developing the best assessment instruments to develop a functional analysis have not been delineated for many problems.
- The methods for integrating data from behavioural assessment methods into a functional analysis have not yet been developed for many behaviour problems.
- Practicality problems exist – functional analysis is time consuming and requires high-level expertise in behavioural assessment, knowledge of the problem behaviour being considered and awareness of contextual issues (e.g. the prison environment, the contingencies that operate to promote and maintain problem behaviour and those contingencies that inhibit pro-social action)
- There are utility and cost-effectiveness concerns.

As with case formulation generally (Luborsky and Diguer, 1998), these problems impact on the reliability and validity of assessments. Future research should focus on the development of methods that assist in the creation of reliable and valid functional analyses. Regarding utility and cost effectiveness, some (e.g. Haynes, 1986) have argued that idiographic functional analysis may be unnecessary in some situations. For example, some simple problems share functionality and respond well to standardised treatments (e.g. simple phobias), whereas other, more complicated and serious problems (e.g. interpersonal violence) may benefit from a function analytic assessment:

> The social and personal significance of behaviours associated with pre-intervention assessment varies across behaviour problems. A 10 per cent failure rate for a standardised intervention programme for nail-biting may not warrant extensive pre-intervention assessment to design individual-ised intervention programmes that would reduce the rate to 5 per cent. However, more extensive pre-intervention assessment may be warranted by a proportional increase in the effectiveness of interventions for suicidal, self-mutilatory or socially violent behaviours.
>
> (Haynes, 1996, p. 393)

Conclusion

Functional analysis is a flexible, constructive and widely used assessment method for clinicians working with offenders in community forensic and secure settings. There are, however, few accounts of its application to applied forensic settings within the scientific and in particular, peer-reviewed literature. This is probably because function analysis is seen as an idiographic assessment approach used to assess an individual's offending behaviour. Functional analysis is, however, a suitable idiographic assessment method for understanding other psychological processes, like failing to engage in treatment. Functional analysis can also be used to understand the behaviour or psychological processes of a group or the purpose of a system. It therefore lends itself to a range of clinical applications and research questions. This chapter has differentiated descriptive from experimental functional analyses and emphasised the need for clinicians to consider the latter to ensure more valid assessment. The offence paralleling behaviour framework has been invoked as a necessary consideration for those clinicians and researchers who want to conduct proper experimental functional analyses. Although potentially appealing, this proposal require empirical scrutiny. There remain many opportunities for research using functional analysis in the forensic context.

Further reading

The following texts provide a general overview of functional analysis. The Daffern *et al.* (2010) book describes the Offence Paralleling Behaviour framework. Within this book is a chapter written by Peter Sturmey. This chapter summarises research on case formulation, and specifically functional analysis, in the forensic context. Furthermore, there are a number of journals with a behavioural assessment focus. These journals include *Behavior Research and Therapy*, *Behavior Analyst Today* and *The Journal of Behavior Analysis of Offender and Victim – Treatment and Prevention*. Finally, the reference list at the end of this chapter contains many papers describing function analytic methods. The following list may provide researchers interested in functional analysis with critical skills and ideas to refine their research.

Bellack, A. and Hersen, M. (1998). *Behavioral assessment: a practical handbook*. Allyn and Bacon: Boston.
Daffern, M., Jones, L. and Shine, J. (in press). *Individualised approaches to offender assessment and treatment: the Offence Paralleling Behaviour framework*. Chichester, UK: Wiley.
Sturmey, P. (1996). *Functional analysis in clinical psychology*. Chichester, UK: Wiley.
—— (2007). *Functional analysis in clinical treatment*. Amsterdam: Academic Press.
—— (in press). Case formulation in forensic psychology. In M. Daffern, L. Jones and J. Shine (Eds). *Individualised approaches to offender assessment and treatment: the Offence Paralleling Behaviour framework*. Chichester, UK: Wiley.

References

Andrews, D. A. and Bonta, J. (2003). *The psychology of criminal conduct*. Cincinnati, OH: Anderson Publishing.
Bakeman, R. and Gottman, J. M. (1986). *Observing interaction: an introduction to sequential analysis*. London: Cambridge University Press.
Bandura, A. (1977). *Social learning theory*. Englewood Cliffs, NJ: Prentice-Hall.

Bellack, A. S. and Hersen, M. (1998). *Behavioral assessment: a practical handbook*. 4th edn. Needham Heights, MA: Allyn & Bacon.

Bushman, B. J. and Anderson, C. A. (2001). Is it time to pull the plug on the hostile versus hostile versus instrumental aggression dichotomy? *Psychological Review*, 108: 273–9.

Clark, D., Fisher, M. J. and McDougall, C. (1994). A new methodology for assessing the level of risk in incarcerated offenders. *British Journal of Criminology*, 33: 436–8.

Cone, J. D. (1998). Psychometric considerations: concepts, contents, and methods. In A. S. Bellack and M. Hersen (Eds). *Behavioral assessment: a practical handbook* (pp. 22–46). 4th edn. Needham Heights, MA: Allyn & Bacon.

Cornell, D. G., Warren, J., Hawk, G., Stafford, E., Oram, G. and Pine, D. (1996). Psychopathy in instrumental and reactive violent offenders. *Journal of Consulting and Clinical Psychology*, 64: 783–90.

Daffern, M. (2010). Risk assessment for aggressive behaviour in personality disorder. In A. Tenant and K. Howells (Eds). *Using time, not doing time: practitioner perspectives on personality disorder and risk* (pp. 15–32). Wiley.

—— (2010). Methods for developing an Offence Paralleling Behaviour formulation for violent offenders. In M. Daffern, L. Jones and J. Shine (Eds). *Offence Paralleling Behaviour: A case formulation approach to offender assessment and treatment*, pp. 105–20. John Wiley and Sons: Chichester, UK.

Daffern, M. and Howells, K. (2007). Antecedents for aggression and the function analytic approach to the assessment of aggression and violence in personality disordered patients within secure settings. *Personality and Mental Health*, 1: 126–37.

—— (2009). The function of aggression in personality disordered patients. *Journal of Interpersonal Violence*, 24: 586–600.

Daffern, M., Howells, K. and Ogloff, J. R. P. (2006). What's the point? Towards a methodology for assessing the function of psychiatric inpatient aggression. *Behavior Research and Therapy*, 45: 101–11.

Daffern, M., Jones, L., Howells, K., Shine, J., Mikton, C. and Tunbridge, V.C. (2007a). Refining the definition of offence paralleling behaviour. *Criminal Behaviour and Mental Health*, 17: 265–73.

Daffern, M., Howells, K. and Ogloff, J. (2007b). The interaction between individual characteristics and the function of aggression in forensic psychiatric inpatients. *Psychiatry, Psychology and Law*, 14: 17–25.

Daffern, M. Ogloff, J. R. P., Ferguson. M., Thomson, L. and Howells, K. (2007c). Appropriate treatment targets or products of a demanding environment? The relationship between aggression in a forensic psychiatric hospital with aggressive behaviour preceding admission and violent recidivism. *Psychology, Crime and Law*, 13: 431–41.

Daffern, M., Howells, K., Stacey, J., Hogue, T. and Mooney, P. (2008). Sexually abusive behaviour in personality disordered inpatients of a high secure psychiatric hospital: implications for the assessment of offence paralleling behaviours. *Journal of Sexual Aggression*, 14: 123–33.

Daffern, M., Howells, K., Manion, A. and Tonkin, M. (2009). A test of methodology intended to assist detection of aggressive Offence Paralleling Behaviour within secure settings. *Legal and Criminological Psychology*, 14: 213–26.

Daffern, M., Jones, L. and Shine, J. (2010). *Offence Paralleling Behaviour: A case formulation approach to offender assessment and treatment*. John Wiley & Sons: Chichester, UK.

Eells, T.D. (1997). *Handbook of psychotherapy case formulation.* New York: Guilford Press.

Gresswell, D. M. and Hollin, C. R. (1992). Towards a new methodology for making sense of case material: an illustrative case involving attempted multiple murder. *Criminal Behaviour and Mental Health,* 2: 329–41.

Hare, R. (1991). *The Hare Psychopathy Checklist-Revised.* Toronto: Multi Health Systems.

Hayes, S. N. (1986). The design of intervention programmes. In R. O. Nelson and S. C. Hayes (Eds) *Conceptual foundations of behavioral assessment* (pp. 386–423). New York: Guilford Press.

Haynes, S. N. (1998). The changing nature of behavioural assessment. In A. Bellack and M. Hersen (Eds). *Behavioral assessment: a practical handbook* (pp. 1–21). 4th edn. Needham Heights, MA: Allyn & Bacon.

Haynes, S. N. and O'Brien, W. H. (1998). Functional analysis in behavior therapy. *Clinical Psychology Review,* 10: 649–68.

Howells, K. (1998). Cognitive behavioural interventions for anger, aggression and violence. In N. Tarrier, A. Welsh and G. Haddock (Eds). *Treating complex cases: the cognitive behavioural approach* (pp. 295–318). Chichester, UK: John Wiley & Sons.

Iwata, B. A., Dorsey, M. F., Sliferer, K. J., Bauman, K. E. and Richman, G. S. (1982). Toward a functional analysis of self injury. *Analysis and Intervention in Developmental Disabilities,* 2: 3–20.

Johnston, J. M., and Pennypacker, H. S. (1993). *Strategies and tactics of behavioural research.* Hillsdale, NJ: Erlbaum.

Jones, L. F. (1997). Developing models for managing treatment integrity and efficacy in a prison based TC: The Max Glatt Centre. In E. Cullen, L. Jones and R. Woodward (Eds). *Therapeutic communities for offenders.* Chichester, UK: Wiley.

—— (2004). Offence Paralleling Behaviour (OPB) as a framework for assessment and interventions with offenders. In A. Needs and G. Towl (Eds). *Applying psychology to forensic practice.* Oxford: Blackwell.

Kern, L., Carberry, N. and Haidara, C. (1997). Analysis and intervention with two topographies of challenging behaviour exhibited by a young woman with autism. *Research in Developmental Disabilities,* 18: 275–87.

Lee-Evans, M. (1994). Background to behaviour analysis. In M. McMurran and J. Hodge (Eds). *The assessment of criminal behaviours of clients in secure settings* (pp. 6–34). London: Jessica Kingsley Publishers.

Lewis, G. and Appleby, I. (1988). Personality disorder: the patients psychiatrists dislike. *British Journal of Psychiatry,* 153: 44–9.

Luborsky, L. and Diguer, L. (1998). The reliability of the CCRT measure: results from 8 samples. In L. Luborsky and P. Crits-Christoph (Eds). *Understanding transference: the core conflictual relationship theme method (2nd edn).* New York: Basic Books.

McDougal, T. (2000). Violent incidents in a forensic adolescent unit: a functional analysis. *Nursing Times Research,* 5: 346–62.

Markham, D. and Trower, P. (2003). The effects of the psychiatric label 'borderline personality disorder' on nursing staff's perceptions and causal attributions for challenging behaviours. *The British Journal of Clinical Psychology,* 42: 243–55.

Mischel, W. (2004). Toward an integrative model for CBT: encompassing behaviour, cognition, affect and process. *Behavior Therapy,* 35: 185–203.

Novaco, R. W. (1976). The functions and regulation of the arousal of anger. *American Journal of Psychiatry,* 133: 1,124–8.

—— (1994). Anger as a risk factor for violence among the mentally disordered. In J. Monahan and H. J. Steadman (Eds). *Violence and mental disorder* (pp. 137–59). Chicago: University of Chicago Press.

Porter, S. and Woodworth, M. (2007). 'I'm sorry I did it...but he started it'. A comparison of the official and self-reported homicide descriptions of psychopaths and non-psychopaths. *Law and Human Behavior*, 31: 91–107.

Powell, G., Caan, W. and Crowe, M. (1994). What events precede violent incidents in psychiatric hospitals? *British Journal of Psychiatry*, 165: 107–12.

Ross, L. (1977). The intuitive psychologist and his shortcomings: distortions in the attribution process. In L. Berkowitz (Ed). *Advances in experimental social psychology*, vol. 10 (pp. 173–220). New York: Academic Press.

Shepherd, M. and Lavender, T. (1999). Putting aggression into context: an investigation into contextual factors influencing the rate of aggressive incidents in a psychiatric hospital. *Journal of Mental Health*, 8: 159–70.

Sheridan, M., Herion, R., Robinson, L. and Baxter, V. (1990). Precipitants of violence in a psychiatric inpatient setting. *Hospital and Community Psychiatry*, 41: 776–80.

Sturmey, P. (1996). *Functional analysis in clinical psychology*. Chichester, UK: Wiley.

—— (2010). *Offence Paralleling Behaviour: A case formulation approach to offender assessment and treatment*, pp. 105–20. John Wiley and Sons: Chichester, UK.

Sturmey, P. Ward-Horner, J., Marroquin, M. and Doran, E. (2007). Structural and functional approaches to psychopathology and case formulation. In P. Sturmey (Ed). *Functional analysis in clinical treatment* (pp. 1–21). Burlington, MA: Academic Press.

Thomas, G. and Hodge, J. (2010). Substance misuse paralleling behaviour in detained offenders. In M. Daffern, L. Jones and J. Shine (Eds). *Offence Paralleling Behaviour: A case formulation approach to offender assessment and treatment*, pp. 105–20. John Wiley and Sons: Chichester, UK.

Thompson, R. H., Fisher, W. W., Piazza, C. C., and Kuhn, D. E. (1998). The evaluation and treatment of aggression maintained by attention and automatic reinforcement. *Journal of Applied Behaviour Analysis*, 31: 103–16.

Tversky, D. and Kahneman, A. (1974). Judgement under uncertainty: heuristics and biases. *Science*, 185: 1,124–31.

Part V
Approaches at the group level

11 Strengths and weaknesses of randomised controlled trials

Clive R. Hollin

Randomised controlled trials (RCTs) have been used in many different fields of research: the aim of this chapter is to look at their use specifically within a forensic context. It follows that some of the arguments rehearsed below are context-bound and should not be generalised outwith the boundaries of forensic research.

In order for applied research to be useful in the real world it must be ensured that the findings it produces are as robust, or *valid*, as possible. Cook and Campbell (1979) described four types of validity: these four are *internal validity*, *construct validity*, *external validity* and *statistical conclusion validity*. *Internal validity* is the level of confidence the research design gives in allowing changes in the dependent variable to be attributed to manipulation of the independent variable. *Construct validity* refers to the theoretical logic of the research and its potential to advance theory. *External validity* is the degree of generalisability of the findings to other settings or individuals. *Statistical conclusion validity* concerns the study's adherence to the rules of measurement and statistical analysis. In a discussion of these four types of validity, Farrington (2006) notes that internal validity 'is generally viewed as the most important type of validity' (p. 332).

The four types of validity are not mutually independent. A study can ensure its internal validity by using, say, strict sampling criteria and painstaking administration of the intervention. However, such high levels of control may introduce a level of artificiality so that the findings cannot be generalised to practice in the real world. The focus in this chapter is on the interplay between the different types of validity when research uses a randomised design. However, the starting point is to ask why randomisation is important in research.

Randomisation

Design principles and issues

A question often addressed by forensic researchers concerns establishing cause and effect between an intervention and an outcome. Does the introduction of CCTV in a town centre reduce antisocial behaviour? Do punitive prison regimes lower rates of reconviction? Does court-mandated treatment for perpetrators of domestic violence reduce assaults? At first glance the way to answer these questions appears relatively straightforward: compare levels of an appropriate measure pre- and post-intervention and if there is a pre–post difference in the predicted direction then the intervention has had an effect. Alas, matters are not so simple.

There are several reasons why apparently straightforward pre–post comparisons may produce misleading findings. For example, suppose a pre–post evaluation of a punitive prison regime showed that reconviction rates had declined over a two-year period following the introduction of the regime. Can we say this change was due to the regime? We could but there may be other factors to consider: what if the type of prisoner allocated to the prison had changed, say from adult long-term violent prisoners to young short-term non-violent prisoners, over the course of the study? What if reconviction rates were falling nationally in the period covered by the study? These are problematic issues with a design based on pre–post comparisons when looking for cause and effect.

One way around the problems with a pre–post design is to introduce a control condition: continuing the example above, the reconviction rates from the punitive prison could be compared with the rates from another prison with a 'business as usual' regime. This change in design would help but some potential problems remain. Suppose the prison system central allocation unit starts to send older prisoners convicted for a violent crime to the prison with the punitive regime, while younger prisoners convicted for a range of offences are allocated to the control prison. Immediately, this pattern of allocation introduces a *confound* as the two groups of prisoners are not equivalent: thus, any eventual difference in reconviction rates between the two prisons may be a function of differences in the prisoners rather than the different prison regimes. This confound in sampling is a threat to internal validity and can only be countered by ensuring that those in the experimental condition are matched with or are equivalent to those in the control condition.

The process of *matching* first entails the identification of one or more key variables, say age, known to be associated with the outcome (reconviction). With one-to-one matching each member of the experimental group is paired with a member of the control group so that both are the same age. If there is not exact one-to-one matching, which can in practice be difficult to achieve – particularly when matching on several variables, an example of this problem is evident in the evaluation conducted by Friendship *et al.* (2003) – then population matching can be used. In population matching differences on key variables between the two conditions are adjusted statistically, typically using multivariate techniques (for an example see Hollin *et al.*, 2008). The residual problem with one-to-one and population matching is that it does not eliminate the possibility that the outcome is being influenced by some other, uncontrolled, 'hidden' variables.

The way to nullify any 'hidden' threat to internal validity is to randomise individuals to condition. As Smith and Davis (2004) explain: 'The logic behind randomization is as follows. Because the participants have an equal likelihood of being selected for each group in an experiment, any unique characteristics associated with the participants should be equally distributed across all groups' (p. 118). Thus, with randomisation every prisoner has an equal chance of serving their sentence in either of the two prisons.

An approach that uses randomisation to condition is often referred to as an *experimental design*. In contrast, an approach that uses either matching or statistical control to create similar groups is called a *quasi-experimental design* (of which there are several varieties).

A final difficulty remains: what if those involved in the randomisation know which condition is which? The prisoners know which regime they are allocated to, the prison staff know what regime they are running and the researchers know which prisoners went to which prison. It's not difficult to see that any of these factors could introduce a bias into the evaluation. The solution to the problem of bias lies in the process of masking or *blinding* (Jadad *et al.*, 2001).

A randomised study where all those concerned know which intervention each participant is allocated to is known as an *open randomised* trial. A randomised study can be strengthened by 'blinding' those involved in the research.

In a *single-blind* trial, one party, usually those delivering the intervention, know which condition participants are assigned to. In a *double-blind* trial, neither those delivering the intervention nor those participating are aware of who has been assigned to treatment. A *triple-blinded* trial is where the participants, those delivering the intervention and the researchers (see Petrosino and Soydam, 2005) are blind to assignment. There is also the rare *quadruple-blinded* trial, with the fourth party being the statisticians.

Randomised controlled trials

When a randomised experiment is carried out on a large scale, typically in the context of evaluating a medical intervention, it is called a *randomised controlled trial* (RCT). Stolberg *et al.* (2004) suggest that clinical trials date back to 'Approximately 600 B.C. when Daniel of Judah conducted what is probably the earliest recorded clinical trial. He compared the health effects of the vegetarian diet with those of a royal Babylonian diet over a 10-day period' (p. 1,539). However, Stolberg *et al.* continue, the clinical trial became established in the nineteenth century, with the French study reported by P. C. A. Louis of bloodletting in the treatment of pneumonia. The origin of the contemporary randomised clinical trial is credited to Sir Austin Bradford Hill (Hill, 1952). One of the main applications of clinical trials is testing medical procedures, particularly drug trials. As Everitt and Wessely (2004) note, it is easier to conduct a trial when, as with drug interventions, the treatment and no-treatment conditions can be simply controlled.

There are now several variations on the basic theme of randomisation, such as *preference trials* where participants may choose a preferred treatment from several alternatives (Leykin *et al.*, 2007).

The ethics of RCTs

The process of randomisation to condition means that some individuals will not receive treatment. The principle of *equipoise* holds that before a trial commences there must be both genuine doubt and an absence of evidence that patients in one group are more likely to benefit than patients in the other group. Thus, there is a fine balance between predicting that a new treatment will improve a condition and having sufficient evidence to know whether it will or will not have the intended outcome. It follows that ethically RCTs can be only be planned and carried out where there is uncertainty about the effect of the intervention.

Design variations

Everitt and Wessely (2004) distinguish *exploratory* and *pragmatic* trials: the former measures the direct effect of the intervention to determine whether, under controlled conditions, it has the intended effect; the latter tests the effect of the treatment when it is introduced into routine clinical practice. The methodological quality of the design of an RCT may vary considerably (Juni *et al.*, 2001; Lewis and Warlow, 2004): the Jadad scale can be used to rate the quality of reporting of RCTs (Jadad *et al.*, 2001).

Randomised trials in criminological research

Farrington *et al.* (2002) make the point that 'While randomized experiments in principle have the highest internal validity, in practice they are uncommon in criminology and also often have implementation problems' (p. 17). In mainstream criminology the randomised experiment grew in popularity from the 1950s and they are now reasonably well cited. Farrington and Welsh (2005) reported that in criminology there were 35 randomised experiments published between 1957 and 1981, growing to 83 publications between 1982 and 2004. These criminological studies span a variety of topics ranging from violence (Cure *et al.*, 2005) to courts, policing, correctional therapy and boot camps (Telep, 2009). Although mainly conducted by criminologists in North America, there is a, not always favourable, history to the use of randomised designs in the UK (Clarke and Cornish, 1972; Nuttall, 2003). Nevertheless, it is clear that researchers in matters criminological often find issue, rightly or wrongly, with the ethics and practicalities of randomisation (Lum and Yang, 2005).

Scientific Methods Scale

It is often stated that RCTs are the gold standard in evaluation research, a view advocated by Harper and Chitty (2005) for evaluations of interventions with offenders. Indeed, Chitty (2005) takes the view that studies that fall below this gold standard are 'suboptimal'. Are randomised studies so superior to other research designs? The Scientific Methods Scale (SMS; Sherman *et al.*, 1997) ranks research designs according to the strength of their internal validity. The SMS begins at Level 1 with simple correlational design moving to Level 5 with the randomised study as the design with the greatest degree of internal validity as follows:

1   a simple correlation between a crime prevention programme and some measure of crime
2   a temporal sequence between the crime prevention programme and the measure of crime clearly observed; or the use of a comparison group but without demonstrating comparability between the comparison and treatment groups
3   a comparison between two or more groups, one participating in the programme, the other not
4   a group comparison, with and without the programme, in which there is control of relevant factors or a non-equivalent comparison group with only minor differences from the treatment group
5   random assignment to groups with analysis of comparable units for programme and comparison groups.

Wilson, Bouffard and Mackenzie (2005) have suggested that studies at Levels 3, 4 and 5 of the SMS are of acceptable scientific quality. Level 3 is equivalent to a *low-quality quasi-experimental* design in which the main threat to internal validity comes from uncontrolled differences between treatment and comparison groups. Level 4 is a *high-quality quasi-experimental* design with statistical or methodological control of established group differences.

The SMS has been applied in the wider criminological literature (Farrington *et al.*, 2002; Wilson *et al.*, 2005). However, as Hollin (2008) explains, the 'real' SMS should not be confused with the flawed version – which uses the SMS to judge the overall quality of a piece of research rather than the level of internal validity – which has been erroneously used to assess reconviction studies (e.g. Debidin and Lovbakke, 2005).

Types of analysis

An RCT provides a comparison of outcome for individuals randomly allocated to either the experimental or control group. One style of analysis within an RCT is called *Intention to Treat* (ITT) in which 'Analysis is based on original treatment assignment rather than the treatment actually received' (Everitt and Wessely, 2004, p. 90). Thus, with ITT the experimental group contains all those *allocated* to treatment, irrespective of whether or not they actually receive the treatment. The second approach, called *Treatment Received* (TR), looks at outcome 'According to the treatment ultimately received' (Everitt and Wessely, 2004, p. 90) by those who have fully participated in the intervention.

ITT is the purest analysis because any formation of subgroups, such as treatment completers and non-completers, within the randomised condition breaches the principle of randomisation and negates the purpose of the design. In fact, ITT and TR analyses provide answers to different research questions: as Sherman (2003) notes, 'The ITT principle holds that an RCT can test the effects of trying to get someone to take a treatment and, thus, provides a valid inference about the effect of the attempt, as distinct from the actual treatment received' (p. 12). A TR analysis estimates, with an associated risk of bias, the effect of the delivery of the treatment. As Sherman notes, an ITT analysis tests the *policy* of offering an intervention, while TR shows what happens when the offer is accepted. This distinction is reinforced by Prendergast *et al.* (2009) who reported that less than one-half of the offenders in a randomised study of drug abuse treatment failed to attend or completed only a small number of the 12 sessions in the programme. A similar low rate of programme completion was also noted in a large-scale evaluation of community-based offending behaviour programmes (Hollin *et al.*, 2008; McGuire *et al.*, 2008; Palmer *et al.*, 2007).

The application of ITT analysis, devised for biomedical trials, in the evaluation of psychological interventions has been called a 'drug metaphor' (Shapiro *et al.*, 1994). Slade and Priebe (2001) compared drug-based therapies typical of medical treatment with social and psychological interventions, reaching the conclusion that 'Regarding RCTs as the gold standard in mental health care research results in evidence-based recommendations that are skewed, both in the available evidence and the weight assigned to evidence' (p. 287).

Example of a randomised study

Van Voorhis *et al.* (2004) conducted a randomised study of the outcome, as measured by arrests, revocations, technical violations and employment at 9 months and return to prison after 18 to 30 months, for 468 parolees randomly assigned to treatment or no treatment. The treatment was the cognitive skills programme Reasoning and Rehabilitation (R&R; Ross and Fabiano, 1985). Van Voorhis *et al.* reported that the ITT analysis showed that R&R had no effect on outcome. However, like other offending behaviour programmes R&R should be completed to have an effect (Hollin and Palmer, 2006), and Van Voorhis *et al.* recorded a high rate of attrition (about 40 per cent) among offenders assigned to treatment. When the data were analysed according to completion status, using a quasi-experimental design controlling for risk factors, a treatment effect was found for treatment completers.

The issues raised by Van Voorhis *et al.* and similar studies has led to calls to move beyond a sole reliance on RCTs and ITT in medical (Cartwright, 2007; Gilbody and Whitty, 2002; Goetghebeur and Loeys, 2002; Norris and Atkins, 2005; Victora *et al.*, 2004) and psychological research (Clark, 2004; Levant, 2004). Such a shift in research practice would entail a renewed emphasis on quasi-experimental designs.

Quasi-experimental designs

There are guidelines and recommendations for conducting high quality quasi-experimental studies (Heinsman and Shadish, 1996; Des Jarlais *et al.*, 2004). Heinsman and Shadish state that the quality of quasi-experimental studies is improved when the following conditions apply: (i) a high level of control over the degree to which participants can self-select conditions; (ii) there is control of any large pre-treatment differences between groups on important variables; (iii) when the study is underway there are procedures to minimise attrition. Goldkamp (2009) makes the point that high rates of attrition, as seen in several studies (Hollin *et al.*, 2008; McGuire *et al.*, 2008; Palmer *et al.*, 2007; Prendergast *et al.*, 2009), calls into question the reliability of the findings from randomised studies in criminology. In a quasi-experimental study there are techniques, such as propensity analysis (Jones *et al.*, 2004; McGuire *et al.*, 2008), that can be used to estimate the effects of non-completion.

Do RCTs give different findings from other designs?

Are the findings from RCTs markedly different from those of quasi-experimental studies? There are several studies that have considered this issue. Heinsman and Shadish (1996) compared the findings from randomised and non-randomised experiments in psychological research concluding that, given equality in design and execution, randomised and non-randomised experiments give similar effect sizes. Weisburd *et al.* (2001) used the SMS to code 308 studies (15 per cent with a randomised design) of crime prevention. In contrast to Heinsman and Shadish, Weisburd *et al.* concluded that non-randomised designs may introduce a bias in favour of the intervention.

In a large meta-analysis, Lipsey (1992) reported that randomisation had little relationship with effect size in the evaluation of offender treatment. Lipsey *et al.* (2001) reported no statistical difference in outcome according to the use of experimental or quasi-experimental designs for evaluations of cognitive-behavioural interventions with offenders. Babcock *et al.* (2004) reported a similar finding in a meta-analysis of interventions for men who perpetrated acts of domestic violence. Wilson *et al.* (2005) compared findings from randomised and high-quality quasi-experimental studies, reporting that both designs gave similar findings. Lösel and Schmucker (2005) conducted a meta-analysis of treatment effectiveness for sex offenders, coding studies using the SMS. They reported that findings did not differ significantly between those studies using experimental and those using quasi-experimental designs.

Weisburd *et al.* also made the point that randomised studies do not facilitate investigation of how an intervention works. An example of this point is provided in a string of studies, using high-quality quasi-experimental designs, evaluating the outcome of interventions with offenders designed to reduce reconviction (Hollin *et al.*, 2008; McGuire *et al.*, 2008; Palmer *et al.*, 2007). These evaluations compared the reconviction of offenders who completed treatment with that of offenders who dropped out of treatment. As offenders were not randomised to condition it is possible that the offenders who completed the treatment programmes may have different characteristics from non-completers (Wormith and Olver, 2002). However, given the weight from evidence in support of this particular type of treatment, there would have been ethical issues to confront had treatment been withheld for research purposes. Marshall and Marshall (2007) have rehearsed similar arguments specifically in the field of sex offender treatment. Further, as Gondolf (2004) notes, it is entirely realistic to study naturally occurring treatment subgroups. Research that seeks to balance internal and external validity can contribute significantly to practice.

Strengths and limitations of RCTs in a forensic setting

There are practical difficulties in some applications of RCTs in a forensic context: these issues include courts passing sentences to enable randomisation of offenders to an experimental condition, or researchers being able to 'sentence-override' to allocate offenders to condition. There are problems associated with withholding treatment: if an offender is denied treatment for evaluative purposes and they commit further crimes then the question will rightly be put as to whether these crimes could have been prevented. Allocation to the control condition may also disadvantage the individual prisoner as their not taking part in treatment may sway decisions about parole, level of custodial security and so on. It is not unlikely that there would be a legal challenge to attempts to deny treatment to an individual offender for research purposes.

The implementation of an RCT can be problematic. Gondolf (2001) notes that randomisation may actually introduce a bias into a study if offenders who would have been allocated differently are pooled for the sake of the research. Gondolf (2001) also notes that with a randomised study dropouts continue to be part of the treatment condition. If offenders drop out of treatment in the community then there may well be an increased likelihood that they will experience more severe consequences such as going to prison. Thus, the consequences of dropping out of treatment may well influence the eventual outcome of a study, particularly if ITT analysis is used.

Farrington and Jolliffe (2002) examined the conditions required for a randomised outcome study of a prison-based therapeutic unit. They pointed to several practical issues, including cost and time, in running the study to the required standard across eight prisons and involving several hundred prisoners. In an example of the strain in balancing internal and external validity, Farrington and Jolliffe suggested that the difficulties in conducting the research would be eased if the length of the intervention were shortened. As Gondolf (2004) has suggested, the introduction of an RCT may disrupt practice, thereby changing the intervention and the meaning of its evaluation.

In an excellent paper, Asscher *et al.* (2007) recounted the issues they faced in implementing a randomised study with young offenders participating in multisystemic therapy (MST). There were legal debates such as whether it is right for sentenced young people to be treated differently when receiving the same sentence. There were practical issues including at what point to introduce randomisation in the young person's pathway through the criminal justice system. Should randomisation be carried out at the first opportunity, say when the young person first comes to the attention of the authorities, or as late as possible when the court has delivered its verdict?

Asscher *et al.* reported professional obstacles, some concerning workload: would conducting the evaluation give busy people more to do and hinder their work? They describe how some professionals, with the implicit view that 'treatment is good', argue against randomisation as it withholds treatment from some young people. Further, some professionals may have misgivings about evaluation lest it shows, counter to their professional opinion, that treatment does not work. The young people and their families (MST involves young people and their families or caregivers) did not all want to take part in the study. Should they be coerced to take part in the evaluation or allowed to opt out and potentially introduce bias into the randomisation? As noted above, a large dropout has the potential to reduce the numbers of participants to a point where the evaluation is worthless.

Once the study was underway there were threats to its progress as seen in maintaining the co-operation of the various agencies involved in delivering the intervention. A high rate of attrition amongst the research staff also worked against the study: Asscher *et al.* observed that 'There was also a high staff turnover, mainly among the research assistants. The assistants became unmotivated because they had to put a lot of effort into reaching the families, who were often not that interested in the research' (p. 123). It's as well to remember that researchers are people too.

Future directions

Rather than focus just on RCTs, it is more useful to think in terms of an overarching research strategy which may encompass several designs. For example Everitt and Wessely suggest various stages for the development and evaluation of complex interventions using different research methodologies as appropriate:

1   *Theory.* The development of the theoretical basis of the intervention.
2   *Modelling.* The development of and understanding of the intervention and its effect using small-scale surveys, focus groups and observational studies.
3   *Exploratory trial.* Preliminary evidence is gathered in support of the intervention.
4   *Definitive RCT.* A randomised study is conducted.
5   *Long-term implementation.* Can the intervention's effects be replicated over time and in different settings?

Slade and Priebe (2001) provide a suitable closing that applies equally well to forensic as well as mental health research:

> Mental health research needs to span both the natural and social sciences. Evidence based on RCTs has an important place, but to adopt concepts from only one body of knowledge is to neglect the contribution that other, well-established methodologies can make.... RCTs can give better evidence about some contentious research questions, but it is an illusion that the development of increasingly rigorous and sophisticated RCTs will ultimately provide a complete evidence base. (p. 287)

Further reading

Books

In writing this chapter there were several publications that, I felt, captured the debate and which are cited in the text. I have selected several of these publications as particularly worth following up.

Asscher, J. J., Dekovi , M., van der Laan, P. H., Prins, P. J. M. and van Arum, S. (2007). Implementing randomised experiments in criminal justice settings: an evaluation of multi-systemic therapy in the Netherlands. *Journal of Experimental Criminology*, 3: 113–29. Any researcher contemplating research involving randomisation is advised to read this paper.

Clarke, R. V. G. and Cornish, D. B. (1972). *The controlled trial in institutional research – paradigm or pitfall for penal evaluators?* Home Office Research Study 15. London: HMSO. Like Martin Peters, the elegance of the thinking is ahead of its time.

Everitt, B. S. and Wessely, S. (2004). *Clinical trials in psychiatry*. Oxford: Oxford University Press. Everything you ever wanted or needed to know about clinical trials in 189 pages. Bargain.

Farrington, D. P. and Welsh, B. C. (2005). Randomized experiments in criminology: what have we learned in the last two decades? *Journal of Experimental Criminology*, 1: 9–38. A comprehensive overview of the use of randomised studies in mainstream criminology.

Slade, M. and Priebe, S. (2001). Are randomised controlled trials the only gold that glitters? *British Journal of Psychiatry*, 179: 286–7. Asks all the right questions.

Websites

The websites below contain a great deal of information about effective strategies to reduce crime. Inevitably, the material includes discussions of research design, including the role of randomised studies.

The Cochrane Collaboration is an international network of researchers concerned with reviewing the evidence on the effectiveness of healthcare provision, including treatment aimed at antisocial and criminal behaviour. The Cochrane Reviews, of which there are over 4,000, are updated and available online in The Cochrane Library at www2.cochrane.org/reviews.

There is a fantastic collection of material on crime prevention available at www.preventingcrime.org.

The US Department of Justice has a wealth of material: the link www.ncjrs. gov/pdffiles/171676.PDF is to the publication *Preventing crime: what works, what doesn't, what's promising* by Lawrence W. Sherman, Denise C. Gottfredson, Doris L. MacKenzie, John Eck, Peter Reuter and Shawn D. Bushway.

References

Asscher, J. J., Dekovi , M., van der Laan, P. H., Prins, P. J. M., and van Arum, S. (2007). Implementing randomized experiments in criminal justice settings: an evaluation of multi-systemic therapy in the Netherlands. *Journal of Experimental Criminology*, 3: 113–29.

Babcock, J. C., Green, C. E. and Robie, C. (2004). Does batterers' treatment work? A meta-analytic review of domestic violence treatment. *Clinical Psychology Review*, 23: 1,023–53.

Cartwright, N. (2007). *Are RCTs the gold standard?* Centre for Philosophy of Natural and Social Science, Contingency and Dissent in Science, Technical Report 01/07. London: London School of Economics.

Chitty, C. (2005). The impact of corrections on re-offending: conclusions and the way forward. In G. Harper and C. Chitty (Eds). *The impact of corrections on re-offending: a review of 'what works'* (pp. 73–82). Home Office Research Study 291 (2nd edn). London: Home Office.

Clark, D. M. (2004). Developing new treatments: on the interplay between theories, experimental science and clinical innovation. *Behaviour Research and Therapy*, 42: 1,089–1,104.

Clarke, R. V. G. and Cornish, D. B. (1972). *The controlled trial in institutional research – paradigm or pitfall for penal evaluators?* Home Office Research Study 15. London: HMSO.

Cook, T. D. and Campbell, D. T. (1979). *Quasi-experimentation: design and analysis issues for field settings.* Boston, MA: Houghton Mifflin Company.

Cure, S., Chua, W. L., Duggan, L., and Adams, C. (2005). Randomised controlled trials relevant to aggressive and violent people, 1995–2000: a survey. *British Journal of Psychiatry*, 186: 185–9.

Debidin, M. and Lovbakke, J. (2005). Offending behaviour programmes in prison and probation. In G. Harper and C. Chitty (Eds). *The impact of corrections on re-offending: a review of 'what works'* (pp. 31–55). Home Office Research Study 291 (2nd edn). London: Home Office.

Des Jarlais, D. C., Lyles, C. and Crepaz, N. (2004). Improving the quality of nonrandomized evaluations of behavioural and public health interventions: the TREND statement. *American Journal of Public Health*, 94: 361–6.

Everitt, B. S. and Wessely, S. (2004). *Clinical trials in psychiatry*. Oxford: Oxford University Press.

Farrington, D. P. (2006). Methodological quality and the evaluation of anti-crime programs. *Journal of Experimental Criminology*, 2: 329–37.

Farrington, D. P. and Jolliffe, D. (2002). *A feasibility study into using a randomised controlled trial to evaluate treatment pilots at HMP Whitemoor.* Home Office Online Report 14/02. London: Home Office.

Farrington, D. P. and Welsh, B. C. (2005). Randomized experiments in criminology: what have we learned in the last two decades? *Journal of Experimental Criminology*, 1: 9–38.

Farrington, D. P., Gottfredson, D. C., Sherman, L. W. and Welsh, B. C. (2002). The Maryland Scientific Methods Scale. In L. W. Sherman, D. P. Farrington, B. C. Welsh and D. L. MacKenzie (Eds). *Evidence-based crime prevention* (pp. 13–21). London: Routledge.

Friendship, C., Blud, L., Erikson, M., Travers, L. and Thornton, D. M. (2003). Cognitive-behavioural treatment for imprisoned offenders: an evaluation of HM Prison Service's cognitive skills programmes. *Legal and Criminological Psychology*, 8: 103–14.

Gilbody, S. and Whitty, P. (2002). Improving the delivery and organisation of mental health services: Beyond the conventional randomised controlled trial. *British Journal of Psychiatry*, 180, 13–18.

Goetghebeur, E. and Loeys, T. (2002). Beyond intention to treat. *Epidemiologic Reviews*, 24: 85–90.

Goldkamp, J. S. (2009). Missing the target and missing the point: 'successful' random assignment but misleading results. *Journal of Experimental Criminology*, 4: 83–115.

Gondolf, E. W. (2001). Limitations of experimental evaluation of batterer programs. *Trauma, Violence, and Abuse*, 2: 79–88.

—— (2004). Evaluating batterer counselling programs: a difficult task showing some effects and implications. *Aggression and Violent Behavior*, 9: 605–31.

Harper, G. and Chitty, C. (Eds) (2005). *The impact of corrections on re-offending: a review of 'what works'*. Home Office Research Study 291 (2nd edn). London: Home Office.

Heinsman, D. T. and Shadish, W. R. (1996). Assignment methods in experimentation: when do nonrandomized experiments approximate answers from randomized experiments? *Psychological Methods*, 1: 154–69.

Hill, A. B. (1952). The clinical trial. *New England Journal of Medicine*, 247: 113–19.

Hollin, C. R. (2008). Evaluating offending behaviour programmes: does only randomisation glister? *Criminology and Criminal Justice*, 8: 89–106.

Hollin, C. R. and Palmer, E. J. (Eds) (2006). *Offending behaviour programmes: development, application, and controversies*. Chichester: John Wiley & Sons.

Hollin, C. R., McGuire, J., Hounsome, J. C., Hatcher, R. M., Bilby, C. A. L. and Palmer, E. J. (2008). Cognitive skills offending behavior programs in the community: a reconviction analysis. *Criminal Justice and Behavior*, 35: 269–83.

Jadad, A. R., Moore, R. A., Carroll, D., Jenkinson, C., Reynolds, J. M., Gavaghon, D. J. and McQuay, D. M. (2001). Assessing the quality of reports of randomized clinical trials: is blinding necessary? *Controlled Clinical Trials*, 17: 1–12.

Jones, A. S., D'Agostino, R. B., Gondolf, E. W. and Heckert, A. (2004). Assessing the effect of batterer program completion on reassault using propensity scores. *Journal of Interpersonal Violence*, 19: 1,002–20.

Juni, P., Altman, D. G. and Egger, M. (2001). Assessing the quality of controlled clinical trials. *British Medical Journal*, 323: 42–6.

Levant, R. F. (2004). The empirically validated treatments movement: A practitioner/educator perspective. *Clinical Psychology: Science and Practice*, 11: 219–26.

Lewis, S. C. and Warlow, C. P. (2004). How to spot bias and other potential problems in randomised controlled trials. *Journal of Neurology, Neurosurgery and Psychiatry*, 75: 181–7.

Leykin, Y., DeRubeis, R. J., Gallop, R., Amsterdam, J. D., Shelton, R. C. and Hollon, S. D. (2007). The relation of patients' treatment preferences to outcome in a randomized clinical trial. *Behavior Therapy*, 38: 209–17.

Lipsey, M. W. (1992). Juvenile delinquency treatment: a meta-analytic inquiry into the variability of effects. In T. D. Cook, H. Cooper, D. S. Cordray, H. Hartmann, L. V. Hedges, R. J. Light, T. A. Louis and F. Mosteller (Eds). *Meta-analysis for explanation: a casebook* (pp. 83–127). New York: Russell Sage Foundation.

Lipsey, M. W., Chapman, G. L. and Landenberger, N. A. (2001). Cognitive-behavioral programs for offenders. *Annals of The American Academy of Political and Social Science*, 578: 144–57.

Lösel, F. and Schmucker, M. (2005). The effectiveness of treatment for sexual offenders: a comprehensive meta-analysis. *Journal of Experimental Criminology*, 1: 117–46.

Lum, C. and Yang, S. (2005). Why do evaluation researchers in crime and justice choose non-experimental methods? *Journal of Experimental Criminology*, 1: 191–213.

McGuire, J., Bilby, C. A. L., Hatcher, R. M., Hollin, C. R., Hounsome, J. and Palmer, E. J. (2008). Evaluation of structured cognitive-behavioral treatment programmes in reducing criminal recidivism. *Journal of Experimental Criminology*, 4: 21–40.

Marshall, W. L. and Marshall, L. E. (2007). The utility of the random controlled trial for evaluating sexual offender treatment: the gold standard or an inappropriate strategy? *Sex Abuse: A Journal of Research and Treatment*, 19: 175–81.

Norris, S. L. and Atkins, D. (2005). Challenges in using nonrandomized studies in systematic reviews of treatment interventions. *Annals of Internal Medicine*, 142: 1,112–19.

Nuttall, C. (2003). The Home Office and random allocation experiments. *Evaluation Review*, 27: 267–89.

Palmer, E. J., McGuire, J., Hounsome, J. C., Hatcher, R. M., Bilby, C. A. and Hollin, C. R. (2007). Offending behaviour programmes in the community: the effects on reconviction of three programmes with adult male offenders. *Legal and Criminological Psychology*, 12: 251–64.

Petrosino, A., and Soydam, H. (2005). The impact of program developers as evaluators on criminal recidivism: results from meta-analyses of experimental and quasi-experimental research. *Journal of Experimental Criminology*, 1: 435–50.

Prendergast, M., Greenwell, L., Cartier, J., Sacks, J., Frisman, L., Rodis, E. and Havens, J. R. (2009). Adherence to scheduled sessions in a randomized field trial of case management: the criminal justice-drug abuse treatment studies transitional case management study. *Journal of Experimental Criminology*, 5: 273–97.

Ross, R., and Fabiano, E. (1985). *Time to think: a cognitive model of delinquency prevention and offender rehabilitation*. Ottawa: Air Training and Publications.

Shapiro, D. A., Harper, H., Startup, M., Reynolds, S., Bird, D. and Suokas, A. (1994). The high water mark of the drug metaphor: a meta-analytic critique of process-outcome research. In R. L. Russell (Ed), *Reassessing psychotherapy research* (pp. 1–35). New York: Guilford Press.

Sherman, L. W. (2003). Misleading evidence and evidence-led policy: making social science more experimental. *Annals of The American Academy of Political and Social Science*, 589: 6–19.

Sherman, L. W., Gottfredson, D. C., MacKenzie, D. L., Eck, J. E., Reuter, P. and Bushway, S. D. (1997). *Preventing crime: what works, what doesn't, what's promising*. Washington, DC: Department of Justice, National Institute of Justice.

Slade, M. and Priebe, S. (2001). Are randomised controlled trials the only gold that glitters? *British Journal of Psychiatry*, 179: 286–7.

Smith, R. A. and Davis, S. F. (2004). *The psychologist as detective: an introduction to conducting research in psychology.* 3rd edn. Upper Saddle River, NJ: Pearson.

Stolberg, H. O., Norman, G. and Trop, I. (2004). Fundamentals of clinical research for radiologists: randomized controlled trials. *American Journal of Radiology,* 183: 1,539–44.

Telep, C. W. (2009). Citation analysis of randomized experiments in criminology and criminal justice: a research note. *Journal of Experimental Criminology,* 5: 441–63.

Van Voorhis, P., Spruance, L. M., Ritchey, P. N., Listwan, S. J. and Seabrook, R. (2004). The Georgia cognitive skills experiment: an application of Reasoning and Rehabilitation. *Criminal Justice and Behavior,* 31: 282–305.

Victora, C. G., Habicht, J. and Bryce, J. (2004). Evidence-based public health: moving beyond randomized trials. *American Journal of Public Health,* 94: 400–5.

Weisburd, D., Lum, C. M. and Petrosino, A. (2001). Does research design affect study outcomes in criminal justice? *Annals of The American Academy of Political and Social Science,* 578: 50–70.

Wilson, D. B., Bouffard, L. A. and Mackenzie, D. L. (2005). A quantitative review of structured, group-orientated, cognitive-behavioral programs for offenders. *Criminal Justice and Behavior,* 32: 172–204.

Wormith, J. S. and Olver, M. E. (2002). Offender treatment attrition and its relationship with risk, responsivity, and recidivism. *Criminal Justice and Behavior,* 29: 447–71.

12 Evaluation of regimes and environments

Matt Tonkin and Kevin Howells

Introduction

The concept of personality will be familiar to most people, as will some of the central elements that one might name if asked to describe the 'personality' of someone they know. For example some people might be described as warm, gregarious and supportive, whereas others might be described as hostile, suspicious and controlling. Adjectives such as these are commonly used to describe people and their dispositions, but they are also words that can be used to describe an environment or regime. Just as a person might be described as warm and supportive (or cold and hostile), so too might a given environment.

This is how Rudolf Moos viewed the evaluation of regimes and environments (Moos, 1975, 1989). However, he used the term social climate to refer to the 'personality' of a setting or environment. It is with the perception, measurement and evaluation of social climate that the current chapter is concerned. That is, how can practitioners and researchers define, measure and test the social climate of a particular forensic environment? And what issues complicate this task?

These questions will be explored by considering the types of method, design and analysis that might be used to evaluate forensic environments and regimes, the importance of doing so, the history of evaluating environments, the strengths and limitations of this work and the important future directions that work might take. Throughout the chapter, real-life examples from forensic practice and the academic literature will be used to illustrate the material. We begin with a brief history of regime evaluation.

The history of regime evaluation

The formal evaluation of environments and the measurement of social climate were pioneered in the USA by Rudolf Moos during the 1960s and 1970s. At that time, Moos developed the Ward Atmosphere Scale (WAS; Moos, 1974; Moos and Houts, 1968), a 100-item questionnaire that measures 10 aspects of social climate (see Table 12.1). This was the first questionnaire of its kind to provide an objective method for measuring an environment's 'personality'. The questionnaire was developed through a combination of behavioural observation on several

Table 12.1 Six social climate questionnaires and their scales

WAS/CIES (Moos, 1974, 1987; Moos and Houts, 1968)	Prison Preference Inventory (PPI; Toch, 1977) and Prison Environment Inventory (PEI; Wright, 1985)	Prison Social Climate Survey (PSCS; Saylor, 1983)	Essen Climate Evaluation Schema (EssenCES; Schalast et al., 2008)	Measuring Quality of Prison Life (MQPL; Liebling and Arnold, 2002, 2004)
Relationship dimensions:	1) Privacy	*Inmate version:*	1) Therapeutic hold	1) Respect
1) Involvement	2) Safety	1) Background data	2) Patient/prisoner cohesion	2) Humanity
2) Support	3) Structure	2) Quality of life	3) Experienced safety	3) Support
3) Spontaneity	4) Support	3) Personal well-being		4) Relationships
	5) Emotional feedback	4) Staff services and programmes utilised		5) Trust
Personal growth dimensions:	6) Social stimulation	5) Personal safety and security		6) Fairness
4) Autonomy	7) Activity			7) Order
5) Practical orientation	8) Freedom	*Staff version:*		8) Safety
6) Personal problem orientation		1) Socio-demographics		9) Well-being
7) Anger and aggression[1]		2) Personal safety and security		10) Development prison
		3) Quality of life		11) Development family
System maintenance dimensions:		4) Personal well-being		12) Decency
8) Order and organisation		5) Work environment		13) Power
9) Programme clarity		6) Community environment and housing preferences		14) Prisoner social life
10) Staff control		7) Special interest section		15) Belonging
				16) Quality of life

Notes: 1 The CIES does not contain this scale.

psychiatric wards, staff and patient interviews, and the academic literature. The questionnaire was repeatedly trialled with different groups of patients and staff to identify the most useful questions. The final version of the WAS was sufficient for measuring the social climate of psychiatric settings, but it required minor alterations for different contexts. The most relevant of these alterations was the Correctional Institutions Environment Scale (CIES; Moos, 1987), which is a revised version of the WAS that is suitable for use in forensic settings. The CIES measures nine of the original ten WAS scales, which can be combined into three super-ordinate measures of social climate (relationship dimensions; personal growth dimensions; and system maintenance dimensions; see Moos, 1975, and Tables 12.1 and 12.2 for further details).

The WAS and the CIES are probably the most widely used questionnaires for measuring and evaluating social climate. However, despite their widespread use, they have received criticism on a number of grounds, including a lack of reliability and validity, a thin theoretical basis and the fact that juvenile populations were used to develop the CIES (e.g. Liebling and Arnold, 2004; Saylor, 1983; Wright and Boudouris, 1982). In response to criticisms such as these, William Saylor and the US Federal Bureau of Prisons developed a new questionnaire to measure social climate, the Prison Social Climate Survey (PSCS; Saylor, 1983). An inmate version (comprising five sections and 189 questions) and a staff version (comprising seven sections) were developed, which tapped slightly different aspects of experience and interaction within the prison environment (see Tables 12.1 and 12.2). Common areas in the two questionnaires included feelings of personal safety and security, quality of life and well-being.

Before the PSCS was developed, however, and shortly after Moos published his WAS, Hans Toch published an alternative measure of social climate, the Prison Preference Inventory (PPI; Toch, 1977). The PPI works on the assumption that prisoners (like any other person) have different needs and wants and that certain environments naturally cater for these needs better than others. Thus, the PPI assumes that it should be possible to identify which environments and which prisoners are mutually suited. It aims to do this by having respondents rate 56 pairs of statements in terms of preference (where each statement describes a particular type of prison environment or prison characteristic). For example, the respondent might be asked if they prefer guards who are consistent or guards who are friendly. The 56 pairs allow each respondent to be rated in terms of their preference for eight psychosocial aspects of the prison environment (see Tables 12.1 and 12.2). An individual's PPI profile, therefore, says something about the sort of prison environment they prefer.

There were significant problems with the PPI, however, in terms of reliability and validity. There were also significant statistical problems created by pairing items in the way that Toch did (see Wright, 1985, for a summary). These problems led to the development of the Prison Environment Inventory (PEI; Wright, 1985), which was intended to address these issues and provide a revised version of the PPI that was statistically sound.

Table 12.2 Six social climate questionnaires and summary information

	WAS/CIES[1]	PPI	PEI	PSCS	EssenCES	MQPL
Number of items	CIES[1] 1) Form R = 90 2) Form S = 36 3) Form I = 90 4) Form E = 90 WAS 100 items	56 item pairs	48 items	Inmate version 189 items Staff version Unknown	15 items (plus 2 filler items)	102 items
Samples used with	Male and female general and forensic psychiatric patients and staff from the US and staff in these institutions Male and female forensic psychiatric patients from conditions of maximum security in Sweden and staff in this institution Male and female general and forensic psychiatric patients (including adolescents) from various conditions of security in the UK and staff in these institutions	Male and female prisoners from the US	Male prisoners from the US	Male prisoners from the UK and the US (including UK CATs B, C, D)	Male and female German forensic psychiatric patients and staff Male and female patients and staff from high security psychiatric hospitals in the UK	Male prisoners and prison staff from across the UK

Reliability and validity					
In summary, there is considerable evidence to support the construct validity of these measures. However, despite their widespread use, there is surprisingly little evidence to support factor structure and internal consistency. Indeed, some studies even demonstrate quite poor internal consistency and fail to replicate the hypothesised factor structure.	In summary, there is some evidence that the PPI has construct validity, but there is also evidence to the contrary. The evidence for internal consistency is also not strong.	In summary, there is evidence for adequate factor structure and internal consistency for most scales. But there is a lack of research using this measure, which means it has not been trialled in a variety of settings.	In summary, there is good evidence that the PSCS has adequate factor structure cross-culturally (at least for the inmate version). There is also evidence for the factor structure and internal consistency of the staff version. But this evidence is only limited to certain scales and construct validity has not received considerable attention.	In summary, the evidence of reliability and validity is good, with support for the factor structure and evidence for internal consistency and construct validity. But there is a need to test the EssenCES with a wider variety of samples.	In summary, there is no explicit evidence to suggest that the MQPL is unreliable and there is some support for its construct validity. However, it has received very little empirical attention.

Notes

1 There are four versions of the CIES. Forms R and S measure perceptions of an actual (real) programme, with the former a long version and the latter a short version of the questionnaire. Form I measures perceptions of the ideal programme. Form E measures expectations about a programme.

The information in this table was correct at the time of writing and to the best possible knowledge of the authors. However, this table should not be viewed as a comprehensive summary of information available for these measures, as the authors recognise that some information may have been omitted erroneously.

Wright's PEI maintained the eight original dimensions identified by Toch, but gave the individual items a complete overhaul. The new set of questions that Wright developed were refined and tested on various samples of prison inmates from several medium- and maximum-security prisons in New York State. This led to a final 48-item version of the PEI, which measured the eight psychosocial aspects of prison environment originally proposed by Toch in a seemingly more reliable and sound way (see Tables 12.1 and 12.2).

The four measures of social climate described so far were all developed in the USA, but in Europe, a similar (albeit more recent) history of regime evaluation exists. As described by Liebling and Arnold (2004), evaluation of prison regimes in the UK began in 1992 when the prison service introduced a number of key performance indicators and targets on which all prisons would be monitored and evaluated regularly. Theoretically, these indicators and targets were designed to provide institutions with a sense of direction and purpose for guiding their activities, as well as a formal structure for evaluating and comparing prisons across the UK (Liebling and Arnold, 2004). These initial indicators and targets have gone through various revisions over time and the sophistication with which they are measured and scored has increased. Furthermore, specific bodies and organisations have been established to run these regular audits, such as the Standards Audit, the Prisons Inspectorate and Independent Monitoring Boards. There has also been an increase in the scope of these evaluations. Whereas initially the targets and indicators were concerned with issues such as security and staffing, more recent evaluations have begun incorporating qualitative aspects, such as interviews with prisoners that ask about perceptions of safety and how respected and cared for they feel in the prison environment (Liebling and Arnold, 2004).

These recent changes have spurred the development of several new questionnaires, designed specifically to measure social climate and aspects of the prison regime/environment in the UK. For example, Liebling and Arnold (2002, 2004) developed the English Measurement of Quality of Prison Life (MQPL), which assesses 16 aspects of the prison environment (see Tables 12.1 and 12.2). Interestingly, staff and prisoners in these studies seemed to agree on what aspects of the prison environment mattered, and their scores on this measure were related to key targets and performance indicators.

Most recently, Dr Norbert Schalast has developed the Essen Climate Evaluation Schema in Germany (EssenCES; Schalast *et al.*, 2008). This questionnaire has since been translated into a variety of languages, including English, and versions are available for both male and female services and for psychiatric and prison settings, which differ in their wording very slightly (e.g. the word 'ward' that is used in the psychiatric version is replaced with the word 'unit' in the prison version). The EssenCES measures three aspects of the social climate in forensic settings: (1) therapeutic hold (five questions; e.g. 'Often, staff seem not to care if patients/prisoners succeed or fail in treatment'); (2) patient/prisoner cohesion and mutual support (five questions; e.g. 'There is good peer support among patients/prisoners'); and (3) experienced safety (five questions; e.g. 'At times, members of staff are afraid of some of the patients/prisoners'). Unlike many of the other measures, support for the reliability and validity of this questionnaire exists in both German and English psychiatric settings (Howells *et al.*, 2009; Schalast *et al.*, 2008). However, it should be noted that the English version of EssenCES cannot yet be considered fully validated for use in UK secure settings; primarily because its validity in a prison setting has not been examined. But this may soon change as a large-scale validation project, which will shed light on the validity of the English EssenCES in a variety of prison and secure NHS sites around the country, is nearing completion.

This brief history of regime evaluation clearly demonstrates that there is a growing body of work in this area and there now exist several different question-naire-based measures that can assess various aspects of the forensic environment and social climate. This raises the question of why it is actually important to monitor and evaluate social climate and what types of method are available for doing so.

The importance of regime evaluation

Regular auditing and evaluation is a fundamental process that almost all major public and private services undergo, and forensic services in the prison and healthcare systems are certainly no exception. In forensic settings, service evalu-ation often involves the evaluation of specific treatment programmes, such as sex offender treatment programmes, anger management or cognitive skills training, where various questionnaire-based and behavioural measures are used to assess whether the programme has facilitated the expected changes. These sorts of treat-ment evaluations are, of course, an important part of evaluating forensic settings; however, the wider environment (or climate) in which these programmes occur is also important. But despite the importance of a regime's social climate, it has traditionally been given far less attention during service evaluations. This is surprising because it is logical to expect that social climate would have an impact on the outcome of treatment programmes. That is, if treatment programmes are run in an unhealthy environment, where residents feel unsafe, uncared for and unsupported, then any potential benefits that might arise from treatment would probably be at best attenuated and at worst lost altogether.

Indeed, this expectation is supported by a multitude of studies that demonstrate a relationship between social climate and a variety of clinical and organisational outcomes, including staff and resident satisfaction (e.g. Middleboe *et al.*, 2001; Moos and Houts, 1970), institutional violence and the frequency of assaults on staff (e.g. Friis and Helldin, 1994; Lanza *et al.*, 1994), staff performance and morale (e.g. Moos and Schaefer, 1987), occupational stress in staff (e.g. Kirby and Pollock, 1995) and, most importantly, treatment outcomes such as drop-out, release rate and reconviction (e.g. Beech and Hamilton-Giachritsis, 2005; Melle *et al.*, 1996). It is, therefore, clear that a healthy social climate is potentially important for the successful functioning of forensic settings and that, like many other aspects of treatment, it should be monitored on a regular basis.

Environments and climate as independent variables

There are models in the literature relating to how environmental conditions might affect outcomes of offender rehabilitation programmes. One model is the Multifactorial Offender Readiness Model (MORM; Day *et al.*, 2010; Ward *et al.*, 2004). This model suggests that successful outcomes for offender rehabilitation programmes depend in part on the level of engagement of participants in the programme itself. Indices of low engagement include drop-out, poor attendance, minimal participation in sessions and failing to complete homework. Engagement is seen as being driven by two types of readiness conditions, those *internal* to the participant (their beliefs about treatment, self-efficacy etc.) and those which are *external* (characteristics of the situation, the organisation and the treatment programme itself). Within this model internal and external conditions may be reciprocally related, in that the beliefs and attitudes of therapy participants may influence the social climate of the unit within which they live. Equally, the social climate may support or hinder the treatment attitudes and motivation of individuals. From this perspective, the social climate of a unit or service is potentially a factor that may impact on readiness to engage with and benefit from treatment.

Climate as a dependent variable

The regular monitoring of social climate (for example on a six-monthly or yearly basis) is a practice that some forensic units have adopted in recent times. For example Rampton and Broadmoor Hospitals (two of the three high-security psychiatric hospitals in the UK) both regularly monitor social climate and feed the results back to senior management staff, ward staff and patients. In the US, the US Federal Bureau of Prisons also regularly monitors social climate by annually selecting a random and representative sample of prison employees from each US jurisdiction to comment on the climate of its prisons (Britton, 1997).

Some forensic services, therefore, choose to monitor social climate in a longitudinal way, where the attitudes of patients and/or staff are sampled on a regular basis over a period of years. However, the regular monitoring of social climate at fixed intervals is just one type of method that can be used to evaluate social climate. An alternative approach is to treat climate as something that can change in accordance with the environment and, in some cases, something that can be explicitly manipulated. For example, how does the social climate change when a service is moved to a new building, when staff are restructured or when a new policy or method of working is introduced?

These very questions were addressed within Rampton Hospital when the National High Secure Women's Service was relocated to a new building and significant staff and patient restructuring occurred. These changes were significant and it was expected that they would impact on social climate. It was, therefore, decided that social climate would be measured prior to the move and some time afterwards in order to assess the impact of service change on social climate. A range of climate-related questionnaires were distributed to patients and staff and the scores obtained on these measures before the move were compared with those obtained after the move. In short, there were few differences pre- and post-move, with a positive climate maintained despite the significant upheaval associated with the move and subsequent restructuring. A similar method was adopted by the Personality Disorder Service within Rampton Hospital when a new model of therapeutic care was introduced – the RAID (Reinforce Appropriate Implode Disruptive) method of managing extreme behaviour (Davies, 2001). Social climate (amongst many other factors) was measured pre- and post-RAID to assess whether this new method of working had led to a significant improvement (or deterioration) in climate.

Thus, there are two basic methods that can be used to evaluate the social climate of an environment or regime. The climate can either be measured in a longitudinal way at regular fixed intervals, or it can be measured in a time-limited, cross-sectional way where the effect of a particular intervention (be it clinical or organisational) is assessed by comparing pre-intervention climate with post-intervention climate. The next question that arises is what specific research questions can be addressed using these methods of regime evaluation?

The types of research question that can be addressed in regime evaluation

In terms of the longitudinal approach, the primary question that this method is suitable for addressing is whether and to what extent social climate fluctuates over time. But the longitudinal method can also be used as a way of monitoring (and even pre-empting) conditions which may give rise to behavioural problems in a service, such as aggression and self-harm. Indeed, the studies reported above showing a relationship between social climate and aggressive behaviour (Friis and Helldin, 1994; Lanza *et al.*, 1994), suggest that aggressive incidents become more likely when social climate deteriorates. If this is true, then long-term monitoring might provide a way of identifying areas of a regime in need of specific attention. This could help managers plan regime changes to prevent such incidents arising.

On the other hand, the cross-sectional approach is more suitable for assessing the impact of a given intervention. As discussed previously, this could include the impact of staff/resident restructuring, a new method of working or a new physical environment on the climate of a given institution. But it might also be the impact that a specific treatment programme has on social climate. Indeed, many introductory treatment programmes within forensic settings are aimed at increasing positive peer relationships and helping new prisoners/patients adjust to their surroundings. As such, social climate is quite conceivably an outcome that one might expect to improve after successful completion of these treatment programmes. In this sense, social climate can become part of a standard battery

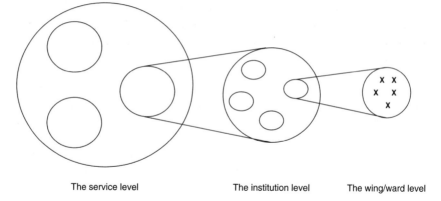

The service level   The institution level   The wing/ward level

Figure 12.1 A schematic representation of the various levels at which regime evaluation can function.

of measures that could be administered pre-treatment and post-treatment to judge whether treatment has been successful.

The range and diversity of research questions that can be addressed in regime evaluation is, therefore, substantial. However, within each of the two fundamental methods described above there are various 'levels' at which regime evaluation can function (see Figure 12.1). At the highest level, the climate of whole services containing many different individual institutions can be evaluated, for example the climate within all Category A prisons. Beyond that, the climate of an individual institution within a particular service can be focused upon, such as the climate within one category A prison in the prison system or a high security hospital in the health service. At an even more refined level, the climate within a particular wing/ward of a given institution can be examined (e.g. a particular wing in a prison or a ward in a forensic mental health service). At the most detailed level, the perceptions of an individual prisoner or patient living on a specific wing/ward can be evaluated. The level at which one evaluates a regime will depend on the specific purpose of evaluation. For example when evaluating the impact of a specific treatment programme the researcher might be more concerned with how an individual perceives social climate. However, when monitoring the impact of a new policy there might be more interest in the perception of climate over an entire ward, institution or service.

Design issues and decisions in regime evaluation

The first major methodological decision to make when attempting to evaluate a regime is which measure of social climate to use. As discussed, there are numerous questionnaires that measure climate (or related constructs) and, in fact, the six questionnaires discussed previously are but a few of the many possible measures that could be selected. So, the question is, then: how do we choose the most appropriate questionnaire given this vast array of options? Initial considerations may be cost and accessibility. Not all social climate questionnaires are free and easy to access; notably, the WAS is a commercial product, which means it costs to purchase and use. Others, although free to use, may require some effort to obtain and necessitate contact with the author who designed the questionnaire. The urgency to complete a project may make ease of access an important issue.

But there are more substantive issues worth considering when selecting a questionnaire. The first is whether the questionnaire is valid and reliable. That is does the questionnaire measure what it is supposed to measure (construct validity) and does it do so in a consistent way, regardless of to whom it is given and when (test-retest reliability, cross-cultural and cross-sample validity)? A published measure does not necessarily have high reliability and validity. Indeed, as discussed above, many climate questionnaires have been criticised for their lack of reliability (e.g. the WAS, CIES and PPI). Furthermore, even those that do have evidence for their psychometric adequacy may not have been validated for use in all settings (e.g. we cannot assume that a questionnaire validated on a sample of juvenile male offenders is suitable for use with a sample of adult females with mental health difficulties). The relatively sparse amount of research in this area means that is quite unlikely you will find a measure that has been validated sufficiently on a sample that exactly matches the population you hope to test. It is important, therefore, to at least pay heed to these issues and select a measure that is generally reliable and valid with a sample that resembles the population you are proposing to study.

The structure and nature of the questionnaire are also important. Although the six measures listed in Table 12.1 overlap substantially, there *is* variation between them. For example some measures such as the EssenCES are a general measure of social climate, whereas others provide a more refined and differentiated view of a given environment (e.g. the MQPL). Whether a general or refined measure of social climate is the most appropriate, however, will depend on the type of environment being evaluated. More detailed measures of social climate almost invariably mean longer questionnaires that are more arduous to complete. In secure settings this can be problematic because prisoners and patients may not have the motivation or abilities to complete long questionnaires (Schalast *et al.*, 2008). Indeed, from personal experience, we suggest that the most challenging aspect of evaluating social climate in forensic settings is ensuring a sufficient response rate. But some key tips to increasing participation are to involve participants in the process of regime evaluation as much as possible, for example by consulting them on how they would like to be approached and what questions they would like answering, and, crucially, keeping them fully informed of how the evaluation has progressed (including feedback on the final outcomes, which will help to persuade others to take part in future evaluations). Nonetheless, it is clear that a fine balance needs to be struck between detail and more pragmatic issues when selecting the most appropriate questionnaire for evaluation purposes.

Having selected the questionnaire that is most appropriate for the evaluation, the next decision is who to give it to. This might seem a simple decision, but some services see a high turnover in residents and staff. Furthermore, not all staff and residents necessarily interact with an environment continuously. Some patients may be in long-term seclusion or some staff may work only on night shifts or may not even work on the ward/wing at all. Clearly, not all people who *could* be given a questionnaire on climate *should* be given one. Therefore, the question is: how do we judge whether someone has sufficient experience with a given environment/regime to provide a reliable estimate of climate? Unfortunately, there is no well-established rule that can be followed when making this decision. However, several researchers have adopted protocols that give some guidance. Brunt and Rask (2005), for example, excluded staff and residents with less than one month's experience either living or working on a given ward. Likewise, Howells *et al.* (2009) included only staff who had clinical contact with patients (e.g. nursing, psychiatry, social work, psychology staff and so on). Again, this is a decision that will depend to some extent on the nature of the environment and the type of evaluation. One key aim should be to try to sample as many differ- ent professional and resident groups as possible because different people will almost invariably have different perspectives of the social climate (Britton, 1997; Wright and Saylor, 1992). This is the only way to ensure that you get a fully balanced view.

Having chosen the questionnaire and the people to give it to, the next issue is how to administer it. Should the questionnaire be mailed to respondents or should a member of staff supervise administration? If the latter, should it be someone who knows the respondent well or someone who does not? Also, should respond- ents complete the questionnaire in groups or individually? Should items be read aloud or left for reading and completion by the participant alone? Although these may seem to be minor points of detail, they have the capacity to significantly affect the outcome of an evaluation. In terms of issues such as whether the respondent is supervised and whether the questionnaire is read out to them or not, the answers will depend on the nature of the population, with some groups requir- ing assistance in reading and responding. But issues such as whether the measure administrator should be someone well-known or not and how the completed questionnaires should be returned are less clear-cut. Nonetheless, they are impor- tant because some prisoners/patients (and even staff) may be less honest about their perceptions if interviewed by certain people. Indeed this was a finding clearly demonstrated by Moos (1975), who found that social climate was reported in a much more negative light on wards where respondents were allowed to remain anonymous compared to wards where they were required to give their name. It is, therefore, important to allow anonymous responding where possible and to at least ensure confidentiality. But this in itself can cause problems, particularly if a respondent later decides that they want to withdraw from the evaluation or indicates that they may be a risk to themselves or others. In cases such as this, it is important to be able to identify which questionnaire corresponds to that participant. One approach is to give participants a unique, but anonymous, code that can link individuals to their respective questionnaire, while retaining a degree of anonymity.

The next issue to consider is when data collection should stop. That is how many responses are needed to provide a reliable and accurate measure of social climate? Does everyone have to respond? Is 50 per cent sufficient? 75 per cent? Or is the absolute number of responses more important (e.g. are eight responses from a ward/wing sufficient)? Again, unfortunately, there is little in the way of guidance to help in this decision. But, Moos (1975) does make some recommendations for the CIES. He suggests that a tentative guide might be to sample at least 50 per cent of residents in units with more than 30 residents and 15 staff, and 25 per cent in units with more than 40 residents and 20 staff. By adopting these thresholds, Moos found intra-class correlation coefficients (ICC) of 0.80 and 0.90, respectively, which indicates that the respondents provided similar responses to the questionnaire and were quite homogeneous as a group (i.e. had similar perceptions of the social climate). But there are problems with these thresholds. First, they are only applicable to the CIES; there are no reliable thresholds available for any of the other climate questionnaires reviewed in this chapter. Second, the 25 per cent and 50 per cent thresholds were selected quite arbitrarily and there was no attempt to systematically test how the ICC varied over a wide number of thresholds. Indeed, the 0.90 coefficient observed for 25 per cent samples is very high, which suggests that good levels of reliability might have been obtained with less than a 25 per cent sample. The third problem is that in many secure settings (particularly secure psychiatric hospitals) ward sizes are much smaller than in prison or other correctional settings. Indeed, it is not unusual to have wards with fewer than ten patients. Appropriate guidelines for smaller units are, therefore, sadly lacking. The only real advice we can offer is simply to get as many completed questionnaires as possible on small units.

Once all of these issues have been navigated and the completed questionnaires collated and analysed, the final step is to interpret the findings. There are further problems at this stage of the evaluation. First, the measurement of social climate is not as advanced as that in other areas of clinical/forensic psychology, such as the measurement of psychopathy and risk. These latter concepts have been specifically tied to assessment and formulation from the start of their development. Consequently, they have well-established guidelines to aid in their interpretation (e.g. a score of 30 or above on the PCL-R is generally used to indicate the presence of psychopathy; Hare, 2003). Unfortunately, no such guidelines exist for measures of social climate, so there are no convenient thresholds to indicate when, for example, social climate is so poor that aggressive or self-harming incidents are imminent. Indeed, the relationship between disruptive behaviour and social climate is still not even fully established yet, so this may never happen. But, there are instances where authors have attempted to provide arbitrary guidelines to aid the interpretation of psychometric scores. Eklund and Hansson (1996), for example, suggest that scores on the WAS subscales that are under or equal to 3.33 are 'low' (i.e. generally indicative of a negative social climate), whereas scores of 3.34–36.66 are 'intermediate' and scores of 6.67 or above are 'high' (note that total scores are out of 10 for each WAS scale). Although these guidelines can help, they still do not tell us what psychometric scores actually mean in terms of real and tangible clinical outcomes (predictive validity).

The number and scale of the issues that require careful consideration in regime evaluation is, therefore, significant. But they can be addressed and will become less significant as research in this area increases. Once the data have been collated, however, the next task is to analyse that data.

The types of analysis involved in regime evaluation

Given the wide array of methodologies and questions that can be can addressed in regime evaluation, a correspondingly wide range of statistical approaches may be relevant. In terms of both the longitudinal and cross-sectional approaches, simple tests of difference can be useful to determine whether a particular individual, ward/wing or service has changed from one time to the next (using Analysis of Variance F-Tests, t-tests or their non-parametric equivalents). Time series analysis (see Ostrom, 1990) might also be useful for tracking fluctuation in climate over time (although this approach does not seem to have been used yet in the literature). Regression analysis can be used in situations where there is interest in using social climate to predict certain outcomes, for example aggression or self-harm (see Field, 2005, for a helpful guide to various types of regression analysis). Factor analysis and measures of internal consistency are appropriate where the question is whether the findings are reliable and valid (see Coakes and Steed, 2007, for a practical guide to factor analysis). Given the various levels at which a regime can be evaluated, multi-level analysis can also be useful where it is desirable to look at climate across several different levels, for example at individual, ward and institutional levels.

Having considered the methods, statistics and design issues that are involved in regime evaluation at a relatively abstract level, the next section will provide an illustrative example using data not previously published to provide a more concrete example of how social climate can be evaluated in a given forensic setting.

A worked example of regime evaluation: the case of the Peaks Unit

To illustrate the process of regime evaluation in a more hands-on way, data collected as part of a larger study that is aimed at validating the EssenCES for use in UK forensic settings will be described.

The data we will describe were collected on the Peaks Unit, a maximum-security forensic psychiatric unit within Rampton Hospital in England that houses individuals with high risk ('dangerous') severe personality disorders (DSPD). For a description of the DSPD system, see Howells *et al.* (2007). This unit is one of four high security DSPD sites established in 2003 to deal with individuals who pose a grave threat to the safety of others and who suffer from severe personality disorder that is functionally linked to (i.e. causes) their high risk behaviours. The monitoring of social climate is particularly important in such settings, for a number of reasons. First, secure forensic psychiatric institutions have had a controversial history in terms of their capacity to create and maintain therapeutic, as opposed to custodial, climates. Second, DSPD services, buildings, resident groups and staff were largely new, with some uncertainty as to how they might evolve. For these reasons, the climate on the Peaks Unit has been evaluated at regular intervals since March 2006 using the EssenCES questionnaire of social climate (amongst other questionnaires).

The primary purpose of the data reported here was to contribute to the larger validation study, but for the purposes of this worked example several local issues will be discussed, so as to illustrate the kinds of questions that can be addressed in regime evaluation. These issues are:

1   How has social climate on the unit fluctuated over time since 2006?
2   Do patients and staff differ in their perceptions of the social climate?
3   Are there different perceptions of social climate across the six wards that comprise the unit?

The questionnaires were administered to all patients on the unit and all staff working with patients in a clinical capacity (including nursing, psychology, psychiatry, social work and other clinical staff). They were administered by a research assistant working on the unit who was known, but relatively unfamiliar, to all patients and staff. Some patients had the questionnaire read aloud to them, whereas others completed it in their own time, depending on their preference. Questionnaires were completed anonymously, though the respondents' ward was recorded.

The first question that was addressed was how social climate had fluctuated over time since measurement began in March 2006. There were six time-points at which the social climate of the Peaks Unit had been sampled, which allowed climate to be compared and plotted over a four-year period (see Figure 12.2). From this figure we can see that minor fluctuation has occurred in perceived social climate on the Peaks Unit over three and a half years. In particular, we see that patients have been rated as less cohesive over time, whilst the environment generally has been seen by patients and staff as offering an increasing amount of therapeutic support (as indicated by two statistically significant repeated-measures Analysis of Variance F-Tests). However, there has been little change in how safe patients and staff feel and the overall level of social climate reported over this period (as indicated by a non-significant repeated-measures Analysis of Variance).

But, these scores are difficult to interpret without some point of reference. We can, therefore, compare these scores with those reported in German psychiatric units (Schalast *et al.*, 2008; see Figure 12.3). When we do this, we see that the

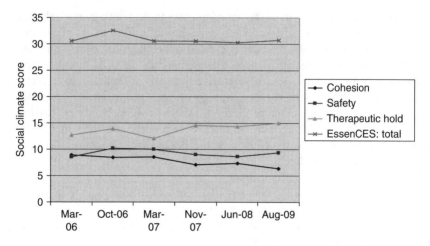

Figure 12.2 Social climate on the Peaks Unit.

Note: Scores on the three components of social climate (cohesion, safety and therapeutic hold) can range from 0–20 and on the EssenCES total can range from 0–60.

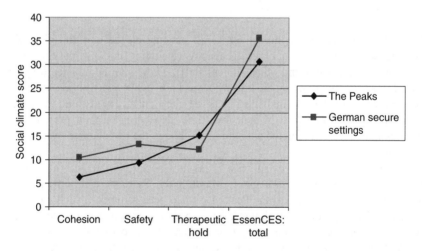

Figure 12.3 Social climate on the Peaks Unit compared with German secure psychiatric settings.

Peaks Unit is rated as offering a greater degree of therapeutic support than German psychiatric units (Peaks mean = 15.03; German mean = 12.10), but patients on the Peaks are rated as less cohesive (Peaks mean = 6.32; German mean = 10.40) and patients and staff feel more at risk of aggression (Peaks mean = 9.38; German mean = 13.10). Also, the social climate generally is rated as less positive (Peaks mean = 30.73; German mean = 35.60; see Figure 12.3). This is perhaps not surprising, however, given the higher risk and severity of 'disorder' among the respondents at the Peaks in comparison to those in the German psychiatric settings sampled by Schalast *et al.* (2008). It should be noted, however, that it was not possible to confirm whether these differences were statistically significant because the authors did not have access to Schalast *et al.*'s (2008) original data. Had this been available, though, t-tests (or the non-parametric equivalent, the Mann Whitney U test) would have been appropriate for statistical comparisons.

The remaining two issues that were addressed are whether patients and staff differ in their perceptions of the social climate and whether people from different wards have a different perspective on climate. Such differences would be expected. Patients and staff, for example, are quite likely to have very different perspectives because the unit is home for one group and merely a work location for the other. Also, one group is detained involuntarily, whilst the other is free to leave when they want. Likewise, different wards on the unit have different functions; for example one ward is an admissions ward, another is an intensive care ward for patients presenting as particularly challenging, and others are wards designated for patients undergoing treatment. Furthermore, within each ward there are different mixtures of patients and staff. All these factors could be expected to create different perceptions of climate on the six wards that comprise the Peaks Unit.

Indeed, when we compare the perceptions of staff and patients (see Figure 12.4), we notice that they differ most noticeably in terms of perceived safety and therapeutic hold, with staff feeling less safe than patients, but reporting a higher level of therapeutic support (as indicated by statistically significant t-tests). Furthermore, there are differences in perceived social climate across the six wards (although none of these differences achieved statistical significance according to an independent-samples Analysis of Variance;

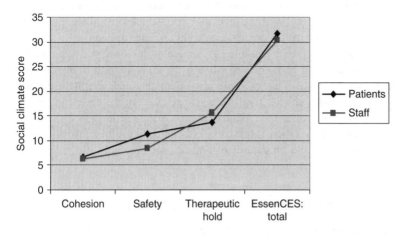

Figure 12.4 Patient and staff perceptions of social climate on the Peaks Unit.

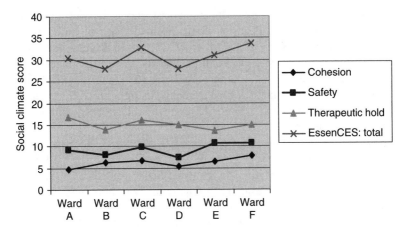

Figure 12.5 Perceptions of social climate across the six wards on the Peaks Unit.

see Figure 12.5). For example we see that wards B and D have the lowest social climate scores. Ward B is the admissions ward on the Peaks, so it is perhaps not surprising that the climate is less favourable in comparison with the other wards because patients are new and still have to become accustomed to their surroundings. Ward F, on the other hand, seems to receive the highest social climate rating. This ward is the 'step-down' ward that is for patients who have progressed well in treatment and are being considered for transfer to conditions of lower security. Again, it is not surprising that the social climate is more positive, because patients are relatively more settled and co-operative. What is slightly surprising, perhaps, is that Ward A received a fairly modal social climate score. This ward is designated as the high dependency, intensive care ward for patients. Patients are subject to much more restrictive timetables and security measures, so it is somewhat surprising that this does not impact detrimentally on the climate. However, the relatively high staffing level may counteract some of these negative effects because patients have a greater availability of care options.

This very short illustrative example has hopefully demonstrated some of the many questions that can be addressed when it comes to regime evaluation and measuring social climate. This example also illustrates that, despite the many issues discussed in this chapter (that were also relevant in the collection of this data), it *is* possible to measure the social climate of secure settings in a successful way. Furthermore, studies such as this can yield clinically useful information. But what are the strengths and limitations of findings such as these and the general approach to regime evaluation discussed in this chapter?

The strengths and limitations of regime evaluation

Many of the strengths and limitations that exist in regime evaluation have been touched upon throughout this chapter. This section will, therefore, provide a simple summary of the most pertinent issues. One of the most important issues is the clear lack of research in this area. This causes many problems, including a lack of well-validated measures that are appropriate for use in a wide range of forensic settings with various groups of residents in the UK and beyond. In addition, we lack normative data that can aid in the interpretation of psychometric scores, and illuminate if and how social climate impacts on important clinical and organisational outcomes, such as aggression, self-harm, staff turnover and staff sickness. These issues all combine to make it very difficult at present to conduct and interpret studies that evaluate forensic environments and regimes. Furthermore, the nature of social climate means that change over time is likely. It is a dynamic variable, which makes the regular monitoring of social climate essential. This can make regime evaluation a time-consuming activity. Nevertheless, the growing body of research showing that social climate can impact on a wide range of important issues, including stress, staff performance and treatment outcome, suggests that this effort is worthwhile.

Future directions

The many problems detailed in this chapter and summarised briefly in the previous section suggest some crucial future directions for research and study. First, and most importantly, future work needs to test the reliability and validity of questionnaires designed to measure social climate. These studies need to test the applicability of the questionnaires in a variety of forensic settings, including prisons and secure hospitals of varying levels of security that contain various residents of different ages, ethnicities and genders with diverse needs (such as personality disorder, mental health issues and learning disability). They also need to determine how much variation one can typically expect as a result of 'real' change versus measurement error over repeated administrations of these questionnaires. Only once these questionnaires are properly validated can we be confident that regime evaluation is reliable and worthwhile.

These sorts of study, however, are valuable not only for testing reliability and validity, but they also allow for the development of comprehensive normative data that can help aid future studies and practitioners to interpret their local climate findings. Furthermore, they allow different types of service to be compared and contrasted, which will build up a more in-depth understanding of how staff and residents perceive and react to secure environments.

As we have suggested, research needs to determine what (if any) relationship exists between social climate and service outcomes, such as treatment success, aggression, stress, staff sickness and so on. They also need to determine whether social climate questionnaires can reliably distinguish between 'healthy' and 'unhealthy' climates based on these service outcomes. These will be difficult questions to answer, not least because it will be very hard to tease out whether climate is 'causing' these outcomes or whether it is a product of them. Nonetheless, they remain important questions to address because if climate does not relate to these outcomes then this would offer a strong argument against devoting the time and effort that is necessary to monitor and evaluate climate on a regular basis.

Acknowledgements

The authors would like to thank Sara Northey for her helpful comments on an earlier draft of this chapter.

Further reading

Howells, K., Tonkin, M., Schalast, N., Milburn, C., Lewis, J., Draycott, S., Cordwell, J., Price, M. and Davies, S. (2009). The EssenCES measure of social climate: a preliminary validation and normative data in UK high secure hospital settings. *Criminal Behaviour and Mental Health*, 19: 308–20.

Liebling, A. and Arnold, H. (2004). *Prisons and their moral performance: a study of values, quality, and prison life*. Oxford: Oxford University Press.

Moos, R. H. (1975). *Evaluating correctional and community settings*. New York: Wiley.

—— (1976). *The human context: environmental determinants of behavior*. New York: Wiley.

Schalast, N., Redies, M., Collins, M., Stacey, J. and Howells, K. (2008). EssenCES, a short questionnaire for assessing the social climate of forensic psychiatric wards. *Criminal Behaviour and Mental Health*, 18: 49–58.

Toch, H. (1977). *Living in prison: the ecology of survival*. New York: The Free Press.

Wright, K. N. (1985). Developing the Prison Environment Inventory. *Journal of Research in Crime and Delinquency*, 22: 257–77.

Institut für Forensische Psychiatrie website: www.forensik-essen.de.

References

Beech, A. R. and Hamilton-Giachritsis, C. E. (2005). Relationship between therapeutic climate and treatment outcome in group-based sexual offender treatment programs. *Sexual Abuse: A Journal of Research and Treatment*, 17: 127–40.

Britton, D. M. (1997). Perceptions of the work environment among correctional officers: do race and sex matter? *Criminology*, 35: 85–105.

Brunt, D. and Rask, M. (2005). Patient and staff perceptions of the ward atmosphere in a Swedish maximum-security forensic psychiatric hospital. *The Journal of Forensic Psychiatry and Psychology*, 16: 263–76.

Coakes, S. J. and Steed, L. (2007). *SPSS: analysis without anguish (Version 14.0 for Windows)*. Milton, QLD: Wiley.

Davies, W. (2001). *The RAID manual: a relentlessly positive approach to working with extreme behaviours*. Leicester: APT Press.

Day, A., Casey, S., Ward, T., Howells, K., and Vess, J. (2010). *Transitions to better lives: readiness for treatment and offender rehabilitation*.Collumpton: Willan Press.

Eklund, M. and Hansson, L. (1996). The ward atmosphere in a psychiatric day care unit on the basis of occupational therapy: characteristics and development during a five-year period. *Nordic Journal of Psychiatry*, 50: 117–25.

Field, A. (2005). *Discovering statistics using SPSS*. 2nd edn. London: Sage.

Friis, S. and Helldin, L. (1994). The contribution made by clinical setting to violence among psychiatric patients. *Criminal Behaviour and Mental Health*, 4: 341–52.

Hare, R. D. (2003). *Manual for the Revised Psychopathy Checklist*. 2nd edn. Toronto, Canada: Multi-Health Systems.

Howells, K., Krishnan, G. and Daffern, M. (2007). Challenges in the treatment of dangerous and severe personality disorders. *Advances in Psychiatric Treatment*, 13: 325–32.

Howells, K., Tonkin, M., Schalast, N., Milburn, C., Lewis, J., Draycott, S., Cordwell, J., Price, M. and Davies, S. (2009). The EssenCES measure of social climate: a preliminary validation and normative data in UK high secure hospital settings. *Criminal Behaviour and Mental Health*, 19: 308–20.

Kirby, S. D. and Pollock, P. H. (1995). The relationship between a medium secure environment and occupational stress in forensic psychiatric nurses. *Journal of Advanced Nursing*, 22: 862–7.

Lanza, M. L., Kayne, H. L., Hicks, C. and Milner, J. (1994). Environmental characteristics related to patient assault. *Issues in Mental Health Nursing*, 15: 1,319–55.

Liebling, A. and Arnold, H. (2002). *Measuring the quality of prison life*. Home Office Research Findings No. 174. London: Home Office Research, Development and Statistics Directorate.

—— (2004). *Prisons and their moral performance: a study of values, quality, and prison life*. Oxford: Oxford University Press.

Melle, I., Friis, S., Hauff, E., Island, T. K., Lorentzen, S. and Vaglum, P. (1996). The importance of ward atmosphere in inpatient treatment of schizophrenia on short-term units. *Psychiatric Services*, 47: 721–26.

Middleboe, T., Schjodt, T., Byrsting, K. and Gjerris, A. (2001). Ward atmosphere in acute psychiatric in-patient care: patients' perceptions, ideals and satisfaction. *Acta Psychiatrica Scandinavica*, 103: 212–19.

Moos, R. (1974). *Ward Atmosphere Scale manual*. Palo Alto, CA: Consulting Psychologists Press.

—— (1975). *Evaluating correctional environments: with implications for community settings*. New York: Wiley.

—— (1987). *Correctional Institutions Environment Scale*. Palo Alto, CA: Consulting Psychologists Press.

—— (1989). *Ward Atmosphere Scale manual*. 2nd edn. Palo Alto, CA: Consulting Psychologists Press.

Moos, R. H. and Houts, P. S. (1968). Assessment of the social atmospheres of psychiatric wards. *Journal of Abnormal Psychology*, 73: 595–604.

Moos, R. H. and Houts, P. A. (1970). Differential effects of the social atmosphere of psychiatric wards. *Human Relations*, 23: 47–60.

Moos, R. H. and Schaefer, J. (1987). Evaluating health care settings: a holistic conceptual framework. *Psychology and Health*, 1: 97–122.

Moos, R., Shelton, R. and Petty, C. (1973). Perceived ward climate and treatment outcome. *Journal of Abnormal Psychology*, 82: 291–8.

Ostrom, C. W., Jr (1990). *Time series analysis: regression techniques*. 2nd edn. Thousand Oaks, CA: Sage.

Saylor, W. (1983). *Surveying prison environments*. Unpublished manuscript. Washington, D.C.: Federal Bureau of Prisons, Office of Research.

Schalast, N., Redies, M., Collins, M., Stacey, J. and Howells, K. (2008). EssenCES, a short questionnaire for assessing the social climate of forensic psychiatric wards. *Criminal Behaviour and Mental Health*, 18: 49–58.

Toch, H. (1977). *Living in prison: the ecology of survival*. New York: The Free Press.

Ward, T., Day, A., Howells, K. and Birgden, A. (2004). The multifactor offender readiness model. *Aggression and Violent Behavior*, 9: 645–73.

Wright, K. N. (1985). Developing the prison environment inventory. *Journal of Research in Crime and Delinquency*, 22: 257–77.

Wright, K. N. and Boudouris, J. (1982). An assessment of the Moos Correctional Institutions Environment Scale. *Journal of Research in Crime and Delinquency*, 19: 255–76.

Wright, K. N. and Saylor, W. G. (1992). A comparison of perceptions of the work environment between minority and non-minority employees of the Federal Prison System. *Journal of Criminal Justice*, 20: 63–71.

13 Evaluating the quality of criminal justice programmes

Andrew Day

Introduction

It is probably fair to say that criminal justice programmes are scrutinised more closely these days than they have been at any time in the past. It is widely accepted that not only do all areas of public service have to deliver services that meet the needs of their clients and the broader community, but they also have to demonstrate that the services and programmes that are offered achieve their intended outcomes. Managers and policy makers alike have become interested in issues of effectiveness, accountability and transparency, and despite concerns expressed by some practitioners that their professional autonomy is being eroded, terms such as 'best practice' and 'good practice', originally developed to assist business and manufacturing to be more internationally competitive, are now commonplace across criminal justice settings.

In healthcare settings, including forensic mental health, notions of 'empirically supported' and 'evidence based' treatment have been around for many years. Although these terms can sometimes be used rather loosely, specific criteria have been developed to describe the level of evidence that is required for an intervention to be described in this way (see, for example, work conducted under the auspices of the Cochrane and Campbell collaborations). Whilst this approach to quality assurance has not escaped criticism (e.g. Pawson, 2006), research knowledge is now routinely applied to professional healthcare practice through clinical practice guidelines. These are 'systematically developed statements formulated to assist health practitioners, consumers and policy makers to make appropriate decisions about health care', and are 'based on a thorough evaluation of the evidence from published research studies on the outcomes of treatment or other health care procedures' (NHMRC, 2000, p. 21). In essence, such guidelines are a set of practice-based action statements that need to be adhered to if a service is to make any claims of applying 'best practice'.

In prison and probation and parole settings, the notion of evidence-based practice is perhaps most apparent in relation to the identification of a series of offender rehabilitation practice principles that have been derived from meta-analytic reviews of the outcomes of a series of programme evaluations (e.g. Andrews and Bonta, 2010). The resulting principles have been widely endorsed by prison and probation services around the western world (Ogloff and Davis, 2004; Wormwith *et al.*, 2007); form the basis for most programme accreditation, inspection and review processes; and have directly informed the writing of programme standards. In brief, practitioners who work in prison and probation settings are generally expected to focus their therapeutic efforts on those who are most likely to reoffend (the higher risk offenders), target those factors that are directly associated with offending, and deliver interventions in ways that have been shown to be most likely to bring about change. Although these three core principles (of Risk, Needs and Responsivity) are the most well known, Bonta and Andrews (2007) and Andrews *et al.* (2011) have identified a total of eighteen different evidence-based principles that are thought to be associated with improved service outcomes (adapted from Matthews *et al.*, 2001):

1 Effective interventions should be behavioural in nature.
2 Levels of service should be matched to the risk level of the offender.
3 Offenders should be matched to services designed to improve their specific criminogenic needs such as antisocial attitudes, substance abuse, family communication and peer association.
4 Treatment approaches and service providers should be matched to the learning style or personality of the offender.
5 Services for high-risk offenders should be intensive, occupying 40 to 70 per cent of the offenders' time over a three- to nine-month period.
6 Programmes should be highly structured, and contingencies enforced in a firm but fair way.
7 Staff members should relate to offenders in interpersonally sensitive and constructive ways and be trained and supervised appropriately.
8 Staff members should monitor offender change on intermediate targets of treatment.
9 Relapse prevention and aftercare services should be employed in the community.
10 Family members or significant others should be trained in how to assist clients during problem situations.
11 High levels of advocacy and brokerage should occur when community services are appropriate.

Type of method

At first glance, then, the task of evaluating the quality of criminal justice systems might appear to be reasonably straightforward: (a) ensure that there are programmes and services to match the range of needs that the client group presents with; (b) ensure that every programme offered is evidence-based and has been evaluated to establish its effectiveness with the local client group; and finally (c) audit delivery to ensure that programmes are delivered according to a set of quality standards or practice guidelines, where these are available.

This approach to quality assurance is illustrated in this chapter through reference to a system of programme review and audit that has been developed to assess the quality of correctional (prison and/or probation and parole) programmes whose primary aim is to reduce the risk of reoffending. Although a range of performance measures has been developed to assess a broader range of criminal justice system outputs and outcomes (see, for example, the standards developed by the Council of Juvenile Correctional Administrators in the USA), this particular method represents a standardised way for assessing the quality of offender rehabilitation programmes against criteria that are empirically based.

Background

Over the last 20 years criminal justice services around the world have made a considerable commitment to the development and delivery of a suite of offender rehabilitation programmes offered in both institutional and community settings. Indeed, offender rehabilitation has re-emerged as one of the primary goals of correctional agencies around the world and programmes which have been specifically designed to reduce the risk of reoffending are now commonly, if not routinely, offered to offenders serving medium or long-term sentences (Heseltine *et al.*, 2011). In addition to these offence-focused programmes (such as those offered to violent and sexual offenders), the number of transitional support services and programmes for those leaving prison has also grown dramatically (Borzycki, 2005).

It is now widely accepted, at a policy level at least, that the general principles of Risk, Needs and Responsivity (RNR) should be used to guide service delivery. However, considerable concerns have been expressed about the policy implementation gap that exists in many criminal justice services. As Andrews and Bonta (2010, p. 46) put it: 'Unfortunately, in the "real world" of routine correctional practice, adhering to the principles is a challenge'. An illustration of this can be found in the results of a meta-analysis of the effects of community supervision conducted by Bonta *et al.* (2008). They found little evidence that current supervision practices reduce recidivism, explaining these somewhat disappointing findings by reference to what were apparently low levels of adherence to the principles of risk and need, and an underuse of behavioural techniques and prosocial modelling methods (Listwan *et al.*, 2006). The implementation gap is, however, not a problem that is peculiar to probation and parole: a review by Morgan *et al.* (2007, cited by Andrews and Bonta, 2010, p. 51) of 374 correctional programmes concluded that the majority (61 per cent, n = 230) failed to reach even a basic level of adherence to the RNR principles, with less that 1 per cent (n = 6) of forensic mental health service documents making any reference to targeting criminogenic need. They concluded that the majority of the programmes reviewed did not adequately assess offender risk, need or responsivity factors, did not utilise effective treatment models, did not use behavioural strategies and did not adequately train staff members or evaluate their performance.

Smith *et al.* (2009, p. 162) have further noted that criminal justice programme effectiveness is often 'compromised by staff drift and organisational resistance at both the frontline and administrative levels', and that the issue of programme integrity is an 'ongoing problem of major proportions'. Such observations highlight the need to develop methods that can reliably assess programme quality, identify areas that require development, and ensure that those interventions which are offered are those that are known to be the most effective.

Type of research question addressed

The questions addressed in this chapter relate to how the quality of a particular programme or treatment can be assessed by an audit and review process. An assessment tool is used to illustrate how such questions might be answered by comparing programmes against accepted principles of good practice.

Design principles and issues

The Correctional Program Assessment Inventory (CPAI-2000, Gendreau and Andrews, 2001) is a particularly useful protocol to use in any attempt to determine the quality of offender rehabilitation programmes. It is a 131-item assessment/audit protocol which assesses programmes against eight different domains: organisational culture, programme implementation/maintenance, management/staff characteristics, client risk/need practices, programme characteristics, core correctional practices (including relationship and skill factors), interagency communication and evaluation. The principles of effective intervention outlined on page 272 serve as a template, and the goal of the assessment is to ascertain the extent to which these principles have been implemented. It is important to note that any administration of the CPAI-2000 should be conducted by trained assessors, and this is recommended in circumstances in which there is a need for a thorough external review of programme quality, or indeed to establish the extent to which a particular programme might be suitable for evaluation. Nonetheless, checklists have been developed by accrediting bodies (e.g. the Home Office), and can be easily adapted for use by an individual service.

A worked example: reviewing a prison programme to treat violent young offenders

The example provided here is a review of a high intensity cognitive-behavioural rehabilitation programme that is offered in a prison setting to young offenders who have been convicted of violent offences. Programmes for violent offenders are routinely provided in forensic and clinical settings and the rationale for, and content of, such programmes has been described by a number of researchers and practitioners (e.g. Polaschek and Collie, 2004). Given the heterogeneity of violent offenders, interventions tend to be broad-based, diverse in the selection of therapeutic targets and tailored to the characteristics, risk levels and demonstrable needs of participants, as well as their readiness to address their behaviour (Serin and Preston, 2001).

Programme description

Structure

The programme itself is delivered three times per week over a period of seven months. It is described in the manual as a cognitive-behavioural group-based programme which aims to help participants understand their violent behaviour, establish remorse and empathy towards victims, and develop a relapse prevention plan to manage their risk of violence. The programme is intended to be offered to those who are assessed as moderate-high or high risk of reoffending. Offenders who are ineligible for the programme include those with active psychiatric symptoms, limited cognitive ability or limited English speaking skills.

In addition to the sessions with offenders, family members are given information about the programme and invited to attend a parenting workshop which aims to improve their communication skills. Prison officers are also given regular briefings about the programme.

Content

The programme content is well documented in a programme manual, and procedures are in place that clearly articulate the client assessment and selection processes, and summarise both session content and broader offender management issues. The programme comprises three main phases: the first phase aims to heighten motivation to change; the second to help participants identify and challenge their thinking styles that led to violent offending; and the final phase to equip them with the skills that are required to help them manage the risk of reoffending. The programme encourages participants to look at issues relating to their past experience, types of thinking and attitudes to violence, and participants are invited to adopt a model of conflict resolution which they then practise. The programme is, therefore, reasonably typical of the type of programme that is often offered to violent offenders (see Polaschek and Collie, 2004).

Self-assessment

As part of the review process, programme developers and staff were invited to complete a self-assessment exercise, which asked them to respond to a series of questions pertinent to each of the principles of effective intervention outlined above. The following are sample questions relating to how participants for the programme are selected:

1   Is it easy to establish the target client population?
2   Are client selection criteria available?
3   Have risk and needs have been assessed?
4   How is risk assessed (both general risk and risk of violence)?
5   How are criminogenic needs assessed?
6   Is level of risk matched to programme intensity?
7   How are responsivity factors assessed?
8   How are responsivity factors considered in programme delivery?

Programme checklist

Responses to each of these questions were then used to inform follow-up interviews with programme staff which aimed to identify areas of strength, as well as those aspects of the programme that could benefit from further development. The overall assessment is then summarised in a simple checklist in which a rating of *present* represents a clear indication (as evidenced either in the manuals or from the interviews) of the extent to which the programme exhibits each required feature. *Partially present* represents a degree of ambiguity as to whether or not the programme exhibits that feature (for example where discrepancies exist between the manual and practice are noted), and *Absent* is used when there is clear evidence to indicate that the characteristic was not present. A final rating of *Unknown* is included to cover circumstances in which insufficient information is available to make a judgement. In Table 13.1, the ratings for one category of the assessment are reproduced, relating to staffing needs. It identifies staff support and supervision areas that required further development in this particular programme.

Strengths and limitations of the approach

The approach described here represents a relatively straightforward and efficient approach to quality assessment that allows both service providers and service managers to reflect on and review their current processes (e.g. Indiana Probation Services, 2010). It can help to identify programme strengths and deficits, evaluate funding proposals, assist programme staff to articulate what they do and understand the logic that underpins programme activities, identify credible rationales for treatment and stimulate relevant research. It is not, however, necessarily a thorough or objective assessment of programme quality or, indeed, any guarantee that the programme will be successful in meeting its objectives.

A particular strength of using an audit approach such as that offered by the CPAI-2000, however, is the existence of evidence to support the validity of the approach. Two studies have examined the extent to which CPAI scores correlate with reductions in recidivism (Lowenkamp *et al.*, 2006, Nesovic, 2003; cited by Smith et al., 2009), both of which found that total CPAI scores correlated

Table 13.1 Programme checklist (staffing considerations)

Programme elements	Present	Partially present	Absent	Unknown
Staffing considerations				
Area of study/training relevant to programme delivery		X		
Individualised training needs analysis			X	
Documented staff training needs			X	
Detailed staff training course manual			X	
Staff receive formal training in theory and practice of intervention employed, along with additional on-the-job training, workshops etc.		X		
Criteria for ensuring staff competence at the end of training			X	
Guidelines for review of staff performance			X	
Personal qualities of staff outlined	X			
Ongoing supervision for staff		X		
Staff able to modify or adapt programme structure as required	X			
Manual specifies number of staff required to deliver programme	X			

positively with reductions in recidivism in those who completed the programme. Such studies are important as they demonstrate that programmes which adhere closely to best practice principles are those which are likely to be more effective. In other words, achieving higher levels of integrity is likely to be important if programmes are to succeed in producing their intended outcomes.

One weakness of the approach to audit outlined here relates to the limited scope of the process. It is a method that has been developed to assess individual programmes rather than systems of service delivery. Some of the broader issues that arise in relation to how programmes inter-relate, the interface between programme delivery and sentence planning, case management processes and the relationship between programme attendance and throughcare into the community are not addressed directly. In addition, the dependent variable used in the studies that have identified the principles of best practice in offender rehabilitation is that of reduced rates of reoffending. Some services, notably forensic mental health services, juvenile justice services, and many offender transitional support services, have aims that are substantially broader than reducing rates of reoffending. As such the approach to quality assessment outlined here may need to be supplemented with other methods of assessing quality that are linked to these others aims (e.g. improved health and well-being, social functioning, healthy development).

There are, of course, also many other types of criminal justice service than individual treatment programmes. The quality of some of these other initiatives is much more difficult to assess. Consider, for example, the use of mandatory arrest as a means of reducing rates of repeated assault in the area of domestic or family violence (Sherman, Schmidt and Rogan, 1992). In the US (State of Minnesota) in the 1980s three groups of police officers responding to domestic violence reports[1] were required to act in one of three ways: arrest the perpetrator, provide advice or send the perpetrator away. Evaluations of the initiative found that there was a significantly lower rate of repeat calls for domestic violence incidents amongst the group where arrest occurred, compared to the other groups. Other US cities subsequently adopted the same strategy and whilst the mandatory arrest policy reduced repeat domestic violence call outs in some places, it unexpectedly increased it in others. Sherman *et al.* (1992) suggested that these results could only be explained by the different community, employment and family structures that existed in the various cities, and the example clearly illustrates how the effects of any intervention can vary by context. It also shows how aggregated estimates of effect size may be misleading when applied to a local population, and speaks for the need for ongoing local evaluations to be conducted.

Although the method outlined here represents one way to help programme delivery become more evidence-based, it is important to remember that criminal justice policy does not always aspire to be evidence-based (see, for example, Pawson's 2006 analysis of the evidence supporting the effectiveness of Megan's Law legislation in relation to community notification of sex offenders). Indeed, even when research does demonstrate that programmes are able to achieve their intended objectives, Pawson (2006, p. 7) suggests that there are

> precious few examples of it leading to actual decisions to 'retain, imitate, modify, or discard' programmes and, indeed, there are numerous examples of programmes that have been shown to be ineffective which are still funded, whereas others that are widely thought to be 'successful' are sometimes discontinued.

This is partly because most evaluation research occurs after policies have been put into place (i.e. following programme design and implementation), and partly because in practice most evaluators experience significant constraints to their ability to provide conclusive answers to the key questions, whether they be related to budget, timelines or methodology.

An important additional factor here is on 'value for money', and it has been suggested that 'ultimately, the key considerations associated with continuing and/ or rolling out [criminal justice programmes] will centre on cost and outcomes' (Monash University and Victorian Institute of Forensic Mental Health, 2007, p. 91). This is likely to be particularly true in a socio-political environment (such as exists in most parts of the world) in which the value of services for offenders is not universally recognised (Ward and Maruna, 2007), and budgets for the development and delivery of programmes are typically modest. As such, decisions about the quality of criminal justice services and programmes can sometimes be influenced by economic, rather than evidence-based, considerations. An economic or cost–benefit analysis of a programme is an extension of other forms of programme evaluation that involves a calculation of the monetary value of the costs and benefits of delivering a programme (in terms of the benefits to taxpayers and crime victims of future crimes avoided). Benefits can then be compared to the costs of programme delivery, in order to determine the bottom-line economics of different programmes. The potential benefits include reduced costs associated with the police, the courts and corrections, and crime victim costs which can be divided into monetary costs (e.g. health care expenses, loss of earnings) and quality of life cost estimates (e.g. a monetary value for pain and suffering; see Drake *et al.*, 2009).

Future directions of the approach

In many respects, the RNR approach has revolutionised correctional practice. It has promoted the idea of community safety as the primary driver behind correctional case management, and placed offender rehabilitation programming at the centre of the sentence planning process. There is a need to continue to build the evidence base from which statements about good criminal justice and rehabilitation practice can be developed (see Andrews, 2006; Bonta *et al.*, 1998), and significant gaps in knowledge remain (Andrews and Dowden, 2007), as well as inconsistencies and deficiencies in how the model is operationalised. The audit approach described in this chapter relies on the completion of evaluation research that can be used to determine the basis for evidence-based practice, as well as the policy endorsement that is required to implement models of service delivery.

Critics of the RNR model have, in a range of different ways, drawn attention to how the model struggles to inform the actual process of programme delivery, and how psychological and behaviour change might take place (e.g. Day *et al.*, 2006). There would appear to be scope for developing the notion 'good practice' in programme delivery to include aspects of therapeutic process. Assessments of quality programming are perhaps too focused on aspects of delivery such as adherence to programme manuals, and the quality of the relationship formed between the practitioner and the offender is often under-emphasised and under-valued (Kozar, 2010). In short there is a need to ensure that notions of quality do not become oversimplified.

There may also be lessons to be learned here from the development of clinical practice guidelines, such as those that are emerging for use in forensic mental health settings (e.g. Duggan *et al.*, 2009), but have yet to emerge in relation to rehabilitation programme delivery. It is clearly important that those who are involved with the delivery of criminal justice services are able to apply the available research evidence in ways that directly guide their practice if outcomes for both programme participants and the broader community are to be maximised. Quality assurance and audit measures can be used to help the criminal justice system to run more efficiently, establish priorities and reinforce the mission, goals and objectives of service providers. In short, it makes it possible to describe successes and failures in quantifiable terms. The approach to quality assurance that is outlined in this chapter represents one way in which this might be achieved.

Further reading and resources

For principles of effective rehabilitation see:
Lescheid, A. W. (2000). Compendium 2000 on effective correctional program-ming: implementation of effective correctional programs. Available at www. csc-cc.gc.ca/text/rsrch/compendium/2000/introeng.shtml 2000 (accessed 21/4/11).

For programme audit methods see:
Matthews, B., Hubbard, D. J. and Latessa, E. (2001). Making the next step: using evaluability assessment to improve correctional programming. *The Prison Journal*, 81: 454–72.

For systematic reviews, see www.evidencenetwork.org.

For a discussion of evidence based policy see:
Pawson, R. (2006). *Evidence-based policy: a realist perspective*. London: Sage.
Trinder, L. and Reynolds, S. (Eds) (2000). *Evidence-based practice: a critical Appraisal*. Oxford: Blackwell Science.

For the evidence basis for offender rehabilitation programmes see:
Andrews, D. A. (2006). Enhancing adherence to risk-need-responsivity: making equality a matter of policy. *Criminology and Public Policy*, 5: 595–602.

For a performance based assessment process see standards developed by the Council of Juvenile Correctional Administrators in the USA (www.pbstandards. org).

References

Andrews, D. A. (2006). Enhancing adherence to risk-need-responsivity: making equality a matter of policy. *Criminology and Public Policy*, 5: 595–602.
Andrews, D. A. and Bonta, J. (2006). *The psychology of criminal conduct.* 4th edn. Newark, NJ: LexisNexis/Matthew Bender.
——— (2010). Rehabilitating criminal justice policy and practice. *Psychology, Public Policy, and Law*, 16: 39–55.
Andrews, D. A. and Dowden, C. (2007). The risk-need-responsivity model of assessment and human service in prevention and corrections: crime-prevention jurisprudence. *Canadian Journal of Criminology and Criminal Justice*, 49: 439–64.
Andrews, D. A., Bonta, D. and Wormwith, J. S. (2011) The Risk Need Responsivity (PNR) model: does adding the Good Lives model contribute to effective crime prevention? *Criminal Justice and Behaviour*, 38: 735–55.
Bonta, J. and Andrews, D. A. (2007). *Risk-need-responsivity model for offender assessment and rehabilitation.* User Report 2007–6. Ottawa, Ontario: Public Safety Canada.

Bonta, J., Law, M. and Hanson, R. K. (1998). The prediction of criminal and violent-recidivism among mentally disordered offenders: a meta-analysis. *Psychological Bulletin*, 123: 123–42.

Bonta, J., Rugge, T., Scott, T., Bourgon, G. and Yessine, A. K. (2008). Exploring the black box of community supervision. *Journal of Offender Rehabilitaion*, 47: 258–70.

Borzycki, M. (2005). *Interventions for prisoners returning to the community*. Canberra: Australian Institute of Criminology.

Day, A., Bryan, J., Davey, L. and Casey, S. (2006). Processes of change in offender rehabilitation. *Psychology, Crime and Law*, 12: 473–89.

Drake, E. K., Aos, S. and Miller, M. G. (2009). Evidence-based public policy options to reduce crime and criminal justice costs: implications in Washington State. *Victims and Offenders*, 4: 170–96.

Duggan, C., Pilling, S., Adshead, G., Brown, A., Coid, J., Connelly, N., Dearden, C., Duncan, A., Dyer, M., Ferguson, B., Flanagan, E., Fonagy, P., Hadjipavlou, S., Kane, E., Li, R., Maden, A., Mavranezouli, I., McGuire, J., Meader, N., Pettinari, C., Retsa, P., Rooney, C., Stockton, S., Taylor, C. and Wright, N. (2009). Antisocial Personality Disorder (ASPD): treatment, management and prevention. NICE Clinical Guideline 77. NICE, National Collaborating Centre for Mental Health.

Gendreau, P. and Andrews, D. (2001). *Correctional Program Assessment Inventory (CPAI-2000)*. St John, Canada: University of New Brunswick.

Heseltine, K., Sarre, R. and Day, A. (2011). Prison-based correctional offender rehabilitation programs: the 2009 national picture in Australia. Report for the Criminology Research Council. Canberra: Australian Institute of Criminology.

Indiana Probation Services (2010). Best practices guide. Available at www.in.gov/judiciary/center/pubs/best-practices/cpai.html (accessed 1/2/10).

Kozar, C. (2010). Treatment readiness and the therapeutic alliance. In A. Day, S. Casey, T. Ward, K. Howells and J. Vess. *Transitions to better lives: offender readiness and rehabilitation* (pp. 247–74). Cullompton, UK: Willan Press.

Listwan, S. J., Cullen, F. T. and Latessa, E. J. (2006). How to prevent prisoner re-entry programs from failing: insights from evidence-based corrections. *Federal Probation*, 70: 19–25.

Lowenkamp, C. T., Latessa, E. J. and Smith, P. (2006). Does correctional program quality matter? The impact of adhering to the principles of effective intervention. *Criminology & Public Policy*, 5: 575–94.

Matthews, B., Hubbard, D. J. and Latessa, E. (2001). Making the next step: using evaluability assessment to improve correctional programming. *The Prison Journal*, 81: 454–72.

Monash University and the Victorian Institute of Forensic Mental Health (2007). *An evaluation of the Corrections Victoria Violence Intervention Program: final report*. Melbourne: Corrections Victoria.

Morgan, R., Flora, D., Kroner, D., Mills, J., Varghese, F. and Stefan, J. (2007). *Treatment of mentally disordered offenders: a research synthesis*. Paper presented at the North American Conference of Correctional and Criminal Justice Psychology, Ottawa, Ontario, Canada.

Nesovic, A. (2003). *Psychometric evaluation of the Correctional Program Assessment Inventory (CPAI)*. Unpublished doctoral dissertation, Carleton University, Ottawa, Ontario.

NHMRC (2000). *A guide to the development, implementation and evaluation of clinical practice guidelines*. Canberra: Commonwealth of Australia.

Ogloff, J. R. P. and Davis, N. R. (2004). Advances in offender assessment and rehabilitation: contributions of the risk-needs-responsivity approach. *Psychology, Crime & Law*, 10: 229–42.

Pawson, R. (2006). *Evidence-based policy: a realist perspective.* London: Sage.

Polaschek, D. and Collie, R. (2004). Rehabilitating serious violent adult offenders: an empirical and theoretical stocktake. *Psychology, Crime and Law*, 10: 321–34.

Serin, R. C. and Preston, D. L. (2001). Managing and treating violent offenders. In J. B. Ashford, B. D. Sales and W. Reid (Eds) *Treating adult and juvenile offenders with special needs.* Washington DC: American Psychological Association.

Sherman, L. W., Schmidt, J. D. and Rogan, D. P. (1992). *Policing domestic violence: experiments and dilemmas.* New York: Free Press.

Sherman, L. W., Schmidt, J. D., Rogan, D. P., Smith, D. A., Gartin, P. R., Cohn, E. G., Collins, D. J. and Bacich, A. R. (1992). The variable effects of arrest on criminal careers: the Milwaukee Domestic Violence Experiment. *Journal of Criminal Law & Criminology*, 83: 137–69.

Smith, P., Gendreau, P. and Swartz, K. (2009). Validating the principle of effective intervention: a systematic review of the contributions of meta-analysis in the field of corrections. *Victims and Offenders*, 4: 148–69.

Ward, T. and Maruna, S. (2007). *Rehabilitation.* London: Routledge.

Wormwith, J. S., Althouse, R., Simpson, M., Reitzel, L. R., Fagan, T. J. and Morgan, R. D. (2007). The rehabilitation and reintegration of offenders: the current landscape and some future directions for correctional psychology. *Criminal Justice and Behavior*, 34: 879–92.

14 Treatment and rehabilitation evaluation and large-scale outcomes

James McGuire

The objectives of the present chapter are twofold: first, to survey the kinds of methods employed in carrying out large-scale evaluation research, where random allocation to groups is not practicable; second, to describe how the findings of evaluation research are combined and integrated, to permit the drawing of conclusions about what is being learnt in a given field of inquiry. Throughout, our focal point of interest will be the impact of efforts towards treatment or rehabilitation of individuals who have repeatedly broken the law.

Evaluation research

Researchers in criminology often have immense datasets at their disposal, using official sources such as annual crime reports published by government departments. Within such datasets there may be numerous variables operating, and it can be difficult to discern the effect of any specific component. *Evaluation research*, sometimes called programme evaluation (Rossi *et al.*, 2004) is a specialised type of activity with the explicit objective of estimating the effect of a designated type of service delivery, or of some other change that has been initiated within a system of services such as criminal justice or secure mental health.

Evaluation research can address a range of purposes associated with society's response to any problem, criminal conduct being just one example. It can adopt a variety of models. Stecher and Davis (1987) proposed a taxonomy of five types (experimental, goal-oriented, decision-focused, user-oriented and responsive), while Posavac and Carey (1997) listed as many as eleven separate variations. Several of these serve purposes other than the inspection of outcomes. They may, for example, be focused on different stakeholders' perceptions of an agency, understanding how decisions are made within it or other 'process-oriented' questions. Some approaches within this employ qualitative rather than quantitative methods of investigation. The present chapter focuses on one selection from within this spectrum of approaches, one which has a measurable outcome as its focus, and is primarily, though by no means exclusively, quantitative in methodology.

Ideally, the possibility of evaluation would be built into the model of service delivery from the outset, such that when embarking on evaluation, researchers can be guided by the logic of a programme's design (McGuire, 2001). Often, however, 'real world' services do not follow that pattern. Selecting a method of evaluation is likely to depend on a wide array of factors, and will often be carried out in circumstances that are by no means favourable for research (Rossi *et al.*, 2004).

Steps in evaluation methodology

An abundance of methods and designs can be used in evaluation research. Whichever one an evaluator chooses will depend on the precise question he or she (or the commissioning agency) is seeking to answer. Notwithstanding the plethora of design possibilities, in outcome-evaluation research the fundamental objective remains the same across all formats. It is to test for the presence of a cause–effect relationship between the service or intervention of interest (the independent variable) and the target or outcome of interest (the dependent variable). The essence of sound research design is that it is an attempt to reduce or if possible eliminate the explanatory potential of factors other than the independent variable. If it were practicable to control all other variables while manipulating only the single factor of interest to us – as can be done in labora-tory-based experiments – evaluation research, though still challenging, might be more orderly and exact than it generally is.

Within this broad framework many different types of study are conceivable and the prospective researcher will find it necessary to make some decisions in order to focus the work he or she wants to do. To address the numerous complexities that might arise within this would require many volumes. For present purposes we will narrow down the process of planning an evaluation study into a sequence of four main steps, all of which should as far as possible be planned in advance.

Step one – research questions and study objectives

The fundamental first step when contemplating evaluation research – in fact, pivotal to any research study – is to ask ourselves a question such as: what are my objectives? and what is it I want to know? Many of the other decisions about how to conduct a study flow from our answers to these elemental questions. It is worthwhile expending effort in articulating them as clearly as possible. The more precisely we do this, the greater the ease with which other aspects of the research can be logistically and coherently planned.

Thus a loosely framed question, for example as to whether an intervention works, might need considerable refinement. First, we need to define the interven-tion; a surprising number of research reports are very vague regarding this – and then ask what we expect it to do. Will it reduce criminal recidivism? Ensure more appropriate allocation? Decrease levels of drop-out? Improve well-being?

Lower running costs? Improve efficiency? Many other elements of a research project depend crucially on the clarity with which we define our aims. Large-scale outcome studies, where evaluation involves substantial samples or will be conducted over multiple sites, pose particular challenges and require additional careful thought.

Step two – study design

Having formulated our question the next essential step is to decide how best to answer it. This is the core issue addressed within the domain of research design and methodology. The major types of design in current widespread use can be conceptualised within a common framework, as suggested by Gliner *et al.* (2009) and depicted in diagrammatic form in Figure 14.1.

Randomised designs apply basic principles of inferential logic in order to identify causal patterns. Randomised controlled trials (RCTs) are widely regarded as the strongest test of an experimental hypothesis concerning the effectiveness of interventions in applied settings and the relationships between independent and dependent variables. RCTs are discussed in Chapter 11 and will not be considered further here.

Quasi-experimental designs possess most of the features of RCTs, with the exception of random allocation to conditions. Thus they compare outcomes between or across groups to which membership has been assigned on some other basis, such as a sentencing decision, assessed risk level or participant choice. There is no assurance that the groups being compared are evenly balanced in terms of other factors that might influence the observed outcome.

There are several variant types of design under this broad heading. They include non-equivalent group designs in which assignment to two or more conditions occurs naturalistically in the everyday setting of 'routine practice'. Other variants include single cohort, before-and-after (pre-test post-test) designs, using repeated measures analyses, where no comparison group is available. This deficit may be compensated for to some extent through the use of prediction scores (for an example see Hollis, 2007). Alternatively, if there has been a measured baseline, it may be possible to utilise interrupted time-series designs,

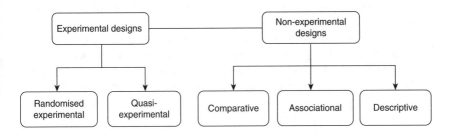

Figure 14.1 Typology of research designs.
Source: based on Gliner *et al.,* 2009.

where the rate of offending (or some other variable) may be monitored for a period preceding, during and following an intervention.

The above is of necessity an incomplete and simplified list; the intricacies of real-world research require evaluators to adapt methods to circumstances, and there are numerous other ways in which designs can be modified.

Non-experimental designs. If neither randomised nor quasi-experimental designs are viable, evaluation research can take other forms. They include comparative or cross-sectional studies, which involve making comparisons between two or more groups at a given point in time, to search or test for differences that might indicate directions for further enquiry. Alternatively, they might comprise associational or correlational research, investigating relationships amongst variables within a group at a specific time-point. Or they could entail descriptive studies, providing a detailed account of a programme, perhaps using qualitative methods, thereby yielding insights that would probably not be gained from the study of measured outcomes alone.

Step three – outcome measures: data collection

After choosing an experimental design, our next planning decision concerns what to measure in the evaluation. Many sources of information can be employed to study the actions that society defines as crime and the problems associated with it. One obvious approach is to examine official statistics supplied by government departments, based on the information gathered by the police and on the working of the penal system. Doing so can provide 'snapshots' of crime at a single moment in time, or can map trends over long periods. Most countries publish crime statistics on an annual basis, so it is possible both to study national patterns and to make international comparisons, for example using the reports of the United Nations Office on Drugs and Crime.

Official crime figures are notoriously difficult to interpret, as many factors influence what is recorded in them. They are universally recognised as only a partial depiction of the amount of crime in a society (Maguire, 2007). That caveat accepted, there is a consensus on the possibility of arriving at a more accurate picture of crime by comparing official statistics with more direct estimates of individual citizens' experience of it. In the United Kingdom this is done in the *British Crime Survey*, begun in 1982 and published annually since 2000.

Using such sources, it is possible to answer several types of question. We might study whether large-scale social change has a discernible impact on crime rates. For example did the transition in statehood from what was formerly the USSR to Russia, and the accompanying switch from a centrally planned to a market economy, lead to any changes in crime rates? Answer: there was a 50 per cent increase in recorded crimes per 100,000 population between 1990 and 1992 (Gilinskiy, 2006). Or do police crackdowns, or their opposite, industrial action ('go-slows' or strikes), have an impact on crime rates? We might expect the former to result in an appreciable drop in rates of crime, whereas the latter would lead to massive escalations in it, perhaps even to extensive public disorder. Answer: the available data suggest that neither has any especially marked effect (Pfuhl, 1983; Sherman, 1990).

Understandably given the central objectives of the criminal justice system and the public's expectations of it, in evaluation studies a prime emphasis is placed on measuring criminal recidivism as an outcome variable. Rehabilitation and reduced reoffending are cast as core purposes for which sentences are imposed by courts of law; although there are several different ways of conceptualising precisely what that entails (McGuire, 2008). There are also disputes concerning how best to bring it about.

Recidivism as a general category of outcome can be defined in a number of ways. Each has its own advantages and drawbacks. This can be problematic when interpreting research, as different studies may not have used comparable methods. So the variable 'recidivism' may be defined in several ways including (a) individuals' self-reports of involvement in crime; (b) rates of re-arrest; (c) numbers of appearances in court; (d) rates of reconviction; and (e) rates of re-incarceration, often used as a proxy measure of crime seriousness. All of these types of data may be reported as raw rates over a preselected time interval (e.g. 12 or 24 months), or as proportionate changes relative to an earlier (pre-intervention) baseline period. Alternatively, they may be compared with predicted rates; or with parallel data from a relevant comparator sample (such as an untreated control group). Reading any journal article or research report, it is important to note how recidivism was recorded, the length of follow-up, the nature of whatever comparisons have been made and other key points of information.

It is sometimes remarked that outcome research of this kind provides insufficient evidence concerning which factors have induced change (assuming that is found). Accordingly, some studies also measure intervening or mediator variables (not to be confused with moderator variables, discussed on page 293). In relation to criminal recidivism these might include risk-need factors such as low levels of problem-solving or self-control skills. Monitoring of them might be accomplished, for example, using psychometric assessments, as reported in relation to the 'treatment targets' of offending behaviour or cognitive skills programmes in prisons and probation (Blud and Travers, 2001; McGuire and Hatcher, 2001). Alternatively, researchers may use direct observations of day-to-day activity or performance in specially designed behavioural measures. The latter approach was used to evaluate the 'decompression' regime in work with high-risk young offenders in Mendota Youth Treatment Center, as described by Caldwell *et al.* (2007).

Another entirely discrete but increasingly important evaluation measure is the use of benefit–cost analysis or variants of it. This is focused on the comparative monetary outlays involved in delivering a criminal justice service relative to the money saved if it is successful. The former is measured by summing the amounts spent on staff salaries, programme materials, buildings (heating, lighting, maintenance), transport and other expenses necessarily incurred. The latter is appraised with reference to the reduced costs of police work, legal personnel, court hearings, victim support (e.g. hospitalisation, counselling) and offender supervision or incarceration. Aos and his colleagues (2001, 2004) have computed relative benefit–cost ratios for interventions with adult and youthful offenders respectively.

Step four – data analysis

Another key feature to be planned, one that is intimately connected with the study design, is how to analyse the data. Where group membership has not been randomly assigned, self-evidently groups cannot be assumed to be equivalent. Nevertheless, it may still be possible to test the extent of matching of the resultant groups on some of the key study variables. In small-scale research, typically we would confirm group equivalence by statistical matching, comparing group means and assuming satisfactory equivalence if differences are non-significant.

With larger samples, however, given the likely sizeable group variances, further steps might need to be taken. One possibility is sub-group matching. This was used in the national evaluation of the Sex Offender Treatment Programme (SOTP) in England and Wales (Friendship *et al.*, 2003). Prisoners who had attended the SOTP (n = 647) were compared with a large untreated sample (n = 1,910) matched by year of discharge and by risk level, divided into four bands using a specialised measure, the *Static-99*. While outcomes for sexual and general recidivism were statistically non-significant, there was an association between SOTP completion and a combined measure of sexual and violent reoffending.

An alternative approach is the use of one-to-one matching. If there is a potentially large pool from which to draw a comparison sample, members of the experimental group can be 'paired' with individuals from within it on specified variables (e.g. age, offence type, number of previous convictions) creating a close approximation to an equivalent group. This was employed by Hatcher *et al.* (2008) in an evaluation of the Aggression Replacement Training (ART) programme, finding a 13.3 per cent reduction in recidivism amongst programme completers relative to the controls.

Of course, it may transpire that our groups are unambiguously non-equivalent; and even where groups appear to be equivalent there may still be residual differences between them, some components of which remain unknown. There are several options for addressing this, using the strategy of statistical control. This might simply entail analysis of covariance; but more elaborate procedures using multivariate statistics are generally applied to differentiate the operation of possible programme effects. Where binary outcomes are evaluated (e.g. recidivism yes/no) logistic regression can be employed. This was used in the SOTP evaluation outlined earlier in this section (Friendship *et al.*, 2003); and in evaluation of the probation-based Pathfinder programmes, utilising very large samples (Palmer *et al.*, 2007). Where there are worries that the same variables predict both programme completion and desistance from reoffending (the notion that certain offenders are likely 'to do well anyway'), this can be investigated using propensity score analysis (McGuire *et al.*, 2008). Readers are referred to the cited studies for explanation of these approaches.

Researchers in a position to pursue studies with large samples should note the complex interplay between statistical power, sample size, significance levels and the risk of Type I and Type II errors. Most psychological research is reputedly 'under-powered' (Maxwell, 2004); by contrast when it is 'over-powered' even a small difference between experimental and comparison samples in the outcome variable may be statistically significant. Conversely, however, when the outcome variable has a low base rate (as in the SOTP evaluation) it may be difficult to discern meaningful differences between study samples and their comparators. For these and other reasons many researchers have advocated replacing the familiar ethos of null hypothesis significance testing (NHST) with effect size statistics and confidence intervals (Gendreau and Smith, 2007; Maxwell *et al.*, 2008).

We now have to imagine that we have completed, written up and successfully published a study of the above kind. We wonder how the results compare with other studies on the same question, and decide to survey and summarise the results obtained from other evaluations. We would then be engaging in a different type of study known as research review.

Methods of research review

Research review is essential for the progress of investigation in any field, in order to judge the collective import of what has been found. In medicine, it has been said that 'good review articles are precious commodities' (Mulrow, 1987, p. 485). Indeed, failure to aggregate research results and apply the lessons so learned has proven a costly and even fatal mistake (Chalmers, 2006). Critical overviews of research are key drivers of the processes of knowledge accumulation, theory construction and practical implementation. They also pinpoint necessary directions for further work.

Literature review procedures can be divided into two broad categories. The traditional approach, loosely called 'narrative review', involves collecting the studies done so far in the area to be reviewed and summarising their findings; noting methodological strengths and weakness of each study; and posing questions or making recommendations for future research. In common with other sciences, for a large part of its history the progress of psychology was steered through review articles adopting this format. This is still the method of choice for reviewing an area that is emergent and relatively new; where the number of studies is small; where the studies are very disparate in methodology; where there are no quantitative data, or a mixture of quantitative and qualitative studies.

In the last three decades, however, given the exponential growth in research output (the 'data explosion') and amidst widespread calls for improved methodological thoroughness, an approach involving statistical review or *meta-analysis* has gained ascendancy as the standard approach to research synthesis. This employs more formalised procedures for collecting and scrutinising studies. Let us assume we want to make sense of several sets of results in a selected area of research. The original studies that form the bedrock of the research process are termed primary studies; interrogation of the data so produced is therefore called *primary analysis*. If for any reason the data are reanalysed for some other purpose (e.g. to answer questions not posed in the initial study; or to check on the results) this is entitled *secondary analysis*. In a third level of examination, data from several studies are statistically compared or combined. This higher level integration of results was given the name *meta-analysis* by Glass (1976).

History of the approach – meta-analysis

Although meta-analysis is widely believed to be a relatively recent innovation, the basic statistical methods involved in it were formulated just after 1900. The eminent statistician Karl Pearson (1857–1936), developer of the chi-square statistic and the product-moment correlation, is also credited with carrying out the first study that incorporated a recognisable meta-analytic review. Pearson (1904) combined several small sets of data on the effectiveness of inoculations against typhoid and analysed them in a single larger set.

However, the method did not come into prominence until the late 1970s and early 1980s. Smith and Glass (1977) published a much-cited review of 375 studies on the outcomes of psychotherapy, which, contrary to claims made at that time, demonstrated that it was largely effective. Glass, McGaw and Smith (1981) published an influential review of 725 tests of the relationship between class size and educational achievement in schools, an issue which despite hundreds of studies in the preceding 70 years had remained unresolved. Meta-analytic integration of results disclosed a very clear curvilinear association between class size and attainment. To test the rigour of the approach, Cooper and Rosenthal (1980) carried out a simulation-based study in which they invited a group of 41 psychologists to review a set of empirical studies. Their objective was to compare traditional (narrative) with statistical (meta-analytic) methods of research review. They found the latter produced fewer errors in providing summary accounts of the findings contained in the papers so reviewed.

Meta-analysis began to be so widely used that even by the time Lipsey and Wilson (1993) carried out a panoramic survey of the effects of psychological and behavioural interventions, covering the fields of education, therapy and training, there were already 302 meta-analyses available for them to dissect. Field (2009) has charted the spectacular rise in references to meta-analysis in social science journals between 1977 and 2007, while Cooper (2010) graphs the growth in *Web of Science* citations for the period 1998–2007. The first statistical review focused on criminal recidivism as an outcome variable appeared in 1985; since then, more than 70 meta-analyses have been published in this field (McGuire, 2009).

Conducting a meta-analysis

Even when designed to answer fundamentally similar questions, primary studies often differ in numerous ways. When a box file or an electronic folder full of studies all purportedly addressing the same question is examined closely, studies will be found to vary along several dimensions. Those are likely to include their date of completion; language of origin; the setting in which the research was done; sample size and composition; the types and amounts of data provided on participants; project design and methodological quality; the degree of detail given on procedures followed; the numbers and types of outcome measure employed; and kinds of data analysis undertaken, including the amount of attention paid to the potential influence of moderators on the results.

Not surprisingly, therefore, elucidating and clarifying any trends with even a modest number of primary studies can present formidable challenges. Several authors (e.g. Cooper, 2010; Durlak and Lipsey, 1991) have provided helpful step-by-step guidance on the meta-analytic process. Adapting such a scheme, the basic procedure in meta-analysis can be condensed into the following general steps.

1 Formulating the problem and research question(s), and clarifying the objective(s) of the review, defining the variables of interest. As we saw above, this is a vital step in planning an evaluative study, and it is equally important when planning a research review.

2 Searching the literature and locating studies. This includes setting inclusion and exclusion criteria for the body of literature to be reviewed; then using several methods of search, likely to include (a) coverage of relevant electronic databases using agreed search terms; (b) supplementary hand-search where necessary; (c) combing the reference lists of existing review papers; and (d) making direct contact by letter or e-mail with known researchers in the field. Initial searches may yield enormous numbers of 'hits'; the likely number remaining after various filters are applied will be much lower.

3 Gathering information from studies. Data need to be methodically extracted from each source and recorded in an electronic spreadsheet using pre-arranged codes. The extraction should be conducted by more than one reviewer; those engaged in it should be given training for the task, and inter-rater reliability checks computed.

4 Evaluating the quality of studies; making comparisons for design quality and methodological rigour, using an explicit framework. This might involve using a checklist of criteria for each study, such as the Design and Implementation Assessment Device (DIAD) described by Cooper (2010); or the division of studies into sub-groups using a scoring system, such as the Maryland Scientific Methods Scale (Farrington *et al.*, 2002).

5 Analysing and integrating the outcomes of studies; selecting methods of measuring effect size; conducting statistical analyses; making adjustments

and variations in effect size estimates (e.g. application of weighting procedures to take account of variations in sample size); choosing statistical models: fixed-effect model versus random-effects model, which rely on different assumptions regarding the anticipated underlying pattern of results.

6   Interpreting the evidence; drawing conclusions where justifiable, offering defensible interpretations where outcomes are less clear-cut; noting limitations of studies available to date due to missing data or biases amongst published studies (see pages 293–4).

7   Presenting and communicating the results; giving additional thought to how best to convey the meanings of results to different audiences.

Computing and reporting effect sizes

The effect size (ES) statistic has been described as 'the meta-analytic coin of the realm' (Rosenthal, 1995, p. 185). It is the prime measure of outcome in reviews. Separate effect sizes are computed for each study reviewed, and the mean ES calculated across all studies, or within specified sub-sets, delineated for example according to methodological quality or type of intervention. There are three main categories of effect size measure (for details of how to compute them see Cooper, 2010; Rosnow and Rosenthal, 2008).

Standardised mean difference. This compares the means of experimental and control samples as a function of the pooled variance of both groups. Several statistics may be used for reporting this, the most frequently used being Cohen's d statistic and Hedges's g. We are very unlikely to find that all the studies identified for review have used the same outcome measure; more often, a diversity of measures will have been employed. However, data from discrepant outcome measures can be converted to standard scores, such as standard deviation units (i.e. defined with reference to the mean of the distribution of the original set of scores). This can then serve as a common metric, allowing meaningful comparisons to be made between studies.

Correlation coefficients. Another widely used effect-size measure is the strength of the association between independent and dependent variables. For continuous variables this can be computed using Pearson correlations (r). However a variant of it, the phi (ϕ) coefficient, can be calculated from two-by-two contingency tables, for example allocating outcomes of experimental and control samples across studies to success/failure or improvement/no improvement categories.

Binary measures. Another possibility, when both independent and dependent variables are dichotomous, is the odds ratio (OR) or allied measures. This is a way of expressing the relative risk of one out of two outcomes within each of two groups being compared. Within each group (e.g. treatment or control) we calculate the odds of one outcome (e.g. recidivism/no recidivism) to the other; we then calculate the ratio of the two sets of odds. Note that an odds ratio ES of one is equivalent to a mean-difference or correlation-based ES of zero.

Like the average from any dataset, the mean ES can be misleading if interpreted in isolation and should be reported alongside upper and lower confidence intervals, together with indices of the dispersal of effect sizes within the set as a whole. Measures of variability or heterogeneity have been developed for this purpose (the most commonly used are Q and I^2). Some ES conventions have become widely accepted (for a convenient overview see Cohen, 1992). For the mean-difference group of statistics an ES in the region of 0.2 is regarded as small; one in the region of 0.5 as moderate; and of approximately 0.8 or more as large.

Moderator effects

Psychologists are accustomed to the notion that in explaining human action, most events are a function of multiple causal factors. Similarly, interventions to change behaviour have variable outcomes depending on context, the mixture of methods, sample composition and innumerable other factors. In addition to the observed main effects in evaluation research, if a full picture is to be obtained we also have to pay attention to interaction and moderator effects related to the outcomes of interest.

An example widely used in the teaching of meta-analysis in medicine is that of the *Bacillus Calmette-Guérin* (BCG), the vaccination against tuberculosis (TB) widely used in public immunisation programmes in many countries since the end of World War II. While this can secure an effectiveness of up to 80 per cent in preventing TB, that peak rate appears to be restricted to countries (such as the UK) which are in temperate climatic zones. The closer a population is to the equator, the less effective the vaccine. A dataset from 13 outcome studies published between 1948 and 1980 is extensively used to illustrate the moderating effect of geographical latitude on the effectiveness of the BCG.

The mediator–moderator distinction is well known in psychological research (Baron and Kenny, 1986). In forensic psychology when, for example, we evaluate an intervention (the independent variable) in its capacity to reduce reoffending (the dependent variable), it is virtually the norm to find that there are also variations in studies arising from differences in the nature of participants (e.g. assessed risk level), context (e.g. institution versus community), dosage (e.g. the number or distribution of sessions) or programme integrity (e.g. quality of delivery) amongst other factors. In a meta-analysis, the mean effects obtained from a preliminary analysis of the identified studies will have to be interpreted in the light of these effects and supplementary analyses conducted to take account of them.

Publication biases

The possibility that the published research on any given question is not representative of the full range of findings concerning it is a major threat to the integrity of all review processes. The term gray (or grey) literature has developed to denote potentially relevant material that is hard to find because it is not logged in readily accessible databases. It includes, for example, technical reports or working papers of government departments or other agencies which might contain findings that would be important in a review. Another problem arises from publication bias (Greenwald, 1975). This refers to the tendency of journal editors and reviewers to favour studies with statistically significant results, and reject ones lacking them. In some instances this even inhibits researchers from submitting papers for publication unless the results are significant (producing what has been called 'fugitive literature'). While this difficulty cannot be completely surmounted, several methods can be used to detect and minimise it. *Funnel plots* are statistical devices yielding a graphical display that can expose whether there are gaps in published studies suggestive of the operation of publication bias. Computing a *fail-safe* or *file-drawer* number, derived from a formula developed by Rosenthal (1979), enables a reviewer to estimate the number of unpublished studies with nil effects that would be necessary to overturn an observed positive mean effect of a given size. The increasing practice of publishing protocols in advance of conducting reviews, by serving notice of a plan for a review, may reduce the extent of these biases occurring.

Reporting results

When we plan an evaluative study or a research review, we probably have an audience in mind: an individual or group we are trying to influence. Psychological reports are generally designed to persuade the recipient or consumer of them to alter his or her beliefs, as persuasively argued by Ownby (1997). This assertion potentially applies even more forcefully in forensic psychology, whether at the level of individual psycho-legal assessments, or when summarising the results of research. Regarding meta-analysis, Gendreau and Smith (2007) provide invaluable advice on presenting and communicating results of reviews in a manner most likely to influence the 'people who count'. That meta-analytic reviews and their findings have had a substantial impact in the field of criminal justice has been shown (in a systematic review) by Smith, Gendreau and Swartz (2009).

The presentation of meta-analytic findings may have a crucial importance in their impact. To enhance clarity, correlation coefficient effect size measures are often translated into a two-by-two matrix known as the Binomial Effect Size Display (BESD; Rosenthal and Rubin, 1982). This represents the proportion of experimental and control samples in success/failure or improvement/no improvement categories of outcome, as shown in Figure 14.2.

Standardised mean difference statistics can be converted into a measure of comparative changes in experimental versus control groups, and thereby expressed as 'percentage change relative to control'. This can be portrayed graphically and is useful for comparing effect–size differences (see McGuire (2004) for a bar chart showing comparative outcomes for different treatment modalities). Odds ratios are best presented using forest plots, which display each ES with its confidence interval and also denote sample-size information in the

	Experimental	Control
Success/improvement		
Failure/no improvement		

Figure 14.2 The Binomial Effect Size Display (BESD).
Source: Rosenthal and Rubin, 1982.

Meta-analysis

Study name	Statistics for each study					Odds ratio and 95% CI
	Odds ratio	Lower limit	Upper limit	Z-value	P-value	
Motiuk *et al.*, 1996	0.818	0.312	2.143	−0.409	0.683	
Falshaw *et al.*, 2003	0.989	0.825	1.187	−0.116	0.908	
Van Voorhis *et al.*, 2004	2.073	1.318	3.263	3.152	0.002	
Pelissier *et al.*, 2001 (males)	1.393	1.160	1.674	3.543	0.000	
Hall *et al.*, 2004	1.464	0.799	2.681	1.233	0.217	
Henning and Frueh, 1996	2.352	1.238	4.467	2.613	0.009	
Anderson, 2002	2.013	1.673	2.422	7.419	0.000	
Leeman *et al.*, 1993	3.864	0.961	15.540	1.903	0.057	
Ross *et al.*, 1988	10.286	2.534	41.750	3.261	0.001	
	1.460	1.322	1.612	7.464	0.000	

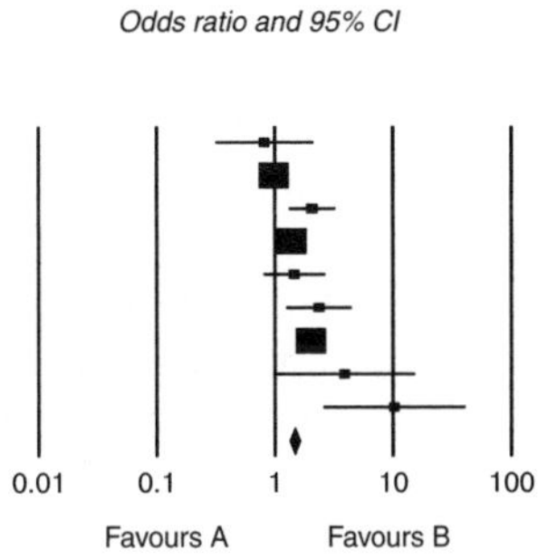

0.01   0.1   1   10   100

Favours A   Favours B

Figure 14.3 Illustration of a forest plot. (A = control; B = treatment).

proportionate weights of each component symbol. An example is shown in Figure 14.3, using a sample of studies from the review by Lipsey, Landenberger and Wilson (2007) which will now be briefly outlined.

An illustrative meta-analytic review

Lipsey, Landenberger and Wilson (2007) reported a meta-analytic review of the impact of cognitive-behavioural programmes on criminal recidivism. Their review located 58 studies published between 1980 and 2004. The majority were quasi-experimental designs, with only 33 per cent using randomisation, and an average follow-up interval of 12 months. There was a mean odds ratio of 1.53, corresponding to a 25 per cent reduction in recidivism from an average of 40 per cent in control groups to 30 per cent in experimental groups. There was significant heterogeneity in outcomes with a Q value of 214.02. There were no significant differences between randomized and non-randomized designs. The distribution of odds ratio effect sizes was displayed in a forest plot (see page 13 of their report). Checks were made to ensure that the obtained results were unlikely to be a function of publication bias, and a number of analyses were run to test the role of moderator variables. Those which emerged prominently were the risk level of the participants, and the quality of implementation of the programmes that were used. Studies with identified 'best practice' features (strong design, zero attrition, intent-to-treat analysis, recidivism defined as arrest, high quality of delivery) yielded a mean odds ratio of 2.86, corresponding to a 52 per cent decrease in recidivism (from a control mean of 40 per cent to an experimental mean of 19 per cent).

Critique of the approach

Not everyone agrees that meta-analysis has been a useful innovation, and there have been some sharp criticisms of it. Reviews are absolutely dependent on the basic studies they encompass, and can be misleading if their sources are over-interpreted. Egger, Dickersin and Smith (2001) have vividly demonstrated how conclusions from a meta-analytic review of a number of small-scale trials were subsequently contradicted by results from a single study containing a much larger sample. Similarly, patterns of findings can be dramatically altered depending on whether or not unpublished studies are included. This can be especially problematic where pharmacological companies suppress research findings on the limited or possibly non-existent effectiveness of a drug.

The two most frequently repeated criticisms of meta-analysis are, loosely termed, those of 'garbage in – garbage out' and 'apples and pears'. The first warns us that if the basic research on which a review depends is of poor quality, no review of it is likely to be able to compensate for its weaknesses and draw any conclusions with confidence, and any attempt to do otherwise is likely to be suspect. The second refers to the sometimes very marked diversity amongst primary studies that can render attempts to synthesise findings from them virtually meaningless. Undoubtedly, these are serious problems if they arise, and readers of any meta-analysis should be aware of them. Like any other research method, meta-analysis has to be used properly and carefully if its findings are to be valid and useful. When done well its findings constitute major contributions to evidence-based practice and can be incorporated in the Cochrane or Campbell databases which are described more fully in Chapter 15.

Quality control protocols

Concern as to the quality control of published work has led the research community to develop benchmarks for the design and reporting of studies. Over recent years this had led to the appearance of a number of *consensus statements* regarding the different principal types of design. Recognition that RCTs are not uniformly well done, and thus not an unerringly definitive hallmark of good outcome evaluation, is codified in the issuing of the CONSORT statement (Moher *et al.*, 2001; Schulz *et al.*, 2010). This stipulates a set of minimum standards to which controlled trials should adhere, and makes recommendations concerning how best to execute and report them. A parallel protocol, the TREND statement (Des Jarlais *et al.*, 2004) has been issued with reference to quasi-experiments. The recent publication of the PRISMA statement (Liberati *et al.*, 2009), though oriented primarily towards studies of medical interventions, is an attempt to ensure the quality control of systematic reviews and meta-analyses, and should be valuable in applied psychology also.

These statements are important not just as touchstones of quality for established researchers. By stipulating what good research should consist of, they provide step-by-step checklists of what to do and how to go about it and so are also useful reference points for anyone embarking on an evaluation project.

Further resources

There are many books on research design in psychology and adjacent disciplines. The basic principles described in them, drawn from experimental, laboratory-based work are also applicable in programme evaluation, though additional issues need to be addressed. For the logic of evaluation design in practical settings, a particularly good source is the book by Shadish, Cook and Campbell (2002). This is a revised version of an earlier, classic text co-authored by Donald Campbell, whose name was adopted by the eponymous Collaboration.

For an overview of evaluation research, the textbook by Rossi, Freeman and Lipsey (2004) is invaluable; see also the text by Gliner, Morgan and Leech (2009). Many methodology books contain a chapter on meta-analysis. See for example those by Breakwell, Hammond, Fife-Shaw and Smith (2006) and Millsap and Maydeu-Olivares (2009).

For more thorough coverage of meta-analysis, the Cooper, Hedges and Valentine (2009) book is the most comprehensive coverage of the subject available and the first edition was the standard reference work in the area. The volume by Borenstein, Hedges, Higgins and Rothstein (2009) is a thorough, methodical and well-explained introduction and is linked to a software package. Another very helpful source is the book by Cooper (2010).

The Campbell Collaboration electronic library can be accessed at www.campbellcollaboration.org/library.php.

References

Aos, S., Phipps, P., Barnoski, R. and Lieb, R. (2001). *The comparative costs and benefits of programs to reduce Crime*. Olympia, WA: Washington State Institute for Public Policy. Available at www.wsipp.wa.gov/rptfiles/costbenefit.pdf (accessed 22/4/11).

Aos, S., Lieb, R., Mayfield, J. Miller, M. and Pennuccii, A. (2004). *Benefits and costs of prevention and early intervention programs for youth*. Olympia, WA: Washington State Institute for Public Policy. Available at www.wsipp.wa.gov/rptfiles/04-07-3901.pdf (accessed 22/4/11).

Baron, R. M. and Kenny, D. A. (1986). The moderator-mediator variable distinction in social psychological research: conceptual, strategic, and statistical considerations. *Journal of Personality and Social Psychology*, 51: 1,173–82.

Blud, L. and Travers, R. (2001). Interpersonal problem-solving skills training: a comparison of R&R and ETS. *Criminal Behaviour and Mental Health*, 11: 251–61.

Borenstein, M., Hedges, L. V., Higgins, J. P. T. and Rothstein, H. R. (2009). *Introduction to meta-analysis*. New York, NY: John Wiley and Sons.

Breakwell, G. M., Hammond, S., Fife-Shaw, C. and Smith, J. A. (Eds) (2006). *Research methods in psychology*. 3rd edn. London: Sage Publications.

Caldwell, M. F., McCormick, D. J., Umstead, D. and Van Rybroek, G. J. (2007). Evidence of treatment progress and therapeutic outcomes among adolescents with psychopathic features. *Criminal Justice and Behaviour*, 34: 573–87.

Chalmers, I. (2006). *The scandalous failure of scientists to cumulate scientifically*. Paper presented at the 9th World Congress on Health Information and Libraries. Available at www.icml9.org/program/activity.php?lang = pt&id = 21 (accessed 22/4/11).

Cohen, J. (1992). A power primer. *Psychological Bulletin*, 112: 155–9.

Cooper, H. M. (2010). *Research synthesis and meta-analysis: a step-by-step approach*. 4th edn. Thousand Oaks, CA: Sage Publications.

Cooper, H. M. and Rosenthal, R. (1980). Statistical versus traditional procedures for summarising research findings. *Psychological Bulletin*, 87: 442–9.

Cooper, H. M., Hedges, L. V. and Valentine, J. C. (Eds) (2009). *The handbook of research synthesis and meta-analysis*. 2nd edn. New York, NY: Russell Sage Foundation.

Des Jarlais, D. C., Lyles, C., Crepaz, N. and the TREND Group (2004). Improving the reporting quality of nonrandomized evaluations of behavioral and public health interventions: the TREND statement. *American Journal of Public Health*, 94: 361–6.

Durlak, J. A. and Lipsey, M. W. (1991). A practitioner's guide to meta-analysis. *American Journal of Community Psychology*, 19: 291–332.

Egger, M., Dickersin, K. and Smith, G. D. (2001). Problems and limitations in conducting systematic reviews. In M. Egger, G. D. Smith and D. G. Altman (Eds). *Systematic reviews in health care: meta-analysis in context* (pp. 43–68). 2nd edn. London: BMJ Books.

Farrington, D. P., Gottfredson, L. W., Sherman, L. W. and Welsh, B. C. (2002). The Maryland Scientific Methods Scale. In L. W. Sherman, D. P. Farrington, B. C. Welsh and D. L. MacKenzie (Eds). *Evidence-based crime prevention* (pp. 3–21). London: Routledge.

Field, A. (2009). Meta-analysis. In R. E. Millsap and A. Maydeu-Olivares (Eds). *The Sage handbook of quantitative methods in psychology* (pp. 405–22). London: Sage Publications.

Friendship, C., Mann, R. E. and Beech, A. R. (2003). Evaluation of a national prison-based treatment program for sexual offenders in England and Wales. *Journal of Interpersonal Violence*, 18: 744–59.

Gendreau, P. and Smith, P. (2007). Influencing the 'people who count': some perspectives on the reporting of meta-analytic results for prediction and treatment outcomes with offenders. *Criminal Justice and Behavior*, 34: 1,536–59.

Gilinskiy, Y. (2006). Crime in contemporary Russia. *European Journal of Criminology*, 3: 259–92.

Glass, G. V. (1976). Primary, secondary and meta-analysis of research. *Educational Researcher*, 5(10): 3–8.

Glass, G. V., McGaw, B. and Smith, M. L. (1981). *Meta-analysis in social research*. Newbury Park: Sage Publications.

Gliner, J. A., Morgan, G. A. and Leech, N. L. (2009). *Research methods in applied settings: an integrated approach to design and analysis.* 2nd edn. New York and London: Routledge.

Greenwald, A. G. (1975). Consequences of prejudice against the null hypothesis. *Psychological Bulletin*, 82: 1–20.

Hatcher, R. M., Palmer, E. J., McGuire, J., Hounsome, J., Bilby, C. A. L. and Hollin, C. R. (2008). Aggression Replacement Training with adult male offenders within community settings: a reconviction analysis. *Journal of Forensic Psychiatry and Psychology*, 19: 517–32.

Hollis, V. (2007). *Reconviction analysis of Interim Accredited Programmes Software (IAPS) data.* London: Research Development Statistics, National Offender Management Service.

Liberati, A., Altman, D. G., Tetzlaff, J., Mulrow, C., Gotzsche, P. C., Ioannidis, J. P. A., Clarke, M., Devereaux, J. J., Kleijnen, J. and Moher, D. (2009). The PRISMA statement for reporting systematic reviews and meta-analyses of studies that evaluate healthcare interventions: explanation and elaboration. *British Medical Journal*, 339: b2700. doi: 10.1136/bmj.b2700.

Lipsey, M. W. and Wilson, D. B. (1993). The efficacy of psychological, educational, and behavioral treatment: confirmation from meta-analysis. *American Psychologist*, 48: 1,181–1,209.

Lipsey, M. W., Landenberger N. A. and Wilson S. J. (2007). *Effects of cognitive-behavioral programs for criminal offenders. Campbell Systematic Reviews*: doi: 10.4073/csr.2007.6.

McGuire, J. (2001). Development of a program logic model to assist evaluation. In L. L. Motiuk and R. C. Serin (Eds). *Compendium 2000 on effective correctional programming* (pp. 208–20). Ottawa: Correctional Service Canada.

—— (2004). *Understanding psychology and crime: perspectives on theory and action.* Maidenhead: Open University Press/McGraw-Hill Education.

—— (2008). What's the point of sentencing? Psychological aspects of crime and punishment. In G. Davies, C. R. Hollin and R. Bull (Eds). *Forensic psychology* (pp. 265–91). Chichester: John Wiley & Sons.

—— (2009). Reducing personal violence: risk factors and effective interventions. In S. Hodgins, E. Viding and A. Plodowski (Eds). *The neurobiological basis of violence: science and rehabilitation* (pp. 287–327). Oxford: Oxford University Press.

McGuire, J. and Hatcher, R. M. (2001). Offence-focused problem-solving: preliminary evaluation of a cognitive skills program. *Criminal Justice and Behavior*, 28: 564–87.

McGuire, J., Bilby, C. A. L., Hatcher, R. M., Hollin, C. R., Hounsome, J. C. and Palmer, E. J. (2008). Evaluation of structured cognitive-behavioral programs in reducing criminal recidivism. *Journal of Experimental Criminology*, 4: 21–40.

Maguire, M. (2007). Crime data and statistics. In M. Maguire, R. Morgan and R. Reiner (Eds). *The Oxford handbook of criminology* (pp. 241–301). 4th edn. Oxford: Oxford University Press.

Maxwell, S. E. (2004). The persistence of underpowered studies in psychological research: causes, consequences and remedies. *Psychological Methods*, 9: 147–63.

Maxwell, S. E., Kelley, K. and Rausch, J. R. (2008). Sample size planning for statistical power and accuracy in parameter estimation. *Annual Review of Psychology*, 59: 537–63.

Millsap, R. E and Maydeu-Olivares, A. (Eds) (2009). *The Sage handbook of quantitative methods in psychology.* London: Sage Publications.

Moher, D., Schulz, K. F. and Altman, D. G. (2001). The CONSORT statement: revised recommendations for improving the quality of reports of parallel group randomized trials. *BMC Medical Research Methodology*, 1: 2. Available at www.biomedcentral. com/1471–2288/1/2 (accessed 22/4/11).

Mulrow, C. D. (1987). The medical review article: state of the science. *Annals of Internal Medicine*, 106: 485–8.

Ownby, R. L. (1997). *Psychological reports: a guide to report writing in professional psycholog.* 3rd edn. New York, NY: John Wiley and Sons.

Palmer, E. J., McGuire, J., Hounsome, J. C., Hatcher, R. M., Bilby, C. A. L. and Hollin, C. R. (2007). Offending behaviour programmes in the community: the effects on reconviction of three programmes with adult male offenders. *Legal and Criminological Psychology*, 12: 251–64.

Pearson, K. (1904). Report on certain enteric fever inoculation statistics. *British Medical Journal*, 2288: 1,243–6.

Pfuhl, E. H. (1983). Police strikes and conventional crime – a look at the data. *Criminology*, 21: 489–503.

Posavac, E. J. and Carey, R. G. (1997). *Program evaluation: methods and case studies.* 5th edn. Upper Saddle River, NJ: Prentice Hall.

Rosenthal, R. (1979). The 'file drawer problem' and tolerance for null results. *Psychological Bulletin*, 86: 638–41.

—— (1995). Writing meta-analytic reviews. *Psychological Bulletin*, 118: 183–92.

Rosenthal, R. and Rubin, D. B. (1982). A simple, general purpose display of magnitude of experimental effect. *Journal of Educational Psychology*, 74: 166–9.

Rosnow, R. L. and Rosenthal, R. (2008). Assessing the effect size of outcome research. In A. M. Nezu and C. M. Nezu (Eds). *Evidence-based outcome research: a practical guide to conducting randomized controlled trials for psychosocial interventions* (pp. 379–401). New York, NY: Oxford University Press.

Rossi, P. H., Freeman, H. E. and Lipsey, M. W. (2004). *Evaluation: a systematic approach.* 7th edn. Thousand Oaks, CA: Sage Publications.

Schulz, K. F., Altman, D. G., Moher, D. for the CONSORT group (2010). CONSORT 2010 statement: updated guidelines for reporting parallel group randomised trials. *PLOS Medicine*, 7(3): e10000251. doi: 10.1371/journal.pmed.1000251.

Shadish, W. R., Cook, T. D. and Campbell, D. T. (2002). *Experimental and quasi-experimental designs for generalized causal inference.* Boston, MA: Houghton Mifflin.

Sherman, L. W. (1990). Police crackdowns: initial and residual deterrence. *Crime and Justice: A Review of Research*, 12: 1–48.

Smith, M. L. and Glass, G. V. (1977). Meta-analysis of psychotherapy outcome studies. *American Psychologist*, 32: 752–60.

Smith, P., Gendreau, P. and Swartz, K. (2009). Validating the principles of effective intervention: a systematic review of the contributions of meta-analysis in the field of corrections. *Victims and Offenders*, 4: 148–69.

Stecher, B. M. and Davis, W. A. (1987). *How to focus an evaluation.* Newbury Park, CA: Sage Publications.

15 Systematic reviews and meta-analysis

Michael Ferriter

What is a systematic review?

Many hierarchies of quantitative evidence now rank systematic reviews of randomised controlled trials (RCTs) as the highest form of treatment outcome evidence, though traditional literature reviews are ranked near the bottom. To understand why systematic reviews are held in such high regard we need to understand how they differ from traditional literature reviews and the relationship between systematic reviews and meta-analysis, two terms that are sometimes mistakenly used as similes. Not all systematic reviews include a meta-analysis and not all meta-analyses are carried out in the context of a systematic review. Let us first consider what is a systematic review.

The defining feature of a systematic review is that its methodology is both transparent and replicable so that a reader with just baseline skills can replicate the review and confirm or refute the findings and also update the review in the light of new studies. It is a review as an experiment and reported in the traditional experimental notebook format. The methodology describes inclusion and exclusion criteria, search terms and prospectively stated outcomes, all of which are described in unambiguous detail. In contrast, the methodology of the traditional literature review, written by an expert in the area, is opaque, and unless the reader has equal or greater expertise in the area it is difficult to tell whether the topic has been thoroughly reviewed or reflects the author's biases.

Although traditional literature reviews in medicine, summarising the state of knowledge in specific disease areas go back to at least the eighteenth century, systematic reviews have only come to the fore in the latter half of the twentieth century (Egger *et al.*, 2001a). A major publisher of systematic reviews is the Cochrane Collaboration, an international network of groups and volunteers supported by a number of governments worldwide that produces gold standard systematic reviews of treatment outcome studies in all the major health domains, including mental health. The Cochrane Collaboration has also led the way in exploring methodological issues in reviewing and the methodologies described in this chapter reflect the recommendations from the Cochrane Collaboration. Other sources of reviews in the UK use similar or identical methodologies and include the York Centre for Reviews and Dissemination (CRD) and the Health Technology Assessment (HTA) Programme. There are also counterparts of the

HTA Programme in other countries. Of particular relevance to those working in the criminological and forensic field is the Campbell Collaboration, which seeks to carry out evaluations of interventions, modelled very closely on the Cochrane model, in the fields of social policy, penology and crime control.

The importance of the protocol in the systematic review process

The first stage in the systematic review process is to draft a protocol and the Cochrane Collaboration requires the publication, following a rigorous peer review process, of a review protocol. The protocol contains what will become the background and methodological sections of the final review. All deviations from the protocol in the final review must be fully described and justified. Those carrying out reviews outside of the Cochrane Collaboration would be well advised to follow a similar process and structure. The protocol stage provides an opportunity to clarify the aims and methodology of the review. If the review is a commissioned project the protocol can be the basis for a constructive dialogue between the commissioner and reviewer, clarifying what is required and what can be delivered.

For the purposes of this brief introduction to systematic reviewing the procedure for reviewing the literature on treatment outcome research will be described as this is the most developed area. However, systematic reviewing techniques may be applied to other areas of research and these are described below. The protocol should contain background information on the condition, intervention, rationale for the intervention and current state of knowledge on the intervention. There should be clearly stated aims and objectives to the review. Inclusion and exclusion criteria should be defined in unambiguous detail describing the types of studies (e.g. RCTs, crossover trials, random centre trials, described later in this chapter), types of participants (e.g. diagnosis, age, gender, ethnicity), the intervention of interest, the comparators (e.g. another intervention, treatment as usual, no treatment, placebo) and outcome measures including period of measure (e.g. end of trial, short-, medium- or long-term follow up). Examples of exclusion criteria might be all studies published before a given date plus justification for this, significant comorbidity or by language, though issues of potential language bias must be taken into account (see page 309).

The protocol must also list the databases to be searched and the extent to which the grey literature will also be searched. The grey literature is usually understood to mean the literature not formerly published in books or journals. Examples include conference abstracts and proceedings and governmental reports and documents. A specimen of the search terms for one of the major databases such as PsycINFO should be included in full with the search terms for other databases either included as appendices or available online or on request from the author.

The protocol should contain prospective statements on data analysis, how dichotomous and continuous data will be extracted from the primary studies and standardised, the method of meta-analysis if applicable, detecting and dealing with heterogeneity of studies and detection of publication bias. Ideally, the protocol should indicate which of the authors will undertake which part of the review process and that the selection of studies process would be carried out by at least two persons independently with a third adjudicating where the assessments are discordant.

What sort of studies should be reviewed in the systematic review?

For treatment outcome studies, randomised controlled trials (RCTs) are considered the 'gold standard' because it is the only design that can control for unknown confounders. Acceptable methods of randomisation are those where the sequences are unpredictable and include computer-generated random sequences, tables of random numbers, drawing lots from an envelope, coin tossing, shuffling cards or throwing dice (Jüni *et al.*, 2001). Some studies are more accurately described as quasi-randomised where the method of allocation is predictable and may introduce a systematic bias. Examples of quasi-randomised methods include allocation by case record number, date of birth, date of admission and alternate allocation. Some systematic reviews have included quasi-randomised studies as well as RCTs but as proper randomisation would require so little extra effort on the part of the researchers, one must wonder what other methodological short-comings the study may have. Other reviews specifically exclude quasi-randomised studies.

However, RCTs are not without their problems. One common criticism is that many RCTs are carried out at centres of excellence with highly competent and motivated staff and that interventions that are shown to be effective in this context may prove less successful or ineffective when rolled out to the standard treatment environment. What are needed are pragmatic trials where the interventions are trialled in environments and with staff more typical of the usual setting.

Another criticism of RCTs is that the participants in trials may be atypical of the population with the disease in their willingness to be randomised. For instance it would be an unusual person who would agree, with equanimity, to be randomised to either radical surgery or a less harsh medical intervention. However, most trials offer less extreme options but even here participants may have a preference and may feel that they have been randomised to the less optimum arm of the trial. This is not uncommon where it is impossible to blind the participant to allocation and the trial compares a novel treatment to a standard intervention. There is a natural tendency to see the novel treatment as superior despite the fact that until the trial is complete we do not know which intervention is the best. One way of dealing with this is a patient preference trial where the participants are asked, having been fully informed about the trial and the intervention arms, whether they are prepared to be randomised or would prefer to select which arm of the trial to enter. In theory this is an elegant solution but, in practice, recruitment to be randomised may be very low.

Another criticism is that RCTs are unethical because they randomise some participants to a placebo or no treatment arm, thus depriving these participants of an effective intervention. However, most trials are of the novel treatment versus standard treatment design or standard treatment plus novel treatment versus standard treatment design. In these designs all participants do receive some form of intervention. Where there is a placebo or no treatment arm to the trial the assumption that the novel treatment may be beneficial is not necessarily the case and those in the no treatment group may be better off than the novel intervention group. This applies as much to psychological interventions as it does to pharmacological interventions; psychological interventions may not be harm free.

However, one way of dealing with these concerns in a pharmacological intervention is a crossover trial. Where the condition is long standing and a small delay in testing the intervention would not be critical one can, with a suitable wash-out period in between, give the novel drug to one group and the placebo to the other group in the first phase and in the second phase reverse the interventions. In this way all participants receive the novel intervention and all receive the placebo but in a different order.

The nearest equivalent design for a psychological intervention is a waiting list control trial. Clearly, it is not possible to 'wash out' a psychological intervention in the same way that a drug free period will guarantee no active component. Instead, the participants are randomised into a group to be treated or to be put on a waiting list for the first phase and in the second phase the group on the waiting list are given the intervention. Where there is a shortage of trained therapists and demand outstrips supply this design makes a virtue out of necessity.

Another variation on the randomised trial is the randomised centre trial where the unit of allocation is not the individual participant but rather the centre or facility where the intervention or comparator are taking place. Examples of this approach might include different methods of service delivery in primary care centres. The problem with this design is precisely that the unit of allocation is the centre not the participant and that the sample size must be calculated on the number of centres not the number of participants, which may mean the trial is not adequately powered.

Evaluating the quality of a study

There have been a number of different tools developed to evaluate the quality of randomised controlled trials and other research designs. Currently, the Cochrane Collaboration requires their reviewers to evaluate trials against a number of risks of bias and biases are divided into five types (Higgins and Altman, 2008).

- *Selection bias* refers to systematic differences of baseline characteristics between the groups that may have arisen because the allocation was not truly random or the trialists or participants could foresee the allocation.

- *Performance bias* refers to systematic differences between the way the groups of participants are treated other than the interventions and can include failure to blind the participants and/or the staff to allocation.
- *Attrition bias* refers to the data on participants not completing the trial being excluded from the results. One simple way of taking this into account is using the last data available as the end of trial data.
- *Detection bias* refers to systematic differences in the way outcomes are measured between the groups. Wherever possible those measuring the outcomes should be blind to allocation of the participants.
- *Reporting bias* refers to the selective reporting of outcomes in the study and it is important to check the prospectively stated outcomes in the methodology against the data reported.

Other possible sources of bias should also be reported including declared or known possible conflicts of interest such as sponsorship or funding from pharmaceutical companies and being a practising therapist in the school of therapy being evaluated.

Trialists are increasingly aware of what systematic reviewers need to see reported in the published papers and over time it will be easier for reviewers to carry out a full risk of bias evaluation. However, when going back in time earlier papers often did not report in such detail, for instance reporting that the trial was randomised but not the method of randomisation. As a result, a trial may appear to be a poorer quality study than it really was. It is important to contact the authors of the paper to clarify these procedural details.

There is a strong temptation to reduce the risk of bias evaluation to a single score but this should be resisted. We cannot assume that each risk is of equal weight and, indeed, the risk and weight may vary between trials. Instead the review should report the evaluation in narrative form.

Change data

Many trials report both the end of study trial results and change data. In large scale trials one might assume that the randomisation process will even out any significant differences at baseline between the participants in the different arms of the trial. The problem is in small trials where randomisation alone may not prevent significant differences between the arms at baseline. Here, the change from baseline is a more appropriate statistic, but to be included in the meta-analysis we need the sample size, mean and standard deviation of the change scores for both arms. The first two statistics are not problematic but frequently authors do not provide the required standard deviations. There are methods of deriving these from the P values, standard errors, confidence intervals or *t* statistics (see Higgins and Deeks, 2008) but again the appropriate statistics may not be available. In circumstances like this the reviewer should attempt to obtain the standard deviations or even the original data from the authors of the original paper, but if this is not forthcoming then the default is to use end-of-study

Table 15.1 Example of a trial of an intervention versus a control group

Intervention group			Control group		
Before	*After*	*Change*	*Before*	*After*	*Change*
2	8	6	6	9	3
3	6	3	7	8	1
4	7	3	7	7	0
4	8	4	6	8	2
3	5	2	5	9	4
6	9	3	6	6	0
2	6	4	6	7	1
4	7	3	6	8	2
3	5	2	7	8	1
3	5	2	5	7	2
3.4	*6.6*	*3.2*	*6.1*	*7.7*	*1.6*

Note: mean scores in italics.

data only. The problem here is that the result of using end-of-study data may be significantly different from the result reported by the original authors using change data and the reviewer must draw attention to and explain this discrepancy in the review.

Table 15.1 shows a simple, fictitious example of a trial of an intervention versus a control group with ten participants in each group and where a high score shows improvement. The mean scores are shown in the bottom row. Without the standard deviation for the difference between the scores before and after the trial we can only enter the results for the end of the trial into the meta-analysis. In this case the intervention group participants have a mean score 6.6 and the control group a mean score 7.7, suggesting that the intervention does not work. However, if we look at the difference scores, the participants in the intervention group showed a mean improvement of 3.2 but the control group only showed a mean improvement of 1.6, a different story entirely.

Meta-analysis

Meta-analysis is a statistical process by which the results of a number of studies can be aggregated together to produce an overall treatment effect size. An effect size is a measure of the contrast in outcome between two different groups of participants receiving different interventions. The origins of meta-analysis are in the early statistical work of Gauss and Laplace. Its first application was in astronomy and the first textbook on the subject was written by the Victorian Astronomer Royal George Biddell Airy. The first application in the medical field was by Karl Pearson in 1904 who pooled the results of studies on the effect of serum inoculations against enteric fever in a meta-analysis. The actual term 'meta-analysis' was first used by the psychologist Glass in 1976 (Egger *et al.*, 2001a). For an introduction to meta-analysis see the York CRD's guidance for undertaking reviews in health care (2009).

One of the major benefits of meta-analysis is that it can be used to aggregate a number of small studies, each of which might be considered underpowered in itself (i.e. with insufficient participants to detect, with confidence, whether an intervention works or not) but which when pooled would have the statistical power of an adequately powered study. However, the first and absolute prerequisite of any meta-analysis is that the included studies should have the same sorts of participants, intervention, comparator and outcome (shortened to the acronym PICO). Any violation of this risks what Eysenck (1995) referred to as adding apples and oranges, producing a spurious and misleading result. When in doubt it is better not to meta-analyse and to present the treatment effect size for each study separately.

The results of a meta-analysis are shown as a forest plot. The plot shows, for each study, the treatment effect as a dot or circle with a horizontal line passing through the dot or circle to show the confidence intervals. The wider the line, the wider the confidence intervals. At the centre of the plot itself is a vertical line marking the line of nil effect. Whether the dot or circle is to the left or the right of the line of nil effect depends on whether the study results favour the intervention or the comparator. If the line showing the extent of the confidence intervals crosses the line of nil effect then the result could have occurred by chance alone. If the horizontal line does not cross the vertical line we can be confident that, for that study, there is a true treatment effect. At the bottom of the plot is a diamond shape which shows the treatment effect for all the studies combined. Again, whether the diamond is to the left or right of the line of nil effect will tell us whether the combined results favour the intervention or the comparator. Whether the diamond itself spans the line of nil effect tells us if we can have confidence in the combined results.

Even when studies appear to have homogeneity of PICO, underlying differences between the studies may lead to heterogeneity. The first and most obvious sign of this would be an outlier result on the forest plot showing one or more studies with a markedly different treatment effect size from the main group. Statistical methods are available for assessing the impact of heterogeneity of studies in a meta-analysis such as the I^2 statistic. If heterogeneity appears to be present the first and most obvious precaution is to check that the results have been accurately transcribed from the published paper to the statistical software and also to check the published paper for any explanation for the outlier result. Sensitivity analysis, comparing the results with or without the outlier, is also recommended. For more detailed information on detecting and dealing with heterogeneity in a meta-analysis see Deeks *et al.* (2008).

Please note that an outcome is not a specific outcome measure and a meta-analysis can include different outcome measures provided they are for the same outcome. For instance the outcome may be an improvement in depression but included trials may use different depression scales. Provided the scales all measure the same construct it is possible to include them in the same meta-analysis through using a specific statistic, the standardised mean difference (SMD).

Potential problems with meta-analysis

The strength of a meta-analysis is that it can be used to aggregate small studies which individually would be dismissed as underpowered but that collectively might be the equivalent of an adequately powered study. Large-scale and often multi-site or even multinational clinical trials are costly, present enormous organisational challenges and present difficulties in maintaining the methodological integrity of the study over many sites. All other things being equal, quality control and methodological integrity are easier to maintain in a small-scale local trial. Does this mean that a meta-analysis of small studies might be preferable to a large-scale clinical trial? Do meta-analyses produce the same results as a large-scale clinical trial?

Studies have now been carried out (Egger *et al.*, 1997a, LeLorier *et al.*, 1997) that compared large clinical trials with meta-analyses of a number of trials in the same domain. The problem is that though in some cases the meta-analysis reassuringly approximated very closely to the results of the large scale trial, in others the results were discordant though consistently showing greater treatment effect sizes in the meta-analysis compared to the large scale trial. In answer to the second question, does a meta-analysis of small trials produce the same result as one large trial, the unhelpful answer appears to be that sometimes they do and sometimes they don't!

The unidirectional nature of the disparity between large trials and equivalent meta-analyses is the clue to the probable underlying reason – publication bias. Publication bias refers to the suspicion that studies which show a significant treatment effect size are more likely to be published than studies showing no treatment effect. There is similar bias in favour of large-scale studies. These biases may be because editors and their peer reviewers may, incorrectly, view studies showing significant treatment effects as more interesting and important than those that do not. Alternatively, this misapprehension may be on the part of the researchers dissuading them from attempting to publish, the so called 'file draw' effect. This systematic bias probably explains why some meta-analyses show discordantly larger treatment effects sizes than equivalent single large trials where the results of all participants are pooled regardless of whether the treatment is effective for an individual participant or not.

Software such as Review Manager is capable of generating funnel plots, a diagrammatic way of indicating if publication bias may be present. A funnel plot is simply a scatter diagram which plots each study by treatment effect size on the horizontal access and by some measure of sample size on the vertical axis. If there is no publication bias present than the scatter plot should approximate to the shape of an inverted funnel. However, if publication bias is a factor then we would expect to see an absence of studies in the bottom

y-axis

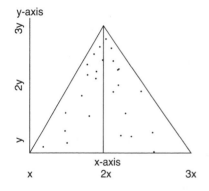

Figure 15.1 Generic funnel plot.
Source: http://en.wikipedia.org/wiki/funnel_plot

right-hand corner of the plot where the small scale studies with no treatment effect should be. Figure 15.1 shows an example of a funnel plot.

There are a number of strategies that the scientific community can adopt as a whole to erode the problem of publication bias. The first is for editors and reviewers to value and publish small-scale trials or trials that show no treatment effect or that go against current received wisdom. Other strategies include 'trials amnesties', by which researchers can declare their unpublished research and make known its existence to reviewers, and registers of research that allow the reviewer to check studies that have commenced against studies that have been reported in the literature.

Another potential source of significant bias is language bias, mainly but not exclusively limiting included studies to one language, English. In our shamefully monolingual country this is often done out of sheer necessity in the face of high costs of professional translation. This would not be a significant problem if one could assume that the distribution of treatment effects size for a given population of treatment effect trials was the same in every language. If this were the case then trials reported in English could safely stand proxy for trials reported in any language. Unfortunately, this assumption may not be true. A study by Egger *et al.* (1997b) identified authors whose first language was German but who had published in English as well as German. Their findings were that that the authors were more likely to publish their studies with significant treatment effects in English language journals with, presumably, wider international readership and more likely to publish their non-significant results in German language journals, with by and large a smaller readership. If this is true for other languages, and it is difficult to imagine why German-speaking authors should be unique in this, then concentrating on purely English language papers, or just one or two languages, risks a significant bias in favour of enhanced treatment effect sizes.

A theoretical risk which, to the best of the writer's knowledge, has not received much attention in the literature is what may be termed 'over powered' meta-analysis.

One of the first steps in planning a single clinical trial is to establish the minimum number of participants that need to be recruited to detect a clinically significant treatment effects size. This is achieved by gaining some sort of estimate of what the minimum outcome difference score between the intervention and the control group would be needed to be regarded by clinicians and/or patients as a significant treatment effect. Along with the level of confidence (usually 95 per cent) it is an easy calculation to derive how many participants need to be recruited for each arm.

For any researcher, recruitment of participants is a challenge and trials rarely recruit more than the minimum number of participants, the minimum sample size, because of this. In fact the major cause of anxiety for most trialists is that their trial will not meet this minimum sample size. However, as a thought experiment, imagine what would happen if the researchers recruited participants above the minimum sample size by several orders of magnitude? With the confidence interval held constant, the risk is that the trial would identify a treatment effect size as being statistically significant but which is clinically insignificant. This, of course, is unlikely to happen in a real world clinical trial, but is a theoretical risk in a meta-analysis containing many large scale trials.

The questions asked at the beginning of this section were: do meta-analyses produce the same results as a large-scale clinical trial and by implication are they a satisfactory proxy for a large-scale trial? As we have seen there is not a straightforward answer to these reasonable and straightforward questions and the results of any meta-analysis must be interpreted with caution. Is there evidence of publication bias, were there language restrictions, what was the total number of participants in the meta-analysis? All these questions must be taken into account before the conclusion can be reached that the meta-analysis has answered the question.

Beyond treatment outcome studies

The Cochrane Collaboration are currently exploring ways of systematically reviewing diagnostic tests and combining individual comparative studies with results plotted as receiver operator characteristics (ROC) curves. The ROC curve is a way of plotting the characteristic of a diagnostic test in terms of its sensitivity, the ability to detect a true case and its specificity, the ability to exclude those who are not a true case (see Lang and Secic, 1997 for an introduction to ROC curves). The format of such studies is often to compare a gold standard diagnostic test with a novel diagnostic test that may be cheaper, quicker, less invasive or less risky than the gold standard test and would therefore be superior provided it matched the sensitivity and specificity of the gold standard. An example in general medicine may be comparing a biopsy test (gold standard) with a less invasive or risky blood test. The problem in mental health is the dearth of gold standard diagnostic tests and the need to use, instead, a best available test usually decided on by clinical consensus. The problem occurs when the novel diagnostic test is superior to the best available test. All the reviewer will know is that the tests are discordant but with no way of knowing which is superior.

A question that is often asked is whether it is possible to carry out a review of qualitative research and there are many examples of attempts to do so. Undoubtedly some of the methodology used in systematic reviewing can be translated with relative ease to qualitative research. These include explicit and replicable search strategies, inclusion and exclusion criteria and quality assessments. However, Murphy *et al.* (1998), in their thorough review of qualitative methods in health research, explicitly reject the methodology of the systematic review as being inappropriate for qualitative research. They describe one school of thought within the qualitative research community in which, because of the complexity of the interactions, the participants and their circumstances in any qualitative research are unique and as such the results of qualitative research cannot be generalised to any other context. In addition, any attempt to identify and review qualitative research that may appear superficially similar would be potentially misleading.

Murphy *et al.* also describe an alternative point of view. The results of qualitative research can be generalised provided there is sufficient contextual detail for the reviewer to form a subjective judgement on inclusion or exclusion. The notion that the reviewer should make a subjective judgement on inclusion or exclusion violates the basic tenet of the systematic review and raises another question about the appropriateness of systematic reviewing to qualitative research.

However, where progress has been made has been in the inclusion of qualitative research as an adjunct to quantitative data in systematic reviews. Qualitative research can inform the process of defining the question and also provide an important third dimension of the experiences of the trial participants (and for that matter, the trialists) to the otherwise two-dimensional data on effectiveness. In many ways these developments are still work in progress but for a fuller explanation of these approaches see Noyes *et al.* (2008).

Ethical considerations

Unlike primary research, systematic reviews do not require ethics committee permission, presumably on the assumption that the primary studies included have already gained ethical approval. Most journals now require confirmation from the author that the study has been approved by an ethics committee.

The Declaration of Helsinki, Section 30 (WMA, 2008), states that research not carried out in accordance with the ethical standards of the Declaration should not be published and by this one might also assume should not be included in systematic reviews. There are rare instances where the data from tainted, unethical research have been approved for secondary analysis. Permission was given to use data on Nazi hypothermia research carried out in the concentration camps which did have potentially life saving utility and could not be replicated on healthy volunteers because of the life threatening risk and intolerable pain (Cohen 2009).

Such historical precedents are extremely rare but of more immediate concern is the emergence of a large corpus of historical research and clinical trials from former totalitarian regimes where there may be no guarantees that the research has been carried out to internationally agreed, ethical standards. Here, the responsibility is firmly on the reviewer to seek reassurance that the research does meet our ethical requirements or exclude the study altogether.

Empty reviews

A number of systematic reviews have been published in areas where there a few or no studies and they are therefore inconclusive and might be thought of as having little value. A corollary of this is that one should only carry out systematic reviews on interventions where we either know or strongly suspect that evidence exists. However, there are equally compelling arguments in favour of empty or near-empty reviews.

The first argument is that though we might think we know that there is no evidence out there we could be wrong and it is only after the review has been carried out that one can say for certain that there is currently little or no evidence. Empty reviews also inform those who commission research of what areas are in urgent need of primary studies. Certainly within the Cochrane context an empty review provides a methodology and framework that can be utilised in the future when clinical trials have been carried out. An example of an empty review on a forensic topic is Ashman and Duggan's (2008) Cochrane review of interventions for learning disabled sex offenders which found no randomised controlled trials.

Examples of systematic reviews of interventions in forensic mental health

It would be impossible to describe all the systematic reviews that might be of interest to those working in forensic mental health services but it is possible to list the main commissioners of research in this area with some examples.

During its brief life the National Forensic Mental Health R&D Programme commissioned 13 reviews, both systematic and traditional, covering the following topics: the epidemiology of mentally disordered offenders; women and secure psychiatric services; effectiveness of nursing interventions with personality disorders; therapeutic community effectiveness; register of RCTs relevant to the management of offenders and systematic review of aspects of treatment relevant to management of those with the dual diagnosis of violence and serious mental illness; health and care of mentally disordered offenders; managements for people with disorders of sexual preference and for convicted sex offenders (also published as a Cochrane review); clinical effectiveness and cost consequences of selective serotonin re-uptake inhibitors in the treatment of sex offenders (also published as an HTA review); psychological treatments for sex offenders (also published as a Cochrane review); prevention strategies for the population at risk of engaging in violent behaviour; review of reviews in forensic mental health; effectiveness of pharmacological and psychological strategies for the management of people with personality disorder; and research relevant to the mental health of young offenders. Copies of these reviews can be downloaded from www.liv.ac.uk/www/fmhweb/research.htm#cpr. Even where these reviews may be out of date they are worth exploring for their methodology.

The review of strategies for the management of people with personality disorder has recently been updated in two reviews of pharmacological (Duggan *et al.*, 2008) and of psychological interventions (Duggan *et al.*, 2007). In turn, these reviews will be updated as part of a portfolio of Cochrane reviews in 2010–11. Also as part of this portfolio will be four systematic reviews on interventions for sex offenders, pharmacological, psychological and surgical interventions and a review on interventions for adolescent sex offenders. A final review in the portfolio of interest is on anti-epileptics for aggression and associated impulsivity (Huband *et al.*, 2010). Sirdifield *et al.* (2009) have recently updated a review by Brooker *et al.* (2003) on mental health problems in prisoners.

Readers interested in searching for systematic reviews on forensic topics would be advised to start at the Campbell Collaboration website (www. campbellcollaboration.org). The Cochrane Library, available on the net (www3. interscience.wiley.com/cgi-bin/mrwhome/106568753/AboutCochrane.html), indexes not only Cochrane systematic reviews but also HTA reports, overseas equivalents to the HTA reports, York Centre for Reviews and Dissemination reports and other systematic reviews.

Further reading

There are several good introductory textbooks on systematic reviewing. Already mentioned is the York CRD's guidance for undertaking reviews in health care (2009) which also has the advantage of being available as a free download. Another good introductory texts is Khan *et al.* (2003). For the more advanced reader Egger *et al.* (2001b) and Higgins and Green (2008) are essential reading.

References

Ashman, L. L. M and Duggan L. (2008). Interventions for learning disabled sex offenders. *Cochrane Database of Systematic Reviews*, issue 1, art. CD003682. DOI: 10.1002/14651858.CD003682.pub2.

Brooker, C., Repper, J., Beverley, C., Ferriter, M. and Brewer N. (2003). *Review of the literature on interventions for prisoners with mental disorders.* Report prepared for Department of Health/Home Office Prison Healthcare Taskforce.

Cohen, B.C. (2009). *Ethics of using medical data from Nazi experiments in Jewish Law.* Available at www.jlaw.com/Articles/NaziMedEx.html (accessed 21/4/11).

Deeks, J. J., Higgins, J. P. T and Altman, D. G. (2008). Analysing data and undertaking meta-analyses. In J. P. T. Higgins and S. Green (Eds). *Cochrane Handbook of Systematic Reviews of Interventions* (pp. 276–89). Chichester: Wiley Blackwell.

Duggan, C., Huband, N., Smailagic, N., Ferriter, M. and Adams, C. (2007). The use of psychological treatments for people with personality disorder: a systematic review of randomised controlled trials. *Personality and Mental Health,* 1: 95–125.

—— (2008). The use of pharmacological treatments for people with personality disorder: a systematic review of randomized controlled trials. *Journal of Personality and Mental Health,* 2: 119–70.

Egger, M., Davey Smith, G., Schneider, M. and Minder, C. E. (1997a). Bias in meta-analysis detected by a simple graphical test. *British Medical Journal,* 315: 629–34.

Egger, M., Zellweger-Zähner, T., Schneider, M., Junker, C., Lengeler, C. and Antes, G. (1997b). Language bias in randomised controlled trials published in English and German. *Lancet,* 350: 326–9.

Egger, M., Davey Smith, G. and O'Rourke, K. (2001a). Rationale, potentials and promise of systematic reviews. In M. Egger, G. Davey Smith and D. G. Altman (Eds). *Systematic reviews in health care: meta-analysis in context* (pp. 3–19). London: BMJ Publishing Group.

Egger, M., Smith, G. D. and Altman, D. (Eds) (2001b). *Systematic reviews in health care: meta-analysis in context.* London. BMJ Publishing.

Eysenck, H. J. (1995). Problems with meta-analysis. In I. Chalmers and D. G. Altman (Eds). *Systematic reviews* (pp. 64–74). London: BMJ Publishing Group.

Higgins, J. P. T. and Altman, D. G. (2008). Assessing risk of bias in included studies. In J. P. T. Higgins and S. Green (Eds). *Cochrane handbook of systematic reviews of interventions* (pp. 187–241). Chichester: Wiley Blackwell.

Higgins, J. P. T. and Deeks, J. J. (2008). Selecting studies and collecting data. In J. P. T. Higgins and S. Green (Eds). *Cochrane handbook of systematic reviews of interventions* (pp. 174–5). Chichester: Wiley Blackwell.

Higgins, J. P. T. and Green, S. (Eds) (2008). *Cochrane handbook of systematic reviews of interventions.* Chichester: Wiley Blackwell.

Huband, N., Ferriter, M., Nathan, R. and Jones H. (2010). Antiepileptics for aggression and associated impulsivity. *Cochrane Database of Systematic Reviews,* issue 2, art. CD003499. DOI: 10.1002/14651858.CD003499.pub3.

Jüni, P., Altman, D. G. and Egger, M. (2001). Assessing the quality of a randomised controlled trial. In M. Egger, G. Davey Smith and D. G. Altman (Eds). *Systematic reviews in health care: meta-analysis in context.* London: BMJ Publishing Group.

Khan, K., Kunz, R., Kleijnen, J. and Antes, G. (2003). *Systematic reviews to support evidence-based medicine: how to review and apply findings of healthcare research.* London: Royal Society of Medicine.

Lang, T.A. and Secic, M. (1997). *How to report statistics in medicine.* Philadelphia: American College of Physicians.

LeLorier, J., Grégoire, G., Benhaddad, A., Lapierre, J. and Derderian, F. (1997). Discrepancies between meta-analyses and subsequent large randomized trials. *New England Journal of Medicine,* 337: 536–42.

Murphy, E., Digwall, R., Greatbatch, D., Parker, S., and Watson, P. (1998). Qualitative research methods in health technology assessment: a review of the literature. *Health Technology Assessment,* 2(16): 1–272.

Noyes, J., Popay, J., Pearson, A., Hannes, K. and Booth, A. (2008). Qualitative research and Cochrane reviews. In J. P. T. Higgins and S. Green (Eds). *Cochrane handbook of systematic reviews of interventions* (pp. 570–91). Chichester: Wiley Blackwell.

Sirdifield, C., Gojkovic, D., Brooker, C. and Ferriter, M. (2009). A systematic review of research on the epidemiology of mental health disorders in prison populations: a summary of findings. *Journal of Forensic Psychiatry and Psychology*, 20(S1): S78–S101.

WMA General Assembly (2008). WMA Declaration of Helsinki – ethical principles for medical research involving human subjects. Seoul: 59th WMA General Assembly.

York CRD (2009). York CRD's guidance for undertaking reviews in health care. Available at www.york.ac.uk/inst/crd/SysRev/!SSL!/WebHelp/SysRev3.htm (accessed 21/4/11).

16 Conclusion

Kevin Howells, Kerry Sheldon and
Jason Davies

All three of the editors of this book have worked as practitioners, researchers and evaluators in forensic mental health (hospital and community services for mentally disordered offenders) and criminal justice (prison, probation) settings. In our experience many practitioners (psychologists, nursing and medical staff, prison and probation workers, social workers, occupational therapists) have an interest in research and in evaluating their own work and the services in which they work. Indeed many forensic practitioners may even have research and evaluation as part of their job description or may be enrolled in an academic programme at a local university with a required research component. Postgraduate programmes in the forensic field (for example Master's and Doctoral programmes in Forensic Psychology) typically have extensive research expectations, often with an emphasis on the students engaging in a research project in the service in which they work or are training as a practitioner. Research and evaluation are often identified as a priority too by those who commission and manage services. The term 'what works' is widely used in human services and in government spending as is 'evidence-based practice'.

For such concepts to move beyond the status of pious platitudes, however, there needs to be consideration of how such research and evaluation is to be conducted in real-world service settings and by whom. In our experience, there are two models of research practice in actual services. The first involves large-scale, multi-centre projects, often externally funded and conducted by full-time researchers based in a university or research institute. Such projects are obviously necessary, even essential, in generating findings and theories that are capable of generalisation across settings, services and even countries. We would suggest, however, that such work needs to be complemented by a research effort more local in nature and conducted by researcher-practitioners who are embedded in the services which are under scrutiny. Essential for the latter is the recruitment of clinicians or practitioners with research and evaluation skills. There is a parallel between what we are advocating here and the influential, international and enduring 'scientist-practitioner model' in clinical psychology training, according to which it is considered desirable that research and clinical skills co-exist within the individual professional rather than be bifurcated, such that clinician and research roles are located within different individuals – you are either a practitioner or a researcher, but not both. The potential strengths of the scientist-practitioner model have been widely and repeatedly discussed, as have its potential limitations. For the scientist-practitioner model to work in forensic services, it is essential to identify the distinctive core research skills and methods required in forensic practice. We are hopeful that the contributions contained within this book amount to a modest step in identifying some core areas of research expertise for the practitioner – the topics covered are clearly not exhaustive of the field.

Research methods need to be located within a broader philosophical and theoretical base and researcher-practitioners need to be wary of an overly narrow and positivistic scientism in our definitions of the scientist-practitioner. Despite this, the vast majority of the procedures and practicalities for undertaking a research project (outlined by Davies, Sheldon and Howells, Chapter 1, this volume) will be relevant irrespective of the particular forensic setting and of the philosophical and methodological preferences of the researcher. However, there is a need to ensure that philosophical and theoretical assumptions are made explicit especially when considering the many ethical issues that arise and need to be considered, at every stage of the research process. Protecting the dignity and moral status of research participants is important in all areas of research but the issues are likely to be sharper in forensic settings such as prisons and secure health facilities, where equality of moral status is less readily recognised and the environment itself may undermine it. As Ward and Willis (Chapter 2) suggest, a wide range of issues require thought and mindful attention although there is no appropriate 'cookbook' for navigating and resolving the many ethical dilemmas faced.

Even though the work of forensic practitioners and researchers is broad and varied, assessing and managing risk have become core activities for large numbers of practitioners working in forensic settings. Not everyone agrees with the focus upon risk in forensic practice and the way it has taken centre stage in many settings, nor the recent societal apparent pre occupation with risk elimination (see discussion of this by Ward and Willis in Chapter 2). What is clear, however, is that the scientific validity and credibility of risk assessment and management depend on underlying research findings. The dynamic nature of risk assessment and the wide range of research questions in this area are described by Doyle (Chapter 3). They provide the new researcher in this area with an understanding of the many challenges for research in relation to risk. Issues such as the methodological pitfalls in design, selection of risk factors, measuring outcomes, sampling and statistical methods, and critically the problems with the notion of prediction itself remind us that research to inform and structure clinical judgement is both challenging and important.

In contrast to the way in which the attention of many practitioners has focused upon assessment, treatment and risk, areas such as profiling, legal and court processes have become much more the preserve of academic researchers. This, however, is at odds with the training of researcher-practitioners such as forensic psychologists for whom such areas are core components of the training syllabus.

These also deserve attention because of the research methods that have been adopted and developed, which could be transferred by practitioner-researchers to address a wide range of other questions. For example the use of Facet Theory and associated empirical tools in offender profiling as discussed by Brown (Chapter 4) provides a framework which has had little use in the wider forensic arena. That this approach can be adapted for both quantitative and qualitative data, to use primary and secondary sources of data and to embrace multi-faceted questions, suggests that the potential of this method for research has been under exploited to date.

Practical issues and the apparent complexity of practice settings have tended to steer practitioner-researchers away from experimental research. However, researchers such as Palmer and colleagues (Chapter 5), who address court-related questions, have continued to develop rigorous experimental designs which have become the norm to some extent in this area. Although the level of control afforded by such methods must be balanced with the concerns about external validity, the use of the laboratory and carefully managed contexts are important elements in the arsenal of methods for practitioner-researchers.

The use of qualitative methods has experienced explosive growth within social science research not only in the number of papers published but also in the development and expansion of methods and approaches. In an ideal world practitioner-researchers would utilise methods guided by the question under study; however, within forensic settings the application of qualitative methods has a relatively short history and is still evolving. Despite this, the need to embrace qualitative approaches in order to explore a broad range of questions within forensic practice is clearly articulated by Howitt (Chapter 7). He also raises the desirability of shifting between qualitative and quantitative methods, depending on the research questions being asked, rather than seeing them as mutually exclusive. However, one challenge for the practitioner-researcher raised explicitly by adopting a qualitative stance is to articulate their epistemological position and their methodological choices. Of the suite of approaches under the qualitative umbrella, Grounded Theory has received a lot of attention. Gordon's work (Chapter 6) illustrates the value of making staff, rather than exclusively offenders, the focus of research enquiry and provides a clear introduction to the philosophy and practice of Grounded Theory.

Our perception is that the individual is re-emerging as a focus in many areas of forensic practice, and so attention to research methods which have an individual, idiographic emphasis compared to more conventional nomothetic, group-based methods is critical. This is also reflected in the increasingly widespread notion of individual formulation-based treatment interventions in the forensic as well as the clinical field (Daffern *et al.*, 2010; Sturmey, 2010). In part this is a response to the acknowledged complexity of many forensic populations, for example the 'dangerous and severe personality disordered' group, which, until recently, has been an important priority group in forensic service delivery (Tennant and Howells, 2010). The focus on individuals, however, requires a corresponding research and methodological base. Single case evaluation is not new, particularly in the mental health field, but is only now emerging as valuable in forensic work. Davies and Sheldon (Chapter 8) spell out some of the requirements and necessary conditions for single case evaluations, including issues of baselines and measures. Notwithstanding important issues of internal and external validity, single case methods are capable of rigour and are not necessarily a soft alternative to conventional group methods. Several structured idiographic methods are described by Hammond (Chapter 9), with a particular emphasis on measurement of change. He stresses that such methods complement rather than replace conventional psychometric methods. Both of these approaches acknowledge the importance of individual formulation which is developed by Daffern (Chapter 10) through a description of one of the more promising approaches to formulation of the individual case – functional analysis. As Daffern indicates, functional analysis is not new and is widely practised by clinicians but rarely engenders research activity in forensic settings. As Daffern suggests, there is a need to move towards the experimental test of proposed functional relationships, including the phenomenon of offence paralleling behaviour (Daffern *et al.*, 2010) – this is a task well suited to the forensic scientist-practitioner.

The need to utilise macro as well as micro perspectives within forensic research cannot be overstated. Whilst attention to the individual, small group and service is critical to forensic research, one of the major successes of forensic practice in the past two decades has been the development, implementation and evaluation of major therapeutic and rehabilitative programmes for offenders. What often started as small-scale therapeutic efforts with a small group of offenders in one institution or service have become major programmes with hundreds or even thousands of people completing treatment. Such interventions are now delivered in a large number of countries, often along similar lines (Risk, Needs and Responsivity principles). The research effort in getting to this point has been immense and there are many lessons to be learned from it by the novice researcher. McGuire (Chapter 14) describes the history, methods and current standing of evaluation research of this sort. Meta-analysis is obviously a critical skill for the researcher in this area as is familiarity with issues of effect size.

In forensic treatment contexts as in other clinical settings, the Randomised Controlled Trial (RCT) is widely reported as being the 'gold standard' for treatment outcome research. Few new researchers, though there are notable exceptions, have the opportunity and tenacity to conduct an RCT in a criminal justice or forensic mental health setting. However, a grounding in the rationale for, and difficulties with, RCTs is important for the practitioner-researcher. Hollin (Chapter 11) provides a detailed account of the RCT approach and practical obstacles, though hopefully not to the point of entirely discouraging the aspiring researcher.

There is, arguably, a bias towards the study of intrapersonal factors in much forensic research. Offender characteristics, cognitions, emotions, behaviours and responses to rehabilitation are common foci, with a relative neglect of situational factors. The potential value of studying environments, particularly regimes in custodial and institutional settings, is addressed by Tonkin and Howells (Chapter 12). The availability of reliable and valid measures has been an important issue for those wishing to conduct research projects. These authors' overview of the field identifies potentially useful measures, particularly of therapeutic climate. Climate is an important independent and dependent variable and potential research projects addressing both are suggested.

Evaluations of criminal justice programmes are increasingly requested and commissioned, whether by organisations that fund the programme who may be concerned about effectiveness and costs, or by managers of the programmes wishing to improve quality and impact. As Day (Chapter 13) indicates, correctional services in particular have been, and continue to be, under scrutiny in many countries. Evaluation in this context is inevitably multi-faceted, with many aspects of the organisation, the programme, the staff and outcomes being assessed. The RNR framework has generated systematic approaches to evaluation, as Day suggests, but there is room for innovative developments in the future.

A text on research methods in this arena would not be complete without paying attention to the approaches being used to understand the lessons contained within a body of research, particularly systematic reviews and meta-analyses. The essential methodologies for both research tasks, as well as the difficulties that can arise, are described in some detail here by Ferriter (Chapter 15). Both systematic review and meta-analytic skills are increasingly an expectation of those involved in postgraduate courses in forensic areas. Ferriter's review provides a valuable jumping-off point for the uninitiated.

The reaction of the editors to the many chapters of this book has been two-fold. First, it provided us with a reminder of the extent and diversity of research endeavour in the forensic field. The range of concepts, rationales and methodologies is wide indeed and this presents a challenge to the novice researcher who might feel, unreasonably, that they need to master them all. This is unlikely to be the requirement for someone wishing to address a very particular research question. Nevertheless, we think it is useful to begin to delineate the methods that might be relevant to someone wishing to develop comprehensive research expertise related to forensic practice. Second (and finally), engaging with those who have provided chapters for this book and reading and reviewing their contributions in detail has made us all aware of the extent of our ignorance, whilst also providing the reassurance of knowing where we might look to improve our knowledge. We are hopeful that the reader may have a similar reaction.

References

Daffern, M., Jones, L. and Shine, J. (Eds) (2010). *Offence paralleling behaviour: a case formulation approach to offender assessment and intervention.* Chichester: Wiley.

Sturmey, P. (2010). Case formulation in forensic psychology. In M. Daffern, L. Jones and J. Shine (Eds). *Offence paralleling behaviour: a case formulation approach to offender assessment and intervention*. Chichester: Wiley.

Tennant, A. and Howells, K. (Eds) (2010). *Using time, not doing time: practitioner perspectives on personality disorder and risk*. Chichester: Wiley.

Index